Mood and Mobility

Mood and Mobility

Navigating the Emotional Spaces of Digital Social Networks

Richard Coyne

The MIT Press
Cambridge, Massachusetts
London, England

This book was set in Stone Serif and Stone Sans by Toppan Best-set Premedia Limited.

Library of Congress Cataloging-in-Publication Data is available.

ISBN: 978-0-262-02975-9 (hardcover)
ISBN: 978-0-262-55201-1 (paperback)

To Diana

Contents

Preface

The simple proposition of this book is that designers, practitioners, educators, researchers, and reflective users of ubiquitous digital networks and devices need to pay greater attention to the issue of mood. The technologies in question include smartphones, tablets, laptops, cameras, audio recorders, and the increasing array of sensing and actuating technologies that monitor and modify the states of our bodies, our social interactions, and our environments. I include social media, news and entertainment channels, and media for crowdsourced creative coproduction and prosumption in this complex matrix. In total, this sociotechnical array of interconnected equipment, systems, and practices has an inevitable influence on the way we feel.

I focus in this book on mood rather than emotion. The study of mood brings issues to light in ways that foreground a diversity of cultural contexts and opinions. Mood is a concept so rich and undetermined that it's necessary to scan insights and controversies from many disciplines. As I've discovered, nearly everyone with whom I speak about the topic of this book has something valuable to say about mood.

I'm grateful in particular to the following students and colleagues, who provided inspiration for the book and in some cases invaluable feedback: Maria Androulaki, Fabrizio Gesuelli, Philip Goulding, Richard James Hanrahan, Christos Kakalis, Dorothea Kalogianni, Anastasia Karandinou, Shi-Mei Lee, Richard McLauchlan, Stella Mygdali, Christopher Neale, Peter Nelson, Dimitra Ntzani, Graham Shawcross, and Neil Thin. Collaborators Jenny Roe (Stockholm Environment Institute, University of York), Peter Aspinall (Heriot-Watt University), and Catharine Ward Thompson (The University of Edinburgh) provided insights into experimental method and the mood effects of being in outdoor spaces. The book arose as part of our collaborative project *Mobility, Mood, and Place* (EP/K037404/1), supported through the EPSRC/AHRC/SRC/MRC scheme *Design for Well-Being: Aging and Mobility in the Built Environment*. I'm particularly grateful to Panos Mavros for inspiring some of the early experimental work.

Introduction

As I sit on the East Coast rail service from London to Edinburgh, I notice other passengers playing video games, watching films, listening to music and audiobooks, tapping the screens of their e-readers and tablet computers, and conversing with others not present. Users of pervasive digital media work while on the move. They communicate, process information, are entertained, and keep in touch. I am among them. What we do with our mobile devices reproduces what by now are common, ubiquitous, and habitual practices. These actions ostensibly make journeys go faster, provide opportunities to catch up, shield us from surrounding distractions, provide time to restore, and prepare us for whatever awaits at the end of the journey. I propose that we also receive, modify, intensify, and transmit moods via these media.[1] Device-equipped travelers participate in a kind of shared digital mood modification.

A few of these travelers are undoubtedly checking into Facebook, a high-profile social media platform (at least at the moment). Facebook invites its users to select an emoji icon (emoticon) to indicate how they are feeling as they update their "status" (i.e., as they post a message). Status messages include pictures, links to other people's posts, news reports, and just about anything that can be communicated via the web. A news feed is a listing of your friends' update statuses and is visible on your Facebook homepage. It serves as a personalized gossip column and arguably a means of communicating feelings and information among networks of friends.

Facebook stirred up controversy recently when it published an academic article with Cornell researchers about "massive-scale emotional contagion through social networks."[2] The article drew attention to people's susceptibility to mood changes transmitted through social media. It also informed its readers that Facebook had secretly manipulated users' moods.

Facebook filtered news feeds according to the "emotional content" of the status messages people viewed in their news feeds. It's an easy step then for commentators and critics to accuse the social media provider of "mood manipulation."[3]

We consumers are of course familiar with the idea of mood alteration via the mass media and in advertising, as well as in public events, such as festivals, sports, parades, and royal weddings. Some politicians and corporations support and sponsor public events to buoy people along toward some major decision point and outcome, such as voting in an election or buying a particular product. Cultural geographer Nigel Thrift shows how the manipulation of people's emotions has always been a key element of politics—for example, the channeling of fear and aggression as part of military training and the various means of preparing a population for war.[4] Vance Packard's influential book *Hidden Persuaders* (first published in the 1950s) made the case that advertising sells products by manipulating our feelings.[5] The theme of persuasion also underlies Matthew Weiner's *Mad Men* television series, which is about a 1960s advertising firm. Realizing that all cigarette companies are confronted by the same problem of adverse medical evidence, the firm's creative director, Don Draper, advises his clients to sidestep the facts. He says, "Advertising is based on one thing: happiness. And you know what happiness is? Happiness is the smell of a new car. It's freedom from fear. It's a billboard on the side of the road that screams with reassurance that whatever you're doing, it's okay."[6] Coercion works in subtle ways, not least by first associating the product (and the whole apparatus of consumption) with a mood of well-being.

There's a social dimension to the construction of such moods. This applies no less to the consumption of ubiquitous digital media devices and services. Many consumers are beguiled by the prospect of some new item of digital kit. Group coercion also kicks in. For sociologist Rich Ling, it's "the ubiquity of our mutual expectations that are pushing the use of these devices."[7] Therefore, the adoption of ubiquitous digital media is subject also to the pressures of "ubiquitous expectations." In the case of communication devices, the fact that everyone else is using them means that I think I should do so, too. If the rest of the family is sharing photos on Facebook, then I also need to sign up, to at least acknowledge those pictures of babies, holidays, and pets. Peer pressure doesn't actually require critical mass. According to Ling, you need only think that the right people are using the technology. Advertisers can step in with the message that everyone's doing it—or that the right crowd is.

People enter into the mood to buy, depending not just on how much of their income they can dispose of in shopping malls and online retail, but according to how they feel in the circumstances. In order to consume, people need to be kept happy. In their book of the 1980s, *Manufacturing Consent*, Noam Chomsky and Edward Herman suggested that advertising works, as long as there's no real controversy that deflects consumers from the "buying mood."[8] Light entertainment in the mass media has a role here, and it's easy to assume that each of us consumers of digital entertainment on the train is also being lulled into a state that ensures our acquiescence to the imperative to consume yet more goods. Some Internet skeptics go further. In *The Filter Bubble*, Eli Pariser suggests that as online advertisers become more adept at gauging your mood through online sentiment analysis, they will be able to deliver messages when you are "especially suggestible." He asserts, "The same data that provides personalized content can be used to allow marketers to find and manipulate your personal weak spots."[9]

In this context, the users of social media are perhaps not entirely in control of their moods, but neither are they simply passive consumers primed and groomed to conform to the dictates of others. I hope to show in the rest of this book that mood management is more subtle than either scenario. Moods have complex agency. They circulate with indirect influences, including from and through online media and devices. We are not just passive receivers of moods that are foisted upon us: We are complicit in the making of moods.

The Mood of the Digital Age

If emotions can spread, as a mild form of contagion via social media, then surely whole communities can succumb to a mood. It's common to describe the character of groups in terms of their emotional profile. Stereotypes proliferate about the way certain social groups "express emotion" and their attitudes to emotion. In a lighthearted book on stereotypes of the English, anthropologist Kate Fox muses that the "English male" will not express "real emotion." She says, "The game is all about mock anger, pretend outrage, jokey one-upmanship. However strongly you may feel about the product, team, theory or shaving method you are defending, you must not allow your feelings to show."[10] The comparison is usually with other English speakers, such as Americans and Australians, who are apparently more uncalculatingly expressive.

In addition to differences among groups, emotional profiles exhibit temporal variation, captured readily by the idea of "the mood of the times." For example, the mood of the 1960s was encapsulated in Timothy Leary's phrase, "Turn on, tune in, drop out." That was the putative spirit of the late 1960s, the mood of those times, their zeitgeist. If I wished to continue in the spirit of such neologisms, I would assert that the current age can be encapsulated in a series of app names: Turnitin, iTunes, and Dropbox. Or, perhaps this is a time when everyone would rather be elsewhere: turn off, drop everything, and turn up late.

On the subject of ages, perhaps we now occupy the age of the spammer, characterized by frustration and relentless sifting through unwanted emails that ruin the flow of work and personal communications and mess it up for everyone. Perhaps it's an age in which spoilers rule: hate tweets, phishing, cyberbullying, and inflammatory emails. In addition to online business, the Internet is taken over by unfinished business. Incomplete projects clog up servers, along with unanswered emails, unread tweets, dead links, links never clicked, and untended comment fields—not to mention unfulfilled entrepreneurial ambitions. Therefore, for those in an impassive mood, it's the *age of the lazypreneur*. Perhaps it's also the time of *antisocial* media, and a generation has emerged of people who are exercised less by the possibilities offered by the Internet's newness than by expecting it just to deliver what they want. We no longer have the option to opt out. We expect friends, relatives, clients, and customers to have the same connectivity we do, and they expect it of us.[11] Some people try to evade the net's hegemony, to go undetected, or they simply give up on any notion of personal privacy. This is after all a *postdigital age*. Perhaps it's a new age of extreme boredom, as mobile device users wait for downloads, Wi-Fi registration codes, the next release, greater bandwidth, and for those phantom vibrations to give way to actual phone calls.[12] As the air is saturated with promises about amazing gadgets, it's now harder to get excited. Apparently those of the Y generation have diminished capacity to create their own interest or engage in face-to-face conversation. Anything outside the digital maelstrom seems boring. Surfing for entertainment, information, and Facebook updates and tapping at smartphone settings replace dinner conversation.

It is easy to get caught up not only in the mood of the times, but also in the feeling that we ought to be busy characterizing the times in some way or other. Such characterizations compete for our attention. For some commentators, in this age we are returning to the time prior to the appearance of the first personal computers. Thanks to massive air-conditioned cloud-computing bunkers, file servers, and data centers, we are back to the era of the mainframe. A beguiling blog post by media theorist Geert Lovink identifies further the character of the age we are now in: "The Snowden revelations in June 2013 mark the symbolic closure of the 'new media' era. The NSA scandal has taken away the last remains of cyber-naivety and lifted the 'internet issue' to the level of world politics. The integration of cybernetics into all aspects of life is a fact."[13] Lovink identifies a decline in the values held dear to the Internet's founders and early adopters: "decentralization, peer-to-peer, rhizomes, networks." For Lovink, we are now back to what George Orwell predicted about surveillance in his novel *1984*, set in a year that in actual history was also the year that Apple launched its personal computer: "Now, thirty years later, the computer is once again the perfect technical instrument of a cold, military security apparatus that is out to allocate, identify, select—and ultimately destroy—the Other. The NSA, with the active support of Google, Facebook, Microsoft, and allied secret services, has achieved 'total awareness.' Precisely at the moment when the PC is disappearing from our desks, large and invisible data centers take their place in the collective techno-imaginary."[14]

The concerns are genuine, and under the zeitgeist paradigm those anxieties elide readily into a way of identifying certain events as having all-pervasive currency, with factors that overwhelm and contaminate all others, as if everyone is thus affected, and in all places. In the humanities, this approach to a unified characterization of a people and a time comes under the heading of *historicism*.[15] As I'm attempting to show in this section, such putative moods compete for identification and attention.

If the world is now returning to buttoned-down mainframe seriousness, then it's also an age laced with Silicon Valley satire,[16] of the kind purveyed by *The Onion* (theonion.com), which distributes (online since 2007) professional, American-style newscasts about topics such as criminally useless Kickstarter projects,[17] "brain dead" teens who only communicate by rolling their eyes,[18] and fake TED talks on "using social media to cover for lack of original thought."[19] A message box on theonion.com tells foreign readers to subscribe "for only $0.99 for the first month: That's less than a dollar—approximately one day's wages in most non-American countries!"[20] The site delivers a double irony, as you do need to pay. Perhaps the current mood is one of ambiguity and a double play between honesty and hoax. This is the age of the headline as one-liner. Perhaps zeitgeists come and go with such rapidity and specificity that they are really just fads—and faddish jokes about fads. With so many channels of information, zeitgeist gets replaced by what's trending, metatrends—as well as mega- and microtrends. Is this the age of the broken zeitgeist?

In sum, I don't think that the idea of the zeitgeist provides a reliable account of mood. There really is no prevailing mood of a time. At best, the claim to have identified it is a convenient fiction, an acknowledged gross generalization, a provocation, an overstatement to bring into consciousness something strange that would otherwise pass unnoticed. At worst, the idea of the zeitgeist assumes that everyone is in the same condition and that human society is uniform across the planet and drifts from one state of consensus to another. The zeitgeist idea encourages us to see the world through headlines. In fact, we don't all read the same tweets or the same news feeds. In the old Hegelian sense of zeitgeist, it also implies the presence of prophets and elites who have the genius capacity to detect, express, influence, and advise on the current mood. Thanks to the Internet, we all have a voice now—whether or not anyone is listening. Sitting at a laptop on a train with Wi-Fi enabled and with the Internet at your disposal, you may think it possible to tune into what's trending or even to start a trend yourself. However, much depends on what you are looking for, who you are, and the company you keep.

Mood and Mobility

The passengers mentioned in my introductory remarks were on the move and using mobile media. Mood connects with movement.[21] I'll refer a few times to the philosopher William James's (1842–1910) assertion that movement is part of what it is to have an emotion.[22] The "bodily manifestations" of an emotion are inseparable from the feeling. For example, running away and fear are part of the same emotional package. The fear doesn't come first as a separable mental state. Emotions involving attraction are similar. In any case, we are beings with bodies that move. We also feel emotions and talk as if we feel them. Our feeling, moving, communicating, and social-izing bodies speak of an incontrovertible link between mood and mobility. I need scarcely mention the lineage of the word "emotion," traceable to concepts of agitation, displacement, and motion.

So much of our movement now is moderated and abetted by technolo-gies—that is, communication and transport systems. Movement under assistance from technology usually occurs at high speed. Rapid movement activates the senses, as when a dog sticks its head out of a car window and gulps at the wind. Speed also has its sounds. The more advanced and sophisticated the technology, the faster and smoother the ride. Language reflects this. Words with an "oo" in them sound smooth. People who have "found their *groove*" have a *smooth* ride, are on the *move*, and sometimes find travel *sooth*ing. Like speed, a *mood* is a condition with some constancy, whether it's a good or a bad mood.

Travel is also a mood changer or amplifier. In *The Art of Travel*, the phi-losopher Alain de Botton described the psychological pleasure of taking off at Heathrow airport: "The swiftness of the plane's ascent is an exemplary symbol of transformation. The display of power can inspire us to imagine analogous, decisive shifts in our own lives; to imagine that we too might one day surge above much that now looms over us."[23] Traveling well means being safe and feeling it—cocooned in a gliding refuge. Some people like being locked in a metal tube with others in control—attended to, coddled, and fed drinks and snacks (as on a plane or train). To travel, you also have to be isolated from the intense effects of speed, the roughness of the weather, water, altitude, and other extremes. There's security in that and perhaps contentment, conducive for some to a feeling of relaxation.

Movement also amplifies the need for sociability. The economics of travel requires that people congregate. Travel means that there's always something to talk about as the view changes and someone to talk with, if you want that. It may even encourage sociability or tactics to remain iso-lated (e.g., on a crowded bus where people instinctively avoid making eye contact). Fast travel inevitably takes you through different places and across thresholds between places. It makes lots of things the same, but also renders transition effects obvious, as when you pass from the city to the country-side, exit a tunnel, or turn a corner. There's excitement in that.

Technology-assisted travel reveals new prospects. Some people prefer to ride the top of a double-decker bus. Airplanes provide obvious prospect, especially when close to the ground and you can see things. In rapid travel, the foreground appears blurred and the distance comes into sharp relief.[24] Geometers and photographers know that movement makes obvious certain spatial relationships and occludes others.[25] Trains and cars hug the land surface. Planes hang from the sky. In either case, fast travel privileges the sky in the visual field. In chapter 5, I'll talk about vertigo as a leitmotif for mood navigation.

With rapid movement, there's usually a destination in mind. Expectant moods pervade travel, both in prospect and while on the move. Interrupted progress frustrates passengers. You can see the concern in their expressions as they reach for their phones. In fact, travel is also associated with acute awareness of time, which some refer to as boredom, a particularly common mood.[26] There's also melancholy on long journeys; I'll discuss that later as well (see chapter 8). Journeys involve excursion and return. You have to come back at some stage, a possibility that causes some would-be travelers to well up with emotion.

Not everyone is equally mobile, and mobility is not constant at all times.[27] Forced restrictions on movement are among the first warnings of incapacity, oppression, and despair. Memorials, museums, plaques, brochures, information boards, and graffiti indulge the contemporary free-roaming tourist's curiosity about blatant oppressions of other times and places. The circumstances of twentieth-century Europe seem quite different from those of the affluent twenty-first-century European traveler, at least for the time being. World War I started in 1914, with centenary commemorations in 2014. Prisons, boundaries, pursuit, and curfews speak of constraint and extreme sadness: "The lamps are going out all over Europe"[28] spoke to a mood of gloom and an end to free movement.

I hope I've established already why mood matters. To focus on mood is to take a step back from instrumentality and function and to look at what prepares us for action in the first place. Wage earners, homemakers, people of leisure, carers, and the cared for who are not in the mood for whatever the day holds find it difficult to perform effectively—or even to get out of bed. Mood provides the context and the impetus for action, and (as I hope the rest of this book will demonstrate) mood is an active place to be.

Motivations for This Study

To address mood as a context for practical action, I structure the book around ten key mood propositions, or mood maps,[29] progressing from the sociable aspects of mood to the potential for synthetic arousal implied by the human–machine relationship. Each chapter is written with a particular mood as its focus and in a particular mood, progressing from the gentle, agreeable moods of solidarity, empathy, and the enjoyment of knowledge to the more problematic and intense mood conditions of intoxication, addiction, hauntings, anxiety, ignorance, and the high-intensity worlds of wired-up, machine-induced mood modulation. Some readers might doubt the status of these themes as moods. At best, they are mental states, or perhaps modes of action. For example, I include a chapter on color. If color is not a mood per se, then being *intoxicated* by color probably is. Without at this stage arguing for their mood status, it might be sufficient to alert the reader to a current intellectual trend to conflate and reintegrate issues of cognition, emotion, and action.[30] Therefore, perhaps some ambiguity is allowed here.

In what follows, I draw together many threads that connect on the theme of mood, and I'll draw on experiments into mood.[31] Those scholars who associate directly with experimental psychology have discovered (or rediscovered) that rationality entails more than abstract, logical reason and detached observation. Science thereby embraces what was formerly the preserve of the romantic poets, philosophers, and artists: the world of feeling and imagination.

However, it's in the sphere of the humanities that such themes have been pursued avidly and critically. I want to reclaim ground for the humanities in the discussion of mood, mobility, and ubiquitous media. I think this is the rightful territory of a "digital humanities": understanding and interrogating the cultural and social impact of new technologies and, in the words of the "Digital Humanities Manifesto 2.0," being "engaged in driving the creation of new technologies, methodologies, and information systems, as well as in their détournement, reinvention, repurposing, via research questions grounded in the Arts and Humanities."[32] Only secondarily might the digital humanities be concerned with curating online collections, mining large cultural data sets, and challenging the supposedly conservative research practices of the humanities.

I see mood as a lens to interpret developments in digital media. I may also be using developments in digital media as an excuse to enjoy interpretations of mood. From my point of view, the digital is so woven into philosophical reflection that it is difficult to disentangle the two. Any excursion into social and cultural phenomena is bound to have a digital dimension, and the study of digital media is deeply cultural. The technologies may be new, but the cultural backdrop to their formation has a much longer history.

In my own research, I've been drawn to collaborative research projects involving electroencephalography (EEG) that claim to measure brain responses as a means of studying stress, emotion, and recuperation in physical environments. This book helps provide a critical context for that work.[33] Brain studies generally draw on lessons from clinical neuroscience about the emotions, informed in large part by the effects of damaged brain functioning: accidents, lesions, and genetic abnormalities. Brain scientists date their investigations back at least to Charles Darwin.[34]

Of course, studies in the phenomenology of perception and understanding predate the development of brain research. Phenomenology deals explicitly with the subject of mood. Freud's theories about dreams also relate to mood,[35] and the critically inclined have incorporated insights from psychoanalysis with those of Karl Marx to examine and promote social and political transformation. Ideology also aligns in some respects to mood. As critical theorist, Walter Benjamin promotes the idea that a work of art has an *aura* that is easy to associate with mood, a proposition I'll develop in chapter 6.[36]

My discipline is architecture, and some architects have long assumed that places have a "spirit" as a kind of mood.[37] Scholars in the humanities might incorporate mood under the headings of *aesthetics* and *hermeneutics*, and mood-related themes pervade the creative arts.[38] Many scholars and critics are motivated to examine the ephemeral, the atmospheric, and the indefinable qualities of things and environments[39] as a reaction against the apparent limits of computer power and the tenets of modernism. On the other hand, digital technologies seem to promise analysts the means to record, measure, and manipulate mood. Insights from music, film, and the mass media contribute to mood studies.[40] I argue that media content transmitted through networked portable multimedia devices are also media for the circulation of moods. This study therefore continues a project I started with *The Tuning of Place*, in which I applied insights from music and sound to argue that we use our digital devices to tune in to one another and to place. To *tune in* is to fit into, accommodate, and adjust a mood.[41]

What difference can studies into mood make? The avid student of mood has several routes into practical application. As will become apparent in the rest of this book, clinicians and counselors promote mood management on the path to health and well-being. Self-help guides for personal mood management abound. Business books claim that knowledge about moods contributes to effective leadership and management. Mood impinges on commerce and marketing. Neuromarketing adopts biometric techniques to detect emotional responses to marketing stimuli, such as packaging, store arrangements, and advertisements. Investors want to know about the mood of the stock market to optimize decision making. Electronic transactions, Internet search engine activity, social media, and microblogging generate vast amounts of data in real time to be mined and analyzed to gauge something resembling the mood of a population, community, place, or time. *Twitter moods* and mood clues from various data sources circulate in the mass media. Some researchers also wish to invent computers that tune in to the moods of their users and that even display emotions.[42]

Mood Design

What follows is informed by my view that the study of mood makes a practical difference to creative activity, including design and other decision-making processes about place and space. We are not just passive receivers of moods that are foisted upon us, but we make moods, and the discovery and cultivation of a mood state is the mood. A mood is an active thing. For Paul Dourish and Genevieve Bell, researchers on digital interaction design: "Emotion is therefore interactional as opposed to representational. This conclusion does not simply raise implications for design; it is an implication for design."[43] It's easy to assume that designers need to pick up on the mood of a user or client group and design systems such that they accommodate or respond to, perhaps dynamically, that condition. However, people don't just encounter the world then and there with pregiven feelings that fit the moment. Dourish and Bell describe an early interactive game system that allowed people to "see how they feel." They explain: "The system's display is not a presentation of an emotional state; it is directly a performance of one. If we think of emotion in terms of performativity, enactment, and cultural production, we are led to a radically different way to conceive of affect in interaction."[44] Therefore, digital devices, along with buildings, environments, objects, and systems, provide play spaces for experimenting with, probing, and altering moods. In the rest of this book, I hope to elaborate on this active, design-oriented way of thinking about mood.

I also consider the way in which the design of technologies and devices is complicit in mood formation and circulation. Much of the empirical literature on mood seeks to uncover its psychological and physiological reality. I don't believe that experimental psychology is the only avenue through which to explore the theme of mood. In creative and cultural practice, it's often sufficient to equate what is true with what is useful. In other words, the designer and artist can entertain conjecture and imagination on the theme of mood and draw on diverse sources for evidence, including literature, linguistics, philosophy, cultural theory, and practical experimentation—as long there's something to work with. Pushing an idea to extremes, even to breaking point, can offer creative returns. As attested by many artists, even the concept of "uselessness" has its use value. What follows is permeated by a particularly open attitude to the subject of mood, to demonstrate the many ways that it is activated, propagated, disseminated, appraised, and modified.

Plan of the Book

In chapter 1, I examine the differences between emotion, mood, and affect, relating each to the context of interconnected media devices, such as smartphones, tablets, and laptops. I argue that the mass media's ubiquity and its imperative to entertain combine with information and communications technologies to intensify the place of emotion and mood in people's lives. The mass mediatization of public and private life through instantly available networks of information, entertainment, and sociability influence our moods, requiring responsible, astute, and knowledgeable mood management.

Chapter 2 is entitled "Moved by the Mob." We readily attach a group to a mood: celebratory, triumphant, angry, battle-weary, frenzied, or docile. Ubiquitous digital media presents collectivity as a virtue. Concepts such as smart mobs and crowdsourced creativity come to mind. In this chapter, I develop the idea that mood is a social phenomenon before it is individual. Mood fits within the purview of interpretative practices as exercised within communities. I examine recent cases in which close observers have claimed that the mood of dissent generated within groups and crowds incited people to action, protest, and revolution, processes supported by networked digital media.

Chapter 3 is about curiosity. Everything you need to know is available online—or so it seems. Ubiquitous digital media deal in the quest for knowledge. It's helpful to think of curiosity as a mood, and without that mood, the student, reader, visitor, or net surfer can't feel interested. I examine how ubiquitous digital technologies create, invoke, or suppress inquisitive, inquisitorial, voyeuristic, and forensic moods. There are implications here for online learning experiences. Since the cabinets of curiosities in the Renaissance, architects, curators, collectors, educators, and artists have known how to invite curiosity in the way they position objects in spaces and the way they arrange space. I translate these insights to the maintenance and exploitation of curiosity online.

In chapter 4, I address the issue of pleasure. Ubiquitous digital media keep us in touch and inform. They also entertain. The theme of entertainment supports the concept of mood and equates to pleasure in some measure. However, we can be entertained by exposure to fright, horror, sadness, and disgust. Film lovers and other media consumers participate vicariously in moods, but we also transition between moods. Insofar as narrative involves mood, it transports the viewer and listener through a series of emotional experiences. Mood effects work through contrast. In this chapter, I expand the discussion of mood to pleasure and happiness as social concerns, examining how ubiquitous digital media impact on the way we think about well-being.

Chapter 5 considers vertigo. Positioning yourself at an extreme height provides a metaphor for the human condition—devoid of firm ground or certainty. Play, including computer gaming, commonly invokes the anxiety and thrill of vertigo. Simulated speed and extreme sports participate in the logic of exaggeration. What appeals to me about such intense encounters is that they bring new aspects of our world into sharp relief, even if just for a moment. This chapter examines the intense moods that accompany ubiquitous digital media, including anxieties and addictions. Unusual, disruptive encounters can be experienced through many media—sometimes just ordinary moments revealed in a new light or the everyday seen from above.

Atmospheres and ambiences are the intangibles in our environment, well-illustrated by the behaviors of sound, perpetrated not least by ubiquitous digital media, and the subject of chapter 6. The human psyche is similarly characterized by intangibles—those moods that hang over the human being like a cloud, shrouding him or her as in a haze. The unconscious is that other great spatial metaphor, the incomprehensible complexity concealed under the smooth veneer of consciousness. This discussion helps position the claims that digital media contribute to the ambience of a place and to the theatricality of places under the influence of media.

In chapter 7, I consider color and mood. Thanks to backlit LCD, projections, and other display technologies, we are now exposed to the dynamic control of color. Color provides a metaphor for pleasure, health, and vitality. Color is undoubtedly complicit in pleasurable experiences, though there are color-filled moods that are somber, violent, and portentous. Efflorescences of color also indicate contamination, virulence, and toxicity. Some think that color pertains not only to harmonious balance, but also to imbalance. This chapter examines color and mood and their convergence in ubiquitous digital media as instrument, metaphor, and provocation.

In chapter 8, I examine melancholy. The relentless quest for happiness barely leaves space for melancholy, and yet some scholars link melancholy to creative accomplishment. This chapter examines loss, ghosts, irony, forgetting, and long-distance travel, each of which is in the company of mood. Insofar as online digital media provides a vehicle for self-disclosure and diarizing, it circulates melancholy. The mass media also purvey health alerts, news, explicit crime dramas, war documentaries, TV fantasies of vampires and werewolves, violent action films, cruel cartoons, and shooter and car crash video games. However, the main thrust of this chapter is to demonstrate the status of melancholy as a reflective condition, a feeling about feelings, and a metamood.

Chapter 9 is about suspense. In expectant mood, we are primed for the big tease, the sequel, indicating a basic human propensity to will some event into existence. Not only media but also consumer products succumb to this chain of expectations. Version numbers keep a project open and edge it ever onwards. Such sequencing tactics are indicators of a propensity within the human species to project forward, to anticipate, which are in a way also about constructing a future and even building the idea of the future. Without having a fore-project, there would be no understanding—which is to say that no one would understand anything: a movie, a trailer, a book, or a blog. I show that the framing through which we construct our expectations constitutes a mood.

In chapter 10, I address ignorance as a mood, head on. The producers of games, films, and multimedia interactives make their entertainments to be viewed over and over. Thanks to multiple media channels, story lines can be elaborated via backstage interviews, explainers, spoilers, and reviews. If you miss the detail, the storyline, or the events, and muddle the characters, then you can catch up later. Incomprehension is not necessarily a disadvantage. It allows scope for the imagination, speculation, discussion, interpretation, and reinterpretation, which is partly what stories are for. Strategies for promoting and validating incomprehension are as important as strategies for acquiring understanding. In this chapter, I examine how ubiquitous digital media thickens as well as disperses our fogs of ignorance.

Chapter 11 is about machines. There's something intriguing about a machine that claims to put you in the mood. Not all machines function as expected, of course, an observation that invites reflection on the nature of machine failure. This concluding chapter reassesses the role of ubiquitous digital media in realizing the age-old quest for automated stimulation of the senses and our attempts to satisfy the craving, whether in isolation or solidarity, to be forever in the mood for whatever is thrown our way.

Beyond Mood Control

To summarize, these chapters support five main propositions about mood. The first is that the devices and technologies we use really do affect people's moods. If you want to understand how people adjust their moods or how people influence the moods of those around them, or you want to explain the mood of a community, then it's worth paying attention to technologies and their selection, design, and configuration.

Second, the influence technologies exert is not always as direct as people have claimed of the Facebook mood manipulation I described at the start of this introduction. The mood you are in is attributable to your environment, social context, personal experiences, and background. A mood is the frame that constitutes the state of mind you are in, and technologies are part of this framework.[45] Devices are in the environment, they affect how we socialize, and they influence how we see ourselves. Inevitably, digital devices have a major role in the modulation of mood. Readers who want confirmation of this point can jump to the start of chapter 11.

Third, I assert the importance of contrast. We practical humans don't really want stasis. Different moods, positive or negative, suit different occasions. We need somber moments of melancholy, as well as flashes of unalloyed pleasure. I bring the theme of contrast into prominence in the discussion of color in chapter 7. Mood effects are transitional and derive character from shifts from one condition to another. They also motivate such transitions.

Fourth, moods are active. We human beings make, create, and trigger moods in the contexts of our actions. That includes social interactions, the uses of language, and artifacts—all the paraphernalia of human sociability.

Fifth, people talk about their moods and have feelings about them. The discourse about mood is deeply reflexive, which also brings mood into the arena of irony. I canvas the idea of metamoods in chapter 8 on melancholy.

Incidental Insights

I expect a series of secondary threads to fall out from these discussions about mood. Ubiquitous digital technology delivers media content: films, music, documentaries, drama, comedy, and the whole panoply of entertainment. Such content tugs at our emotions. Thus, media content provides an easy entry point for considering mood and ubiquitous digital media. I'll make frequent reference to the mass media but will not depend on it entirely to reinforce the technology–mood connection.

In the process of proving these propositions, I indulge an architectural preoccupation: that of geometry. My proposition in chapter 5 is that vertigo, as a mood, provides the inquirer with special access to the shape of things, to the character of space. Its investigation involves a basic mapping exercise—aligning one spatial model over another. Vertigo is that disoriented, unsettled feeling we get in the face of rapid change. It's also about going around in circles and swinging from a height above the ground. The spatial geometries this implies correlate with certain useful propositions in philosophy and cultural theory, pertaining to symbolism, the hermeneutical circle, surveillance, and the human body. I call on this geometrical schema a few times, notably in discussions about the unconscious, color, personality, and suspense. The mapping of themes, one to the other, is germane to how ubiquitous digital media affect our moods. Therefore, the geometrical schemas are relevant to mood and mobility and intersect with the concerns of the designer, many of which, after all, relate to space.

I suspect this geometrization is a bit novel for the circumspect reader who might find it too oblique to the topic of mood and mobility. Little will be lost by skipping over these parts. In addition to following a line of argument in support of singular propositions, I'm interested in the tangents along the way. I invite the reader to think of the content of this book as a series of metaphors that help explain what mood is, providing discursive terrain maps and mood guides. The metaphors are in themselves the names of recognized moods, so they are mood metaphors in a double sense.

In the course of the book, I review themes prominent in the growing literature, the popular press, and online about ubiquitous digital media: identity, privacy, security, freedom of information, globalization, democratization, censorship, addiction, netporn, child protection, grooming, bullying, fanaticism online, and misinformation. However, I approach these themes at an obtuse angle to see how they appear when refracted through the material of mood.

Method of Investigation

The opportunity now to experiment with new forms of Internet scholarship is without precedent. This book is an attempt to tap into this seam of new reading and writing practices. I've canvassed many of the ideas explored here in smaller-sized chunks in regular blog postings, which I've also used for communicating with students on courses and with others undertaking research projects in digital media and culture and in architecture.[46] Comments from contributors have also informed my inquiries. Access to sources online has escalated in recent years.[47] The techniques now fit the subject matter. There's now an opportunity to make connections between psychoanalysis, experimental psychology, sociology, anthropology, cognitive science, cultural geography, literature, history, and design. Search engines now accomplish some of the work of unearthing the linkages, or at least suggesting connections amid the vast range of work pertinent to mood and emotion.

The various disciplines on which I draw have their own discursive frameworks and problem definitions. What role do moods play in cognition? How can you still feel suspense when you know the outcome of a story? Are moods unconscious? Why do we enjoy being sad? Is the mood that's encouraged by watching a film or listening to music really the same thing as moods that accompany events in our own lives? Do visual images, colors, and sounds have direct neurophysiological connections to mood? What elements in the environment trigger mood states directly? I allude to these questions and even posit some answers, but I'm interested mostly in how these questions and the discussions they provoke impact on thinking about digital media design and how they are informed by developments in digital media.

I recognize that the threads from experimental psychology, phenomenology, cultural theory, and interaction design start from different assumptions; neither are they entirely compatible discourses. However, where possible I'll attempt to show how they map onto one another and where there are major differences. Key representative texts include those by experimental psychologists such as James Russell on affect[48] and Stephen and Rachel Kaplan on environment,[49] the philosophers Hans-Georg Gadamer[50] and Martin Heidegger[51] on the phenomenology of interpretation, and Brian Massumi[52] and Jonathan Flatley[53] from cultural studies, with inevitable reference to Sigmund Freud on repetition, the unconscious, and the pleasure principle.[54] The goal of examining emotion in relation to the design of electronic devices comes from the impetus provided by Rosalind Picard on affective computers,[55] Donald Norman on emotion design,[56] and Paul Dourish and Genevieve Bell on the anthropology of interaction design.[57] My own philosophical position is that of the hermeneut, placing interpretation at center stage.[58]

I've examined digital media through a series of lenses in previous books: metaphor, pragmatism, romanticism, economics, and sound. Mood provides a new window through which to view developments in digital media and social networks. The theme of mood acts as a particular kind of probe into the ever-changing world of networked digital media.

1 What Is a Mood?

In the introduction, I identified the value of mood as a way of guiding investigations into mobile media but made no particular distinction between emotion and mood. It's time to catch up with the subtle distinctions between emotion, affect, and mood, and to examine what their study says about ubiquitous digital technologies. Talking about emotion is subtly different from the way we talk about mood, as I'll show in this chapter.

Talking about Emotion

I've always had trouble with emotion. It's fine to be passionate about your work, to want happy clients and students, and to seek the greatest pleasure for the greatest number. However, to create, write, or say something in order deliberately to provoke an emotional response in people is a different matter. Consider my own discipline of architecture. Emotions don't feature prominently in architectural thinking—at least not traditionally. Form and function are important, as well as ornament. On a more abstract level, there's aesthetic experience, significance, memories, and even something called the "spirit of a place." However, raw, unsophisticated emotions—such as feeling happy, sad, angry, frightened, or contented—are too transient and vague when designing long-lasting functional edifices that populate the cityscapes and landscapes of the built environment. Emotion belongs to entertainment and amusement parks. Along with many of the fine arts, architecture inherits Plato's suspicion of the impermanent world of base sensations in favor of rational, abstract, transcendent, important, and long-lasting *ideas*.[1]

Many factors come into play in determining how you feel in a place anyway, including the company you keep, the time of day, your state of health, hormone levels, your last meal, medication, and life events, most of which are beyond the control of the designer. Could architects hope to sustain particular emotional responses among the users and occupants of their buildings? Digital media hold different possibilities. Laptops, tablets, smartphones, and the networks that support them are highly responsive media, foregrounding possibilities for customized and finely tuned interactions between people and machines that are only now being explored in the more static arts.[2]

Not all the arts are ill at ease with emotion; consider music. In his book *The Singing Neanderthal*, Steven Mithen argues that "if music is about anything, it is about expressing and inducing emotion."[3] There are numerous studies and books on music and emotions.[4] Think of how readily we are prepared to describe a piece of music as happy (e.g., Beethoven's *Ode to Joy*) or sad (e.g., Mozart's *Requiem*). Sometimes, we simply mean that the music makes us feel happy or sad or has the potential to influence someone in this way. However, to describe a piece of furniture or a teapot as happy, as suggested by the cognitive theorist Donald Norman, requires some imaginative thinking, and we would be disinclined to describe a building as happy or sad. A similar reluctance applies to fine art. Is Frans Hals's (1580–1666) painting *The Laughing Cavalier* a happy picture? Are we as comfortable with so classifying a painting as we are with the pop song "I Gotta Feeling" by The Black Eyed Peas?[5]

Bodies and Emotions

Rather than focus on emotions, designers (including architects) may prefer to think of how the environment impacts on the body. In fact, observing bodies is one of the main ways by which seasoned people watchers know what others are feeling: stooped shoulders signify depression; lazing around on sofas indicates a relaxed demeanor; standing in silence while looking upward can signal awe. Why not bypass those supposed inner emotional states and design directly for the body? After all, the physical environment encourages bodies to act: dash across public squares, linger by a pool, walk gingerly across an open-meshed steel walkway, sit at tables, lean over balconies, and reach up to shelves. If it's important how people feel in spaces, then it's sufficient to design furniture, equipment, and public and private spaces for the movement, posture, and comfort of the human body. Perhaps the emotions will follow. Digital devices are part of the furniture of the physical environment, and the way people relate to the devices they carry with them has implications in bodily terms.

There's clearly a close coupling between feeling and embodiment anyway. Numerous psychological studies confirm that we can make a good guess at what others are feeling from their facial expressions, postures and behaviors. It also seems that deliberately changing your facial expression, posture, and behaviors (or being coerced to do so) can not only fool others, but also affect how you, the bearer of those signs, feels.[6] At the very least, posture can affect how people *report* what they feel.

A seminal series of experiments by psychologist James Laird indicates that under laboratory conditions, participants instructed to adjust their facial muscles into either a smile or frown position will find certain situations either more or less amusing.[7] Forcing a smile inclines people to be happy. Psychologist Fritz Strack and colleagues conducted a similar series of experiments, in which participants were required to position a pen protruding from their mouths.[8] One of the positions involved gripping the pen with their teeth; the other with the lips only. The former produces something like a smile, the latter a frown. Again, those with the smile reported higher levels of amusement while looking at different stimuli (cartoons). Something similar applies to pharmaceutical adjustments to facial expressions, as when botulinum toxin (Botox) is injected into a person's forehead to reduce frown lines. According to a popular book on the virtues of this procedure, "If you smile broadly, at that moment you will feel happier. You need your smile to help you 'feel' the emotion."[9]

Posture can also affect motivation. Experimenters have reported that human subjects required to slouch for several minutes prior to solving certain puzzles were less likely to persevere with those tasks. Subjects required to sit with chests raised and heads up seemed more motivated to complete the puzzles, even though sitting up straight for long periods of time induces fatigue.[10] Whether or not it involves emotion, the comportment of the body has some influence on motivation, competence, and well-being. Therefore, a design that influences the body's movement and comportment may influence the emotions of the person using it. Does sitting on a bar stool imply a different posture, and hence emotional state, than sitting on a sofa?

Perhaps smartphones, tablet computers, and other digital devices have an effect on our moods by virtue of the facial expressions and postures they require us to adopt when we are using them. Sitting for long periods of time, concentrating and with your head down, and glowering at an iPhone or Kindle screen may incline you to a negative state of mind, whatever the content in your line of sight. For good reason, those arts and technologies that produce spaces and objects for physical use focus on form, function and the body, especially where equipment, furniture, buildings, and open spaces involve human interaction.

Not every creative discipline is so focused on the body, nor do they make such demands on bodies. You can look at a painting in any position, watch a film from a chair or a sofa, or enjoy a dance from the sidelines. You can of course move and dance to music, but you can also listen while in repose, jogging, or perched on a ladder. We usually consume media while passive. Perhaps the immediate environment is incidental, as long as it doesn't distract too much. The emotional stimulation takes place via the screen and through the audio channels.

Media and Emotion

Emotion seems to assert itself most powerfully in the realms of mass media entertainment.[11] Entertainment is a performance or other presentation intended to induce enjoyment, an emotional condition. If we are comfortable associating pieces of music with emotions, then we will be even more inclined to do the same in the case of the expressive and immersive medium of film. According to film theorist Annabel Cohen, "Emotion characterises the experience of film, as it does the experience of music."[12] What is said of film likely applies to other dramatic narrative forms, including documentary, news reports, reality television shows, soap operas, cartoons, sports, game shows, and computer games—anywhere there is narrative, plot, character, and scenery. This is where emotion creeps in to almost every corner of design and creative production—through the back door via the mass media.

We are in an age of media convergence, in which mass media entertainment is channeled to desktop computers, laptops, tablets, and smartphones, not to mention television sets and home entertainment units and broadcast in airport lounges, shops, and leisure centers. The same devices that deliver important emails about a problem at work, a confidential medical report, the company's financial statements, an academic paper, or a catalog of artworks also delivers episodes of a tear-jerking TV soap opera, a

YouTube clip of a boy with a sandwich being chased by an emu, someone's gorgeous flower pictures, a soul song, and an exciting video game.

These are not simply independent channels of information to be filtered and managed. The channels influence one another. I propose that work and leisure are being *mediatized* and in the process bring emotions to the fore in people's thinking.

Consider the mediatization of professional and business life. Whether for profit, esteem, or advancement, chief executive officers, board members, investors, professionals, freelancers, small business owners, and employees want their work to get noticed. The tools exist for anyone with access to the Internet to publish messages, comments, articles, and whole volumes for everyone to see; to garner feedback; and to construct a network of followers, readers, and fans through social media. Individuals can construct a persona and organize their own publicity machine. All of this operates under the scrutiny of numbers: page views, hits, visitors, friends, followers, citations, and subscribers.

Businesses know their sales figures and media producers, publishers and advertisers analyze audience figures, but the Internet amplifies this submission to numerical analysis. Sometimes, this quantification helps assess the competition, but it's also about individuals. Quantities are conspicuously present on the Internet—to be viewed, compared, gloated over, embarrassed about, and provide evidence for influence, reputation, and impact, or their lack.

Such statistics are easy to come by. As a regular user of the Internet, I was recently able to discover that over 10.38 million viewers in the UK watched *The FIFA World Cup* on ITV1 (BARB),[13] the most often viewed video on YouTube had over 2,000 million hits (Gangnam Style by Psy), the Guardian newspaper recently averaged 185,313 sales per issue (and the figure is falling),[14] and the top-selling book series is still *Harry Potter* (over 450 million, according to a Wikipedia entry). The number of times a book or article is cited appears under each item returned by the Google Scholar search engine item (averaging about six in the life sciences[15]). The numbers vary dramatically, but they are public and easy to get a hold of. The data pertains to individuals, organizations, and products.

It's significant that this mediatization relates to individual people as much as to corporate entities. Social media (Facebook, LinkedIn, Beebo, Myspace, Google+, Renren, etc.) were ostensibly started as a way of putting individuals in touch with each other. Corporations, institutions, and other groups have been admitted willingly to the social network ethos, providing advertising revenue and attracted by opportunities for targeted marketing. As I will show, assessing the emotions experienced by an audience or group also presents as something to be quantified.

Emotional Labor

The quantification of emotion also brings it under the purview of economics. If you run a tutorial, advise students, front a counter to answer queries, or deliver marks and feedback, then you are an emotional laborer. Lecturers attempt to deliver and manage enthusiasm, curiosity, passion, and hope among students and colleagues. They may also encourage respect, fear, and even anger about their subjects. In the academic service economy, emotional labor may also require academic and support personnel to appease distress, dissatisfaction, and complaint. After all, people do talk about emotions in economic terms: emotional *cost, expenditure, burden, capital, deficit,* or *investment.* In her study into emotion, sociologist Arlie Russell Hochschild took emotional labor as a defining characteristic of work undertaken by anyone responsible for "voice-to-voice or face-to-face" service.[16]

The metaphor of emotional labor rings true. When I worked in an architect's office designing houses, at times we thought of ourselves as providing clients with their dreams. At times, we also felt as if we were family counselors and had to arbitrate conflicting views among the clients. Designing a family's ideal home involves massive emotional investment by client and architect. Emotional labor is just a small part of an architect's or lecturer's role and skill set, but in some jobs it's key. Hochschild connects with Karl Marx's characterization of labor on the production line, in which the worker has become subservient to the machine. On a production line, laborers have to suppress their own physical freedoms of movement and operate as a compliant instrument of production. What Marx said about physical labor on the production line correlates with labor in the service sector, in which workers are required to deliver "service with a smile" whatever the circumstances.

Hochschild studied the training and work practices of airline attendants whose emotional investment is palpable: "For the flight attendant, the smiles are a *part of her work,* a part that requires her to coordinate self and feeling so that the work seems to be effortless. To show that the enjoyment takes effort is to do the job poorly. Similarly, part of the job is to disguise fatigue and irritation, for otherwise the labor would show in an unseemly way, and the product—passenger contentment—would be damaged! Because it is easier to disguise fatigue and irritation if they can be banished altogether, at least for brief periods, this feat calls for emotional labor."[17]

Two coffee shops near my office belong to well-known chains. One is adjacent to a bus stop and always has customers. The other is down a side street. The second shop is popular, but the staff work harder to befriend the customers, guess their regulars' orders, joke, respond to "thanks" with "you are very welcome," and of course affect a smile. I assume that this is part of a concerted policy and training. Perhaps being superpleasant involves remuneration, management encourages competition among staff, and it's a criterion in recruitment. Businesses gain a competitive edge (or survive) by affecting friendly service.

Hochschild implies that the client–service relationship is prone to inequalities. The pay may be adequate, but it doesn't necessarily take into account the energy expended and the cost to the frontline emotional laborer. Perhaps at least emotional investment should feature in negotiations over pay and conditions. Emotional labor exacts a toll. It makes demands similar to *deep* or *method* acting, according to Hochschild, which leaves the actor drained after prolonged performance. In many cases, there's the strain of masking one's actual feelings. Genuine, heartfelt empathy with customers, patients, those in care, and students spills into the worker's private life. The emotional worker may even require a support group to help cope with these stresses. It all costs.

Hochschild argues that "most of us have jobs that require some handling of other people's feelings and our own, and in this sense we are all partly flight attendants."[18] She identifies the reception personnel who have to reinforce the company's dependable and friendly image. But she also refers to other professional roles: "The social worker whose look of solicitous concern makes the client feel cared for, the salesman who creates the sense of a 'hot commodity,' the bill collector who inspires fear, the funeral parlor director who makes the bereaved feel understood, the minister who creates a sense of protective outreach but even-handed warmth—all of them must confront in some way or another the requirements of emotional labor."[19]

Hochschild's book *The Managed Heart* was first published in 1979, though it was republished in 2012. She references online life in other publications, but the book hasn't been updated to reflect the transfer to online services. From a Marxist viewpoint, we are currently in the final phase in the diminution of the laborer's autonomy. Physical laborers, knowledge workers, and emotional laborers succumb to automation and replacement by the machine—or its prospect. She mainly writes about problems on the supply side of emotional labor. Customer frustration at distant, inept, and unsympathetic online customer service eventually filters through to service design. However, some consumers for some of the time welcome interaction with service providers that don't inquire how you are and seem to mean it. At the very least, we can say that emotional labor is being reconfigured and adjusted in the online world.

Emotional Capital

The ethos of the individual gets amplified online and readily elides into those related media phenomena of *celebrity*, *personality*, and *popularity*, as enjoyed or endured by prominent media personalities, sportspeople, musicians, and artists. Social media users are encouraged to provide public profiles. We become our own public relations department. There's now the option (and in some areas the necessity) to manage our public personas to win clients, customers, readers, voters, and audiences, not just by presenting a list of skill sets but by a projection of self that is personable, approachable, friendly, sometimes quirky, different, and special. An Internet profile is now a curriculum vitae that tugs at the emotions, and it really can read like an entry in a popularity contest, thanks to friends lists, followers, and "likes." What is it to be liked? The words we use in the formulation of an answer often draw on the positive emotions: trust, warmth, fun, empathy. The professional virtues of rationality, commonality, skill, competence, and intelligence are in there somewhere, but in mediatized culture it's insufficient just to be good at your job.

Perhaps only a minority participates in this emotionalized culture of self-promotion, and with varying levels of confidence and competence, but professionals can benchmark their own practices against others who do self-promote. A recent conversation with a friend who wants to publish as a fiction writer revealed that he knows and is impressed by others who promote their art through the Internet and social media, but he claimed as yet to lack the confidence or knowledge to do this himself. There are also those who on moral, political, functional, or ideological grounds resist the pressure to subscribe to social media as a promotional vehicle. The presence of something to be resisted is also a kind of influence. Whether it works or is even necessary, social media profiling is in the air. It's part of the mythology of the current digital climate, and it requires emotional investment; that is, you have to be prepared to manage emotional capital.

Directly and indirectly, ubiquitous digital media invite reflection on emotions, along with sociability, narrative, networking, and celebrity. These entities are revealed in new and influential ways. In any case, as tools of mass media content delivery, those mediatized apparatuses we carry in our pockets, handbags, and backpacks influence the way we feel. At the very least, they deliver music, film, and dramatic narrative, which for many is a way of influencing emotion.

There's nothing new here; rather, it's an amplification and cultural reconfiguration. As I have highlighted elsewhere, we are living within a kind of transformed, technoromantic age.[20] Romanticism as a cultural movement since the eighteenth century never really ended. The scientific Enlightenment generated as a spinoff a potent counterforce that elevated the importance of subjectivity, personal genius, the human imagination, and emotion.

Romanticism's most recent revival stems in part from people's disaffection with impersonal, rationalistic modernism in creativity, design, and philosophy. Attempts to replicate human intelligence in machines by symbolic, logical processes have perhaps reached their limits. In its more extreme forms, romanticism aligns with digital media to support the prospect of melding the human psyche with machines, a kind of transportation to a utopian realm in which all is one—restored, whole, and complete. As well as thought extending into the whole environment,[21] there's the persistent concept of the human organism melding with the world and beyond. Digital arts theorist Charlie Gere reminds us in an interesting article on the brain as metaphor that the idea of a *global brain* keeps cropping up in the eighteenth- to twenty-first-century imaginary.[22]

Emotional Design

In the more sober realms of science, developments in brain studies have played a large part in demonstrating the role of emotion in human rationality. Tools for detecting, measuring, and mapping neural processes are now readily available.[23] Brain-imaging technologies such as electroencephalography (EEG) were once confined to hospitals and specialized laboratories. Now, EEG is available as a low-cost peripheral attached wirelessly to a laptop computer or smartphone, encouraging its use in research contexts outside of the clinic. EEG measures faint electrical impulses from sensors positioned on the surface of a person's scalp. More sophisticated brain-imaging techniques such as fMRI (functional magnetic resonance imaging) offer greater capability but are more expensive.[24] With EEG, maps of the brain show sites of activation as suitably wired-up human subjects report their feelings or respond to standard emotional stimuli, such as a piece of music. Less directly, neural data from subjects with an apparent emotional deficit (as in autism) provides information about how the emotions function and to what end.

Brain science provides renewed impetus to studies into design processes. In his book *Emotional Design*, Donald Norman couples aesthetic study with emotion as neglected aspects of good design. In his earlier writing about design from the point of view of cognitive science, he says he "addressed utility and usability, function and form, all in a logical, dispassionate way." But this was followed by an epiphany in the 1990s, apparently thanks to advances in neuroscience: "We scientists now understand how important emotion is to everyday life, how valuable. Sure, utility and usability are important, but without fun and pleasure, joy and excitement, and yes, anxiety and anger, fear and rage, our lives would be incomplete."[25]

Researchers into ubiquitous computer interaction Paul Dourish and Genevieve Bell also seek to give emotion the attention it deserves, though without calling on the cachet of brain science: "Emotion is a key master category in Western thought—one that lines up with and is linked to other critical distinctions around which our thinking is organized, particularly in its distinction to cognition and rationality."[26] They argue that the discipline of anthropology has a great deal to teach us about machines and emotions. Designed artifacts have to respond to this emotional need. Others have advocated that computers should recognize and respond in some way to the emotions of the user and even provide reciprocal emotional responses, indicating pleasure, satisfaction, insistence, or consolation. In writing about such emotional computers, Rosalind Picard, director of the Affective Computing Research Group at MIT, argues that "if we want computers to be genuinely intelligent, to adapt to us, and to interact naturally with us, then they will need the ability to recognize and express emotions, to have emotions, and to have what has been called 'emotional intelligence.'"[27]

Dourish and Bell challenge some of Picard's assumptions about machines and emotions. Not least, there are cultural factors in play that any machine-encoded emotional capacity would find difficult to take into account. In fact, the idea that emotions come predefined and can be coded into computers already indicates a particular cultural bias. People in different cultures and groups not only express emotions in ways that vary, but also exhibit differences in the ways they identify and speak about emotions. For Dourish and Bell, cross-cultural ethnographic study highlights "a different way of thinking about emotion as a cultural category, a different role for emotion, and a different evaluation of its meaning."[28] There's something about emotions that gets negotiated and activated by circumstance. I'll explore some of these propositions in relation to anger in chapter 2.

I don't think we need to be wedded to the idea of emotional machines to recognize that ubiquitous digital devices and media play a role in people's emotional lives. My point here is that the word "emotion" and emotional concepts (such as happiness, sadness, anger, and fear) have increasing currency in the context of ubiquitous digital media. This is an assertion about culture and language without necessarily committing, for the time being at least, to the psychological or physiological reality of such phenomena or their mechanisms.

Affect

Attraction is another useful metaphor in the emotional landscape. When you like someone, something, or some place, then you are affectionately disposed toward that person, thing, or place. To have an affection for something is to be attracted to it. Affectionate people are easily drawn to others, and *affectation* is an exaggerated and ostentatious fondness for something. The Latin word for *emotion* is *affectus*. The Rationalist philosopher Baruch Spinoza (1632–1677) dealt extensively with the theme of *affectus* in his treatise on *Ethics*. He described *affectus* as the means by which "the power of action of the body is increased or diminished, aided or restrained."[29] Affect can be the power surge that compels and strengthens our actions.

Affect is an inclination that you cannot necessarily yet identify as an emotion. According to Donald Norman, "affect is the general term for the judgmental system, whether conscious or subconscious." He distinguishes it from emotion. On the other hand, "emotion is the conscious experience of affect, complete with attribution of its cause and identification of its object."[30] The concept of affect helps us account for those minuscule decisions we make to which we would not even bother to ascribe emotion, but for which motivation is essential—for example, getting up to pace around the room, tying your shoelaces, changing the batteries in your wireless keypad, choosing a breakfast cereal, and brushing your teeth. Whether as habits or deviations from the norm, every act is characterized by a disposition, an orientation, a tendency, and this comes within the purview of the human "affective system."

The psychologist Wilhelm Wundt (1832–1920) introduced the idea of *core* affect in the late 1800s.[31] He explained affect in terms of a simple axis system. For any event, we might be motivated at a high or low level of *activation* or something in between. We might exhibit a high state of excitement at the prospect of going on a holiday. We may be placid or calm while resting after a picnic lunch. These are on the positive side of the activation line. More negatively, our excitement might manifest itself as being tense and jittery. On the low activation side, we could simply feel tired and lethargic. You can map out any emotion on a two-dimensional space with axes labeled "activation" and "pleasure." There's high and low *activation* on the y axis and positive and negative *pleasure* on the x axis.[32] This is a simple schema and bypasses the necessity and complexity of identifying the object to which the affect is directed. At this affective level, being excited about a holiday is perhaps no different than being excited about a reunion with an old friend or the prospect of a satisfying meal.

The core affect schema has been developed further and with experimental evidence by psychologists James Russell and Geraldine Pratt.[33] In their key paper on the subject of core affect, they introduce a diagram that uses the horizontal axis to indicate pleasure, with greater pleasure to the right and displeasure to the left. The vertical axis indicates intensity, with highest intensity at the top and lowest at the bottom. The two axes cross at the midpoint of either parameter. They assert that human "core affect" is (simply) the experience of pleasure and intensity in different degrees.[34] I've tried to color this description of affect with an example of going on holiday, but for Russell and Pratt, "core affect per se is not about anything. . . . core affect can be experienced in relation to no known stimulus—in a free-floating form."[35] There's a geometrical simplicity to this formulation, which I revisit in chapter 5 when I discuss vertigo and the geometry that entails. The schema trades in simple contrasts: pleasure–displeasure and high–low intensity. The idea of such a contrast schema is captured in the following quotation from Sigmund Freud: "We are so made that we can derive intense enjoyment only from a contrast and very little from a state of things."[36] The idea of contrast cuts across psychological experience in many ways. It also reflects the structuralist concepts of language, based on binary oppositions and contrasts.[37]

What then is an emotion? That's what we make of the affect—on reflection and by our actions. Emotion comes from the wealth of human language, culture, narrative, reflection, and the situation of the person undergoing the affect. That's what identifies any particular pleasure–displeasure–intensity (the core affect) as a particular emotion. Our whole cognitive apparatus kicks in to account for our feelings, including the way we talk about our emotions or give them expression. On the one hand, the core affect diagram is reductive, in that it turns the whole complex of human feelings into a couple of linear scales. On the other hand, it amplifies the role of culture and society in the way we give labels to emotions, recognize their existence, create our emotional categories, and even create emotions. This simplification puts the burden for understanding emotions onto a rich area of culture and interpretation. As Dourish and Bell indicate, "culture is what helps me tell the difference between anger and indigestion; it is generative of the experience. Critically, then, such putatively private aspects of experience such as emotion are always already cultural; cultural aspects of interaction are prior, not consequent, to perception and action."[38]

As well as foregrounding culture and language, the core affect schema has therapeutic implications. Russell and Pratt's core affect diagram shows about 20 emotional responses to environments, such as "comfortable," "peaceful," "depressing," and "frightening." These responses are arrayed as labeled points around the axis system according to correlations with the core affects, as measured and recorded from groups of human participants. The diagram indicates that one emotional response could easily be mistaken for another. "Boring" and "desolate" appear quite close as responses to environments. Both are fairly low on the pleasure and intensity scales. If the situation you are in makes you feel destitute and insignificant, then it could just be a case of relabeling your current condition. You may just be bored, for example; that is, you are experiencing low-intensity displeasure. On the other hand, the schema could indicate that boredom is actually a profound and difficult condition, comparable to other, more complicated emotional states, such as depression. The diagram also suggests resolutions.

To get out of the mood you are in, crank up the pleasure element of your experience by moving to a different environment; for example, shift from the bedroom to a park, though this strategy can lead to other extremes, not least of which is fright. Other means of shifting your feelings along the axes—by resorting to alcohol, for example—can themselves have long-term negative effects—such as addiction. It's not great advice to tell someone who is bored to shift to a pleasurable state by taking drugs or alcohol.

Cultural theorist Brian Massumi concurs with the nonspecificity of affect. In his book *Parables of the Virtual*, and referencing Spinoza, he thinks of affect as *intensity*, asserting that it follows a different logic to discussions about emotion or, for that matter, about meaning and signification. He reinforces the importance of affect: "There seems to be a growing feeling within media, literary, and art theory that affect is central to an understanding of our information- and image-based late capitalist culture, in which so-called master narratives seem to have foundered."[39]

I contend that in order to meet such deficits we need also to understand mood. According to Russell and Pratt, a mood is simply "prolonged core affect without an Object."[40]

Talking about Mood

Until that last sentence, I've avoided using the key term "mood" in this chapter. By most accounts, emotion has an object. It's a way of talking about affect by invoking causality. I'm angry about losing my files, sad about the flood damage, happy about your promotion, or afraid of the savage dog. Sometimes, we even say that the object or circumstance *causes* the emotion. Mood, on the other hand, is described as an affect without an apparent object or cause. Flatley agrees: "It is objectless: we don't have a mood about any one thing in particular but, rather, about everything in general."[41] Sometimes, it's a matter of duration. According to Mithen, a mood "is a prolonged feeling that lasts over minutes, hours or even days," whereas an emotion "may be a very short-lived feeling."[42] (I've avoided the word "feeling" as well; think of "feeling" as "affect.")

Sometimes, we use different words for mood and emotion. Happiness is a mood, whereas joy is an emotion felt at hearing some good news. The emotion might trigger the mood, but then we might also say that the mood makes us receptive to the good news. Unless you are of a happy disposition, or in a good mood, you will not take the news joyfully. If I am in an unhappy mood, then the news of your promotion might make me feel even sadder. Certain mood states may make us receptive to emotions to which they are not immediately related. Therefore, a happy mood might make us more inclined to be interested in the people around us and to feel greater empathy toward them.

How do ubiquitous digital media impinge on the issue of mood? Insofar as they involve physical devices, such as smartphones and laptops, they are part of the physical environment. Whereas hardware, product, architectural, and landscape designers might have difficulty with emotions, they can more easily hold some influence over mood. I mentioned the enigmatic architectural concept of "the spirit of a place." Think also of the mood of a place and how designers might discover, analyze, and create a mood or a series of moods by the choice of materials: the warmth of wood, the rough earthiness of stone, or the freshness of clean cotton. In fact, designers sometimes resort to a so-called mood board on which various materials are laid out and displayed, including sketches and images as a way of informing a client of the proposed mood of an environment before committing to its design. Movie producers do something similar when they commission graphic artists to create detailed renders during the preproduction phase of the story's key moments and atmospheres.

Form also has the potential to contribute to mood. Think of shapes with brittle, aggressive edges, smooth planes, or sensuous, inviting curves and recesses. Apple designer Jony Ive justified the design of a recessed carry handle in the casing of the highly successful iMac G3 by noting that "if there's a handle on it, it makes a relationship possible. It's approachable. It's intuitive. It gives you permission to touch." Even though it cost a lot to build the handle that he knew was not functionally necessary, "it was part of the iMac's friendliness and playfulness."[43] Such elements presumably attempt to contribute to the mood engendered by a product. Users could perhaps say that it was a "friendly" computer. In terms of mood, we might say that the handle contributed to the product's mood of welcome. Any designer mood effect also depends on relationships, objects in combination. There's something attractive about a translucent Bondi blue iMac G3 on a desk in a loft apartment and in proximity to a ribbed Eames chair. That's a different mood from a pile of redundant and dusty iMac G3s in a recycling dumpster.

Mood and Music

A computer's welcoming startup and friendly alert sounds form part of the ensemble of design elements that have a role in the mood of an environment. Enthusiasts even collect computer sounds. There are YouTube videos of iMac G3s and other devices starting up. With solid-state circuitry, digital devices rely increasingly on synthetic sounds to signal their operations, but disk drives still hum and click and computer cooling fans whir. Sounds contribute to moods, and mood is related intimately to music. Music in restaurants is supposed to set the mood. There's "mood music" in elevators, hotel lobbies, and supermarkets. Films, TV commercials, and video games deploy music to encourage a mood. Mithen makes the case for mood and music: "We all know that specific types of music can induce specific types of mood; we play soft, romantic music on a date to induce sexual love, uplifting optimistic music at weddings, and dirges at funerals."[44]

Musicologist Tia DeNora analyzed the use of portable stereos in her study of music in everyday life. Many of the participants she interviewed would remark on the role of music that is under their control as a means of reinforcing or transforming states of mind, emotions and moods. One person described "how she uses music to induce and heighten a sad emotional state."[45] Music is a way of representing to yourself and others how you are feeling, the mood you are in.

There's lots of scope for analyzing music in terms of the moods it supports or invokes. Mood relates to musical scales and the intervals between notes. A *mode* is a particular set of notes, usually within a conventional Western musical scale.[46] Mood and mode are closely related. Modes have names such as Mixolydian, Dorian, and Phrygian. At the end of his book on politics, Aristotle indicates how the various modes cause different reactions in listeners who "are inclined to be mournful and solemn when they listen to that which is called Mixo-Lydian; but they are in a more relaxed frame of mind when they listen to others, for example the looser modes." The Dorian produces a more "equable feeling" and the Phrygian "puts men into a frenzy of excitement."[47] Mournful, solemn, relaxed, equable, excited: music and moods seem to be closely connected. In line with this tradition, contemporary musicologists attribute moods in music to intervals between notes, such as major and minor intervals and scales. The major scales are uplifting, and the minor scales create a mood of sadness.[48] In everyday usage, people might refer to mood in terms of setting a *tone*. Tonality in music generally refers to the note that dominates a musical scale or mode,[49] as in the obvious case of the drone in a bagpipe, a particularly melancholic sound to many ears.

So far in this section, I've been careful to avoid the implication that moods are *caused* by designed elements, ensembles of elements, or sounds. The best we can say is that these components are complicit in the formation of mood, within a field of co-complicit influences. I put this forward as a subtle variation on the argument from Dourish and Bell, that emotions are "interactional as opposed to representational."[50] Whatever the psychological literature says about emotions, the concept of mood lays claim to the idea of an open arena of influences and actions.

Mood and Voice

If music is complicit in the formation of a mood, then so is the voice. I occasionally use a text-to-speech reading app on my smartphone so that during periods of intense reading demands I can have journal articles and essays read to me while I walk through the city to work or undertake mundane chores. The default voice that comes with the app has a slightly alarming directive tone, so I downloaded a softer voice that uses the more familiar accent that I grew up with. It's a bit like a soothing inner voice, to which I feel innately receptive. The many dimensions of voice as presented through ubiquitous digital media further draw attention to the importance of mood.[51] In German, the word for *mood* is *Stimmung*, derived from *Stimme*, which means *voice*. It's a term that crops up in phenomenological discourse, to which I shall return in subsequent chapters.

Language is servant to the voice. *Mood* has a particular meaning in language grammar. English grammar distinguishes between three moods: the delivery of facts (indicative), telling someone they should do something (imperative), and the expression of a desire (subjunctive). Consider each mood in turn related to the verb *to sit*: you are sitting; sit here; if you sat here, then you would see the view. There are of course many other ways in which language conveys or influences mood other than these structural categories, but it's clear that a speech full of indicatives (factual statements) encourages a different mood than a list of commands (imperatives) or an attempt at persuasion via a series of conditional subjunctives. Roy Batty, the melancholic replicant in the film *Blade Runner* (1982), addresses his genetic eye designer thus: "If you could only see what I've seen with your eyes."[52] It's a clever line delivered in the subjunctive mood. Elsewhere, he says: "I've seen things you wouldn't believe" (indicative). Most of us deploy such grammatical constructs without thinking about them, but it's clear that choices in grammatical mood help establish or reinforce the mood of a conversation, advertising campaign, or message.

Popular management theory identifies several styles of leadership. Among them is the "directive" style, a command-driven mode of interaction that requires team members either to comply or rebel. This is sergeant-major style leadership in the *imperative* mood. Participative, democratic, or consensually oriented leadership is more likely to trade in communications in *subjunctive* mood. Social media status updates, text messages, and tweets are also indebted to the workings of grammatical mood, as are other modes of human–machine interaction. The command-driven interface of older-style operating systems implies a different mood than the graphical, kinetic, and contingent interfaces of friendly PCs, laptops, and tablets: the menus, mouse clicks, taps, and swipes of contemporary devices form an altogether more *subjunctive* mode of interaction. Interfaces and interaction design that deals in voice recognition and text-to-speech conversion wrestles with the issues around the mood of the voice.

Among the other mood-setting grammatical constructions is the idea of *grammatical voice*. Copy editors and automated grammar checkers in word processors advise writers to use the *active* rather than the *passive* voice.[53] It's clearer, more engaged, and friendlier.

Mood and Atmosphere

Sound fields also behave as moods. After all, sounds can be pervasive, ephemeral, and of indefinite source. Sounds contribute to the atmosphere of a place. In fact, sound provides a good metaphor for mood. Further evidence for the importance of sound in understanding what we mean by mood comes from the concept of *aura*. The *Oxford English Dictionary* (OED) gives the first definition of *aura* as "breath" or "breeze."[54] The word *aural* pertains to the ear and hearing. It's what's in the air, like sound.[55] This set of associations helps me make sense of Walter Benjamin's assertion that in the age of mechanical reproduction artifacts have lost their "aura": that indefinable and singular quality of a thing, its capacity to induce or participate in the creation of a richly positive mood. Here, the concept of mood aligns with meaning and significance, the time-honored value of a thing, and memories. Mood as aura pertains to meanings that you cannot quite pin down and feelings about those meanings.

A human being may have an aura, a charisma, well expressed in luminous as well as aural terms: that "indefinable something" that lights up a room when he or she walks in or a person over whom hangs a pall of gloom. The metaphor of aura attaches to celebrity culture. It also connects with our collective, mediatized participation in online social networks and the management of self, personality, and online presence. To have a place online, you have to project yourself as noticeable and interesting. I referred previously to someone entering a room, a key moment in the recognition of the mood of a party, audience, workplace, or laboratory. I remember the effect in text-based online chat rooms when someone with a new or unusual name or language style would enter the room. Such intruders, lurkers, extroverts, or spoilers could alter the mood of the "room." They disrupted the ambience of the virtual space. Others would remain silent, move into "private" conversations, or leave abruptly.

In spatial terms, mood is often given further expression in terms of *ambience*. An ambience is something that's around us, or perhaps we are moving through it as we *perambulate* through the air or atmosphere. The meteorological metaphor of mood as *atmosphere* suggests immersion in a microclimatic condition—fog, humidity, balminess, aridity, wind—induced by the presence of a heat source, mountains, lakes, trees, and buildings.[56] In his article "The Architecture of Atmosphere," Mark Wigley maintains that atmosphere starts "precisely where the construction stops." It's worth quoting an extended passage for its metaphors. He says of atmosphere that "it surrounds a building, clinging to the material object. Indeed, it seems to emanate from the object . . . the atmosphere of a building seems to be produced by the physical form. It is some kind of sensuous emission of sound, light, heat, smell, and moisture; a swirling climate of intangible effects generated by a stationary object. To construct a building is to construct such an atmosphere. Atmosphere might even be the central objective of the architect. In the end, it is the climate of ephemeral effects that envelops the inhabitant, not the building. To enter a project is to enter an atmosphere. What is experienced is the atmosphere not the object as such."[57]

Moods, like atmospheres, cling, emanate, emit, and involve intangibles, such as sound, light, heat, and vapor. Buildings and their furniture provide the physical context of living, but when we speak of how we experience those objects it's often in relation to the moods they invoke. Insofar as this reference to atmosphere applies to architecture, we could say the same of industrial design and digital media products. There's the need for function, to be sure, but (as with the iMac handle) it's the mood that draws the user in and encourages engagement.

To facilitate, design, or create such atmospheres in space seems like arranging spaces and artifacts to attract users as they traverse gravitational fields. Mood making is a bit like those simulations that attempt to explain the warping of three-dimensional space by rolling marbles across deformed surfaces. Artifacts in space provide sloping surfaces that incline us to a particular place or orientation. Such distortions create a kind of mood landscape that nudges the traveler in certain directions—as affective *traceur*.[58]

Summary

My main message in this chapter about the matter of mood is that moods matter. From the point of view of ubiquitous digital media, technologies are complicit in negotiating mood swings, jumps, and nudges, not least in their role as channels of increasing mediatization. According to new media and dance theorist Susan Kozel, "Studies into affect are burgeoning, not simply in philosophical or theoretical domains but with the realization that the affective lives of citizens are increasingly 'choreographed' by technologies of all sorts."[59] Choreography provides a good metaphor, especially if we think of contemporary dance and movement that has an improvisatory component and the role of the body and its props in mood setting.

In this chapter, I've outlined the differences between the key terms *emotion*, *affect*, and *mood*. Mood is emotion without an object. Affect reduces emotion to activation and pleasure–displeasure, but that foregrounds the roles of culture and language in giving expression to and creating mood landscapes. I've also canvassed attitudes of different disciplines to emotion. If you are interested further in the differences between emotion in music and the rest of the arts, then I invite you to read to the end of this chapter.[60]

Coda: Why Music Reaches the Parts That Buildings Can't

Physical spaces are charged with meaning and emotion for most of us—some spaces more than others. However, it's rare to enter a building or encounter spectacular scenery and experience the same intensity of emotion that many of us feel on hearing a piece of music, particularly music that fits the mood of the moment or the occasion or that is tuned to our predilections. Putting the two together (music and place) can be electric. Choral music or even soft music playing quietly over the public address system in a cathedral can overwhelm the visitor or worshipper emotionally. The right ambient hum or beat, just a few of the right chords as a music track can amplify, intensify, or counteract the mood of the city. That's why films have music, and with personal stereos we can carry our soundtrack and mood switches around with us. Perhaps that's why some of the time we prefer silence or to let the sounds of the environment do their work. Sometimes, music is too powerful in driving our emotions.

Musical Mechanisms

Why does music achieve what space on its own can do only rarely? Psychologists Patrik Juslin and Daniel Västfjäll offer a plausible framework for understanding the emotional potency of music, at least from the point of view of evolutionary psychology.[61] They don't mention buildings, but I'll draw on their article to affirm the superior emotional potency of music over architecture. They summarize the literature on music and emotions and stack it into a six-tiered framework, starting from primitive neurological reflexes and building to the more culturally nuanced and varied.

First, at the base of our experience is a neurological connection between sounds and emotions in most animals, humans included. Emotions (or affects) are what alert us to something really important: threats, safety, and other causes of fear and pleasure. Sudden noises, loud sounds, dissonance, quick rhythms, high-pitched sounds, deep rumbles, and changes in any of these patterns provide automatic cues that something important, dangerous, large, or threatening is happening or about to be and produces "increased activation of the central nervous system" as a kind of reflex.[62] This is primitive and animal-like brain–body behavior. What has this to do with music? It seems that music is built on these fight-or-flight sonic cues and mechanisms, controlled, exaggerated, moderated, and reinforced by further layers of experience and perception.

Presumably, spatial experience implicates similar basic, raw reflexes—looking down from a height, approaching sharp objects, sudden movements, and threatening gestures—but by then you are already in the danger zone and other responses kick in. The emotional intensity accompanying sound acts as preparation and warning. Think of the arousal induced by a persistent fire alarm, even when there's no visible danger. A similar dominance of sound over space may also be evident in the case of comforting, soothing, and homely spatial experiences.

Second, Juslin and Västfjäll refer to a kind of "conditioning" placed over these primitive reflex reactions and emotions involving sound. This is a process whereby "an emotion is induced by a piece of music simply because this stimulus has been paired repeatedly with other positive or negative stimuli."[63] The taste and texture of rice pudding may remind the adult diner of childhood hours in the security of a happy home. In the same way, "Morningtown Ride" by The Seekers and other songs a bit like it, or its familiar cadences, evoke feelings similar to when the music was first experienced.

Spatial experience might achieve something similar—returning to the home of your youth, seeing familiar old brands in a nostalgia museum, flicking through all those digital photo albums—but the anywhere–anytime aspect of music implies a kind of portability and availability of this conditioning and recollection process that overwhelms and dominates visual stimulation.

Third, stimulus effects often start to operate in sympathy with one another. Music sounds a bit like speech in some respects. We are tuned to respond emotionally to an angry voice: "If human speech is perceived as 'angry' when it has fast rate, loud intensity, and harsh timbre, a musical instrument might sound extremely 'angry' by virtue of its even higher speed, louder intensity, and harsher timbre."[64] Juslin and Västfjäll describe music as a "particularly potent source of emotional contagion."

They describe this emotional contagion in relation to the sympathetic response we have to visual stimulus, such as feeling like tapping our feet when we see someone dancing. Presumably, spatial experience in general involves such processes. However, because of our affinity with the human voice, listening to the "Winter" movement of Vivaldi's *Four Seasons* gets us going with an intensity of emotion that a snow scene, a violent painting by Francis Bacon, a wall covered in angry graffiti, or a stroll through the Baths of Caracalla in the evening light can't quite match—however sublime.

Fourth, Juslin and Västfjäll also describe how music has been known to generate visual imagery. Therefore, thanks to various associations, someone listening to Beethoven's *Pastoral Symphony* is able to conjure up images of pleasant meadows in the sunlight. Here, music is subservient to spatial experience, but Juslin and Västfjäll don't speak of the converse—imagining or humming a particular (emotional) piece of music while walking in the countryside or sitting on the beach. They do, however, refer to research that proposes that musical emotion is a particular category of emotion.[65] Music that makes us happy does not come with the trappings or "beliefs" of everyday events that make us happy, such as passing an exam, being among people who care about us, or enjoying sunlight. Perhaps it's this detached, musical emotion devoid of association with actual life events that we seek, rather than emotions embedded in everyday life.

Fifth, they also associate music with episodic memory. A tune, a chord, or a cadence prompts recollection of particular events: an embarrassing school musical, a happy romance, a cheerful outing. There's a correspondence here with spatial mnemonics, the memories conjured up by spatial experience. Apparently, recollections in adulthood are most vivid for the period between the ages of fifteen and twenty-five—the "reminiscence bump."[66] Adults later in life exhibit strong emotional responses to the pop music they were exposed to during that period. Presumably, spatial experience and physical memorabilia provide similar emotional recollections, but without the ubiquity of music and repeated exposure and its opportunities to bed down and contribute to our emotional reservoirs.

Sixth, music is redolent with familiar forms and patterns that lead us to expect certain things to happen. If the note C is followed by E, then we expect the next note in the sequence to be G to make a triad. The G7 guitar chord ought to resolve to the C chord. The satisfaction or denial of these rules provokes a sense of satisfaction or frustration. There's something similar about spatial experience and spatial languages. Perception is driven substantially by expectations.

Faking It

There are some differences between musical emotions and emotions induced while in a spatial or architectural setting. Emotional responses to music can be switched on and off; they are immediate. Emotions associated with spaces and places are longer term and in a sense weaker, ready to be reinforced or counteracted by music. In a way, the studies to which Juslin and Västfjäll refer reinforce the ancient proposition of the superiority of music among the arts. Perhaps, after all, any claim architecture may have on the emotions is of the musical kind. Perhaps in creating sublime, beautiful, dramatic, or homely places we are simply trying at best to echo what music achieves.

Juslin and Västfjäll's ontology of musical emotions suggests a progression from the primitive to the more culturally sophisticated. Importantly for philosopher Martin Heidegger and the phenomenologists, perception is driven overwhelmingly by expectation, which would reverse this series of priorities.

As a blog post, this coda prompted some discussion online:

Comment 1: Of course, architecture has often been thought of as frozen music, from Goethe's "I call architecture frozen music" (1836) to Schelling's "Architecture is like frozen music" (1802–1803).

Comment 2: In terms of emotion, then, architecture is the more fluid medium, open to a range of emotional responses. Mainstream music, theater, film, and other media forms seek to make us feel a certain way. Looking again at the evocative film *Powaqqatsi*, it's telling us to be in awe of those landscapes, temples, and monuments, in a compelling but fixedly romantic way. Music fixes mood; architecture gives it space. Of course, much contemporary experimental music does something else again and is more akin to architecture, as it tends not to presume an emotional response.

2 Moved by the Mob

News and gossip aid social cohesion. People in the catchment community of print-based mainstream media, broadsheets, tabloids, local newspapers, and circulars receive approximately the same news items, in the same configuration, and at about the same time, according to publication schedules. Something similar happened with mainstream news broadcasts prior to asynchronous streaming and downloads. Writing in the 1980s, media theorist James Carey observed that reading the news was more like a ritual than a means of transmitting information. One of the values of scheduled mass media, and the news, is that people can gather round the dinner table or water cooler and talk about the same information.[1] As with most rituals, there's solidarity in that, and consolation.

Do local news feeds on social media fulfill a similar purpose? To the extent that anyone relies on a Facebook news feed as a source of sociability, it's a bit isolating—a private rather than a public ritual. On Facebook, if you happen to have a circle of friends who are always posting upbeat messages and pictures, then you might be inclined to join in and contribute to the positive melee with your own affirming contributions. The reverse might apply if your online friends have a negative outlook. Social media information streams are personalized to reflect the content of your particular collection of Facebook "friends." We all see different news, so retiring to your offline circle doesn't provide quite the same opportunities to debrief, repair, or talk through shared anxieties. The "personalized experience" provided by Facebook news feeds doesn't fulfill that particular ritual function. If social media is a petri dish for "emotional contagion,"[2] then for all its putative sociability, social media can leave you out in the cold—or under quarantine.

Isolation versus Sociability

For Carey, a ritual view of the media also affirms "communication as a process through which a shared culture is created, modified and transformed."[3] He adds that "news is not information but drama." It creates "an arena of dramatic forces and action,"[4] and we each assume roles within that ritual play. How then does social media operate dramaturgically?

Social media communicators who wish to participate in the drama of life online could do worse than to follow Aristotle's advice to public speakers. To fully engage, you need to establish rapport, which requires you to understand the emotional condition of your audience, to know how they are feeling.[5] Know your audience and present to them accordingly. For Aristotle, this emotional orientation involves being "disposed in a certain way": the speaker to the audience and the audience toward the speaker. Another word for this affective *disposition* is "mood." Latch on to the mood of the crowd. Get the mood right, and the job of persuasion is almost done.

Ideas, memes, stories, and arguments exert their influence in the context of the moods people are in. Something similar could be said of the influence circulated through material objects. Artworks, artifacts, and technologies exert their influence in communities primed for their reception or among those who are ready for art's challenges. People have to be in the appropriate mood in order to respond to whatever influences come their way, whether going with the crowd or resisting it.

Spheres of influence and audience rapport suggest that moods are a public matter. The philosopher Martin Heidegger draws on Aristotle to support the assertion that "Publicness . . . needs moods and 'makes' them for itself."[6] Moods and "publicness" go together. According to Dourish and Bell, one of the problems with the *affective computing* project (computer design that takes account of the emotional responses of users) is that, "like cognition, affect frequently appears in this research as a private experience, as something individual that is internal and closed off from the world."[7] The quarantining of emotions in Facebook status updates and news feeds carries similar risks. In this chapter, I want to reinforce the public nature of moods and highlight the implications for digital social networks.

Empathy

Another term for the rapport between a speaker and audience is "empathy."
Many companies see social media as a way of developing empathy with
their customers and clients.[8] Public figures who use Twitter seem keen to
dispatch signals of empathy to their followers. In fact, in an article circulating on the Internet, the cofounder of Twitter, Christopher Isaac Stone,
asserts the importance of empathy in business ventures,[9] though he insists
there is "more to life than tweets." *Customer engagement* is the business
idiom for sociability, empathy, and rapport. It's worth examining empathy
in some detail. At the very least, it is a current topic among those with an
eye on business.

Empathy is close to *sympathy*, as in the case of the *sympathetic resonance*
that occurs when a musician draws the bow against one string of a violin
and, by virtue of their tunings, one of the other strings will start to vibrate
as well. Less poetically, it's observed when a heavy vehicle passes in the
street and the windows of my apartment start to rattle.[10] Through more
complex processes than mere mechanical vibration, human bodies also
seem to respond to each other involuntarily.

The influential economic and moral theorist Adam Smith (1723–1790)
begins his book *The Theory of Moral Sentiments* with a long chapter on sympathy. He starts with the simple observation that any of us might exhibit an
involuntary muscular response to what we see happening to others: "When
we see a stroke [of a hand] aimed and just ready to fall upon the leg or arm
of another person, we naturally shrink and draw back our own leg or our
own arm; and when it does fall, we feel it in some measure, and are hurt by
it as well as the sufferer."[11] It's enough to see someone else's discomfort in
order to instantly and unselfconsciously flinch.

Smith continues with the observation that a circus audience will writhe
and twist with the motions of a performer who walks precariously across
a rope. To update his observation, think of the immersive nature of cinema, television, and computer games, the power of which resides in the
human capability to respond physically and viscerally to what we see others doing. When immersed in the experience, we attentive audience members put ourselves *in the shoes of* the protagonists, and even though we are
seated, our feet do move with the action. Presumably, a similar empathy
develops around one's on-screen avatar in second-person video games. It's

virtualized empathy that enables the online role player to consider herself a resident in Second Life, World of Warcraft, or EverQuest.

Smith extends the physical phenomenon to the more cognitive sympathies engendered when we observe the condition of a friend who may have won an award, lost money, or be ill. These sympathies are emotional. They operate to "enliven joy and alleviate grief" in both the observer and the observed.[12]

The skeptic may wonder how relevant Smith's interest in human empathy is to his support of capitalism, with which he is most keenly associated. In his later work *The Wealth of Nations*, Smith insists that we have to consider the interests of our potential collaborators, business partners, clients, service providers, and constituents—that is, those from whom we want something or who we wish to persuade. We need to "address ourselves . . . to their self-love, and never talk to them of our own necessities but of their advantages."[13] In the same way that speakers need to strike up rapport with their audiences, and as any beneficent entrepreneur knows, sellers need to empathize with their markets. Empathy makes economic sense.

A breakdown in reputation highlights the public importance of empathy. Powerful individuals are popular targets for the charge that they lack empathy. In the film *The Iron Lady*, the scriptwriter Abi Morgan had former British prime minister Margaret Thatcher say: "Do you know that one of the great problems of our age is that we are governed by people who care more about feelings than they do about thoughts and ideas?"[14] The sentiment is nicely ambiguous, but its negative connotation is not lost on a viewing public familiar with Thatcher's period as prime minister, described by some of her rivals as "heartless."[15] In a more recent situation and of a different leadership, a UK politician made headlines by challenging two top leaders' lack of resonance with the mood of the public, asserting that not only are the prime minister and the chancellor of the exchequer (state treasurer) "two posh boys who don't know the price of milk, but they are two arrogant posh boys who show no remorse, no contrition, and no passion to want to understand the lives of others."[16] In light of a worldwide economic recession, similar charges have been leveled at banking executives and high-salaried CEOs who command privilege, power, and economic control but apparently lack empathy with ordinary people: do they buy their own groceries?[17]

The ability to share a mood implies an ability to empathize with other people and their situation. Individuals who do not identify emotionally with the group look mean, miserly, and out of touch. In the earlier quote from Adam Smith, I left out his insistence that we should appeal to people's self-interest rather than their sense of humanity. Smith is closely associated with "heartless" capitalism, and the "dismal science" of economics.[18] He became the target for nineteenth-century reformers dismayed by the social inequalities perpetrated by capitalism and mass production, but in spite of his reputation as a free marketeer, sociability, rapport, and empathy were at the core of Smith's moral philosophy.[19]

Concepts of empathy are important in the spheres of economics and business and in understanding how moods circulate, as I'll show subsequently.

Mirror Neurons

Smith begins with the involuntary flinches of someone observing a physical indiscretion or an audience watching a daring physical performance, then moves into a discussion of cognitive empathetic responses, such as feeling sorry for the plight of others and responding accordingly. In linking physical and cognitive behaviors in this way, he appeared to anticipate the findings of contemporary neurological research. Economic theorist Elias L. Khalil links Smith's concepts of the bodily basis of empathy to brain research dating to the mid-1990s.[20] It seems that brain studies have uncovered evidence that suggests a kind of emotional codependence within human communities.

As any student of science knows, the brain is made up of millions of interconnected nerve cells called *neurons*.[21] Brain researchers have identified a type of neuron specialized in replicating what people observe in others—as if in support of Smith's proposition about empathy. Therefore, if I observe a person lifting a cup to her mouth, then the same pattern of neural activity that appears in her also takes place in my brain; I carry out the same action mentally. Fortunately, other processes generally (but not always) inhibit the operation from getting as far as my motor system. I don't start aping every movement of those I see around me. Apparently, this kind of mimetic neural activity happens all the time. We are copycat organisms by nature.

The neurons responsible for this propensity toward motor mimicry are known as "mirror neurons" and cluster in vast number in the premotor cortex, a region found in the brains of primates that is concerned with eye and body movement coordination (the visuomotor system).[22] Mirror neurons are found in the brains of higher primates, such as apes, and neuroscientists think they are highly active in humans. According to the researchers responsible for their discovery, Giacomo Rizzolatti and Laila Craighero,[23] this mimicry in the motor system is the start of a series of parallel neural processes that also deliver fellow feeling, emotion, and language competence. They also contribute to your ability to put yourself in the minds of others—to guess what they are thinking, interpret their gestures, believe in minds other than your own, and be "self-aware." Much is claimed of the significance of the mirror neuron system (MNS).

According to Rizzolatti and Craighero, the ability to mimic movement is not a primitive capability. Dogs and cats won't instinctively wave their paws about to copy your hand movements (unless trained), but advanced primates do this without training.[24] It seems as though the MNS is a step up from instinctual codependence within other animal species.

Motile mimicry is also a matter of habit, in that we are apparently most inclined to mimic what we are already practiced at doing: "When observers see a motor event that shares features with a similar motor event present in their motor repertoire, they are primed to repeat it."[25] An accomplished (or practiced) dancer is most inclined to bob around in his or her seat at the sight of others dancing and feel inclined to join in.

Apparently, the MNS is less active in some people than in others. People with Asperger syndrome and autism have limited ability to socialize and experience empathy. For a narrative version of the syndromes, think of Commander Spock in *Star Trek*, Sheldon Cooper in *The Big Bang Theory*, and Detective Saga Norén in *The Bridge*, who seem incapable of putting themselves in other people's shoes. Perhaps any community needs a spectrum of empathizers and detached thinkers to function, and any of us is capable of drifting in and out of an empathic outlook. Smith counsels us to be moderate in our expressions of sympathy. Consider too the supposedly unempathic members of the upper classes in the novels by Evelyn Waugh and P. G. Wodehouse, for whom the Great Depression is a minor inconvenience, but getting rained on during a day out in the countryside is a global catastrophe.[26]

The MNS hypothesis supports the view that the human cognitive apparatus is hardwired for sociability. We are not so many individuals who have to work hard at bringing ourselves together into community, by social or any other media; sociability is the norm.

The philosopher of mind Andy Clark develops a powerful argument that thinking and feeling are phenomena distributed within communities. He invokes the discovery of mirror neurons in support of a theory of distributed cognition. Any particular brain is a node in a vast, interconnected network of places, people, and technologies on which it depends. In place of the brain as an organ of pure, independent reason or the mind as software in the hardware of the brain and body, we are part of a system of environmentally suited, codependent, task-oriented "widewear." He argues against "the vision of the human brain as an organ of pure reason" to be replaced by "the brain as a locus of action-oriented and activity-exploiting problem-solving techniques, and as a potent generator and exploiter of cognition-enhancing wideware."[27] If the case can be made for the distributed nature of cognition and problem solving, then the same can be said of emotion and mood. We are empathic beings who participate in collective moods, a kind of cultural wideware.

Advocates for the power of electronic communication and digital media have for many years alerted us to the interconnected codependence facilitated by global networks. Marshall McLuhan insisted that the electronic age ushers in a global village condition in which we wear "all mankind as our skin."[28] Social media introduces a kind of intimacy to mass communications and raises the issue of empathy to a higher power.

Kinetic Empathy

Dance provides an interesting case for the bonding of movement, empathy, and mood. Search on the web for something about spontaneous dance, and you eventually alight on the saying "you've gotta' dance like there's nobody watching," a statement of devil-may-care self-confidence, expanded, varied, and attributed to several sources.[29] Type "dance like nobody's watching" into YouTube and you'll encounter videos of people apparently caught unawares, dancing and moving, usually alone, and sometimes plugged into their smartphones and MP3 players. Untutored, private dancing amuses us, and it's unfair and invasive to make it public, but the phenomenon draws into relief something about the body, mood, and empathy. In fact, the phenomenologist Otto Bollnow (1903–1991) saw dance as a primitive and challenging mode of human mobility that expresses oneness with environment.[30] Dance transforms our relationship with space: "We experience a new space, which as such fundamentally differs from that of our everyday lives."[31] As participant or observer, dance renders space as something other than what walking to work, vacuuming the carpet, cooking a meal, or other everyday experiences offer. Of interest to a philosopher trying to get back to basics, the main difference (from the everyday) is that dance is without purpose, in the sense that it involves the expenditure of effort but does not get the mover anywhere. For all the discipline required of virtuoso performance, dance comes to represent the free spirit, independence, and lack of inhibition.

Dance is movement in itself, "rests in itself and, without indicating an external aim beyond itself, fulfils its meaning in itself."[32] Apparently, the urge to dance is deeply metaphysical: "In dancing, we experience a breakthrough from the everyday practical world of purposeful action and structure."[33] Dancing is not a means to an end. Bollnow argues that dance is another means of erasing the tension between subject and object. I mention these assertions about dance because Bollnow says something similar about mood: "Mood is itself not something subjectively 'in' an individual and not something objective that could be found 'outside' in his surroundings, but it concerns the individual in his still undivided unity with his surroundings."[34]

Bollnow also draws on the psychologist Erwin Straus (1891–1975), and both were probably thinking of folk and ballroom dancing and perhaps 50s rock and roll. Also search YouTube for *crazy dance moves*. If there's any truth in the zeitgeist idea, you could be forgiven for thinking this is a dancing age, much of it highly skilled—but even just moving in front of a computer screen or gyrating to the stimulus of a music track on an iPod at a bus stop propagates the mood of the dance.

Uninhibited dance conforms to the idea of instinctual empathic responses to people and environment. People's obsession for dance in online media provides evidence, if we need it, of the human propensity for mimicry and infectious behavior. Like mood, dance is contagious.

Tuning In to Moods

Adam Smith refers to the "pitch" of our passions.[35] If our empathic response to a friend who has just lost his or her job lacks conviction, then we can be construed as insensitive. If we are too demonstrative, then we can give the impression that our own distress at the news is more important than the condition of the sufferer. Smith advocates responding somewhere in between, a subtle matter of judgment wrought by experience and wisdom and for which there are after all no rules. Getting something to the right pitch suggests tuning; empathy is a matter of fine-tuning our response to the condition of others.

I dealt with tuning in relation to ubiquitous digital media in the *Tuning of Place*.[36] There, I developed Heidegger's use of the word "attunement." *Attunement* is a term promoted within phenomenology to account for a potential, a horizon, and an atmosphere that prepares you for a particular feeling, emotion, or action. In fact, "attunement" parallels the German word for mood. It's *Stimmung* in Martin Heidegger's writing. As I've shown, *Stimme* is German for "voice," so Stimmung easily relates to harmony and tuning. Attunement is the condition in which we are tuned to each other, the environment, the circumstances, the "wideware," the atmosphere, the moves of a place, pleasant or unpleasant, for good or ill.[37] To be attuned is to pick up on a mood.

If mood avoids the issue of agency, who or what causes the mood or where it resides, then it also conflates notions of mood as something resident in the perceiver and mood as an external feature within an environment. As I indicated in the introduction, Otto Bollnow, follower of Heidegger, seeks to bring the two positions together. To repeat the assertion, "Mood is itself not something subjectively 'in' an individual and not something objective that could be found 'outside' in his surroundings, but it concerns the individual in his still undivided unity with his surroundings . . . One speaks of a mood of the human temperament as well as of the mood of a landscape or a closed interior space, and both are, strictly speaking, only two aspects of the same phenomenon."[38]

It's tempting to think of attunement as an individual and private affair. "Self-interest" and individualism have become the hallmarks of capitalism and neoliberalism. Adam Smith begins his chapter on sympathy: "How selfish soever man may be supposed."[39] For Smith, the value of empathy is assessed first in terms of the pleasure it might bring to the person offering it. Later, he asserts that one of the functions of society is to provide a mirror against which the individual can compare herself.[40] We don't know how well off, attractive, or unfortunate we are until we meet others. Feelings about society at large derive from feelings about individuals: "Our regard for the multitude is compounded and made up of the particular regards which we feel for the different individuals of which it is composed."[41] The romantic tradition set itself up against such economic reductions but also asserted the primacy of the individual. Emotions are a personal matter. The poet is alone "in vacant or in pensive mood" and enjoys the "bliss of solitude" in William Wordsworth's (1770–1850) poem *I Wandered Lonely as a Cloud*.[42]

Heidegger departs from the premise of individualism, of either economic rationalism or romanticism. He thinks that emotions are too transient and centered on the individual. To be more precise, he maintains that the idea of emotion presumes too much: individuality, subjectivity, something internal and invisible. Phenomenology wants to get to the bottom of a phenomenon under study, its grounding on which other understandings can be built. For Heidegger, attunement is a pre-emotional, primordial, shared condition that provides the precondition for a certain feeling, emotion, or action.[43] Such ideas are not so far removed from the insights of evidence-based brain research. In an illuminating article aligning the insights of Heidegger with those of contemporary neuroscience, philosopher Matthew Ratcliffe summarizes the primordial nature of moods: "Moods are not subjective or psychic phenomena but are instead prior to the sense of a theoretical subject-object distinction."[44] Heidegger elaborates further on the subject of mood: "A mood assails us. It comes neither from 'outside' nor from 'inside,' but arises out of Being-in-the-world, as a way of such Being."[45]

As I indicated at the start of this chapter, Heidegger draws on Aristotle to emphasize the "publicness" of mood. The emotional connection between speaker and audience implied by Aristotle is a kind of tuning in.[46] Heidegger underlines mood's silent primacy in sagacious tones: "Publicness, as the kind of Being which belongs to the 'they,' not only in general has its own way of having a mood, but needs moods and 'makes' them for itself. It is into such a mood and out of such a mood that the orator speaks. He must understand the possibilities of moods in order to rouse them and guide them aright."[47] A mood may be invisible in any particular social situation and often goes unremarked. For Heidegger, the phenomenon under discussion (mood) is generally a condition that precedes anything that might be explained as being caused by something. As an emotion without object, mood fits the bill. Social beings simply are *attuned*, a state occasionally manifested as melancholy, outrage, joy, restlessness, expectancy, excitement, or resistance.

We twenty-first-century neoromantics are so wedded to the personal, private, and inner world of emotions that it's difficult to think of mood and emotion as something created and sustained by groups of people or as directionless, unintentional, and an aspect of our environment. As I've attempted to show, moods at least ostensibly have a more public aspect than emotions. According to Ratcliffe, "moods are no longer a subjective window-dressing on privileged theoretical perspectives but a background that constitutes the sense of all intentionalities, whether theoretical or practical."[48]

Developing similar insights to Heidegger, the sociologist Alfred Schutz (1899–1959) draws attention to the "mutual tuning-in relationship" that becomes manifested as a sense of sociability or a "We."[49] Schutz uses music to explain this attunement. Any musician reading a score "has not only to interpret his own part which as such remains necessarily fragmentary, but he has also to anticipate the other player's interpretation of his—the Other's—part and, even more, the Other's anticipations of his own execution."[50] Considering the ready association between music and emotion, I would add that the players tune to a mood—each other's moods—as well as to the mood of the piece. For Schutz, tuning in is an interpretive and relational process concerned with contingent human interactions and participation in human solidarity.

In the digital age, we may assume that the agency of attunement is distributed widely, engaging sociability, conversation, the mass media, digital communications, and other means of cultural creation, preservation, and transmission. When considering technology, it helps to think of moods as public before they are private, collective before individual, "wideware" before hardware and software. We draw on whatever technologies are available to assert our solidarity, facilitate our interactions with one another, and to help frame our relationships. To elaborate on the gravitational metaphor I proposed in the previous chapter, a mood is like a planetary-scale gravitational field both influencing and influenced by the bodies within it, subject to momentary deformations, and influencing the bodies that pass through or orbit within it. This metaphor is not after all so distant from Smith's account of society: "Human society, when we contemplate it in a certain abstract and philosophical light, appears like a great, an immense machine, whose regular and harmonious movements produce a thousand agreeable effects."[51]

The idea of the individual, the identification of individuals, our individual selves, and the first-person reporting of the poet are in any case the result of social processes. Cultural geographers Jen Jack Gieseking and William Mangold assert something similar: "Thus individual experience and self-identification—what we refer to as subjectivity—is conditioned by social, political, and economic forces."[52] The sociability of mood draws mood into the domains of power and politics.

Mood and Online Dissent

To tune in to the mood of the crowd is not necessarily to acquiesce to its dictates. In fact, the concept of mood features in social critique. In a society dominated by the importance of reason and rationality, to understand and represent the world in terms of mood seems to go against the grain.

It was the radical and fraught art group known as the Situationalist International (SI) in the 1950s and 60s who asserted the need to reclaim spaces in the city by accessing their emotional qualities against the "bourgeois zone"—that is, what they claimed was "the confused reign of reactionary imbecility." The SI claimed the ground for thinking of mood as a feature of the city, a theme since taken up by urban designers, artists, and social commentators. In heroic style, its leader Guy Debord affirmed the importance of "momentary ambiences of life and their transformation into a superior passional quality."[53] These are words about affect, emotion, and mood. As I've already indicated, ambience (or *ambiance* in French) is one of the words for "mood." According to Debord, the activist must construct "collective ambiences, ensembles of impressions determining the quality of a moment." As if following Aristotle's advice, he takes the example of a social gathering. The activist who wishes to exert influence needs to take "into account the knowledge and material means we have at our disposal, to study what organization of the place, what selection of participants and what provocation of events are suitable for producing the desired ambience."[54]

Here, the rhetoric of mood drifts away from the mere amplification, intensification, and distribution of emotion. It seems that almost any group process qualifies as a mood: the desire for freedom, liberty, and equality, and a sense of unity.

One of the major effects claimed of social media is that they alter people's expectations by exposing them to free communication, new ideas, knowledge about what happens in other parts of the world, and for some a sense of solidarity and unity. Moods moderate and influence people's anticipations. Theorist of digital media Rich Ling highlights the social coercion that follows the adoption of communications technologies. After a while, the expectation and the necessity circulate that everyone is connected and can participate in the promises offered by solidarity.[55] In a report on the use of social media in the Arab world and the uprisings of 2011, author Jeffrey Ghannam maintains that "social networking has changed expectations of freedom of expression and association to the degree that individual and collective capacities to communicate, mobilize, and gain technical knowledge are expected to lead to even greater voice, political influence, and participation over the next 10 to 20 years."[56] Such a climate of expectation elides into a mood for change.

Taken in this broad sense, mood provides a useful way of accounting for the role of social media in supporting political protest and transformation. Ghannam poses the question: "Could social media continue to manifest itself on a scale and in ways that coalesce into a form of pan-Arab unity that has so far been elusive?"[57] During protests and uprisings, journalists readily deployed phrases that appealed to mood: the Arab uprising reflects the public mood, and there's a revolutionary mood, a new mood in the region, a mood of confusion and fear, and journalists would reference the jubilant mood of the protesters.

Moods provide a handy descriptive device, because they lack specificity. Sometimes, a mood is just a "buzz." As reported by Ghannam, "The mayor of the Jordanian capital, Amman, Omar Maani, is known to gain popular buzz on Twitter and is among several top government officials, including former prime minister Samir Rifai, who engaged in social networking."[58] What leader would not want to generate a "buzz" that draws attention to his or her particular agenda!

Anger

When critics and commentators attribute mood to a group, it's often the group in aggressive mood: mobs, herds, hordes, scurrying minions, warring battalions, and over-wrought spectators. We might ascribe a mood to such groups: celebratory, triumphant, battle-weary, subjugated, hysterical, frenzied, enthusiastic, or angry.

The popular video game *Call of Duty* boasts that its special digital effects "bring the adrenaline-pumping combat to life," immersing players in experiences that are "harrowing and dynamic."[59] Such combat games also have a communal, multiplayer aspect. Parents, teachers, and media commentators worry about the relationship between violent video games and aggressive behavior by players who carry this mood to the street. Does aggression on screen translate to offline violence? Psychological studies of game players by Gary Giumetti and Patrick Markey maintain that at most, game players who are angry before they start playing tend to be more aggressive if "exposed to violent video games than if they were exposed to nonviolent video games."[60] Aggression is indicative of a powerful mood that in turn invokes strong concerns and a kind of "moral panic"[61] fueled by the mass media.

It's helpful to progress with the theme of mood's sociable aspects by considering the mood of anger, as exhibited by groups of people. Anger operates as a kind of *intensification*. In addition to the core affect system I described in the previous chapter, psychologists have invented the Positive and Negative Affect Schedule (PANAS) as a mood-categorization system.[62] They identify such "positive" moods as being interested, enthusiastic, inspired, excited, strong, proud, alert, determined, and attentive. On the "negative" scale are moods such as scared, nervous, upset, distressed, guilty, irritable, hostile, ashamed, jittery, and afraid. Hostility stands in for anger and of all the moods listed is the most suggestive of action, implying a vigorous response to an encounter with threat or an enemy, as if expanding or defending territory: fight rather than flight.[63]

In his seminal work on metaphor and emotion, the linguist Zoltán Kövecses identifies key metaphors about anger. Anger appears at times as a hot fluid in a container, a fire, a captive animal, a burden, and a natural force. Kövecses focuses on the individual, but the schema can be expanded to crowds. Anger is less about liberating a captive animal than releasing a herd. An angry crowd reaches boiling point, unleashes its anger, brews as if a storm, spreads itself like wildfire, and burns out. These are active and violent metaphors. In myth, Thor and Mars are the energetic gods of storms and thunder and preside over people's anger. As well as being fiery, anger is a noisy affair.

In her study of large compilations of texts, using corpus linguistic research techniques, Alice Deignan notes that "heat metaphors are more often found in talk about the collective anger of a group of people and its impact, than in talk about the feelings of individuals."[64] She indicates how "fire has the potential to become uncontrollable and very destructive, and it can be started—*ignited*—with a small and apparently innocuous *spark*."[65]

I'm fond of quoting the composer Iannis Xenakis on the nature of crowds. In the following passage, he conveys something akin to an angry mood, but without naming it as such: "Everyone has observed the sonic phenomena of a political crowd of dozens of hundreds of thousands of people. The human river shouts a slogan in a uniform rhythm. Then another slogan springs from the head of the demonstration; it spreads towards the tail, replacing the first. A wave of transition thus passes from the head to the tail. The clamour fills the city, and the inhibiting force of voice and rhythm reaches a climax. It is an event of great power and beauty in its ferocity . . . They are the laws of the passage from complete order to total disorder in a continuous or explosive manner."[66]

This unnamed mood involves entropy and chaos, which equate to the heating of a gas or liquid and operate by degrees, as if waves of intensity: the greater the mood, the higher the entropy and the stronger the effect. The more *intense* the wave, the more likely the crowd is to move toward extreme action. In fact, as indicated in this passage, it's sufficient to substitute "intensity" for "anger." In any case, anger seems to be at the most intense end of a spectrum that trails off at the lower registers toward apathy and cool indifference. Who can tell what people are feeling, but anyone can observe the intensity through people's actions. The effect is the same.

In the summer of 2011 in the United Kingdom, large numbers of youths raided shops for branded sportswear and electrical goods and set fire to shops. Such flash points are common in many countries. The riots followed a demonstration over the killing of a member of an urban gang by police. The gang riots following the event and on the scale presented were abetted in no small part by rapid communications networks, as rioters signaled their moves to one another via secure messaging on BlackBerry smartphones. The less expert joined in under the gaze of CCTV and global media, which increased the chances that individuals would be identified and provided tangible targets for the apparent anger of others in the community as well as the rule of law. The faces of the offenders appeared on television and then in the courts. The scenario is a familiar one, with parallels in other major cities of the world.

In the case of the UK rioters, it's not clear whether they were angry, nervous, or just caught in the thrill of the moment. The Guardian newspaper reported criminologist John Pitts as saying that the looters "quickly see that police cannot control the situation, which leads to a sort of adrenalin-fueled euphoria—suddenly you are in control and there is nothing anyone can do."[67] Nor was it clear whether the people watching the effects on television were angry at the circumstances that might have led to the riots or at the rioters themselves.

Without presuming what was going on in people's minds, we can simply say that anger featured as a linguistic element in the various coping strategies of the actors or players in the intense drama: rioters, their relatives, police, store owners, journalists, bloggers, tweeters, viewers, politicians, civic leaders, and welfare campaigners. One newspaper reported that "widespread anger and frustration at the way police engage with communities was a significant cause of the summer riots in every major city where disorder took place."[68] It's not just that some people actually felt angry, but that the attribution of anger provided a theme to the story. Emotions and their putative attribution provides a way of structuring an account.

In their seminal research on emotions, anthropologists Catherine Lutz and Geoffrey White identify the kinds of social problems that society is quick to explain in emotional terms.[69] Riots, social disorder, and violent crime are problems that news reporters, commentators, researchers, and other storytellers describe using the language of emotions—in particular, the language of anger. As reported, the perpetrators of these acts may be described as angry, and those observing or caught up in the activity "were angry."

If anger is a group phenomenon, then how do we explain a singular moment of anger—that is, anger outside the intensity of the crowd? Lutz and White describe the phenomenon in terms of convention and cultural codes, which are after all shared within some group or other.[70] A person may become angry when someone violates her cultural code—that is, the code to which she subscribes. A person sensitive to this violation (and commentators) will readily explain her response in terms of anger. A shop worker who expects customers to enter into a polite transaction is angry when the customer complains constantly or, worse, grabs the goods without paying and rushes out of the store. It's also possible to be angry with yourself. Moviegoers may well be angry at a disturbance caused by others, but a moviegoer may also get angry at his own lapse in social competence when he forgets to turn off his mobile phone that rings in the middle of a film. Threat or danger to life and limb of oneself or others can also provoke anger. A pedestrian sees a small child run across a busy street and is angry with the invisible parent. Losing a significant relationship also associates with anger, as in a breakup, departure, or death. Being in receipt of and responsible for some kind of resource can engender anger: Why am I looking after this team that always lets me down? Lutz and White argue that these are all social situations. It is difficult to think of a circumstance in which someone is angry, or at least in which we use the idea of anger to explain someone's behavior, that does not involve some group or other or a set of interpersonal relationships.

The Social Shaping of Emotion

The strong contention here is that moods and emotions are social. Is anger a universal emotion, experienced by everyone in the same way? Anthropology inevitably invokes cross-cultural comparisons, in further support of the sociability of mood. Different cultural groups may respond differently to each of the social problems outlined previously. It is tempting to think that anger is a universal mood with a definition to which everyone subscribes, but there are differences. When a person realizes his own lapse in social competence by letting the phone ring in the cinema, he may focus on the audience in the error and apologize profusely or at least feel anger at himself for upsetting the audience and the management. Someone from a different cultural background may be angry that he has let himself down and resolve to do better next time. Someone else may focus on the damage done to the flow of the movie rather than be concerned about the audience involved. Lutz and White think of these differences in feelings and behavior in terms of substantial cultural differences, such as the difference between a Japanese, American, or Pacific Islander response. Lutz and White also apply this insight to age, personality, and subcultural differences.

They also suggest that different cultural groups tie emotions together in different ways. Anger may be linked to fear, shame, or admiration, depending on one's cultural group. The problems outlined previously also carry with them scripted "solutions" or behavior patterns that inevitably involve social relationships and power structures that will vary. In the phone example, the script might require an audible sigh and quick retrieval of the phone to turn it off. If the faux pas was in a board meeting, then the script may warrant that the phone be answered while making a speedy exit from the room, reflecting something about the power relationships among the people involved.

Whatever the nature of this intensity known as "anger," the context of its explanation places it as a property of groups. What we can say of anger, as a mood, applies to any mood. The strong claim of such social constructivism[71] is that an emotion such as anger fits within "a strategy for defending a group's preferred type of social organization."[72] Emotions are "socially shaped and socially shaping."[73] The case of anger as an element within behavior patterns and discursive practices supports further the view of Dourish and Bell that emotion is "interactional as opposed to representational" as a basis of interaction design.[74]

Moods as Frames for Action

The anger of the crowd implies irrationality, but the emotional life of a group is far from chaotic. In describing the initiation ritual known as *naven* in Iatmul culture in Papua New Guinea, anthropologist Gregory Bateson describes the importance of what he calls the *ethos* of a community, which is its "emotional tone,"[75] to be contrasted with *eidos*, which is the standard interpretation of a mood: "The *eidos* of a culture is an expression of the standardized cognitive aspects of the individuals, while the *ethos* is the corresponding expression of their standardized affective aspects."[76] Groups structure their emotional lives in certain ways, as well as their thinking. Following many contemporary theorists, I don't think there's any need to separate thinking and feeling structures in this way, but I like the proposition that groups structure their emotional vocabularies, relationships, and areas of application. In fact, as I will show, we could usefully describe such structures as moods. I adopt the view of psychologist William N. Morris, who, in his book *Mood: A Frame of Mind*, asserts that moods "subtly insinuate themselves into our lives, influencing what we remember of the past, perceive in the present, and expect from the future."[77] That such structures are social and shared adds further support to the publicness of moods.

Scholars from different quarters have identified such structures essential for communication and cooperation, variously described as codes, scripts, frames, genres, models, paradigms, and metaphor structures.[78] Lutz and White use "code" as indicating a set of moral rules. The idea of a script is also helpful in considering the shared character of emotions and conversations about emotions, as in the earlier example about anger and street riots. Scripts have actors, props, and settings, and follow a narrative format. The concept of the frame in cognitive science implies a structure that supports different objects and relationships, including the format of a script. Film audiences might manage their expectations in terms of genre, expecting a "romantic comedy" to have a happy ending, for example.[79]

In each case, the idea is that we navigate between structures, and people who work together and communicate with one another share structures. When they don't, there is a clash—a culture clash—sometimes resulting in anger, as when the store behavior script is violated by a cashier reciting poetry, a romcom ends in tragedy, or someone throws a stag party in the laboratory. In any case, anger features differently as an element in the context of a sports game, a street riot, counseling session, or intimate relationship. To use a mobile phone in a cinema as if at home would be a frame clash: doing the wrong thing at the wrong place and time.

In her study of linguistic corpuses, Deignan indicates that metaphor is "shaped by societal and ideological factors as well as cognitive ones." It is "influenced by linguistic, genre, and ideological factors."[80] Mood metaphors are similarly structured according to social convention. There are entailments of the heat metaphor applied to anger; certain ideas and actions are included and others excluded. It's permissible to talk of the crowd being all fired up, but less likely that you would talk of it glowing like the sun or about measuring its temperature with a thermometer or of harnessing its anger to generate electricity. You might gesture as if fanning someone to cool them down, but would not fear being burned if you made body contact. Insofar as mood participates in the play of metaphor, it is subject to the varying norms of sociability.

Codes, scripts, frames, genres, and metaphor structures, by whatever name, govern our expectations. Being in a particular frame of mind means knowing what to expect. Such expectations are shared, as are the frames that govern them. Adopting a suitable frame of mind, or mood, is a major accomplishment and key to addressing life's challenges.

Summary

In this chapter, I've demonstrated the collective aspect of moods. Any sociable interaction involves some kind of response to the mood of those around you. This is to deal with the basic human capacity for empathy toward others. There's some interesting neurological theory about this involving the mirror neuron system, which provides strong support for just how codependent we are. I think it's helpful to assume that moods are collective before they are private and individual. There is a social and cultural aspect to the definition of mood. In the process, I've examined anger as a group phenomenon that motivates people to action and protest. The contingent nature of anger practices highlights the active nature of people's emotional lives. When people adopt a particular mood, they also adopt a way of framing and thinking about possible actions. In chapter 9, I'll emphasize further how digital technologies are implicated in this framing.

Coda 1: Social Problems Are Wicked

Close observers have claimed that the mood of dissent generated within groups and crowds incites people to action, protest, and revolution, processes supported by digital social media. As I've shown, mood features in the vocabulary of protest. In an academic article about the Arab Spring, George Joffé wonders how "it possible for protesters in Egypt and Tunisia to create what were effective and apparently spontaneous social movements that so rapidly captured the popular mood and thus effected the changes activists sought."[81] One answer resides in the moods circulating with the aid of social media that put people in a frame of mind (a mood) in which they were primed for and expected particular kinds of change. This is not to claim that social media were responsible for the changes.

It's worth reflecting on the complexity of these mood-defining processes. A book by Evgeny Morozov seeks to deflate the enthusiasm of those who claim that Facebook, Twitter, and other social networking tools are responsible for social and political transformations of the kind we saw in Tunisia, Egypt, Bahrain, and Libya.[82] Morozov's book is entitled *The Net Delusion: How Not to Liberate the World*. I'm particularly interested in Morozov's argument that revives a line that emerged in the 1970s, that social problems are in fact "wicked problems." These problems in turn relate to mood.

To suggest that a particular technology (Twitter) is responsible for solving a social problem is to treat wicked problems as if they are "tame," according to Morozov. Factoring a quadratic equation is a tame problem, as is calculating the required dimensions of a concrete beam, traversing a maze, or solving the Rubik's cube puzzle. Tame problems are well-defined, with a single goal and a set of well-defined rules; for example, each side of a Rubik's cube must display a unique color, and you can only rotate nine coplanar cubes at a time.

However, significant and challenging problems, such as designing a building, deciding on a transportation policy, or influencing how people are to think and behave, are invariably "wicked." They are only loosely formulated. There is no "stopping rule." Wicked problems persist and are subject to redefinition and resolution in different ways over time. Wicked problems are not objectively given, but their formulation already depends on the viewpoint of those presenting them. There is no ultimate test of the validity of a solution to a wicked problem. The testing of solutions takes place in some practical context, the solutions are not easily undone, and the verdict on the solution is often contested.

This characterization of the nature of real-world problems was put forward by Horst Rittel and Melvin Webber in their 1973 article "Dilemmas in a General Theory of Planning."[83] Rittel and Webber joined a chorus of dissenters against those who thought that all social problems could be solved by systematized organization, clear procedures, and rational method. They argued persuasively that most professional tasks are only very poorly explained in terms of goal setting, constraints, rules, and search through a well-defined problem space. If studies into affect, emotion, and mood teach us anything, it is that reason is not a purely logical process in any case.

Professionals and political activists practice their art by framing the problems they choose to address. By the time problems of any social consequence (i.e., wicked problems, such as deciding a public health policy or fomenting a more democratic society) are identified, conjectured, and defined, they are already "solved" according to the frame of the professional, politician, or activist. Problem framing is a contingent, fraught, and contested process for which there is no authoritative set of rules, criteria, or methods. To define social and political problems in terms of the need for better communication among citizens (i.e., social networking) already presupposes a solution, thus short-circuiting difficult debate. In so doing, it attempts to tame a wicked problem. According to Morozov, "modern authoritarianism, by its very constitution, is a wicked, not a tame, problem. It cannot be 'solved' or 'engineered away' by a few lines of genius computer code or a stunning iPhone app."[84] Although much in the book is overstated, I think this reasoning resonates with that of the digital sceptic. Technologies do not change society or shift the mood of a people; it is the complex web of human practices, human organization, relationships, customs, and attitudes that bring about transformation.

To bundle such phenomena together as mood serves as well as any other overarching concept: code, script, frame, genre, model, metaphor structure, or paradigm.[85] The mood sets the stage and governs anticipation. Matthew Ratcliffe describes a mood as "a background that binds us to the world, anchoring us in a context of goals, projects and relevant environmental patterns."[86] Mood engenders a feeling of orientation: "It is, quite simply, the rhythm of life."[87]

The strong claim for the study of mood is that, if you get the mood right and tune in appropriately, then you've almost solved the problem. The audience is already persuaded. The hard work is done. The rest is easier. Far from trivializing the role of mood, this indicates its complexity, significance, and "publicness" in human affairs. Were I to write a business manual, I would overstate the case thus: Put your efforts into mood management, which is a complex, difficult, and contingent process, and the solutions will follow. Mood management focuses on *esprit de corps*, solidarity, and communities rather than individuals.

Business-oriented weblog authors are ready to offer advice in these terms. Enter "why blog" into your search engine. The answers invariably invoke concepts of building community, putting a human face on your brand, sharing, and picking up on customer mood. Social digital media present collectivity as a virtue. Concepts such as smart mobs and crowdsourced creativity trade on the strength of public mood. Advocacy of the power of digital media finds support from the sociability of mood. Mood lies within the purview of interpretative practices as exercised within communities. Communities that deploy digital social media are indeed powerful creators and purveyors of mood and influence.

Coda 2: Myths of Collective Madness

There are many explanations for moods of collective irrationality, even involving natural processes such as the cycles of the moon.

Google launched 15-meter-wide helium balloons into the stratosphere to extend the Internet to remote areas. This was called "Project Loon." According to a Google engineer working on the project, Cliffe Biffle, "Balloon-powered Internet sounds positively mad."[88] "Loon" is clever branding. The association between the clinically suspect term *lunatic* and the extraterrestrial is fairly obvious. According to the *Oxford English Dictionary*, lunatic originally meant "affected with the kind of insanity that was supposed to have recurring periods dependent on the changes of the moon."[89]

As I'm investigating mood, I feel I have to look at the moon, or perhaps join with those who howl at it. Some studies provide tantalizing evidence of a link between the cycles of the moon and the moods people are in, though other factors also intervene, such as the weather. According to one study, "in both summer and winter, people seemed to be less helpful when the moon was full than when the moon was less full,"[90] though the data was "ambiguous." It may not be the moon that affects people's moods but factors such as the luminance of the night sky, the tides, the weather, or disturbed sleep. The evidence is probably available if you really want to believe that the moon affects moods.

Lycanthropy

Certain myths strengthen the relationship between lunar cycles and human behavior and help us want to believe it. A fascinating thesis by Erin Flaherty summarizes some compelling links between lunar cycles, menstruation, werewolves, and the Jekyll and Hyde story. Producers of werewolf horror movies generally depict the transformation of a male to a werewolf on the night of the full moon as a transformation to extreme masculinity: predation, aggression, an excess of hair, and a deep voice. The transformed creature is the lycanthrope, a human–wolf hybrid.

However, Flaherty marshals support from several sources to indicate that the werewolf is really about the feminine taken to extremes: "As a woman's menstrual cycle has come to be defined by monthly blood loss, physical changes, vicious temperaments and insatiable appetites, so is the werewolf's transformation."[91] She argues provocatively that the werewolf transformation myth is about man becoming woman, the real "monster" in patriarchal society.

The Jekyll and Hyde story is also about transformation, and the doppelganger motif, as if each of us has within ourselves both the potential to (a) fit in as if normal and (b) stand out as antisocial and monstrous. In Freudian terms, human nature involves tussles between the sober and sane ego versus the more animalistic id part of our natures: a mood of sober reasonableness contrasted with occasional transformation to the converse mood of animalistic irrationality, and even rage. After all, people in a really bad mood are "beastly." They become "monsters."

In more abstract terms, these narratives speak of the relationship between mood and transformation. The putative agency of the moon adds a third term. At the very least, the moon metaphor reminds us that there can be a cyclical aspect to people's moods.

Moon Modulators

The challenge for me is to think about what if anything these ideas contribute to how we understand digital media as mood modifiers. Here are some candidates. First, moods go in cycles, seasons, rhythms, patterns, subject of course to disruption. The digital devices we carry around with us participate in the recording, monitoring, and modulation of cycles. They can make such cycles more visible and obvious. These cycles include the delivery of mood-altering entertainment via television and radio schedules, as well as health and fitness monitoring. Digital devices make calendars, reminders, birthdays, monthly bills, and direct debits more visible and allow us to align with or resist such quotidian and annual organization.

Second, the cycles of the moon represent a system of cycles that is at odds with the diurnal movement of the earth around the sun. I explored this idea in *The Tuning of Place*, introducing terms such as *discrepancy, calibration, temperament, discord,* and *tuning.* The cycles of the moon also feed into festival cycles (e.g., Easter, Hogmanay, and the Gaelic festival of Beltane). Festivals as times of celebration and breaking out of the norm relate to moods.

Third, werewolves are not the only monsters in the human imaginary. If the functions of monsters are to displace, disrupt, and hybridize, as a kind of matter out of place, then digital devices also fit the bill with their own hybrid "monstrosity" and as channels for violent or monster-filled movies and computer games.[92]

Fourth, in any case, the Internet is a medium from which the ardent believer can extract evidence for almost anything, including the proposition that the moon affects collective moods. The medium is a bit "mad" in this and other respects.

A reader left an informative comment on this post: Your article made me think of the ambiguous etymology of "lykos" and "lyki": the first wolf— the second light. Some theories say that the roots of each word [are] different and they just sound similar. Other theories try to draw a link. For example, the interpretations interweave further: "Lykios Apollo" has been interpreted as the god associated with light, but it has also been associated with the story saying that he was born of Lito while she was transformed into a wolf. Other interpretations associate the word with a sculptor who created a sculpture of Apollo, and others with Lycia—the city in Minor Asia. Further associations with the word "lyceum" (lykio) can be made.

3 Captivated by Curiosity

Curious people are open to new experiences, and what better medium to exercise that curiosity than the vast resources of online media and social networks. After all, curious people want to broaden their outlook. They are inquisitive and acquisitive. People at their most curious are learners on the lookout for mental and physical resources that will aid them in solving problems—if not immediately, then later. Curiosity exhibits itself when people explore, collect, sort, and store information, artifacts, images, and perhaps memories and experiences. Most of us exhibit curiosity to some degree, at different times and in different situations. Curiosity is mostly about being open to difference, a proposition I will argue in this chapter.

There's a long tradition of techniques and technologies for supporting human curiosity, not least encyclopedias, books, museums, and libraries. During the Renaissance, wealthy travelers would collect relics, sculptures, skeletal remains, birds' eggs, and other curios that attracted their interest and assemble them in "cabinets of curiosity."[1] Skillful creators, architects, collectors, educators, and artists know how to invite curiosity in the way they position objects in spaces and the way they arrange spaces. As dynamic repositories of information, the Internet and online social media provide obvious tools that further promote, engender, and sustain the human capacity for curiosity.

Broadening Horizons

Experimental psychologist Barbara Fredrickson describes curiosity as a kind of broadening of horizons, or broadening of *repertoires*, as she calls them.[2] She establishes a direct link between positive emotions and this capacity to broaden our "thought-action repertoires." From an evolutionary perspective, over millennia human beings have increased their odds for survival by exercising positive emotions, such as joy, love, and contentment. Such emotions emerge when there's a lack of immediate threat and give us respite from the struggles to survive. Our positive emotions alert us that it's safe to look around and collect information, bond socially, play, and rehearse. On the other hand, the so-called negative emotions of fear, anxiety, and sadness are calls to adopt evasive action. To avoid danger and threats, we are inclined to focus attention, to run, or to expend valuable energy and cognitive resources to resolve immediate problems.[3] We develop strategies to avoid negative emotions, and so we avoid threatening circumstances that engender such feelings.

Events associated with positive emotions attract us and encourage us to want more of the same. They also prompt us to "broaden," which also carries rewards. Such events encourage "approach tendencies." When of a positive and trustful disposition, we will tend to approach the unknown and the different rather than settle for the security of the known: "Evidence suggests that resilient people have optimistic, zestful and energetic approaches to life, are curious and open to new experiences, and are characterized by high positive emotionality."[4] Positivity and curiosity contribute to a cognitive "banking" strategy. When times are good, we not only store up material for harsh winters and dangerous times, but we load up with cognitive resources by scouting around, testing ourselves, and learning.[5]

Curiosity and Positive Moods

Insofar as curiosity is associated with positive moods, it seems that human beings can't help but be curious. According to some researchers, human beings exhibit a bias toward positive emotions in any case and hence curiosity. In most cultures, the instinctive response to "How are you?" is "I'm well, thanks." If you imagine a scale between "sad" and "happy," with "happy" at the upper end, then most people will place themselves somewhere above the midpoint—that is, above the neutral state. There's a lot here about social convention and social cohesion, but psychologists Ed and Carol Diener assert that we really do feel slightly happier than the midpoint. Among other benefits, this bias actually sharpens our awareness of dangerous and unpleasant circumstances, which is necessary for survival. It allows negative events to stand out even more strongly. If we incline to a positive mood, then against that background we are more likely to recognize and respond to danger and the related emotions of fear and anxiety when they occur. Our positive disposition also makes us more inclined to explore. Insofar as positive moods enhance "approach tendencies," they help maintain our curiosity: the tendency to broaden our experience. According to Diener and Diener, all of human history is caught up in this positive drive: "Human approach tendencies are manifest in the rapid exploration and settlement of new frontiers and in the unremitting invention of new ideas and institutions throughout human history."[6] Curiosity expands from a local survival mechanism to embrace the whole of human development.

Where psychologists and poets think of curiosity as an emotion, it is one of the so-called knowledge emotions, such as interest, confusion, surprise, awe, and wonder. Psychologist Paul Silvia explains that people present visible signs when experiencing a "knowledge emotion," similar in kind to facial expressions and gestures evident in other emotions, such as happiness and anger.[7] In the case of the knowledge emotions, such signs indicate concentration and attention: movement of the eyes and the muscles in the forehead, tilting the head, and speaking rapidly. Silvia also associates the expressive qualities of such knowledge emotions with "orientation, activation, concentration, and approach-oriented action."[8] Curiosity is not restricted to humans. Emblematic of curiosity is the cat and its tentative, approach-oriented actions as it inspects new territory.

Human physiology supports our curious impulses. As upright creatures, human beings have several advantages over other animals. We are able to shift orientation rapidly and to look upward, a propensity given significance in myth and art. I'm fond of quoting Vitruvius's (c. 80–15 BC) description of primitive man emerging from the woods, exhibiting advantage over the other creatures: "finding themselves naturally gifted beyond the other animals in not being obliged to walk with faces to the ground, but upright and gazing upon the splendour of the starry firmament."[9] It's as if the human body is equipped to exercise broad-ranging curiosity behaviors, attending to both the bigger picture and the fine detail.

It's helpful to think of curiosity as a mood rather than an impulse to gather information, or even just an emotion. In his book *Affective Mapping*, Jonathan Flatley says, "Only when I am curious can new objects present themselves to me as interesting."[10] He maintains that without the mood of curiosity he can't *feel* interested. Moods are not supposed to have an object, so it's necessary to think of curiosity as a general condition, as opposed to the more specific circumstance of being curious *about* something or interested *in* something. Distinguishing curiosity as a mood is helpful, as it opens the issue of curiosity to the longer time spans of cultural and social contexts. It also positions curiosity within a constellation of contributing conditions: technologies, artifacts, social organization, and physicality. A curious inclination engendered and supported by the environment can enable learning and development independently of any particular target. We can just be in a curious mood.

The association between curiosity, other positive moods, and "approach-oriented actions" suggests that curiosity involves getting out and about. Poets and storytellers often associate curiosity with tentative, cat-like steps, the physical approach, gingerly lifting a piece of bark to see what's underneath, looking in wonder at the starry firmament, roving, roaming, and exploring. It's a cautious but very active mood. Curious creatures don't sit and wait. Curiosity involves going out into the world, rather than sitting indoors in front of a computer or cradling a smartphone while ignoring everything going on around you.

Curious about Nature

Poets and philosophers have long celebrated curiosity. It's the mainstay of a scientific orientation, learning, the romantic spirit, and travel. The romantic philosopher Jean Jacques Rousseau (1712–1778) wrote about curiosity in relation to the education of the teenage adolescent.[11] At the age of about twelve, any child has a surplus of strength and capacity. The parent or tutor's task is to encourage the child to invest this surplus in the future by directing it to physical exploration of the world. If we include within this capacity the child's optimism and propensity for positive emotion, then Rousseau was supporting an early version of Fredrickson's "broaden and build" theory.

Rousseau also asserted that the tutor has no need for globes, spheres, and maps to teach a child an academic discipline such as geography. These are mere "symbols." (He could have been talking about computers.) The child should be shown the real thing: "the scent of flowers, the beauty of foliage, the moistness of the dew, the soft turf beneath his feet,"[12] the song of birds, the rising and setting sun.

It is in children's natures to be curious, including in relation to nature. For many of us desk-bound urban dwellers, the great outdoors provides the model environment for curiosity and inquiry. We harbor the belief that we need to return to the arousing outdoor world of nature in order to reanimate our sense of wonder and curiosity. The American poet Henry Thoreau (1817–1862) retreated to the woods "to live deliberately, to front only the essential facts of life," and "to live deep and suck out all the marrow of life."[13] This sentiment persists. According to naturalists Stephen Kellert and Edward Wilson, "The naturalistic tendency involves an intense curiosity and urge for exploration of the natural world."[14] Nature writer Roger Deakin describes the activity of an ecologist friend: "He himself was insatiably curious about everything, climbing trees to inspect birds' nests, getting up at daybreak to check the tilley-lamp moth trap or leading night patrols across the heather armed with torches and nets to sweep for moths and caterpillars."[15] This at least is the idealized model of the exercise of curiosity and of learning. To update the sentiment, books and computers are fine in their place, but we need to get out more, to explore and to learn.

The exploration of nature provides a benchmark for technologies that support the curious spirit. Against the measure of natural curiosity—curiosity in nature—I want to examine the case that ubiquitous and mobile computing is good for curiosity. Like it or not, we have lost our natural innocence, and live in a highly mediated and mediatized world of ubiquitous digital devices and networks.[16] I'll continue the rest of this chapter developing the obvious point that content is important, and then progress to the more instructive notion that our curiosity is driven by the desire and the necessity to encounter difference. I'll demonstrate how online content encourages curiosity management via personal profiling, via presenting material that is alien and different, by hiding as well as revealing information, and as a medium for raising and responding to questions.

Curious about Content

Like the natural world, the Internet provides content, and lots of it. The exercise of curiosity in the context of digital media is soon rewarded. Ubiquitous digital media circulate data, facts, and knowledge—or more precisely, *information*: Olympic medal scores, the name of that actor in *Total Recall*, how long it takes to get to Mars, how to cook artichokes, how to start a riot, and who has written about curiosity.

As with all information sources, there are limits. Critics and scholars raise questions about the accuracy of that information content, its validity, inevitable biases, and the way it gets filtered, censored, and channeled.[17] Online information is not uniformly available, and portals and subscription services produce elite information enclaves. In any case, not everyone has access to the Internet, or the language skills, contextual understanding, and time to access all that's available or that might be relevant to them. Although the Internet promises more than was ever claimed of print media, its limitations are not so different.

The content of the web is always changing and expanding, and much is available while on the move. If curiosity is sustained by getting out and about, then mobile computing supports that. You can look up information on your smartphone from anywhere and at any time. Mobile computing aids fieldwork and exploration outdoors in the natural environment. There are ample systems, apps, and technologically mediated practices that assist people to get out and about, such as mapping applications, GPS, online bus timetables, exercise monitors, digital photography, tweeting about location, and spontaneous meetings among friends enabled through text messaging and specialized apps.

Ubiquitous access to online information carries with it new practices and demands. The technologies for making all that information accessible, the indexing and search of web pages, supports our capacity for curiosity. Web search engines index pages on the web and rapidly return results to web queries. Effective web search has become a necessary skill. There's a lot of noise online that requires skill to filter out. The search results for *curiosity* most likely begin with information about the Mars Rover that bears that name. During many one-on-one and small group meetings with students, we'll reach a point when we indulge in spontaneous online searches for articles, newspaper reports, spellings, translations, locations, images, and videos. Many times, I'll be trying to answer the charge that there's nothing available on whatever topic we are studying. To filter is to discriminate between contexts of word use, to distinguish advertising blurb from academic papers and formal legal documents, and to identify the difference between weblog posts, magazine copy, news items, crowdsourced encyclopedia entries, and variations in quality and authority among them. Smart web users can quickly identify the difference between rants, informal notes, off-the-cuff comments, and considered prose, and develop the skill to recruit the best search terms, combinations of terms, and the most helpful ways of linking them together. Web search also requires familiarity with the idioms of the language of your inquiry and cultural knowledge. Online researchers also develop tactics for identifying reliable information and ascertaining risks involved in using the information they uncover, often confirming information across several sources.

The ready availability of information content makes demands. Any author or lecturer needs to invest time browsing on the Internet before writing or speaking on a topic, not least to find out what has not been said or written already. Then, there's the capacity to generate new insights, crossing disciplinary boundaries, just through browsing. There are many portals to the Internet, which now elides with databases, interpreted and accessed through various search engines and subscription services. Google Scholar provides access to academic publications. Students and staff in universities and other institutions with access to online journal subscriptions can search, browse, and cite learned articles on many topics. For example, a search on *curiosity* uncovers sources in sports medicine, linguistics, psychology, education, art, design, and anthropology. This newly available intellectual license has the potential to uncover hitherto unnoticed connections, clashes, and syntheses across disciplines.

Not all curiosity is driven by a direct inquiry, though. As for Rousseau's learning adolescent, there's scope for aimless exploration, chance, and *idle* curiosity: just poking about. It seems that curiosity is enhanced when it's rewarded. There's ample opportunity for just digging about on the Internet: following the trails set by interlinked web pages, looking at picture files, videos, aerial maps, street views, company and personal websites, and investigating or lurking around social media sites, not to mention chat rooms, massively multiplayer online role-playing games (MMORPGs), and other virtual environments.

All this information content provides potential routes for learning and the development of expertise. According to Paul Silvia, the development of expertise is a further reward from and enhancement to the curious impulse. Online resources are now an essential part of formal learning and a major resource for professional projects. Silvia draws attention to the paradox that the more you know about a subject, the more you become aware of what little you know.[18] The more knowledgeable psychologists are about emotion, the more aware they become of the shortfalls in their understanding, which drives them to know more. Curiosity also becomes more nuanced and finely tuned. Once they become experts, professionals (e.g., architects) searching online may therefore deviate from an interest in what makes buildings beautiful to the history of ideas about beauty and then to the converse, the lack of beauty, and thence to the subtle line between beauty and ugliness, the social construction of such terms, and the politics of aesthetic judgment. The endless trails available during online research can distract, but in the right hands they provide fruitful links and associations. People are keen to become experts in something, and that quest further encourages them to be curious.

Curious Together

Of course, we are not alone in our curiosity. The impulse to be curious accompanies the drive to be sociable. Rousseau presents the education of the free-spirited child as an individualistic affair, under the guidance and extravagance of a personal tutor. However, Rousseau and the romantic tradition on which he draws neglect the socializing aspects of curiosity. Survival as a species requires that we are interested in people—and other people—and social cohesion depends on such interest. Engagement with social media and online gossip are both indicators and symptoms of the impulse to be socially curious. We want to know what other people are up to, even if from a safe distance. Hence, the forensic search for old school companions on social media sites and the habitual or occasional inspection of Facebook news feeds. Sociability also thrives on shared speculation about facts, showing off knowledge, and sharing information. Curiosity contributes to companionship.

Many self-help guides point to the sociability inherent in asking questions as opposed to always being ready with answers. Perhaps the relationship between sociability and curiosity are undergoing transformation. Why spend time during a dinner party fielding guesses as to who sang "Tennessee Waltz" or won the World Cup in 1966? Anyone interested can look it up later. On the other hand, collaborative web browsing, playing favorite songs from playlists, searching for online videos, and looking at maps and web photographs constitute new social pastimes. Sociability seems to deploy whatever technologies are to hand for amusement, for the establishment of social cohesion, and to support the curiosity of the group.

The creation of online content also has a sociable aspect through cocreation. An interesting online article and images by Bob Stein while working for Atari predicted the use of mobile devices as knowledge sources back in 1982.[19] The images indicate ubiquitous tablet computers and wireless connectivity. Of less prominence in the images are the cocreative aspects of shared encyclopedic knowledge. Online information does not just belong to authors, publishers (of works such as the *Encyclopædia Britannica* or the *Oxford English Dictionary*), and authoritative institutions to be dispatched to mobile tablet computers; everyone can contribute to the growing information pool.

According to Silvia, learners with the capacity for curiosity develop strategies to enhance their interest in important and necessary tasks and to ensure that they persist with tasks,[20] such as filing a tax return, running an errand, or physical exercise. Sociability can enhance the enjoyment of tasks by providing companionship, pooling people's abilities, dividing labor, and getting the job done quicker, but also through sharing the outcome, talking about it, publicizing the results on social media, and garnering feedback. Learners can also introduce challenges by turning the task into a competition against others or oneself: competing against time, assessing what they do against past performance, and cognitively restructuring the task at hand. I would add multitasking, listening to the radio, setting targets, and developing research skills. These all help to make the work environment more engaging. Ubiquitous media provide tools for making routine or tedious tasks more interesting by such sociable means.

The computing environment can also render routine tasks such as composing a report more interesting by introducing page design and layout into the task, image selection, indexing, or discovering how to create a table of contents. Tasks that lack challenge can thereby be made more challenging or encourage outcomes that have qualities other than those demanded by the immediate task at hand and enhance self-satisfaction and appreciation by others. The ability to broadcast the results of online tasks via blogs and social media posts and updates adds a further sociable dimension to the task at hand.

The availability of multiple channels means that one can be listening to music while composing text. There are numerous ways of setting a mood conducive to your way of working and under your moderation. It's also possible in some cases to move to a different physical environment while carrying out a task: sitting on public transport, at a coffee shop, in the park, or in some other sociable context. Following from Fredrickson's theories of

"broaden and build," insofar as digital media increase one's sense of pleasure and sociability, curiosity is enhanced. We manage our curiosity like
other moods by moving in and out of different social contexts. Insofar as
moods are socially constructed and regulated, curiosity is sociable. Everyone knows that enthusiasm "is infectious"; so is curiosity. It's easy to catch
the enthusiasms of those around us. In fact, it takes some effort to work
against the grain of the group's curiosity contours.

People home in to what benefits them in some way. That's what Adam
Smith asserts as "self-interest." We have a special interest in ourselves, the
self, self-preservation, and self-presentation. Psychologists call this *hedonic*
motivation—that is, the motivation to meet some personal need and
thereby derive pleasure. Thus, curiosity also operates in the service of self.

Curious about Identities

We humans are insatiably curious about ourselves as individuals. Social
media and blogging confirm as much, as social networkers check up on
personal statistics, ratings, hits, friends, likes, mentions, retweets, and visits. According to James Carey's ritual view of media we follow online personalized news feeds to check in to the world to see that it is okay and that
our place in it is still secure: "Nothing new is learned but . . . a particular
view of the world is portrayed and confirmed."[21] As further evidence of the
intensity of first-person self-curiosity, the psychologist Sigmund Freud con-
troversially associated curiosity with the sex drive. The young adolescent
is required to sublimate his or her curiosity about their own bodies and in
so doing takes an exaggerated interest in the world around him or her. For
Freud, compulsive research into the world in general is a "substitute for
sexual activity."[22] Whatever the status of Freud's view now, it speaks to the
intensity of adolescent curiosity as identified by Rousseau and in support of
the hedonic sources of curiosity.

Internet entrepreneurs capitalize on the curiosity of potential markets
and audiences. You need to engage your online audience, and one of the
techniques is to feed their curiosity. Social media draw on concepts of celebrity from the mass media. Online mechanisms for self-promotion mimic
the way celebrities cultivate a fan base. Depictions of Internet cultures are
replete with examples of individuals who have made clever use of the Internet to promote themselves and their business through YouTube videos,
apps, free downloads, blogs, and other social media.

In keeping with celebrity culture, social media encourage personal and private disclosures, or at least, the tools for presenting oneself professionally readily elide into tools for personal presentation. It's as if to succeed in professional life you need to invoke other people's curiosity in what you have to offer—of course, selectively. Professionals have to decide whether to let their online professional profile (or persona) deliver insights into their hobbies, holidays, and family matters. The scope for identity formation seems to be expanding, or at least changing. There will always be some group or other, no matter how small, among whom one can entertain unusual or idiosyncratic interests and with whom one can readily identify. There is a group out there, possibly not yet formed and unknown to you, among whom you can enjoy a ration of fame, recognition, or notoriety if you really want it.

Curiosity and mood here intersect with issues of identity. Sherry Turkle, Allucquere Rosanne Stone, and other commentators and critics of life online have said much about the role of the Internet in identity formation.[23] According to the *Oxford English Dictionary*, *identity* is the condition of being a single individual, having an identifiable character or personality, but also understood in terms of the individual's place within a group with which he or she associates.[24] With social media, you have control (or at least a sense of control) over how you project yourself to others, what you choose to make public or private, and the extent to which you might reveal different identities in different contexts. Part of this control involves letting you choose the extent to which you reveal your identity to different groups. Identity is something to be managed, an opportunity and a challenge for social networkers.[25]

Returning to education, it has an inevitable personal dimension. To *educate* is to *edify*.[26] It's a personal thing. To learn something new, no matter how abstruse or divorced from day-to-day experience, is to learn something about oneself, not least what one thinks of the subject at hand. The philosopher Hans-Georg Gadamer argues that all understanding is in a way a self-understanding.[27] In support of this proposition, the philosopher Martin Heidegger defines the entity of everyday human existence (*Dasein*) as that (self) which inquires after its own being.[28] He stops short of calling this very human capacity *curiosity*, which he reserves for a more idle kind of flitting from one topic to another. However, we are most curious when we participate in the world. We want to see how our own stuff looks, fits in, or rates.

Curious learners want to follow their own projects and are motivated to do so—to "suck out all the marrow of life."[29] Ubiquitous digital media provide an environment for this self-actualization to flourish, or to flounder.

Curious about Difference

So far, I've identified the role of information content, expertise, sociability, and personal growth as factors that sustain curiosity on- and offline. These all converge on the issues of *difference*, nascent in much contemporary psychological theory about curiosity. I indicated Diener and Diener's proposition that human cognition has developed to amplify threat and danger by exaggerating differences between our generally positive mood state and situations that require action, such as fleeing and avoiding.[30] They argue that most people are happy most of the time, thereby bringing threats and dangers into sharper relief. We are inclined after all to be curious about that which differs from what we expect. Curious people seek out such differences. They recognize the different in the same and the same in the different.

Computer graphics and the claims made of it provide a helpful model of the role of difference. Audiences often think that computer graphics and animation are remarkable in their ability to mimic reality. However, I contend that such technologies capture our interest insofar as they purvey unreality or, more precisely, present to audiences experiences that are unlike what they experience every day—features of narrative, drama, and film in any case, but exaggerated further in the case of computer-generated imagery (CGI) and digital effects.

On the rare occasion that I perceive something on-screen as resembling an everyday object or event, it is the unfamiliarity engendered by a new set of relationships or by the strangeness of the context that jolts me into a moment of recognition. Audiences are probably most impressed by how alike things are when seen against a backdrop of un-alikeness. Walking down the street, eating a meal, or buying something in a shop stand out when we realize that the walker is about to break into song, the diners hardly touch their food, and the shopper is Harry Potter in Scrivenshaft's Quill Shop.

The importance of difference also comes to the fore in the relationship between film and everyday life. City life features in films, people make films to explore city spaces, and tourists visit film locations. Artists create multimedia interactives about cities that also have a filmic aspect to them. *Night Walk in Marseilles*[31] is a filmic art piece featuring the sounds, music, atmosphere, and graffiti of Marseilles at night, with narration, routes, and diversions, built on Google Street View. Although it's about a place rather than a story with characters, it carries much of the emotional force of a film. Cities are much like films in any case. In his book on "cine-scapes," Richard Koeck outlines the ways that cities and films converge structurally.[32] In a film, shots inevitably are juxtaposed against one another, bringing about smooth transitions or causing surprise: a shot of a smiling face followed by one of a playing child conjures up a different emotion than the same smile followed by a picture of a blood-stained corpse.

Architects, activists, and graffiti artists are adept at creating such urban montages that provoke particular meanings and emotions. Koeck refers to the use of the cut in architecture and gradual transitions (dissolves). He also refers to the narrative qualities of spaces, those aspects that invite people to put themselves on show (spectator qualities), the way architects control views, creating prospect, translucency, and other optical qualities, and of course the way designers alter sonic qualities by configuring spaces and activities. It's sometimes helpful to think of people's experience of space in filmic terms: movement and passage, framing, rhythm, and soundtracks. This city-film discourse provides a further example of the complicity of media in our emotional landscapes. Those of us brought up with film can't help but experience places colored by the expectations provided by film techniques and by films of particular places. Of course, the reverse can apply. The way places get depicted in film can bring to light just how alien our everyday experiences can be. Like cities, films jar us into new realities by the differences they bring to light.

The cinema audience member is like a tourist. Part of this encounter involves the provision of a new backdrop to the ordinary aspects of a person's life, such as physical activity, shopping, eating, and drinking. That one thing may strike us as similar to another—that is, that an image on a screen is similar to something we encounter everyday—produces pleasure of a kind but also invokes a sense of the uncanny. It presents to us as "curious." The "uncanny valley" hypothesis proposes that audiences are less comfortable with humanoid figures on-screen that look almost human. Reviewers have remarked that the nearly realistic characters in the CGI films *Final Fantasy: The Spirits Within, Beowulf,* and *The Polar Express* look cadaverous, or at least unemotional. In *Avatar* the CGI characters are fashioned to be super (or extra) human and so are received differently by audiences. Computer animations, video games, and immersive virtual reality are often applauded because they present experiences similar to what can be accomplished by actors and sets on film, but it is important to reflect on the human capacity to appreciate differences, as opposed to similarities, in these experiences.

As in film, it's not necessary to search far to discover evidence for the primary importance of difference (rather than similarity) as a key factor in human curiosity. The linguist Ferdinand de Saussure demonstrated that it is difference that makes language possible.[33] Concepts of categorization are not possible without difference. The social philosopher Michel Foucault pointed to the triumph of difference over attempts to introduce conformity. The identification of "the same" only serves to make "it possible to measure gaps, to determine levels, to fix specialities . . . all the shading of individual difference."[34]

The philosopher Jacques Derrida, Following Martin Heidegger, makes maximum play on the nature of difference, even to the extent of creating a new word (*différance*) that also implies (in relation to language) "that meaning is always deferred."[35] To focus on difference is to embark on restless discovery. By contrast, the identification of sameness aims for stasis and seems to close off discussion. If we are intent on finding out what is the same about things, then our search ends at the achievement of the goal: photorealism in computer graphics, for example. On the other hand, difference reveals further difference. Difference also opens up the possibility of interplay between discussants who never quite agree. The pursuit of difference is an obvious motivator in curiosity. The supposed realism of computer imagery and screen-based media connect to a wider social concern and in turn to the character of design and all art. Diversity drives curiosity.

Curious about What's Hidden

The absence of a thing is difference magnified. What can be more different from a thing than its lack! But then, something may not be entirely absent but simply hidden. To hide something is a sure way to arouse curiosity. It's about secrets. According to the travel writer Robert Mcfarlane, "Literature and religion are littered with stories of other worlds—uncharted oceans, secret realms, imaginary deserts, unclimbable peaks, unvisited islands and lost cities. The curiosity and attraction we instinctively feel towards the locked room, the garden over the wall, the landscape just beyond the horizon, the imagined country on the other side of the world; these are all expressions of the same desire in us to know somewhere apart, somewhere hidden."[36] Hiddenness is absence in the context of uncertainty.

Nature affords much that is hidden, and Rousseau's counsel to the tutor is to hold off from answering the child's questions directly. Don't reveal too much. Sometimes, we hide things deliberately to make the quest more interesting for ourselves and for others. Most stories include an element of mystery, and not only in the case of detective stories. The "mystery" tag is a major tabloid cliché, not to mention a key element of gossip—or any narrative, for that matter. It's the gradual unfolding of a story that appeals, whether it's a mystery story, a fiction about secret societies, or some tale about conspiracy. The mood that mystery engenders is of suspicion and not quite knowing what's at the end of the journey. Mystery invokes curiosity and is therefore a useful tool for educators. It also infuses the ordinary with gravitas.

One way that digital media amplifies difference and renders it interesting and accessible and amenable to cognitive manipulation is by its capacity to make things invisible: to hide things and to cultivate mystery. Any environment that invokes our curiosity renders simple things we take for granted strange and complex: hidden content, secrets, codes, and discovering what goes on behind the scenes. The mass media has latched on to the desire to get behind the scenery and see what transpires in private. Most of us have an appetite for knowing how things work or at least seeing the preparations for the big event: how the frocks got onto the catwalk, the coach psyched the team, the camera operators stalked the leopard, and the banquet was prepared, and the recriminations after a "firing" on *The Apprentice*. These private spaces are a respite from politeness; they are sites of conflict when the guards are down.

Skilled content providers (producers, writers, directors, and designers) control such exposures and balance the formal, professional, front-of-stage product with the other show: the backstage interviews, the fly-on-the-wall documentary, the confidential. The ethnographer Irvin Goffman developed the idea that we each participate in two modes of behavior: the front of stage and behind the scenes.[37] The metaphor of acting is appropriate, as it suggests we put on a performance in the public sphere but let down our guard in the private. But we are always putting on an act, or at least we act differently in different contexts. The metaphor here is of layers and a priority among layers. Audiences on- and offline want to peel back the covers and see what's underneath. It's the same basic curiosity that compels the child to poke a stick under a log, the investigator to root out a scandal, the archeologist to keep excavating, and the physicist to expose the elusive hidden particle.

This forensic impulse also compels the social critic to search inexorably for the hegemony, the hidden inequalities of neoliberalism, the mood and mind control of advertising and social media. Curiosity is brought to service in forensic investigation in the personal and public sphere.

Video game play also engenders curiosity. Gamers converse in online forums, where cheats are exchanged and players challenge the quality of the game elements, narratives, and game task difficulties. Some online exchanges indicate profound knowledge about the industry and its audiences. Some players wish to be involved in the production process, to go behind the scenes. They are encouraged by their curiosity about the process to participate in "user-generated content." It seems there are always some elements in an audience's awareness not only of the front of stage spectacle of the game but also of the backstage arena, where other, hidden games are acted out. In a previous book, I thought of these hidden activities as metagames, games about games.[38]

Some media content providers recognize the importance of exposing audiences in a controlled way to how things are made behind the scenes: alienating, Brechtian-style stage productions,[39] museums that show off their workrooms, film studio tours, reality TV shows, confessionals, "The Making of *Inception*," naming TV documentaries to arouse curiosity—calling a program about mathematics *The Code* or a nature show *Fossil Wonderlands: Nature's Hidden Treasures*. Perhaps there's a place for interactive media experiences in which audiences shift at will between the front and the back, the main event and the rehearsal, the game and the metagame, or perhaps access to offstage secrets is one of the rewards of the game. The desire to get behind the scenes to see what's really going on is after all one of the perennial drivers of detective stories, conspiracy theories, *The Matrix*, psychoanalysis, and paranoia.

Curiosity and Questioning

The Internet supports the most prototypical of curiosity behaviors: asking a question. The curious web user can direct questioning to a community forum, an individual, some automated agent, or web content through a search engine. Rousseau counseled the judicious use of questioning when confronting the learning adolescent: "When you see that his curiosity is thoroughly aroused, put some brief question which will set him trying to discover the answer."[40] The tutor can ask questions of the pupil, and the pupil can make inquiries of the tutor: "If he asks questions let your answers be enough to whet his curiosity but not enough to satisfy it."[41]

As if to reinforce the importance of questioning, a student left an astute comment on one of my blog postings: "Even though there are thousands of millions of web sites on the Internet, I still fail to find answers at times when I have questions." The search for answers is insatiable. In 2012, Cambridge University launched a campaign to celebrate the physicist Stephen Hawking's seventieth birthday. You could tweet questions to #AskHawking (or send email). The questions appearing were a mixture of the extremely clever, sensible, predictable, witty, sarcastic, and vulgar. Hawking was to serve as an oracle, a role often expected of the Internet itself. However, skill resides in asking the right questions. There are questions that are cleverer than their answers could ever be. Often, the framing of a question presupposes a certain kind of answer. Questions can be traps: When did you stop copying your ideas from the Internet? Sometimes, they are rhetorical: What are we to do with all this information? Sometimes, questions are not there to be answered, but evaded or reframed: How do we solve the problem of social media addiction? What is the mood of this place? In fact, it's often safer, less direct, and more polite to require the person to whom we direct the question to *address* it rather than simply to answer it: How would you address the question of software piracy?

Smart questioning is a well-known path to teaching and learning. Socrates asks his interlocutor Euthyphro, "What's the difference between the pious and the impious?" Sometimes, the answer is in the question. Saint Paul laced his letter to the Romans with a series of such questions that contained their own answers: "Are we to continue in sin that grace may abound?"[42] Sometimes, a question doesn't make sense unless you are already in a frame of mind receptive to the question, let alone the answer. You have to be in the mood. Martin Heidegger subjects his readers to difficult questions, such as those from his collection of lyrical essays, *Poetry, Language, Thought* and elsewhere: "What and whence is the artist what he is?"[43] "Can art be an origin at all?"[44] "What is at work in the work?"[45] "What is truth itself, that it sometimes comes to pass as art?"[46] "What are poets for?"[47] "What is it to dwell?"[48] "How does building belong to dwelling?"[49] "What in the thing is thingly?"[50]

In this case, the challenge for the reader is to enter into a Heideggerian, or phenomenological, frame of mind. How does one do this? By reading the texts, but then adjusting one's frame of mind, even if momentarily, suspending skepticism, meditating on the texts, returning after a break, and not just to comprehend the answers, but to understand the questions. Perhaps the job is done when the committed reader reaches a moment of understanding: when they feel that the artfully formed question is understood.

If you ask Google "How do you bake a pie?" it lists recipes. If you present Google with Heidegger's questions, you get something about graffiti art and vandalism, Wikipedia on martial arts, health and safety in the workplace, someone quoting Martin Heidegger, the Free Online Dictionary definition of "dwell," a suggestion to correct "thingly" to "tingly," and Wikipedia on language acquisition. Posing the same questions to Siri, Apple's voice-activated digital assistant, revealed a lot of information about art museums and parrots (less on poets). I don't think that these answers are too oblique to be useful. Understanding is after all a matter of practical application. Curiosity involves the artful manipulation of questions, adjusting frames of reference (moods), and imagining your own answers.

Intertexts

Contributors to the World Wide Web organize documents, texts, sounds, pictures, and ideas through links and indices that aid search and assist discovery. Readers don't just follow a single line of argument. As in the exploration of nature, you can branch, backtrack, skim the surface, and go in deep. Literary theorist George Landow thinks of literature in this way, as a potentially interconnected set of texts and ideas. That's hypertext, "the use of the computer to transcend the linear, bounded and fixed qualities of the traditional written text" which was after all "linear, bounded and fixed."[51] A hypertextual document is cross-linked, interlinked, within itself and with other documents, so that readers can explore avenues of thought raised by the text and even contribute comments and notes, which are in turn shared and hyperlinked. The web is so structured and instrumentalized, with tags, temporal markers, trace records, and other elements to facilitate navigation and search and to provoke and guide the curious.

The researcher and intellectual follows these writing and reading tactics anyway, well-illustrated by the philosopher Jacques Derrida's sometimes arcane way of constructing arguments.[52] For example, Derrida wants to argue the nature of rhetoric in early Greek texts and how Greek philosophers such as Plato always fall back on the idea that it is really important to write things down. Any attempt to praise the virtues of free-form oration (and speech) resorts to metaphors derived from writing. To this end, Derrida studies Plato's book *Phaedrus* through the detailed analysis of a single word in Plato's text, *pharmakon* (remedy). Throughout his writing, Derrida makes copious and seemingly inexhaustible references. These are not just to provide colorful illustrations. In addition to proving the main point of his argument, he ends up instructing the reader how words are and can be associated. Derrida constructs his arguments via a chain of associations, many of which go beyond what any reader would think of as the correct meanings of *pharmakon*. For Derrida, the word associates with drug, poison, cosmetics, magician, and scapegoat.[53] His investigations are fine grained, sometimes surgical, and seem at times to deviate a long way from the subject at hand. He describes his approach as *intertextual*. This is a useful metaphor to account for Derrida's style, and it is one brought into sharp relief in experiments in new writing forms on- and offline—from experimental literature to slash fiction.[54] However, this interlinking and flow of ideas is nascent in any form of creative and scholarly writing.

Derrida's concepts of intertextuality provide a way of understanding the World Wide Web and hyperlinked social media. Researchers, analysts, and those of a curious disposition resort to intertextual investigations as they trace along connections and fault lines within and between texts. Such resources propel the thoughts of the curious.

Summary

In this chapter, I've argued the case for curiosity as a mood. Curiosity is supported by positive mood states, and the cultivation of curiosity encourages sociability and inquiry. When in such a frame of mind, we are more likely to explore and be open to new experiences. I cataloged some of the major ways that online activity supports the human tendency to be curious. It provides lots of content, of course. It also supports the tendency to provide personal profiles online—to encourage others to be curious about us, but under our management. Online content is useful in representing material about which we audiences might be curious, but it's at its most compelling when it presents what's different. Online content can also hide as well as reveal, and it provides a medium for raising questions. Thanks to its relentless capacity for making connections, online media provide tools for following intertextual traces and associations.

Coda: How the Internet Kills Curiosity

Here's an example of an intertextual movement in thought abetted by the Internet. The word "curiosity" has currency in the modern, technological world. NASA successfully landed a robotic vehicle on Mars on August 5, 2012, early morning Pacific Daylight Time (PDT). The new Mars rover was called *Curiosity*, a name that departed from the usual lexicon of pioneers, conquerors, and the bold (Voyager, Discovery, Apollo, Viking). As it happened, the Mars landing event was the anniversary of the bombing of Hiroshima, a coincidence easily discovered by browsing the Internet, a fact that then got circulated and reinforced by bloggers, whose blogs then appeared in web search engines. In fact, I, among others, was able to check that the dates correspond only if you use Greenwich Mean Time (GMT) rather than PDT. The Mars vehicle landed late evening GMT on August 5, which fits the Hiroshima anniversary. The atom bomb was of course associated with Pandora's box. According to the record from an interview with a Los Alamos scientist on the invention of the bomb, "we've opened Pandora's box, and the genie can't be stuffed back in the bottle."[55] Curiosity can be risky, if not lethal. There's no shortage of information online about Pandora's box, including ancient Greek texts. The text of *Hesiod: Works and Days* (written around 700 BC) tells the story of Pandora's box and is freely available on the web. Pandora was a female archetype. Hephaestus, Athena and Aphrodite gave her form, arts, and graces, but the god Hermes put in her "a shameless mind and a deceitful nature." She was given a box, sometimes translated as a *jar*. Her curiosity got the better of her; she opened the tempting box gifted to her and unleashed plagues and evils (leaving *hope* behind). As was the Devil to Eve, it's actually Hermes, the false guide and trickster god, who was the culprit for purveying "lies and crafty words," seducing the impressionable young woman into starting the world's ills. The closest NASA has come to naming one of its missions after Hermes is Mercury, the Roman copy—rehabilitated as the swift messenger. Hermes is of course the god of hiddenness and of trickery. It's also from Hermes that the word "hermeneutics" derives, which also means interpretation. Hermes is the source and purveyor of curiosity and its dangers.

So, there's a train of thought, a series of intertextual associations encouraged by the Internet: the theme of curiosity, a robot vehicle on Mars, the atom bomb, Pandora's box, the danger of information, and the role of hermeneutics: a curious exploration in a curious medium.

Does anyone list "smart search" under *skillset* in their CV? There's no point in looking up "Pandora" on Google, as it's a popular company name and the name of the planet (moon) in a popular film. There really is a skill in finding the right search terms and linking them together. It also requires a fair degree of cultural knowledge. It seems to me that a couple of hours browsing on the Internet is now mandatory before writing or speaking on a topic. This tactic may also sow confusion, which needs to be managed.

When it appeared in a blog online, this post prompted some observations from readers:

Comment 1: On the substantive point about the knowledge or skill needed to construct intelligent searches, I think this is where a liberal education is indicated, perhaps reversely analogous to the skill required to estimate the result of a computation on a pocket calculator or spreadsheet.

Comment 2: There was a time when scholars worth their salt would have had a "classical" education, meaning they were read in the classics, including the Greek myths, and they probably knew ancient Greek and Latin. This provided a common language, as it were. Maybe the web substitutes for that common language. A writer can drop all sorts of references into an online text. If the reader doesn't get the reference, then he or she can do a quick Google search. Of course, the reader may end up thinking that Pandora is a radio station and be doubly confused.

4 Piqued by Pleasure

When dinner guests congratulate the chef on the quality of the meal, the chef is likely to experience a feeling of pleasure. If the food genuinely tastes good and satisfies their hunger, then the guests may have a similar feeling. It's the same when the social media user receives a "like" for a photograph she just posted on Facebook or the game player progresses to the next level in *Call of Duty*. It's well known that the positive feelings we identify as pleasure reinforce the value of the achievement, such that the bearer of the feeling is inclined to do more of the same. Pleasure encourages you to keep preparing satisfying meals, eat delicious food, publish cool pictures online, and keep playing the game.

Psychologists B. F. Skinner (1904–1990) and Ivan Pavlov (1849–1936) and their followers famously examined the relationships between pleasure, motivation, and reward.[1] They experimented with rats and dogs, conditioning them to push on levers and exhibit involuntarily behaviors such as secreting saliva at the sound of a bell. Rats in mazes and Pavlov's dog are emblematic of conditioned behavior, stimulus, and response, and inform common insights about pleasure. What equine beast of labor wouldn't prefer to eat a carrot than be beaten with a stick—or child prefer a gold star to a reprimand? However, some people also experience pleasure from struggling with a new piece of software, putting their bodies through torturous exercise programs, and identifying with the misfortunes of others. In any case, not all causes of pleasure are good for us.

The world of entertainment brings the complexities of pleasures into sharp relief, as ubiquitous digital media now elide into entertainment. In this chapter, I will show that entertainment exaggerates and amplifies aspects of the computer user's experience, notably the experience of pleasure. Curious people may derive pleasure from eavesdropping on a discussion between two strangers in a restaurant, but a similar discussion scripted and acted on a television soap opera is more likely to keep us engaged. Filmmakers deploy camera angles, framing, cuts, scenery, economy of movement, and all the artifices of theatrical and cinematographic production to exaggerate the important bits and diminish the incidental. That's entertainment.

The Internet has a similar stake in exaggeration. Call it "amplification." After all, the Internet is built on an electronic medium for transmission across distances, making the scarcely audible louder and the impermanent last as long as you want. Social media also foregrounds the process of amplification, enabling you to maintain contact over large distances. Social media give you a bigger voice, increase your circle, leave digital traces to posterity, and in so doing amplify sociability. At least, it's easy to think this. Even these claims indicate that the medium is rife with exaggeration, not least the exaggerated, utopian claims many people make of it.[2] Not everything that's exaggerated is pleasurable, but I hope to show that pleasure and exaggeration are close associates.

Ambient Entertainment

Entertainment comes to the consumer through many channels, not least downloads over the ubiquitous Internet. Sales of online films, music, and games from downloads now exceed shop sales,[3] also impacted by free and pirated downloads. Travelers waiting patiently in airport lounges and couples and groups sitting in dulled silence access online news reports. They also stream, download, and play movies, TV programs, and other rich media information content and entertainment on their smartphones, tablets, and laptops. Media consumers browse and graze across a raft of entertainment offerings. Looking for suitable diversions for the moment also constitutes a kind of entertaining pastime. Flicking across television channels or sorting through music tracks are idle pastimes not devoid of entertainment value.

The Entertainment Trap

There is so much content online, of widely varying quality. Long before digital media, cultural critics Theodor Adorno and Max Horkheimer identified the delusions of the modern age, including the impression that mass-produced goods are different from one another even though they really are all the same: "The mechanically differentiated products prove to be all alike in the end."[4] Adorno and Horkheimer thought the mass media cultivated an appetite for the resemblance of individuality but not its reality: "Pseudo individuality is rife: from the standardized jazz improvisation to the exceptional film star."[5] In similar vein, critical theorist and playwright Antonin Artaud (1896–1948) lamented the ascendancy of film over theater, which was already succumbing to the dictates of mere entertainment as "useless, artificial amusement."[6] Films are also "murdering us with second-hand reproductions which, filtered through machines, cannot unite with our sensibility, have maintained us for ten years in an ineffectual torpor, in which all our faculties appear to be foundering."[7] Whatever its quality and originality, there is no denying the quantity and ubiquity of entertainment delivered digitally, especially considering now the production by readers/consumers (as producer-consumers) of entertainment content.

Everyone is now a producer of sorts. The inventive and media savvy or the idle and irritating contribute their own content, and they review, copy, edit, rework, hack, remix, repeat, and multiply entertainment through social video and audio services, such as YouTube, Vimeo, and Vine. Media offerings are also interactive, as in the case of video games, and tools for digital social networking highlight the convergence of work, play, communications, media, and entertainment. Display screens and digital audio populate lounges, bars, libraries, foyers, and public and private spaces. Entertainment is part of our architecture, and through digital media crowd sourcing we media-savvy "prosumers" and "produsers" can cast ourselves in the role of entertainment architects if we so choose. Relatively prosperous societies are saturated with media and, in particular, entertainment, which we now take for granted as part of the background of everyday life. Consumers of entertainment can direct their attention to or choose to ignore information, entertainment, and infotainment from multiple channel sources.

Entertainment is now ambient. In an interesting essay from 2002 on entertainment and the Internet, film theorist Richard Dyer noted how entertainment was then fusing with everyday communications channels, particularly via the Internet.[8] The earliest forms of this fusion were sonic, in particular the use of background music and radio broadcasts that we might expect to hear anywhere and at any time. Then came personal stereos. Now, the visual aspects of entertainment are ubiquitous as well: "Television, video and the internet are visual as well as audio media that are also in the home, permanently available, that you can take about with you and access at any time."[9]

Even then, he noted that entertainment was no longer apart from the rest of life, at least not spatially and temporally. Neither was it constrained to professional production. It was coproduced, crowd sourced, and user generated: "With the internet, performance is not even necessarily professionally provided (except by technicians facilitating commercial web sites)—music, drama, all kinds of performances and visual expressions are now as likely to be amateur as professional, and anyone may be both a provider and a consumer of entertainment."[10]

Insofar as entertainment affords pleasure, it conditions us to seek yet more entertainment. Media theorist Neil Postman began his book *Amusing Ourselves to Death* by identifying Las Vegas as the quintessential US city defining the nation's aspirations and character, arguing that cultural forms such as politics, religion, sports, education, and commerce had become "congenial adjuncts of show business,"[11] a view popular in the 1980s with an actor in the office of US president. Amusement can bring about our ruin, as it inures and distracts us from what's really going on. As if caught in a spiral of feverish consumption, we gamble away our livelihoods. According to Postman, we acquiescent consumers become numbed to life and confuse the spectacle with what's really happening, enjoying news reports for their entertainment value until we realize that human lives really are being destroyed or until it's our home that floods.

What Is Entertainment?

What is this spiraling, all-consuming, diversionary phenomenon known as entertainment? Entertainment is a subspecies of art dedicated to distraction and pleasure. It takes people out of the ordinary and the routine. Commentators place entertainment in the company of popular culture. Entertainment also has its elite forms, from which some people used to think the tastes of the rest of us derive.[12] Respectable middle-class Victorians thought it acceptable to entertain their friends with a song, but the truly professional performer was under suspicion. Entertainment is often cast negatively, as an indulgence, separate from rational, workaday life, or as a means of diverting the exploited from their plight, sustaining mass consumption and therefore global capitalism. In any case, entertainment belongs to ordinary people. It's a pop-culture phenomenon, now promoted and circulated through digital media and ubiquitous communications.

We can certainly derive pleasure by means other than through entertainment, but entertainment is emblematic of the pleasure quest. Work is pleasurable for many, as are sociability, communication, and learning. Everyday software systems can be pleasurable to use, even the use of a well-designed spreadsheet brought to service in sorting out one's personal finances. However, the link connecting pleasure with entertainment, the mass media, and digital media is now palpable.

Pleasure Indices

Digital media not only circulates pleasure, through the ubiquitous distribution of entertainment, but it also monitors it. In chapter 1 I referred to the quantification of emotions, the application of number to our assessment of people's emotional states. So-called sentiment surveys probe consumer confidence, well-being, emotional states, and people's moods. As well as eliciting opinions about the economy, employment, and politics, such surveys might ask respondents to provide number scores to propositions about their emotional condition: to find out if people think their lives are close to their ideal and how satisfied they are. Have they achieved the important things they want, and if they had to live their lives over, would they make the same choices? When collected across whole communities or regions, this information is aggregated to provide sentiment indicators, including measures of how "happy" people are. In his critical study of happiness and social policy, my colleague Neil Thin remarks that "it is startling how easy respondents seem to find it to put a number on their happiness," and the results are "reasonably consistent and reliable."[13] Policy makers and market analysts use this kind of data for making comparisons between communities, across time, and among different demographically defined groups.

As I discussed in the introduction, social media elicits sentiment data from its users as a matter of course. Over 40 million Facebook status updates are posted across the world every day. Status updates are simply short messages people post on their Facebook profile page, prompted by the following question: What's on your mind? Facebook users registered as your friends can read these status updates in their news feed when they log on. Facebook makes available anonymized collections of such messages for researchers to analyze, providing a database of short texts from which to derive trends, obsessions, and sentiments. Twitter and other microblogging sites provide similar databases.[14] Researchers have mined Twitter feeds to purportedly capture the mood of people across whole continents. For example, computer scientists Alan Mislove and colleagues provide dynamic maps of how moods derived from Twitter feeds wax, wane, and migrate across the United States throughout the day and the week.[15] The research team identified peaks in the "overall tweet mood score" on Sunday mornings. Tweeters are apparently most somber on Thursday evenings.

The technique is not entirely new. Artists thought about expressing community moods before social media took hold. In 2003, architect Lars Spuybroek erected D-Tower in the Dutch town of Doetinchem. The project included a website on which the townspeople would indicate their emotional state each month. Architectural theorist Dana Cuff describes it thus: "Those emotions are in turn displayed in different colored surfaces of the tower: when it is deep red passersby notice the town is feeling more love and happiness than hate and fear."[16] With online communications, people don't actually need to declare or name their moods. For whatever purpose, algorithms mining Internet information provide a means of deducing how people are feeling.

The association of a word with positive and negative emotions is its "valence." A key 1999 report provides a table of words and their positive or negative valences as rated by a wide sample of survey participants.[17] Words like "justice" get a score of around 8 out of 10, without much variation. "Nasty" scores about 3.5, with a fair bit of variation. "Building" rates lower than "car" and "art" and is on par with "body" but is above "bus." To determine the mood conveyed by a collection of messages, an algorithm adds up the word valences from Facebook status updates or Twitter feeds. It seems that individual words and words formed into messages do carry a certain valence, or mood association. The algorithms used by researchers identify the frequency of occurrence of positive and negative words and phrases to derive mood and happiness indices and their distribution across a region or country. The procedure aggregates and processes very large numbers of short text messages. Researchers are working on ever more sophisticated methods of automated content analysis and text data mining based on identifying and parsing patterns within texts and across texts.[18]

These methods for supposedly picking up on the mood of a nation depend on language and what people are willing to write or type in a public medium such as the Internet. In case we think that such techniques just involve words and are not about how people really feel, it's worth considering that words and emotions are closely related. The feelings can follow the words.[19] Does the use of such positive phrases, pleasant platitudes, and polite idioms indicate a positive mood, or cause it, or the reverse? Of course, it's words in combination that really count, along with their context of use. On the Internet there's wit, sarcasm, and humor to cloud the measures, not to mention low-valence idioms and linguistic habits, such as "happy birthday," "great to chat," and "how interesting."

People who are unhappy often withdraw from communication anyway. Recently, I blogged on the theme of moods and status updates. Someone commented: "I know friends who disappear from Facebook when they are feeling depressed—both because the sight of so many 'happy' people makes them feel worse, and also because they don't have the capacity at the time to live up to this level of expectation." People obviously regulate what they write online and how they want to appear.

Limits of Mood Monitoring

In the introduction, I canvassed the issue of putative mood manipulation on social media. There exists the obvious question of what motivates such study and how the results might be used.[20] In benign political contexts, happiness indices could help in directing state resources to areas in which people are dissatisfied with the provision of services, or such statistics could be used to confirm the return on expenditure on public projects. One such study maps the happiness index derived from Twitter analysis in the various boroughs across London, claiming that the results correlate with well-being maps derived from official census data.[21] Perhaps governments can mine social media communications to gather well-being data without asking people to fill in a form at census time.

Insofar as they do capture a mood, such techniques tend toward the mean, a leveling of feeling across a community, an amplification of the average. They also depend on enormous databases, gross behaviors, the unsubtle processes of aggregation. At best, they identify the background moods against which we exercise our own sentiment-rich lives. Sentiment analysis effectively filters out the lone voice. In addition to happiness, it would be interesting to explore *melancholy* through these media, a literary and productive kind of mood of somber reflection—perhaps identifiable in London boroughs with a high proportion of poets—or bankers. I'll investigate melancholy in chapter 8.

Obviously, such techniques don't capture all there is to know about happiness or pleasure. With far less reliance on masses of empirical data, Sigmund Freud suggested that we don't only do things for the pleasures they bring. There's also deferred pleasure. We struggle with a new item of software for the pleasure brought by its mastery, and athletes torture their bodies for the pleasure that comes from exceeding their personal best or winning the race. According to Freud, we are also prone to compulsions that we have trouble describing as pleasures, such as repeating apparently unproductive actions over and over:[22] obsessive hand washing, pacing up and down, shopping, and updating Facebook statuses. To these, we could add obsessive game play, watching television show repeats, listening to the same popular songs over and over, and, if not amusing ourselves to death, then entertaining ourselves into a stupor.

Negative Pleasure

Entertainment amplifies the contradictions of pleasure. Why do we derive pleasure not only from positive experiences but also from the full range of emotions, as delivered in film, song, music, novels, and theater? It seems that audiences can find exposure to negative emotions, such as fright, horror, sadness, and disgust, highly entertaining. Filmmakers encourage their audiences to participate in a succession of moods and emotions, and audiences seem to find pleasure in that.[23]

Some of the authors in *The Routledge Handbook of Emotions and Mass Media* explore entertainment in this light.[24] How does the human species benefit from the vicarious experiences presented in films, video games, news reports, celebrity gossip, advertising and art?[25] The authors concur that the mass media and what they have become in the Internet age build on the idea of entertainment. Their strong message is that mass media are tools not only for conveying information but also for regulating people's emotions. Information that doesn't pluck at the heartstrings will probably go unnoticed, and the art of persuasion doesn't depend on the delivery of facts framed in unassailable logic. Emotion is a crucial part of the media experience. Thrillers, romcoms, and tear-jerkers present us with an array of emotional experiences—positive and negative.

Are the emotions experienced while watching a film as real as if the events were happening to you? The *Routledge Handbook* reports on several experiments showing that the feelings from watching cinema or a television show, though transitory, can be just as real as when facing our own peril, embarrassment, joy, and heartbreak. The central paradox of the mass media is that we choose to subject ourselves to sadness, shock, fear, and disappointment, and we even enjoy it. The handbook offers a range of explanations. I'll discuss three that stand out.

First, imaginative storytelling, playacting, and now the mass media and the Internet act as means of rehearsing appropriate responses to situations we wouldn't otherwise encounter on a day-to-day basis. We are drawn to the learning opportunities provided by the kind of vicarious activity offered by media entertainments. We like to learn and be emotionally prepared for everyday life events. Learning is pleasurable, though not necessarily at every stage in the experience. As I explored in chapter 3, the cultivation and satisfaction of curiosity is closely aligned with pleasure.

Second, storytelling, gossip, and art aid in the manufacture of social cohesion. They give us something to share and talk about. Solidarity brings positive feelings, a necessary inducement for collaboration. As outlined in chapter 2, according to evolutionary psychologists, natural selection within the human species favors such empathy. Exchanging stories and the sociability that ensues registers as pleasure, whether the stories are happy, sad, or frightening.

Third, perhaps there's pleasure in simply experiencing an emotion. Here, pleasure also serves as a metaemotion. In fact, any emotion can operate as a metaemotion. We can have an emotion about an emotion; we can be bored with pleasure, angry at being fearful, worried that we don't care, optimistic about depression, curious about our own insistent questioning, and enjoy being confused. In a seminal paper on emotional awareness, empirical psychologists Peter Salovey and colleagues define several metaemotional conditions, emphasizing that it takes a certain skill to deal with your own emotions. Emotional intelligence means being aware of your emotional states and being able to talk about them. It takes skill in experiencing your emotions clearly, knowing whether you are happy, sad, afraid, jealous, or contented, and an ability to regulate your emotions and change your circumstances to moderate your emotional condition.[26]

Salovey contends that people who are emotion aware in these ways are better able to recover from negative emotional experiences, such as watching a scary movie or a documentary about car accidents or experiencing actual traumatic life events, such as losing a close relative. Emotional intelligence of this kind engenders a kind of resilience. Metaemotional skills help in coping with stress, abetted by friends, counsellors, therapists, and (perhaps) communicating with others via social media. Sometimes, we read a book, look at pictures, watch television shows, or listen to music to modulate our mood. Selecting suitable entertainments, diversions, and pleasures is part of the repertoire of emotional adjustment, and that sense of emotional mastery brings pleasure.

Pleasure and Resistance

So pleasure is a complex condition. Most audiences enjoy paradox and contrast. Cultural theorist Gerald Cupchik emphasizes "the active interpretive roles of individuals and communities" in understanding media and emotions. Media consumption draws on our imaginations, and imagination has a greater opportunity to take over when films and television programs "are seen as polyvalent, indeterminate, and open-ended."[27] In a way, we are perverse creatures, seeking out complexity, paradox, and contrasts. Pleasurable emotional stasis is boring.[28]

Not everyone finds the same stimulus pleasurable. Sometimes, I feel an emotion contrary to what the filmmaker expected me to feel, or I willfully resist what the filmmaker wants me to experience. Defiant audience members may change the channel, walk out of the cinema, talk over the action, or sit there unmoved, no matter how skillful the production. According to Cupchik, our response to emotional material lies in the issue of how a media offering relates to one's "ongoing personal life themes"[29]—or I would say our background of experience. As with any interpretation, our expectation and reception of a work of art is colored by the kinds of memories and recollections it conjures up. Such is the potency for some audience members of the farewell scene at the end of *E.T.* (1982), or the eventual sight of Norman Bates' mother in *Psycho* (1986), the embarrassment of the late-running Brian Stimpson in *Clockwise* (1986), or the sentimentalism of *Bicentennial Man* (1999), about a robot who gradually transforms into something like a sentient human being. Emotional responses are interpretive, hermeneutical, and can be explained by the workings of background, context, and difference.

We also enjoy media content for its skill and artistry, which may support or run counter to the emotions purveyed through the narrative. According to Freud, we can derive pleasure from the technique of a joke as much as we can from its content.[30] Even a "weak" joke can provide pleasure when delivered in the right way and in the right context. I still can't get people to laugh when I say: "The snow outside was so thick. I asked a snowman for the time, and he just looked at me." It's often the way a comedian delivers the joke that gives us pleasure, even for a weak joke; so too for drama. At the end of a murder mystery, I may feel pleasure as much for the clever resolution of the plot as in seeing the killer brought to justice. We can admire and enjoy the skill of the filmmaker and storyteller at the same time that we are repulsed by the horror of the stabbing in the shower (*Psycho*). There's sometimes more pleasure from the telling of the tale than in the tale itself or the events it depicts. The converse also can be the case. I heard recently a professional film reviewer criticize the film *The Impossible* (2012), about the effects of the tsunami on the Pacific coast in 2004.[31] The critic felt her emotions were being overly manipulated, which clearly displeased her. Perhaps we find it unpleasant to feel sympathy for the wrong characters or to be made to laugh at someone's misfortune.

There's also the social–political context that forms part of the emotional setting or mood of a media offering. However potent the artistry, and however emotional the story-telling, audiences may be displeased in *The Impossible* by the focus on a middle-class European family "suffering" from a ruined holiday when all around are thousands of inhabitants losing life and livelihood under the devastation of the tsunami. A filmgoer can be displeased in sympathy with an angry character, displeased at some injustice being presented in the film, or displeased at the film maker for poor artistry, manipulation, or political bias. Then, there's the crass trailer for Arnold Schwarzenegger's film *Last Stand*, which sensationalizes gunfire, epitomizing the social irresponsibility and insensitivity in some filmmaking. What emotions are invoked among socially aware audiences by celebratory violence in films?

Emotions inevitably implicate morality. Abrogation of artistry and professionalism can produce a different emotional effect than the one intended by the author. A professionally produced music track ripped from a CD or download and planted on an amateur video does not usually move me, no matter how well it fits the mood of the piece. A homegrown soundtrack in keeping with the ethos of the video might. Issues of intellectual property and respect for creative enterprise can override other emotional stimuli in both professional and amateur productions.

We are not passive receivers of whatever the mass media serve up and subject to emotions it expects of us, but we are critics and judges. Look at live twitter feeds for popular television programs, such as #downton (*Downton Abbey*). They usually include jokes about the characters, exclamations about unlikely plot twists, cynical asides about the emotion of the events, and criticisms and praises addressed to the playwright. These tweets echo the couch conversation that takes place in front of millions of television sets, and now given vent in the popular UK Channel 4 television program, *Gogglebox*.[32] The ambient wit of the audiences' making is important in understanding emotions and the mass media.

Wit refers to mental faculties of reason, but also humor, saying the right thing at the right time, usually to amuse. Wit is the capacity to fine-tune to context. The theme of tuning crops up in *The Routledge Handbook of Emotions and Mass Media*. Media content provides "emotional framing" or "fine tuning."[33] An audience's nonvoluntary emotional responses to situations provides "preattunements" for the encounters that follow.[34] It's as if emotions put you in the right musical key for the arrangement that follows. You are in the right mood for action.

Grotesque Realism

Wit and humor also draw on exaggeration. In his introduction to Freud's account of jokes, literary critic James Carey says: "By making our enemy small, inferior, despicable or comic, we achieve in a roundabout way the enjoyment of overcoming him—to which the third person, who has made no efforts, bears witness by his laughter."[35] Such are the caricatures by which historical villains such as Richard III in Shakespeare's play by that name are demonized. After soliloquizing about his own deformities, and how his appearance excludes him from the role of lover, Richard remarks that he is "determined to prove a villain." His deformed body and nature leave him with little else. Historian playwrights and storytellers exaggerate the characteristics of their adversaries to make them look grotesque and ridiculous, and from that authors encourage us to derive pleasure.

Caricature and Hyperreality

It's worth examining the relationship between pleasure and exaggeration further. One of the oldest forms of mass entertainment is the carnival, or festival. I live in the "City of Festivals." Since 1947, the city of Edinburgh has played host to an annual International Festival. The city in fact hosts several festivals at the same time, including the Fridge Festival, a departure from the main show. The streets are peppered with performers, handbill distributors, costumed actors scuttling from A to B, and late-running Royal Scots Dragoon guards getting ready for the famous Military Tattoo. The city shifts into a higher register. Festivals are popular in most major cities across the world and attract thousands of visitors. There are also music festivals, open air concerts, parades, pageants, and firework displays. The mass media also delivers and facilitates such public events. Festival experiences are played and replayed online. Thanks to ubiquitous entertainment from television, radio, cinemas, and digital media, it's festival time everywhere, all day and all year round.

The idea of the festival has a long history. Think of the historic importance of religious festivals, pilgrimages, the Roman Saturnalia, carnivals, and pageants. During the traditional festival, ordinary people would break out from conformity and restraint imposed by the state and the church. Festivals offered license and stimulus for the growth of marginal and creative activity that would often slide into the illicit. Festivals and carnivals were participative events in which the strictures of the church, the state, and the usual social orders would be relaxed and even reversed. As outlined by Mikhail Bakhtin (1895–1975) and Mircea Eliade (1907–1986), the symbolic reversal of roles, the suspension of laws and customs under the pretext of carnival pranks, and orgiastic rituals sought "a reintegration of opposites, a regression to the primordial and homogeneous," but such activities were also "a symbolic restoration of 'Chaos,' of the undifferentiated unity that preceded the Creation."[36] Think of carnival costumes and the distortion of human and animal forms. There's something festive and carnivalesque about distorted representations, a demonstration of the appeal of "grotesque realism" enjoyed within "folk culture" to which Bakhtin refers.

The distortion of bodies via contemporary costuming, puppetry, cartooning, and digital animation is a remnant of what Bakhtin attributes to the base humor of the Middle Ages and the early Renaissance. Such irreverent ribaldry is the other side to formal church and state ritual, with their definitions of the sacred and insistence on respect for it, the aspirational and the correct. Contrary to propriety and order, the carnivalesque deals in parody and degradation of the high and the mighty but also of the less than idealized body in total: a concern with the "lower stratum of the body, the life of the belly and the reproductive organs; it therefore relates to acts of defecation and copulation, conception, pregnancy and birth."[37] Bakhtin's point is that these two strands (the formal and the degraded) coexisted in premodern awareness.

The chief literary subject of Bakhtin's study into the grotesque is the lengthy satirical novel by François Rabelais (c.1494–1553), *The Histories of Gargantua and Pantagruel*, ostensibly about two giants and their encounters with ribald monks, wayward priests, conceited rulers, and arbitrary judges. The author's preface begins: "Most noble boozers, and you my very esteemed and poxy friends."[38] Amid the Late Medieval bathroom (garderobe) banter, there's much violence, not least a description of bodily dismembering as a friar defends his wine store against raiders: "He beat out the brains of some, broke the arms and legs of others, disjointed the neck-bones, demolished the kidneys, slit the noses, blacked the eyes, smashed the jaws, knocked the teeth down the throats, shattered the shoulder-blades, crushed the shins, dislocated the thigh-bones, and cracked the fore-arms of yet others."[39] Bakhtin sees the parading of this kind of detail as a typical "anatomization and dismemberment of the human body." There's also a culinary aspect to this butchery, presenting "a grotesque image of the dissected body."[40] It's also about the parts and their exaggeration.

In fact, carnival grotesqueries are typically described in terms outside of the privileged realms of vision and the sound. They deal in the baser senses and exaggerated depictions of the organs that process and produce them: smell (the nose), taste (the tongue and belly). These are the organs treated in the most exaggerated form in carnival costumes and in cartoons. Needless to say, odor, flatulence, excrement, and urine percolate through Rabelais' novel, not to mention allusions to erotic sensations and anything else generated or consumed below the waist.

How does grotesque realism impinge on the pleasures derived through ubiquitous digital media? Media theorists Ross Buck and Stacie Renfro Powers confirm that the media present life in exaggerated form, creating "super-displays"—hence the hyperreality of cartoons, CGI effects, and digital interaction. It's not only in cartoons and satire that bodies and body parts are exaggerated. The emotions felt through mediated presentations can apparently be even more compelling than with real-life events.[41]

There's also an appealing seam of theory from neuroscience to be mined here. Neuroscientist V. S. Ramachandran calls this propensity toward exaggeration "the law of peak shift." According to Ramachandran, this law accounts for the animal (and human) propensity to respond to exaggeration, at least in the visual field. A lab rat can be trained to respond to simple shapes. Researchers have devised a simple experiment. They set up a cage in which a rat is confronted with two painted shapes: an elongated rectangle and a square. If the rat moves toward the elongated rectangle, then it is rewarded with a piece of cheese. If it moves to the square, then it gets no reward. After a trial and error phase, as expected, the rat soon learns to go straight for the elongated rectangle every time. Now, replace the square shape with an even longer elongated rectangle than the food-rewarding shape. The rat will go for it, and with measurably greater vigor. There's a tendency for the rat's cognitive apparatus to assume that the longer the rectangle, the greater the reward, even though there was nothing in the training phase to establish that rule.[42]

The simple extrapolation from this and other experiments—plus some explanation in terms of neural wiring—is that when we animals get used to a visual condition, we regard it as normal, but then we become impressed, pleased with, allured by, or provoked by its exaggerated variant. At the very least, our curiosity is aroused. Presumably, there's a point at which the exaggeration no longer registers as such and the shape appears as a new class of object or something entirely alien. In any case, according to Ramachandran, the lure of exaggeration is one of the key factors in reading the environment.

I think this law of peak shift touches on ideas of the grotesque; faces with inordinately large noses and ears attract our pleasurable interest. Ramachandran refers to the popularity of caricatures of well-known people: politicians, entertainers, and even our friends and relatives. He doesn't address this issue, but there's also something to be said about animals as bearers of exaggerated human traits, zoomorphism, and anthropomorphized animals in cartoons and comics. The law of peak shift also touches on metaphor and play: the child who claims to his mother he's just seen a carrot "as big as God." The tendency to exaggerate is a crucial element of play, according to Johannes Huizinga.[43] Contemporary architecture also presents masterly demonstration of the power in exaggeration. Human inhabitants are accustomed to orthogonality, a world of right angles. In the visual field, these angles and lines appear to converge according to the conventions of perspective. Exaggerating and distorting these vectors certainly produces an effect on the person negotiating such spaces, or perhaps produces a particular atmosphere or mood. Studio Libeskind's Military History Museum extension in Dresden, Germany, provides an impressive example of architectural exaggeration. There's much that is familiar in these spaces, not least the straightness of line and of course the classical contours of perspective, but then you realize the floor is sloping, walls converge, and the rules of form and perspective are grossly exaggerated. In such architectural play, there's a pleasure. If we are conditioned to find reward and pleasure in the converging lines of our perspectival view in the everyday world, then according to the "law of peak shift," that convergence increased magnifies the pleasure.

CGI and cartoons trade in exaggeration. To get the measure of everyone's interest in exaggeration, see what gets top billing on YouTube. In 2013, top ratings went to a dance song about foxes, surreal moves by a Norwegian army platoon, a man showing how animals eat their food, and countless other parodies of pop songs and clips of animals doing strange things and people caught in awkward situations.

Sadistic Pleasures
There's a political aspect to the carnival, which mocks the elites who hold power over the rest of us. There's pleasure in seeing the mighty fall and a malicious joy, even in simulation. Conflict, humor, ridicule, and exaggeration: these are some of the means by which we cultivate pleasure and imagine the leveling of the powerful. Classic animated cartoon formats foreground exaggeration and misfortune. Cartoons confirm that we like to be entertained by failure: Tom and Jerry beating each other up, Wile E. Coyote's incessant self-harm by his attempts to catch the Roadrunner. Insofar as audiences enjoy such scenarios, they participate in schadenfreude, an appropriate emotion with which to conclude this chapter on pleasure.

Exaggeration enters the pleasure circuit via envy. Apparently, you are most likely to experience envy when you encounter someone you think exhibits your own positive characteristics but in exaggerated form: creates better art, plays the violin with greater skill, writes wittier blogs, dresses smarter, or looks cooler in photographs. Psychologists indicate that envy involves social comparison. When someone you envy falls from grace, slips up, loses status, or is embarrassed, then you are most likely to experience a feeling of pleasure at their misfortune. Surprisingly, some psychologists claim they can detect this relationship in fMRI brain scanning, introducing further insights from neuroscience.

Neuroscientists Hidehiko Takahashi and colleagues tested the proposition that "a misfortune happening to an envied person produces greater brain activation associated with schadenfreude than misfortune happening to a person who is not envied."[44] In their study, they recorded activation levels in the part of the brain "where cognitive conflicts or social pain are processed."[45] This is the rear part of the anterior cingulate cortex (ACC).

In their study, the researchers presented a group of students with a range of scenarios. Each student was to imagine someone with superior or inferior levels of ability in sports, music, art, academic achievement, earning money, or popularity. The researchers confirmed that people are most envious of others who are on their own territory of achievement and do better at it. I'm probably not envious of someone who writes superb poetry if I've never thought of myself as a poet; an aspiring but mediocre cyclist might envy someone else who always wins at cycling. Of course, it might not be the cycling with which we identify but the money, the adulation, and the popularity. According to the brain scan activation measures for the students in the study, it's those we envy most for whom we are inclined to feel pleasure when they lose a game, suffer food poisoning, or get caught in a scandal. Takahashi argues that envy motivates us to close social gaps. It prompts you to either enhance your own performance or to sabotage an opponent's performance. Observing the misfortunes of another brings a degree of pleasure, as it contributes to narrowing the gap between ourselves and our rivals.

Insofar as we can trust the mapping of cognitive processes to regions of the brain, the place where Takahashi detected greater activation (the dorsal part of the ACC) is associated with "error detection and conflict monitoring." It seems that envy and schadenfreude are *not* autonomous and automatic feelings triggered by circumstances and events. We really are torn between conflicting emotions. Admiration, envy, and schadenfreude are strongly associated with conflict.

Perhaps it's easier to give full vent to feelings of schadenfreude when its target is distant from our own ken and those in whose lives we don't have any real investment—such as celebrity singers, sports heroes, and renowned artists. The downfall of the rich, powerful, and famous is standard fare in the news. Sports stars are fair game for schadenfreude. Cyclist Lance Armstrong denied charges that he used performance-enhancing drugs. After many years of such denials, he eventually admitted to winning his seven Tour de France titles under the influence of performance-enhancing drugs. Interest in this celebrity's confession was massive. Around 28 million people watched the television interview in which he confessed his guilt. We are more inclined to allow ourselves to enjoy the demise of a celebrity, or at least to gain enjoyment from the confessional, which narrows the gap between the spectacularly successful and the rest of us. Familiarity diminishes schadenfreude, or at least its effects. Socially adjusted adults manage to suppress the tendency to delight in their friends' misfortunes. Perhaps familiarity creates some degree of immunity from schadenfreude for social media users—that and the circulation of humor. The manufacture of celebrity and its dismantling provide an exaggerated version of what all of us experience at a smaller scale.

Schadenfreude is culturally loaded as a concept and without a single-word synonym in English. Its German origin indicates as much. Along with many other scholars, I'm skeptical of the idea that a cultural meme such as schadenfreude can be extracted from the field of complex human relationships, identified as a singular function, and even attributed to a region of the brain. Cultural theorists Steve Cross and Jo Littler indicate the cultural complexity of the concept as "indicative of a society with profoundly unequal concentrations of power."[46] They continue: "The cultural desire for meritocracy or 'making it against the odds' exists simultaneously with desires for degradation and humiliation of those 'above themselves' or deemed to be at the end of their celebrity lives. It is in such a social and political formation that Schadenfreude functions: as the flip side of meritocracy whilst imbricated in its logic. For in this framework of understanding, just as people 'go up,' so too do they 'fall down.'"[47] There's something satisfying and necessary about this economy, which they refer to as the rise and fall of "celebrity stock." It's as a cyclical process, of adulation and humiliation, the turning of the "wheel of fate," an alternation of extremes. I would say it's a pleasurable play in exaggeration.

Summary

In this chapter, I've examined the different "sources" of pleasure through the idea of entertainment. Ubiquitous digital media are clearly vehicles for the delivery of entertainment. Entertainment is present even if we are not attending to it fully. It's sometimes ambient. On a slightly different tack, digital media provides access to metrics for trying to calculate the emotional health of a group of people, made difficult not least by the ambiguities and challenges posed by the idea of pleasure. We socially engaged humans don't really seek emotional stasis but rather pleasure laced with melancholy and other moods. Entertainment has this character anyway. Audiences seem to derive pleasure from tragedy and sorrow as part of a palette of narrative emotional experiences. I've shown how entertainment thrives on exaggeration in keeping with the carnival tradition. In fact, there's some neurological evidence to support the human propensity to respond positively to exaggeration. Finally, I examined the pleasure some people derive from the misfortunes of others. This is schadenfreude, indicative of a cycle between extremes, the positives and negatives of the pleasure spectrum. The varied sources of pleasure indicate again that moods and emotions are interactional rather than representational. Pleasure, like schadenfreude, doesn't preexist as a well-defined category or mood state, but gets negotiated and emerges on reflection. This is good news for interaction design and those critics concerned about the how happy we are with digital social media and our digitally mediated lives.

Coda: Risks of the Pleasure Business

There's danger in exaggeration. Extremes entail risks.[48] Entertainment and pleasure entail similar hazards. We risk amusing ourselves into oblivion: forgetting to socialize, ignoring our health, spending hours in front of the television and playing computer games, or forgetting to talk to the company we are with while busy tapping at our smartphones. People have been known to walk into lampposts while texting and to die from deep vein thrombosis (DVT) while glued to video games.

Socrates, Plato, and Aristotle counseled a middle state between excess and deficiency. A character in a play by Terence, the Roman comic dramatist (185–159 BC), was overjoyed by "moderation all," handed down as the wise advice to exercise "moderation in all things." However, entertainment feeds on excess. Our forced participation in a ubiquitous culture of entertainment online, particularly through our active production and coproduction of entertainment, presentations of the self in public and semipublic forums, highlights costs entailed in the business of providing pleasure.

Anyone can be an entertainer, tell a joke, hold the floor at a party, deliver a karaoke rendition, offer an entertaining speech or lecture, provide online amusements, or appear on YouTube,[49] but as ersatz online entertainers and pleasure providers, what are we getting ourselves in to? The entertainer is a juggler of emotions. Aristotle says as much of the rhetorician. You have to gauge the mood of the audience and in turn project the right mood. For the classical tradition, any discipline so dependent on the emotions for its raison d'etre is suspect. Emotions can sway either way. The entertainer has to be prepared for derision and schadenfreude as well as applause.

Entertainment carries with it the trappings of class inequality. Society places a great premium on entertainers who fit the bill, and some earn extremely high incomes. For most, their entertainment labors are badly paid. Although we may admire and even envy the entertainer's abilities, stories about entertainers place them on the margins of society. Even those who are rich and famous pay the price by giving up their privacy and dignity; why isn't Jennifer Aniston wearing her engagement ring? As depicted in Sylvain Chomet's (and Jacques Tatti's) clever animated film *The Illusionist* (2010), entertainment is closely associated with pathos, dashed dreams, derision, and playing the fool. Drag acts seem to play on comic-tragedy, and audiences do enjoy sad stories about entertainers: *A Star Is Born* (1954), *The Entertainer* (1960), *The Rose* (1979), and *Festival* (2005). "Entertainer" is also sometimes a euphemism for someone in the sex business, or at least someone who is "available." Consider the words and video of Robbie Williams's *Let Me Entertain You*. Entertainment has this association. According to Richard Dyer, "To watch an action movie is to sink back in the seat and say, 'show me a good time.'"[50]

Keeping Out of the Limelight

There are people in the public eye who don't want to be mistaken for entertainers and prefer to be "taken seriously": journalists, educators, activists, politicians, critics, coaches, guides, sportspeople, and bishops. It's interesting and somewhat jarring when entertainers turn into politicians, activists, and public intellectuals, but it's just a role, after all, like delivering information or a challenge. Although, some of us just want a quiet life.

Entertainment can be potent politically and dangerous. "We are all hooligans," said the banner of protesters in New York denouncing the sentencing of the three members of the Russian protest band *Pussy Riot*.[51] The lyrics of the punk prayer they tried to sing in the Moscow Cathedral are online. The cause enlisted the support of many in the business. Entertainment and activism, punk and protest—there's something here about the magnification, power, potential, and danger of the pleasure business.

Some readers left informative comments on this post:

Comment 1: In 2009, a woman called Sister Feng became famous to every Chinese web surfer. She passed out leaflets in Shanghai seeking a marriage partner. However, one day a network marketing agency admitted it engineered the case of Sister Feng.[52] As a result, I am suspicious of anything of interest online, as I have no idea if people are saying what they really mean without playacting.

Comment 2: There does seem to be a sly satisfaction in the remark that Confucius is said to have made that "there is no spectacle more agreeable than watching an old friend fall off a roof." Somehow, it seems important that the friend is an old one.

Comment 3: So, friendship doesn't provide immunity from schadenfreude, nor does old age.

Comment 4: It is interesting that "celebrities" are sometimes created from feelings of schadenfreude, as is the case with some YouTube vloggers, anonymous people who have become famous as subjects of mocking derision.

5 Addicted to Vertigo

One evening in October 2012, a small group of us sat in a bar in Copenhagen after a workshop at the NordiCHI[1] conference and watched Felix Baumgartner, wearing a space suit, tumble from a capsule suspended from a helium balloon positioned over 39 kilometers above ground. We wondered whether he might spin as he fell, which would mean he would lose control and be unable to open his parachute. He didn't spin, and landed safely after exceeding the speed of sound on his fall. That's vertigo: sitting in a bar staring at an iPad for an hour, waiting for someone to jump. Vertigo helps explain our fascination as well: the vertical trajectory, hanging, falling, spinning, and swaying.

If you were ever confused, dizzy, afraid of being on a ledge, thrilled by speed, or mesmerized by being rocked back and forth, then you were probably in a state of vertigo. *Vertigo* is a useful umbrella term to account for a range of emotions, including confusion, disorientation, and dizziness. Like a mood, when it happens, vertigo is all around us. Like digital media, it's ubiquitous. The world is vertiginous in many senses. Vertigo has spatial properties and a long history. We vertically aligned humans are primed for vertigo and experience it in relation to the body's position in space and the geometry of space.[2] In any case, the world rotates, and many cultural practices are aligned directly to that rotation, not least to the rising and setting sun and the cycles of the moon.

Why is vertigo important in understanding the relationship between pervasive digital media and the emotions? I'll show that vertigo inevitably involves objects and equipment, sometimes including digital equipment. Vertigo also relates to habits, obsessions, dependency, and addiction, which many commentators think characterize the human organism's relationship with computers. Vertigo has several connections with mobility: motion sickness, travel anxiety, and keeping up with travel schedules. According to theorists of tourism, the term *tourist* comes from the Latin *"tornus* or lathe, and defines an individual who makes a circuitous journey—usually for pleasure—and returns to the starting point."[3] Travel-weary tourists alighting from a train, plane, or ferry look as though they've been through a mill, as if they are wheat trapped, tossed about, and ground down between rotating disks of stone. Philosophers point to a deep, primordial kind of anxiety, often termed *existential angst*,[4] but I will argue that there's a deep, primordial kind of vertigo, grounded in the body and its symbolic relationship with earth and sky: *existential vertigo*.

Too Much Information

For many digital commentators, vertigo equates to dizziness and confusion. In his early book on cyberspace, Michael Benedikt invoked the feeling of vertigo in his account of the challenges presented by virtual reality: "Bombarded everywhere by images of opportunity and escape, the very circumstances of a free and meaningful human life have become kaleidoscopic, vertiginous."[5] More recently, digital commentator Andrew Kean used vertigo as the guiding metaphor in his book appropriately titled *Digital Vertigo*, alluding to the "increasingly vertiginous nature of twenty-first-century life."[6]

Here, confusion is a state of mind in which audiences and consumers experience a sense of disorder. If you want to persuade an audience about the clarity of your own position, then you can start by impressing on them how confused they are in theirs. The early management theorists tried to persuade professionals that they needed clear-cut and well-documented procedures to inject clarity into the confusion of a fast-moving and ever more interconnected series of business and social relationships: so too in design. According to design theorist J. Christopher Jones, "the intuitive resolution of contemporary design problems simply lies beyond a single individual's integrative grasp"[7]—hence the need for the methods he outlines. Without that sense of confusion, people are not yet ready for clarity. Vertigo provides a rich metaphor for this mood of confusion, but in this chapter I'll show that there's much more to vertigo than confusion. Vertigo pertains to geometry and embodiment, and to ideas that have multiple and profound cultural resonances.

Clinical Vertigo

Clinicians identify vertigo as a condition symptomatic of or triggered by rapid movement of the head (such as spinning your body around), disorders of the inner ear (when you have a bad cold), and particular visual stimuli (such as looking down from heights). Epidemiologists calculate that 39 percent of people over the age of eighty suffer from vertigo[8] as a serious and disturbing medical condition. The inner ear (the vestibular system) senses rotation about the vertical axis (z) and the two horizontal axes (x and y), providing spatial experience in terms of yaw, pitch, and roll, familiar to anyone who's flown an airplane or flight simulator. The horizontal plane is established by gravity. Any upset to either of these axes induces vertigo.

According to the *Oxford English Dictionary*, vertigo simply refers to a state in which an object is turning around, rotating, or whirling.[9] When I am the object, then I'm likely to feel dizzy; my balance is upset, as when alighting from a roller coaster ride. You may experience vertigo when you stand up after being spun round in a swivel chair, drink too much alcohol, or are on a boat in a rough sea. For some people, the experience of vertigo is noticeable when they position themselves at a height, even just a few meters above the ground. For many of us, we just don't like being in a position where there's a risk of losing our balance or falling. Vertigo spans a spectrum from mild anxiety to extreme discomfort, pain, and outright incapacity.

Vertigo is a useful metaphor for many physical, social, psychological, and cultural conditions. You can induce vertigo of your own free will as a game. In *Man, Play and Games*, Roger Caillois defines voluntary vertigo as "an attempt to momentarily destroy the stability of perception and inflict a kind of voluptuous panic upon an otherwise lucid mind."[10] He refers to children spinning around deliberately to make themselves giddy. Vertigo is part of some play activity, and some people actually enjoy the experience, at least for a while. Caillois thinks that people can become obsessed with experiences that engender vertigo, such as car racing, and even addicted to vertigo, or to vertigo-inducing substances, like alcohol and drugs. Updating his insights to the contemporary condition, play, including video games that involve racing or rapid gestures, commonly invokes the anxiety and . thrill of vertigo.

Vertical Chase

We associate vertigo with heights. A few years ago, newspapers carried photographs of climbers queuing along a precarious mountain trail in the snow
to climb Mount Everest.[11] There's something irresistible about verticality.
TV producer and scriptwriter Russell T. Davies famously employed "the vertical chase" in his *Doctor Who* episodes. Characters are pursued up a stair,
ladder, duct, a rope suspended from a dirigible; they shimmy along ledges,
leap across gaps, and teeter on the edge. It's a common device in adventure
films. Vertical action heightens risk, tension, and danger. Think of Peter
Jackson's *King Kong* (2005), in which the ape battles to save Ann Darrow
from a T. rex while all three fall through a ravine tangled with vines.

Superheroes also fly, glide, hang upside down, jump, fall, and catch.
Some games and sports also induce or play on the sense of vertigo: high-
wire circus acts, climbing trees, aerial adventure parks, and car racing. We
could add skateboarding, parkour, and extreme sports and pastimes such as
bungee jumping, climbing Everest, and skydiving. Video games of course
invite simulation of vertiginous experience, and people fly in Second Life.
Several well-known films derive much of their drama from height: *Up*
(2009); *The Eiger Sanction* (1975); *Around the World in Eighty Days* (1956);
Cargo (2009); *Mary Poppins* (1964); and of course the iconic film that bears
the name of the condition under discussion in this chapter, *Vertigo* (1958),
by Alfred Hitchcock, in which the main character's incapacity to climb a
tower or even to stand on a ladder impedes his ability to solve a murder
mystery.

Architecture employs vertigo: towers, stairs, mezzanines, atriums in
shopping malls, and multistory hotels with thin sheets of waist-high glass
to protect patrons from the void, transparent lifts and open-grated flooring
on bridges and gantries. The vertigo effect is induced not only by height
but by seeing objects just out of reach above a gorge, looking up as well
as down, and seeing crane operators, painters, and window cleaners suspended, poised, vulnerable, and isolated. Vertigo connects the advantages
of access and prospect with the hazards of falling or being abandoned on
a ledge that no one else can reach. Scholars in architecture and cultural
studies also research the aerial view.[12] For us earthbound creatures, looking
from above or obliquely still carries novelty. It's a way of looking at things
from a new angle. We don't climb mountains and towers only to see, but
to see differently.

The development of very small video cameras means that high-quality moving images can be gathered and transmitted from just about anywhere, including the front of racing cars; strapped to birds in flight; on missiles, drones, and the helmets of construction workers and skydivers; and while scaling cliffs. The official promotional video for Google Glass shows what it's like when the wearer is flying, swinging, riding a rollercoaster, skydiving, on a trapeze, or on a balloon ride. I suspect that the videos look different from being there, but in any case, being there is different than the view from the ground.[13]

Losing Control

Internet entrepreneur Andrew Keen's book *Digital Vertigo* draws insights from Alfred Hitchcock's film, *Vertigo*, as leitmotif. Keen treats vertigo as a confused condition brought about by the digital moguls of Silicon Valley, by whom we consumers are deluded into thinking society is becoming more consumer oriented, democratic, benign, and sensitive, but as we use the social media tools they provide we lose control of our private information and of ourselves. We are subject to constant scrutiny and surveillance, under the misconception that all this "friction-free" digital sharing on social media is for our good. The film *Vertigo* was set in San Francisco and the Bay area, where Keen thinks much of this digital transformation originates. Keen also references Jeremy Bentham's (1748–1832) idea of the circular panoptic prison, in which the prisoners are under constant surveillance from the all-seeing prison warden positioned in a central tower. He also positions Bentham's utilitarianism as a precursor to the time management and industrial-scale efficiency to which we are all becoming subject, surreptitiously, to our detriment, and amplified through social media. I'll provide an alternative account of the significance of these themes later in this chapter.

In the rest of this chapter, I want to take these architectural metaphors further than Keen. To stretch the centrifugal metaphor to the limit, I posit this concept as central to the issue of mood. Thus, I place the theme of vertigo at the center of this book. Vertigo involves architecture's organizing schema of the circle, getting caught up in circles, and going around in circles, repeatedly. Vertigo relates to being in a circle, even a vicious circle that you can't always get out of.

Existential Vertigo

Like filmmakers, philosophers invoke height to dramatize the human condition. Derrida refers to the "bottomless chessboard on which Being is put
into play"[14] and hovering over an abyss or void: what it is to have no certainties, where the ground is taken from under you. There's a tradition here
of philosophical reflection that makes its way into media theory. Media
theorist Eugene Thacker describes what he calls "dark media" in these
terms: "seeing something in nothing . . . and finding nothing in each something."[15] This is a trope with some circularity: "The function of media is no
longer to render the inaccessible accessible, or to connect what is separated.
Instead, media reveal inaccessibility in and of itself—they make accessible
the inaccessible—in its inaccessibility."[16]

Such circular tropes, metaphors, and literary devices draw on Martin
Heidegger. In a section on anxiety in Heidegger's *Being and Time*, we read
about *fleeing, falling,* and *grounding,* as well as being "not at home," and the
uncanny,[17] key components of the philosopher's "vertical chase." However,
it's really in the idea of the circle that the vertiginous is expressed with
greatest acuity. After all, vertigo refers to rotary motion. The opening title
sequence of Hitchcock's *Vertigo* makes this clear, with the spiraling graphic
and the repeating note sequence in the theme music by Bernard Her-
mann.[18] Vertigo is about spinning before it derives its effects from height.
Circles really are everywhere, in philosophy, architecture, science, engineering, and digital networks, operationally, historically, and experientially.[19]
Here's some further evidence of their ubiquity.

First, circles feature in problem solving. Circles exist in circuits, flows,
and networks and how we think about human relationships, information
processes, and economics. Consider a typical statement about the economic
crisis of 2012: "There are weeks when it can sound as if the European sov-
ereign debt crisis is going around in circles."[20] Problems that can't easily be
solved, like the economic crisis, are not only confusing but also lead you in
circles, even a vicious circle. Resolving the euro crisis is also like "trying to
square the circle," a reference to the impossible task of using only a compass and straightedge to draw a circle and a square that enclose exactly the
same area.[21]

Second, circles entail certain efficiencies. As any amateur geometer
knows, circles enclose the greatest area within the least perimeter, and so
make for efficient structures. They are the shape that cells, planets, and

atoms want to be—in section. Circles of course relate to ellipses (circles seen from an oblique angle), spheres (circles in 3-D), spirals (the path around a circle with a diminishing radius), and sine waves (a graph over time of the y value of a point traveling round a circle).

Third, circles are easy to create and draw but are easy to get trapped in, and the perimeter is so undifferentiated that it's hard to know where to jump off, if that's your trajectory of travel. You just go round and round, vertiginously. The circle is such a universal symbol of commerce and of life that it would be an intellectual triumph to identify phenomena that have absolutely no association with circles. I can't think of any. It seems the human body and psychology are so inscribed in circles that the best hope of escape (if we want to escape) is *tangentiality* and *eccentricity*, or at least to expose the paradoxes within circularity (circular philosophy, rotary logic) itself.

Fourth, the cultural legacies of the circle run deep. As a traditionally educated architect, it's had to avoid seeing the deep significance of the legacy by which all things spin, cycle, and gyrate. For Plato (c. 428–347 BC), God created the universe as a circle moving within a circle.[22] A skilled draftsperson can draw most of the so-called Platonic shapes (such as triangles, squares, and hexagons) with just a straight edge and a compass to scribe arcs and circles. Plato also observed that no one has ever seen a perfect circle, and yet we know they exist. The most "eccentric" circle story is an account in Plato's *Symposium* that humans were originally spherical in shape.[23] They then were split in two, with each half destined to search for its other "soulmate" to complete the circle, an explanation of sexual attraction and of being "in the mood for love," a theme to which I return in chapter 11. The symbolic link between architecture and vertigo is satisfying for me not least because it positions vertigo's moods as something geometrical.

Fifth, standing tall is the body's commerce with vertigo. As I referenced in chapter 3, the classical architectural theorist Vitruvius (circa 80–15 BC) relates the story of man emerging from the forest and exhibiting advantage over the other creatures by standing tall.[24] Standing is the usual starting position for mobility among humans. That's when we are most active. Digital media are complicit in various postural transformations. Not least in this trajectory is the transition from sitting deskbound, tethered to the machine. Now, we carry our digital equipment, wear it, and even render it inconspicuous and invisible. Of course, we can recline with our screens and ear pods as well, but head-mounted cameras, selfie sticks, and mobile media emphasize yet again the human tendency to the vertical and to be at the center of orbital movement, the panoramic sweep. The world and our lives are inscribed within circles, and so there's a sense in which vertigo is the norm, especially in relation to the body.

In the next section, I'll offer a brief architectural excursion into the cultural geometry of the embodied human to emphasize humankind's commitment to a condition of existential vertigo before returning to the theme of ubiquitous digital media.

Spinning Bodies

Standing upright entails an ability to keep balance, to defy dizziness and vertigo. The vertical line of the upright human body is also the start of a circle. The human body's position between ground and sky is crucial in antique thought and is often represented geometrically. The ground is a flat plane, and the sky is a dome. The passage of the sun is an arc across the sky. Its symmetrical rising and setting defines the cardinal points: east, west, and (by simple derivation) south and north. The plane of the ground is a square defined by the four compass directions, the x and y of the vestibular system, and the cosmos above is a circle, joined to the center by the vertical vestibular axis (z) about which our bodies turn. The human body is at the center of this configuration: the body as vertical gnomon (as in a classic sundial) extended between the ground and the sky, in contemporary anatomical terms, with yaw, pitch, and roll.

The body's place in the cosmos is well-represented by Vitruvius's famous description of ideal proportioning, derived from a male body not standing, but stretched out on his back with the center of a circle at the navel. The extremities of the body define the edge of a circle and similarly of a square.[25] Vitruvius left no diagram to show us the precise geometry of the arrangement of the body. Architects have long been interested in the symbolism of the spatial pattern involving the heavens (macrocosm), the earth (microcosm), and the human body. This template (circle, square, gnomon) has a practical aspect. It features in the laying out of a city, and Vitruvius describes how you use the movement of the sun to lay out the square on the ground that forms the basis of a town. For the Romans, it was no coincidence that such cosmic ordering produced optimal arrangements for the passage of restorative breezes through the streets.[26]

Whether the tradition here refers to actual bodies, idealized bodies, symbols, functions, or the body as metaphor would not have been important to the antique mind, for which symbol inhered within all of human experience. There is a variation to this tradition, that of the universe as understood by the philosopher Plotinus (circa 204–270 AD), a follower of Plato though he lived some six hundred years later, for whom it was apparent that the cosmos is made up of concentric spheres, successive stages through which the soul must pass in order to participate in unity with the cosmos. The circle is there in full force, but the body is something to leave behind, disconnected from the divine order, incidental, and even loathed, as the soul ascends to enlightenment and completeness.

The Renaissance was heir to, and in some cases rediscovered, these classical, Vitruvian, and Neoplatonic traditions. The most compelling image of a circular logic comes from the image now on the Italian euro coin, Leonardo da Vinci's representation of Vitruvius's man in 1487.[27] Da Vinci's text accompanying his drawing focuses on the dimensional relationships between body parts and provides no description of what else he might have meant the diagram to convey. The architectural historian Rudolf Wittkower describes this and similar Renaissance drawings: "The Vitruvian figure inscribed in a square and a circle became a symbol of the mathematical sympathy between microcosm and macrocosm."[28] Historian Martin Gem elaborates: "What we discover is an identity of the square and the circle, surpassing mere sensual perception and existing as the unique divine essence that reveals its limited image in the square, and its absolute, limitless reality in the circle."[29] The true moderns of course rejected such cosmologies in place of a scientific, open, and all-seeing worldview, tinged in no small measure with sentiment. For example, Edmund Burke (1729–1797) rejected the Vitruvian model: "Men are very rarely seen in this strained posture; it is not natural to them; neither is it at all becoming."[30]

As if returning to Vitruvius's body as it emerged upright from the forest and gazed "upon the splendour of the starry firmament," Burke's modern body stands on the clifftop beholding the vastness of the sky, the vertiginous spectacle of terror and wonder, immersed in the emotion of a highly individualized sense of the sublime.[31] However, the other side of this modern coin is occupied by the technorationalist, the emotionally detached dealer in numbers, commodities, brands, and the circulation of capital, exhibiting a different kind of mastery.

Panoptic Surveillance

Here's another trajectory that relates geometry to mood and technology. I referred at the start of this chapter to Keen's invocation of Jeremy Bentham's utilitarianism oriented toward control. Bentham's disciplinary practices and processes come together in the concept of the prison, a circular architectural instrument for reform as well as punishment. Here, the circle presents itself with great potency, not as a symbolic, recreational, or instructive apparatus, but as the Panopticon, an architectural "machine" that positions at its focal point the all-seeing eye.

Bentham was a prominent British legal reformer, appropriately labeled a "utilitarian." In keeping with an era of burgeoning industrial production, bureaucracy, efficiency, and the translation of social life to number and calculation, he was the one who advocated that laws should account for maximizing pleasure and minimizing pain for the greatest number. We are each capable of calculating what is to our individual benefit. In a way, the calculation of happiness indices from questionnaires and microblogs is heir to this instrumentalism. Everything is amenable to calculation, even moods. Interestingly, Bentham thought that architecture and the arrangement of things in space could also feature in this calculation, especially for people in prison.

Bentham describes his prison design in great detail in a series of published letters, helpfully available online in facsimile as well as text formats.[32] There's a naive, industrial simplicity to his circular schema: Cells are arranged around a closed courtyard. There's an "inspection lodge" or tower at the center, from which the guard can see every prisoner in his cell. It's not possible to tell if the guard at the hub of this arrangement is present or even watching the cells. Furthermore, the prisoners can't see or hear one another. Bentham suggested that this "inspection principle" could be applied to other building types, such as hospitals, schools, and factories.[33]

Bentham's utilitarianism is vertiginous in three senses, insofar as it enlists the circle for its system of control, in the psychological and physical effects of height on its occupants, and in the vicious cycle of draconian punishment and reform measures of the seventeenth and eighteenth centuries. It's arguable whether the results are better now, but contemporary liberal theory suggests that stripping inmates of privacy and dignity only increases grievances and their likelihood to reoffend.

In the contemporary prison, attending to the mood of the prisoners really matters, evidenced not least by severe and high-profile instances of suicide, hunger strikes, riots, substance abuse, physical abuse, and reoffending. All that confinement seems to intensify negative moods. It's interesting to compare the high profile of such instances with the iconic performance by fifteen hundred inmates in the Cebu Provincial Detention and Rehabilitation Center in the Philippines, which became a YouTube hit in 2007.[34] They danced to Michael Jackson's *Thriller* in strict geometrical order, filmed safely and obliquely from above. There's a female character who dances around the central group in a kind of frenzy, eventually mauled or consumed by orange-clad prisoners wandering around like zombies—that is, giddy bodies as if alighting from a vertiginous, fast-moving carousel, a metaphor for the prison system, perhaps.

Returning to Bentham, like the rudimentary Platonic shape on which it's based (the circle), the Panopticon presents as an idealized type, a form that is only imperfectly realized, if at all. The Panopticon is also a handy emblem of the way power is distributed among bodies in society. It has also become the emblem for the surveillance society. The central tower is the surveillance camera, though now cameras are distributed and networked inconspicuously in shops, busses, streets, hotels, and homes.[35] The myth of the central viewing point persists, though, as if there's a center monitoring and controlling everything.

Ubiquity and Power

Bentham's design was popularized as a target for critique by cultural theorists working through Michel Foucault's ideas about the way power and discipline operate in the modern world. His account of Bentham's panoptic schema for controlling bodies sustains a potent social commentary. The Panopticon is not actually a machine for the powerful to exercise control over the weak or for the domination of one class over another. In fact, in any panoptic arrangement (in a hospital, factory, school, or prison), it matters little who is in the position of observer or if there's even anyone there. The Panopticon provides "an apparatus for supervising its own mechanisms," and "enclosed as he is in the middle of this architectural mechanism, is not the director's own fate entirely bound up with it?"[36]

Foucault elaborates further: "Power has its principle not so much in a person as in a certain concerted distribution of bodies, surfaces, lights, gazes; in an arrangement whose internal mechanisms produce the relation in which individuals are caught up."[37] The multidirectional nature of contemporary surveillance comes into stark relief with all-pervasive digital video cameras.

To stretch a point, there's a lesson here for critics of Silicon Valley culture, such as Keen, who have difficulty finding the center, the source of villainy and control. The technologies we have are of all our making. We are complicit, which is to say that there is social complicity in the various means by which power circulates, including the technologies we use. The noncausal operations of mood come to our aid here as well. Foucault doesn't refer to mood, but its nondeterminate origins fit the idea of power, and its manifestations get propagated and circulated through complex social processes and practices. Moods, power, surveillance, and digital technologies each share in the operations of ubiquity.

Paradox

There's an obvious orbital logic to the spatial account of the body I've been providing: It's all about the circle. There's the Vitruvian Man positioned within a circle and its Renaissance representations. In the industrial age, there's a shift to a utilitarian, mechanical circle, a circuit of visually linked control points, with all attention on the hub. Contemporary communications add further emphasis to this orbital logic, with all those communications towers and base stations for configuring the cell phone networks. Other geometries emerge of course, such as the invisible hyperbolic paraboloids formed by intersecting patterns of concentric, radiating radio waves, but a lot of essential geometries derive from the circle.

Inevitably, there are circles within circles, or at least circles within narratives about circles. In the Cebu prison dance, it's about staggering zombies. In premodern Europe, there was the rotary specter of the body torn apart (quartered) by four horses that begins Foucault's gruesome account in *Discipline and Punish*. As a spectacle only slightly less macabre, Foucault refers to the punitive chain gangs in the early 1800s that would pass periodically through a European town, "a saturnalia of punishment," and "a great merry-go-round."[38]

Jumping to the age of irony, the late 1900s, the film *Logan's Run* (1976) directed by Michael Anderson depicts a dystopian future in which social equilibrium is maintained by requiring everyone at the age of thirty to enter a "carousel" to be "renewed." The carousel is a circular auditorium in which the younger citizens watch their older siblings float, spin, and ascend to the upper, glowing crystalline reaches of the domed space. The audience chants encouragement toward the ascendants, who eventually disappear from view—we think vaporized. The story is a nihilistic allegory, as if Plato and Plotinus got it wrong about the soul's ascent, though life is redeemed ultimately in the story by the discovery of an old man living beyond the city limits.

Insofar as our bodies, spatial and social organization, and politics are bound up in circles, human beings are immersed in vertigo. It's no wonder that circles interest philosophers. Derrida addresses the question of which comes first, thought or language. Such classic chicken-and-egg questions lead the inquirer in an inevitable circle. Here's what Derrida provides as an answer: "The circle, as a vicious circle, a logical circle, by the same token constitutes the rigorously limited, closed, and original autonomy of a field . . . the circle forms a perfectly underivable figure." Such circles are "simultaneously open and closed."[39]

The cosmic paradoxes of the circle were already identified in the Renaissance. By a certain reading, the truths to which the Vitruvian Man refers were meant to transcend what our senses tell us, in a way presenting the inexpressible paradoxes relating the limited and the infinite. According to German theologian Nicholas of Cusa (1401–1464), "Thus, the fabric of the world (*machina mundi*) will *quasi* have its center everywhere and its circumference nowhere, because the circumference and the center are God, who is everywhere and nowhere."[40] The circle is an object of paradox, or at least provides a template for describing the paradox of the world: a center everywhere, and a circumference nowhere. This is a geometrically structured challenge to common sense.

The circularity of question and answer, the cycle of interpretation to which I alluded in the previous chapter, is also open-ended, if not paradoxically formed. Contemporary philosophers who read Derrida appeal to metaphors that draw on the circle and prefer those metaphors that imply eccentricity, a center that's come adrift. Insofar as circles provide efficient boundaries, it's what's excluded that is of interest, bringing the periphery and what's outside it into the center of the circle, the old man outside the city precinct (*Logan's Run*) brought in to rejuvenate the life within.

Movement around a circle repeats, as do the hours, the seasons, and the tides. The circle is also a progenitor of oscillatory movements. Radical philosopher Gloria Anzaldúa describes her own contradictory position thus: "I am a wind-swayed bridge, a crossroads inhabited by whirlwinds. Gloria, the facilitator, Gloria the mediator, straddling the walls between abysses."[41] I'll investigate the relationship between vertigo and swinging in the next section.

In this section, I've attempted to show that vertigo, as complicit in mood, is something more than feeling giddy when up a ladder. It connects with the body's position in space and the history of thought. It implicates power relations, surveillance, technologies, and paradox. It's also about swinging.

Swinging and Oscillating

If you look from ground level at someone running in a circle, then they appear to slow down at the edges of your field of view and speed up in the middle. The rate at which they speed and slow follows a sine curve. This is also the classic arc motion of a swinging pendulum. All regular movement around a circle, whether by animal or machine, follows this oscillatory, repetitive pattern of movement.

What does the body do at height? The body stands, floats, ascends, and falls—but it also hangs and swings. The opening scene of Hitchcock's *Vertigo* involves a chase across rooftops.[42] Bernard Herman's accompanying music repeats a run up and down the musical scale, emphasizing the circularity of vertigo. A misjudged jump leaves the hero hanging from the guttering of a multistory building, while the other policeman who tries to save him slips on the roof tiles and plummets to the ground. The hero is suspended and not swinging, but the empathic mirror neurons of the audience kick in, and they certainly want to swing, and try to enact the geometrical and kinesthetic movement by which the hero could possibly recover his position on the roof. Hanging from a position suspended above the ground is about losing the center, balance, and eccentricity. It's also about teetering between complete verticality and being inclined. If vertigo is a sensation about circles, it's also about swinging.[43]

Ritual Swinging

If circles permeate the vertiginous economy of the human condition, then swinging does as well. The gnomon is a rigid pole centered through the human body ascending from the ground to the heavens, but it's also "the great chain of being," descending from the heavens to earth.[44] A drawing in the book *Retorica Christiana*, written by Didacus Valdes in 1579, shows this chain hooked at the top with a weight at the bottom, traversed by a series of arcs that accommodate the ordering of angels, mortals, and natural kinds connected at each level by the links of this single chain. The arcs suggest a pendulum-like movement, which itself confirms the orbital ordering of the world. There are other iconic pendulums that express this relationship mechanically. The long pendulum suspended from the ceiling of the repurposed chapel in the Musée des Arts et Métiers in Paris provides evidence of the rotary motion of the earth as the pendulum swings slowly back and forth, returning to a slightly different position on each oscillation.

Anthropologists identify the role of swings in certain rituals, the symbolic significance of which is all but lost in contemporary culture. Alfred Gell explains how in Central India Hindu divinities would be depicted perched on swings suspended within ornate frame structures, but like a contemporary child's swing in scale and proportion. To be rocked in that way is apparently something of a privilege, like the rare honor of riding a horse or on the back of an elephant: "To swing, to ride, is to enjoy the vertiginous triumphs the Gods alone can know."[45] A cursory search of websites indicates that religious festivals of swings are still a major aspect of Indian cultural life.[46]

Mediums whose job it was to channel the thoughts of the Gods would spend time imitating this action, sitting on the seats of wooden swings constructed for this ritual purpose. Gell relates swinging to the experience of vertiginous play, which in turn relates to the body's equilibrium and disequilibrium and states of consciousness.[47] Swinging is in the company of other vertiginous activities that seem to induce a state "combining fatigue, over-breathing and auditory stress" that "cause them to experience themselves and their situation in non-normal ways."[48] Excitement and this disorientation to the world around them seem to go together.

This sounds to me a lot like the vertiginous experience of watching a state-of-the-art CGI animation. Each movie becomes more gravity defying than the last, and with 3-D the characters come right at you. In titles such as *How to Train Your Dragon* (2010), *Kung Fu Panda* (2008), *Madagascar* (2005), and their sequels, people, animals, objects, and cameras don't just fly, they swing—in great arcs across the sky, bouncing, ricocheting, and colliding, in jubilant arcs and sinusoidal sweeps. Something similar happens in computer games. The player is immersed in repetitive game operations, some of which involve flying, gliding, and swooping, but there are also the more ordinary operations in so-called nonnarrative games that involve moving abstract tokens around the screen. At the time of writing, *Candy Crush* played on a tablet computer or smartphone was popular and had a reputation for mesmerizing the player. It rewards the player with high scores, lots of congratulatory noises, color, and funky animations. It's a bit like *Tetris*. You just tap on pictures of candy on a grid, and new ones fall to take their place in this rhythmic, animated, eye-candy spectacle that transports the player into a mood of frenzied acquiescence, ready to make some in-game purchases to help them win. Rapidly falling tokens that slide and bounce populate the eye-catching visuals and interactions.

Gell relates the movement of the medium in the swinging rituals to the "oscillation in cybernetic systems," as described by the cyberneticist Norbert Wiener.[49] Such mesmeric swinging provides a feedback process as the participants attune themselves to the system as a whole. The swing is a vestibular apparatus paralleling that of the inner ear.

Thus, the motion of the swing, the rocking to and fro, has cultural significance within the orbital apparatus of existential vertigo, at least within some cultures. It also provides a means of escaping normal consciousness and resonates with game play. In a ritual context, it renders the player or spiritual medium dizzy and susceptible as a potential channel for messages from the Gods. Gell notes that swings bring about both pleasure and danger, which brings us back to the risks of vertigo and excess.

Habits and Addictions

The relationship between vertigo and addiction is clear. Vertigo provides a means of escape. Whereas the vertigo of speed, height, and giddy games is temporary, the effects of chemical substitutes, alcohol and drugs, are long lasting and tend toward destruction. At least, that's how Roger Caillois describes the life of the addict: "In the end, deprived of the freedom to desire anything but his poison, he is left prey to chronic organic disorder, far more dangerous than the physical vertigo which at least only momentarily compromises his capacity to resist the fascination of oblivion."[50] Why is addiction dangerous? For Caillois, vertigo as addiction can induce a loss of self-control, a sensibility numbed to the sober and rational alternative, and in turn a dependency, leading to further intoxication. Those dependent on alcohol are not in a state to make rational judgments that haul them out of their predicament, and so they spiral further into dependency. This is the vicious cycle of addiction.

Chemicals (alcohol and drugs) can have direct effects on the body that amplify their addictive and destructive properties, but then so can other obsessions. Addictions are usually associated with strong drives. We often hear of addiction to food, weight loss, shopping, and pornography. *Addiction* is an emotive term, and is ready to hand as a focus for anxiety and to dampen enthusiasm for something everyone otherwise feels positive about.

As a case in point, the UK's 2012 Ofcom report on the communications market carried the cunning strapline: "Are we addicted to our smartphones?"[51] The adoption of fully featured mobile phones (BlackBerry, iPhone, Android) had rocketed in the preceding 12 months. Furthermore, according to the report, "when asked how addicted they are to their mobiles phones, 37% of adult smartphone users admitted high levels of 'addiction' to their phone, with this rising to 60% of teen smartphone users."[52] It seems people use their phones in the street, the bathroom, in bed first thing in the morning, and in the midst of social gatherings, and that, along with self-reported obsessions, constitutes addiction.

Like anger, discussed in the previous chapter, addiction is a powerfully loaded concept with shameful connotations. "Addiction" has become a kind of streetwise colloquial overstatement to which any of us could subscribe. But people can also be addicted to learning, charitable causes, healthy eating, and exercise. If this is addiction, then perhaps we should embrace it. Instead of "addictions," the adoption of smartphones into everyday use could be presented as the acquisition of new communicative habits or new media practices. Walking quickly in the rain, cleaning your teeth, rubbing your eyes in the morning, and eating with a knife and fork are habits, implying behaviors and emotional conditions more benign than *addiction*.

People now habitually use their smartphones in many contexts. These are practices they fall into without thinking. It's a habit from which they are extricated only by a conscious exercise of will. Academic researchers have long scrutinized the social changes brought about by ubiquitous mobile media. The book on mobile phone usage in Japan edited by Mizuko Ito, Daisuke Okabe, and Misa Matsuda captures the trend toward ubiquity well, even in its title: *Personal, Portable, Pedestrian*.[53] The pedestrian is the ordinary, which is to say the habitual, the taken for granted, as well as the mobile. Mobile phone researcher Michael Bull describes "habitual everyday notions of what it might mean to 'inhabit' certain spaces such as the automobile, the street, the shopping arcade or indeed the living room,"[54] thereby linking habit to habitat—that is, space. Insofar as they occupy the world of everyday things, pervasive media become part of the regular way of doing things, part of the human being's habitual and everyday lifeworld. "A nation habituated to smartphones" is less catchy but provides a more subtle rubric under which to discuss smartphones. Smartphone habits carry less stigma and social embarrassment than smartphone addictions.

I discuss habits and smartphones in a chapter in *The Tuning of Place*.[55] As everyone knows by now, with a smartphone you can download third-party apps that facilitate a range of useful tasks: mapping, locating, recording, listening, talking, browsing, and shopping. The rapid adoption of smartphones is impressive, leading no doubt to subtly new ways of thinking about sociability, how we occupy space, what we see and hear, the ways we tune our interactions with each other and the environment, and the moods we are in.

The topic of habits provides an appropriate conclusion to this chapter. Habits are repeated every day in cyclical fashion, but without recourse to the cycles of destruction implied by addiction. Habituation provides yet another way of accessing or realizing existential vertigo. This excursion into vertigo emphasizes geometry and embodiment, reinforcing the idea that moods are about bodies in the world and habituation.

Summary

I started this chapter by discussing confusion, one of the symptoms of vertigo. Film action at a height increases tension, and it's a device in game play. I explored the pivotal role of vertigo in various cultural forms. Perhaps more significant and unusual, I discussed height, circularity, and the phenomenon of vertigo as symbolic of the human being's position in the world. Architecture gives direct expression to this, in the company of other technologies. I discussed instrumentalism, surveillance, and the way the circle is invoked to explain contradiction and paradox. Then, I touched on the symbolism of the swing, the to and fro oscillations among different pleasures and dangers. This helped me to situate addiction and risk taking in the information age. *Habit* provides a softer vocabulary than *addiction*. If vertigo taps into mood, then it provides a further clue to the centrality of mood in all aspects of being in the world. Perhaps this formulation also provides an alternative to Heidegger's focus on the primary role of human anxiety. For *existential angst* about technology and the world, substitute *existential vertigo* . . . or habituation.

Coda: Equipment Failure

The mechanics of existential vertigo entail equipment. There's the compass and straightedge for measuring out the architect's primordial circle and square, all the tools of architecture and astronomy. There's also the gnomon, chain, the pendulum, the swing, the tightrope, and the tower, not to mention the harness, the safety rail, and suspension wires. What happens if this equipment is not available or breaks down?

Philosopher Gunnar Breivik explores the relationship between extreme sports and Heidegger's concepts of anxiety.[56] Dangerous pastimes that take you to a height require resolute trust in equipment: ropes, crampons, harnesses, and parachutes. Heidegger talks about the breakdown of equipment in the workshop. Breakdown brings to light, or reveals, the nature of the environment we are in at a particular moment. It even makes the moment. Heidegger refers to equipment in the carpenter's workshop (hammers, screwdrivers, and saws) and its failure.

The possibility of fatal failure of equipment in extreme sports adds to the novice's anxiety. In fact, Breivik makes much of the first time element of extreme sports. There's a lot here about anxiety as a primordial condition, exposed by confronting the possibility of your own death due to equipment failure, amplified further by the inevitable "groundlessness" of being up in the air and helplessly dependent on kit, maintenance routines, instructors, and teammates.

Contemporary vertiginous anxieties result from the prospect of absence of that on which the addict depends. A test for our dependency on ubiquitous digital media is what happens when we move to a new context in which such equipment is no longer available.

The Ordinary Seen from Above

Vertigo participates in the logic of exaggeration. We are too high, or the chasm is too deep. We are traveling too quickly, or spinning too fast. For theorist of popular culture Janez Strehovec, writing before the social media revolution, the emerging techno-entertainments and synthetic virtual roller coaster rides seemed designed to commit us "to a maximum extent to the frequencies of perception which have not yet been experienced."[57] Now, we would think of fast-moving live action and CGI films in high frame rate (HFR), high-definition (HD) 3-D with full surround sound. Home entertainment units offer similar capability, and there are kinetically controlled, networked, multiplayer video games. These tools and the artistry that goes with them succeed in exciting the senses beyond what we've ever experienced. At best, they make familiar, everyday encounters look strange: human beings with extensible limbs, horsemen charging into battle in their thousands, cars that talk, steam trains that journey across ice, and toys that spring into life. Extreme encounters bring new aspects of our world into sharp relief, even just for a moment.

However, unusual, disruptive encounters can be experienced through many media and are sometimes just ordinary moments revealed anew. Disruptive encounters can be experienced through gentler media and experiences: art, a stunning piece of music, surveying a flock of gulls off the coast of Scotland, a flotilla of boats on the Thames, being somewhere that you've seen and heard about and now you are actually there: the everyday seen from above. Looking from above carries novelty. It's a way of looking at the world from a new angle. We climb towers to see differently. This is the mood of vertigo. In its various forms and manifestations, it sustains life and makes other senses possible.

As a blog post, this coda prompted some interesting comments:

Comment 1: This reminds me of the suicidal behavior among people who try extreme sports. I remember that Jung believes in the fear of death as a core psychological cause. The normal mode of human locomotion is horizontal rather than vertical. The sky is the domain of birds, and we aspire to be up there. The sea represents the downward direction, and inspires even greater awe.

Comment 2: Yes, rapid movement through the air by flying creatures and machines and across water by humans, crocodiles, and fish is usually horizontal. Why are angels in paintings therefore nearly always vertical, as if always coming in to land?

Comment 3: When the Apollo moon landing revealed that there were no gods or animals on the moon, it ruined a very romantic Chinese fairy tale. Perhaps myth is just another reflection of the collective psychology of human beings?

"I enter a building, see a room, and—in a fraction of a second—have this feeling about it," wrote the architect Peter Zumthor.[1] Zumthor was responsible most notably for the design of the Thermal Baths at Vals, Graubünden in Switzerland (1996), an acoustically resonant series of spaces composed of crisp, clear surfaces, glass, water, light, and air. Critics and visitors regard the building as a bold yet sensitive structure, austere in form and exquisite in detailing. Whether intentionally or not, the baths present an impression that people are pleased to describe as "atmospheric."[2] The building houses a series of swimming pools and bathing rooms. If you look at photographs of these spaces, the lighting is subdued, and haze rises from the heated water. In older, art deco public bathing houses, such as Gellert Spa in Budapest, such atmospheres are more obvious, imbued as they are with the scents and patina of age. On a visit to Gellert Spa, I recall low lighting, a slightly somnambulant, decadent air, humidity, and the earthy whiff of steam and mildew, at least before the baths were renovated.

Mood and Atmosphere

The atmosphere or mood of a place hangs around like a haze, shrouding occupants as if in a cloud. There are some prominent examples from architecture and art that even make spaces out of haze. There's the Blur Building by Diller and Scofidio and Ben Rubin, of EAR Studio, an artificial cloud bank in Lake Neuchatel, Switzerland, built for the Swiss Expo in 2002.[3] *Blind Light*, a mist-filled glass room by sculptor Antony Gormley, was on show at the Hayward Gallery London in 2007.[4] The artwork depended for its impact on fog.

When people were allowed to smoke in public places, haze effects were even more common. The classic black and white film *Brief Encounter* (1945) is mostly set in a railway station, a canteen, and a cinema. Steam, mist, and cigarette smoke permeate the settings as the couple who meet try to resolve their nascent and clandestine relationship. The mist and haze are cinematic metaphors to be sure, but also stark reminders of how hazy the past used to be, at least in the industrial age. Now, haze is more subtle—and healthier. Some hazy spaces also have an acoustical resonance, as if an aural haze. After all, sound relates to breath, wind, and air. Like the air we breathe, the atmosphere of a place is inconspicuous and barely perceptible, but it has an effect. Presumably, spatial forms and shapes, textures, smells, light, sounds, and the whole panoply of architectural elements, including the hum of electronic equipment, contribute to the creation of atmosphere. There are even fog machines for adding atmosphere to concerts, films, and dance clubs. Whether or not such atmospheric spaces contain smoke, water, steam, vapor or fog, it's haze that gives the strongest expression to the spatial presence of mood.

Memories

Haze also provides a spatial metaphor for the workings of memory. Memories linger, like a haze, and then dissipate. Recollections emerge from the mists of time. Haze and memories are where ghosts come from. Where ghosts make an appearance in films and paintings, they are represented as ephemeral and transparent, like a haze, as in Lawrence Olivier's screen version of *Hamlet* (1948), in which the ghost of Hamlet's father appears as a diaphanous shape through a swirling mist.[5]

If you search for "atmospheric painting" under Google Images, then you'll see pages of softly colored, white, purple, and mauve paintings, either professional or amateur, suggesting layerings of haze, storm clouds, and other atmospheric effects. Among them will be some whirling, haze-filled paintings by Joseph Mallord William Turner (1775–1851). Eventually, you'll alight on pictures of ruins.

Ruins also bring to attention the physical decay of memories and the earthy aspects of mood. Ruins make great album covers and stage settings for scenes in drama and opera—and there are lots of ruins in *Lord of the Rings* (2001). The ruin provides a potent metaphor in film as in life. There's a poem by Robert Browning titled "Love among the Ruins" and at least one film by the same title. In art and poetry, as in meteorology, like steam rising from a dewy meadow in the first morning light, atmosphere collects around the ruin from the interaction between air and earth. The profile of a stone ruin emerging through the haze arouses regret, longing, affection, hope, fear, and submission to the inevitable progression of time. In the words of Charles and Alfred Tennyson (1808–1879, 1809–1892) and as any professional photographer or painter knows, "distance on all a mellowing haze bestows."[6]

Ruins in 3-D

For romantic painters, the ruin also captures the spatial expression of mood, redolent with recollections and occupying the interface between air and earth. Classical temples, gothic chapels, castles, abandoned homes, and disused factories collect as ruins. Insofar as moods attach to spaces, ruins provide good exemplars of atmospheric, mood-filled places. In his essay on the subject of ruins, philosopher Georg Simmel (1858–1918) decided that there's a "peace whose mood surrounds the ruin."[7] It's where buildings return to earth, architecture melds with stone, and the earth struggles to reach back into the sky, only to be eroded by the pneumatic forces of time and nature, an equilibrium, or a struggle, he describes as "the striving upward and the sinking downward"[8] and "the struggle between above and below."[9]

The powerful sketches and etchings of the architect Giovanni Battista Piranesi (1720–1778) also capture this sense of mood-filled places, especially his images of the crumbling buildings and monuments of ancient Rome. Even in the case of completed buildings, his sketches depict architecture as if in ruins. From that derives the somber magic of his imagery. As commentator Gail Leggio remarks in relation to Piranesi's drawings of the imaginary prison *Carceri d'invenzione*, "the emotional atmosphere speaks to universal anxieties."[10] The illustrations are of high and lofty spaces with bold arches, stone staircases fashioned as if after the ancient Roman Baths of Caracalla, and wooden galleries. Shafts of light pierce the gloom, exposing inmates and keepers in silhouette, along with wooden drawbridges, pulleys, giant gear wheels, and gallows. The drawings deploy the artifice of haze; surface overlays surface, receding into indistinctness. The whole could well be underground. It's a mood that's repeated in much film scenography. Film reviewer Jonathan Jones sees Piranesi's influence in *Metropolis* (1927),

Blade Runner (1982), and the moving staircases at Hogwarts, and "in today's architecture, you see Piranesi's imagination in Tate Modern, and London Underground's Jubilee line."[11]

Five years ago, when excitement about the 3-D role-playing environment Second Life was in full frenzy, a group of us constructed a playground promontory on the edge of our university's virtual island. We built walls that changed their surface patterns and moved about, a bit like Piranesi's drawbridges or the moving staircases in Hogwarts, but in abstracted form and in response to signals from mobile phones (in physical life). We made a favela of dynamic virtual pop-up architecture. I recall another university department that occupied the adjoining land complaining about our mess. Its members erected a big wall so that we wouldn't be seen. Anyway, I returned a few years later. The whole island was a bit of a graveyard even at its peak, but the contents of our open-air laboratory had decayed. Some of the folding walls had folded into the sea or were suspended in thin virtual air. The algorithmic haze in Second Life reduces the computational cost of rendering distant objects. The virtual scene recedes from full color to complete whiteout over several hundred virtual meters. The diffused whiteness also adds to the atmosphere, the loneliness and sense of neglect. Other forms and fragments were strewn across our promontory. Whether by neglect or malice, we were in ruins.

Travelers and scholars in the everyday lifeworld, independent of computer environments, associate ruins readily with decay and pollution. Without protection and maintenance, ruins are prone to the effects of time and weather. Restoration projects also require the removal of air pollution effects. Architectural scholar Jonathan Hill provides a telling account of Turner's atmospheric paintings.[12] Not only were his depictions of swirling mists accurate portrayals of London's yellow polluted skies and vistas, but Turner left unfinished paintings in his damp studio to gather dirt and grease, which he would later paint over, and then the paint would peel. This carelessness makes conservation of his work difficult now, but also speaks to Turner's recognition of the strong relationship between atmosphere and decay in his practice as an artist.

However, ruins also have a positive aspect, in that they show familiar objects in a new light, providing further insights into mood and digital media. In an illuminating article about physical waste in derelict industrial sites, geographer Tim Edensor notes, "as things decay they lose their status as separate objects, fragmenting and dissolving as discrete entities, becoming part of the soil or absorbed into non-human bodies."[13] These are the bits of rusting machinery, office furniture, discarded personal effects, oily tins, crockery, torn posters, redundant signage, old magazines, and other random industrial and recreational remnants now piled, strewn, exposed, and rotting in arbitrary relationships one to the other. The same applies to dumpsters of old computers tangled up with miscellaneous discarded furniture. Edensor elaborates: "Positioned in these new locations, objects become unfamiliar and enigmatic, they contravene our usual sense of perspective, rebuke the way things are supposed to assume a position in regimented linearity or are separated from each other at appropriate distance."[14] This "accidental surrealism" of waste and ruin challenges our ordered understanding of object, function, value, and presentation.

The incompleteness of ruins, the recollections they invoke of what might have been, and their frequent depictions through haze and mist all present the familiar in an alien light. What else do ruins say about digital media? Further on in this chapter, I'll focus on such alienation effects as a way of understanding how digital devices function theatrically in space.

The Ambient and the Inconspicuous

Haze provides a useful backdrop to the issue of ubiquitous digital devices and mood. Devices such as mobile smartphones and tablets have become part of the background to everyday life. So-called ambient computing incorporates networked digital processing into everyday objects (such as toasters, power tools, and armchairs) and environments (such as the office, schoolroom, and shopping plaza), thickening the everyday background with ambient information, entertainment, services, and functions of which we are scarcely aware.[15] Before ubiquitous digital media, Martin Heidegger alluded to the way objects and devices move in and out of conspicuousness, as if appearing from and retreating into an experiential haze. Haze provides a useful metaphor for key ideas in phenomenology about the way equipment impacts on people's lives. I want to explore the functioning of haze a little further before returning to digital media.

It's helpful to think of inconspicuous aspects of our environment as hazed out. Romantic painters often position ruins within atmospheric haze. I alluded to the benefit in digital renderings of landscapes (Second Life) to have distant objects disappear into a haze, providing a dual benefit of reducing rendering time and increasing the appearance of depth and distance. Painters call the effect "aerial perspective": where colors lose their saturation and contrast and veer toward the blue end of the spectrum. My first recollection of theater was of an amateur production involving fairies and woodland creatures moving behind stretched gauze drop curtains that simulated haze, presumably to invoke depth and to enable objects and actors to appear and disappear as if by magic via changes in the lighting.

Haze operates by causing certain elements, such as distant objects, to recede and foreground objects to stand out—bringing aspects of the environment into sharp relief. In some respects, haze makes things inconspicuous, but also causes other elements to stand out. This is the play of disclosure, a kind of revealing and concealing, which is so much a part of everyday perception.

Haze hides things, but objects appearing through a haze can also appear more stark and conspicuous. We need only look to the night sky for that bizarre symbol of incongruity, the sight of a full moon. It's well known that the moon can look much larger when close to the horizon than when high in the sky. This is the so-called moon illusion. Scholars through the ages have proposed several explanations, generally based on the workings of perspective, but language philosopher Colin Turbayne attributes this size disparity to haze effects.[16] The moon stays at the same size; that is, it occupies the same area on the retina of the eye whether we observe it overhead or near the horizon. We earthbound observers have acquired a particular language of vision. As an object moves further away, it has reduced color saturation, contrast, and brightness, the effect of aerial perspective. Light from the object weakens as it scatters through the thickness of the atmosphere. As I've already indicated, painters and illustrators exploit and exaggerate this feature to give depth to their pictures. When we observe the moon to be near the horizon, its light has to pass through more of the Earth's atmosphere. It appears fainter through the haze. The visual cue implied by this faintness suggests to the human perceptual apparatus that the moon is further away than normal. It is however just the same size as when it appears higher and brighter in the sky. Through the cue of implied distance, we perceive the moon as bigger than normal. Something similar occurs when we see a tower, wind turbine, mountain, or ship through the haze, or even an airplane as a faint silhouette behind cloud. If keen observers are used to seeing them in a clear light, then objects appear bigger when masked by haze. Haze renders familiar sights, such as the moon, strange in this and other ways.

The effects of haze correlate with perception in general. For most people for most of the time, the environment we inhabit, the buildings and equipment we see and use, are part of the background of living and working—the indistinct architecture of the everyday, just blending in as if in a haze. This inconspicuous character of our experience of environment fits in with Heidegger's concepts of the everyday lifeworld.[17] According to Heidegger, our primary experience of the world is undifferentiated. We are absorbed. As we engage in our activities, things are simply available for use. We are unaware.[18] Like many philosophers, Heidegger appeals to visual metaphors. He talks about a clearing, as if we experience the world through a haze, subject to regions appearing with great clarity, only to be covered over again by the fog. We never have a complete picture. Aspects of our environment recede from view, only to be revealed again in a certain light on another occasion. Haze shifts our perception. Sometimes, the moon looks large, other times smaller. Sometimes, the equipment we use, such as a mobile phone or tablet computer, blends into the background; at other times, it comes into our awareness.

The variability of the haze effect modifies the statement at the start of this chapter expressed by Peter Zumthor, that on entering a room "in a fraction of a second" he has "this feeling about it."[19] He may well have a feeling about it, but that is likely to change, and other visitors and occupants may have a different experience. Moods shift and change like haze effects, and people participate in different moods according to their different circumstances and recollections. The mood experienced by the first-time building user or the tourist will be different than that of the habitual user. The familiarity inculcated within a house will be different than that experienced during an occasional visit to a museum. The appreciation of a building will be different when it is first opened for use than after ten years. The experience of a photograph of a building is not the same as inhabiting the building.

As for spaces, so too with equipment. Encountering a new smartphone app for the first time is a rare, singular event. It's the habitual use that will have lasting impact. First impressions are important, and the memory of first impressions, but many more impressions follow. Astute listeners also experience this with music, as when plugged into a playlist. Initially, our selection of music strikes us as conspicuously interesting, but then recedes into the background as we become habituated to the listening. Eventually, its familiar strains may grate on the nerves, and we replace it with another list.

Therefore, the mood or atmosphere of a place is more than first impressions. It's not available for impersonal identification and classification. As one scholar puts it, "architecture depends,"[20] and so do its moods. On what do these moods depend? Moods depend on a complex of cultural practices, social interactions, histories, stories, other places, empathies, circumstances, and memories, as haze is affected by air currents, weather, atmosphere, earth, and the circumstances of our viewing.

Memory Layers

If past experiences contribute to mood as background to current experience, then perhaps those contributing experiences eventually recede from consciousness, retreating into oblivion: complete whiteout.[21] What's at the end of the view, the end of recollection? Some scholars think it's oblivion. For anthropologist Marc Augé, oblivion is the "loss of remembrance."[22] The vastness of the ocean provides one of the great metaphors of oblivion. Augé presents oblivion as an active agent that erodes and reforms memories: "Memories are crafted by oblivion as the outlines of the shore are created by the sea."[23] By this reading, oblivion is not nothing, and its understanding contributes to the nuanced workings of memory.

The gradation from clarity to haze to whiteout, and from perception to recollection to oblivion, fits with Freud's descriptions of the unconscious. What has the unconscious to do with mood and ubiquitous digital media? For a start, there's a thread within psychology that distinguishes between conscious and unconscious moods.[24] In the rest of this section, I'll examine what the idea of the unconscious says about mood. In the section that follows, I'll attempt to dismantle these familiar ideas, or at least modify them via a radical proposition: there is no such thing as the unconscious. What if the unconscious is a fiction, or at least an unhelpful metaphor?

In one of his notes, Freud describes human memory through the concept of the "mystic writing pad." I used to have one of these. It predates Etch A Sketch and tablet computers. The mystic writing pad is a cardboard writing surface covered in a layer of wax. Overlaid on the wax surface is a sheet of thin paper, with a protective layer of clear plastic over that. As you write or draw on the tablet with a stylus, the paper adheres to the wax and leaves dark lines where the stylus has been. To clear the tablet of its drawing and start afresh, you momentarily lift the paper film from the wax surface and start again. An artifact of the process is that the wax surface invariably retains a trace of the drawings that have been made and erased before. Unlike digital storage devices, in time these "memories" recede into the background and become obscured by successive overlays of new drawings. Freud explains this simple structure and process as a metaphor for the unconscious: "the wax slab with the unconscious behind them, and the appearance and disappearance of the writing with the flickering-up and passing-away of consciousness in the process of perception."[25] Our memories recede into unconsciousness as if through successive layering and occlusion, as if retreating into the mists of time and eventual oblivion.

Of course, there are many intriguing features of this drawing process, not least the interactions between the layers of memory. Were we able to recover anything from the palimpsest of scribbles on the writing pad, then we would encounter new associations and connections, a process familiar to anyone in the habit of keeping a regular journal.

Recollection

Although digital records don't fade, the practice of producing regular weblogs or journal entries has something of the character of the mystic writing pad and hence of the recession of memories. At the time of writing this book, I had maintained a weekly blog post for several years. My blog is like any academic diary or journal in that it chronicles my reading and thinking, though written in a way that could be consumed by others, including students. I have attempted to make the posts topical as well, hooking in to recent occurrences, such as the discovery of King Richard III's remains under a car park in Leicester, the Pope's retirement from the Vatican, or a film released recently. The blog was also a way of exploring ideas for this book. In any case, the blog constitutes a list of textual and photographic productions stacked in order from September 2010 on. As with other regular bloggers, people occasionally post comments. The content management system (WordPress.com) encourages the blogger to attach keyword tags to posts to aid search and categorization. I can go back, as if in time, and revise any aspect of the entry without altering its chronological order. I notice that in each post I make reference to relevant previous posts, with suitable links. In 2013, WordPress introduced a feature whereby links appear automatically at the end of each blog. The content manager actively assists my recollection on the basis of some automatic text-analysis software. The resultant blog archive is inevitably richly hyperlinked within its own content and to resources beyond, including other people's blogs, an Amazon author site, Facebook, and Twitter. The blog has become an important tool for me to communicate with myself and with others.

For the blog author, trawling through this compendium is like casting back through the mists of time. Like any data archive, it bears some of the characteristics of the mystic writing pad, but with greater permanence. Unlike a paper diary, I can search this memory bank instantly using Google Custom Search and even combine search terms to mine for ideas in combination. Following Freud's metaphor, the most recent blog post is at the conscious, perceptual level, with previous posts receding back in terms of relevance to the current circumstance and constituting further depths of the unconscious. Social media provide similar analogies. Facebook's Timeline provides a sense of going back to fading memories. In the case of Twitter microblogs, the archive for any account is limited to 3,200 tweets, and so appears to diminish back in time. Tweets recede more rapidly into oblivion.

Concepts of the unconscious provide a fruitful explanation of mood as something normally hidden from view. After all, it takes some sophistication to identify what mood one is in at any moment. Freud's idea of the unconscious has strong explanatory power for the modern imaginary. As well as a haze, the idea of the unconscious suggests a layer beneath the visible edifice, a foundation that supports the parts above ground. Here, the metaphors of atmosphere and haze meet the apparent solidity of the earth. The unconscious is also the structure, mostly invisible, residing underground or behind the cladding. It's the incomprehensible complexity concealed by the smooth veneer of consciousness.

By this reading, moods are like the unconscious. They operate beneath the surface, as a substrate. They operate through the unconscious, with unconscious sources, and come into awareness when something triggers a strong perception or experience: a response to someone else's minor misfortune at misplacing their car keys recalls your own experience about becoming lost on your way to an examination, which is in turn attributed to an experience in which you failed to live up to your parents' expectations, which in turn relates to unresolved issues with your parents, and so on. Such is the trajectory of Freudian psychology and psychoanalysis.[26] Nothing is as it seems. The unconscious is the repository of memories and past perceptions, the hidden source of psychological symptoms, the sepulcher beneath the whitewash, and the cracks under the wallpaper.

What Lurks Beneath

The metaphor of the unconscious is of a rendering that covers over the irregularities of the rubble wall beneath, keeping us one step away from ruin. The unconscious is also a metaphor about rooms: the progression from the reception area, the shop front, the presentable public parts of an organization to the back rooms occupied by hard-working or indifferent functionaries, where the work gets done in private, where there's sometimes conflict and mess. If exposed, this backstage activity might betray the coherence of the organization's public appearance—its public performance, as it were. The architectural unconscious in the home is the closet that conceals the metaphorical skeleton, or simply the place under the stair where souvenirs reside, forgotten. For philosopher Gaston Bachellard, "our memories have refuges." If you live in an elaborate house, then such refuges may well include a "cellar and a garret, nooks and corridors."[27]

The uncovering of the unconscious also draws on an archeological metaphor. For someone undergoing therapy, the psychoanalyst or counselor has to dig away to find out what's beneath the surface, to find the ruined foundations of lost structures. It also invokes diagnosis. Signs and symptoms are surface manifestations of an underlying disease. Cracks in the wall require further probing to uncover causes such as ground movement, water seepage, or a collapsed tunnel. Moods are themselves root causes, hidden structures, frameworks, and frames of mind.

Structuralist language theory also points to deep structures on which the superficial configuration of syntax, idiom, and accent are built.[28] These latter are the ornaments of language (to invoke a further architectural metaphor). Beneath the surface lie the elusive but common semantic rules that support all the variations and differences between the world's languages—the subcommunicable semantics that indicate our common humanity and practices. From this perspective, there's always something simmering beneath the visible social habits, customs, rituals, styles, and movements. These are also the elusive "deep structures" of art, architecture, and all storytelling: the primordial, symbolically rich substrata of hearth, home, sacrifice, and beauty, or those distinctions between male and female, the sacred and the profane, the microcosm and macrocosm, the raw and the cooked, which might underlie all of culture or become subverted or suppressed by contingency and commercial necessity. These hidden elements are what make up the structures of our moods. Think of moods as underground forces that at times erupt to the surface as our visible behaviors. By this reading, moods are not therefore incidental emotional ornamentation to human experience, but the deeply grounded social and cultural conditions that prompt us to act.

Moods therefore are not only virtuous. For critical theorists, this substrate is permeated, if not infected, with the effects of capitalism and class domination. Social and political commentators have latched on to the idea of the unconscious. The neo-Marxist polemic of architectural historian Manfredo Tafuri refers to "the contingent and historical realities . . . hidden behind the unifying terms of art, architecture, and city."[29] Tafuri's argument is about class struggle and the domination of capital rumbling under the surface. For Tafuri, considering architecture's complicity in capitalist production, the role left for cultural commentary and criticism is to bring to light the "general aims proposed by the dominant forces in any given phase of development."[30] Marxism advocates the posture of the forensic investigator: skeptical, suspicious, and perpetually critical. Corruption, delusion, and dissent lurk within the moods of a place; nowhere is innocent.

For Sigmund Freud, the unconscious is further associated with urges, desires, and conflicts. The role of psychoanalysis is to uncover these as a means of healing various psychological disorders via catharsis. Even without the idea of underlying pathology, it's easy enough to assume that most of what goes through our minds is hidden, only occasionally bubbling to the surface during a process of conscious reflection or deliberate decision making. Moods are formed through this psychic economy and flow beneath the certainties and structures of everyday living. Moods occupy this ambivalent position. They envelop and support, drift and erupt, reveal and conceal.

Similar to the fixity of moods to places, the potency of the layered metaphor (of the unconscious) as an explanatory tool for moods is difficult to resist. It's bolstered by the authority within cultural theory of Freud on the unconscious, structuralist theories of language and culture, and the highly influential neo-Marxism of critical theory and the Frankfurt School.[31]

Abandoning the Unconscious

So far, I've been playing along with the clandestine, subterranean, unconscious, and sometimes sinister side of mood, but that's not the only way to account for mood. The haze affect doesn't need to be aligned exclusively to memory layers. Some philosophers, psychologists, and linguistics think of the unconscious as a fiction, convenient at best.[32] There's no need to explain how the mind works by resorting to multilayered processes. Similarly, language and culture do not require the idea of substrata as a basis of their critiques. The layering metaphor leads to paradox, not least the idea that the analyst descends or excavates to bedrock, a certain foundation—the truth, or oblivion. As I explored in chapter 5, for some philosophers, at bedrock resides the vertiginous abyss. Skeptics on the unconscious are critical not only of Freud's ideas about the unconscious as permeated by dark recesses and forbidden thoughts but of the notion that there is any cognitive activity at all that can be usefully labeled as "unconscious."

Let's consider some alternative metaphors for what people too easily describe as the unconscious, thinking first of memory. It's easy to assume that before computers we diarists used to *store* our *memories* in paper journals and boxes and albums of photographs. As I explored in relation to blogging, now we can store "memories" online and contribute to a bigger pool of social memories. We can see other people's memories and add our own. You can also attach memories to objects via barcodes, QR codes, and RFID tags. Scan a barcode attached to a display item in a museum and you can see, hear, or read what others remember about it.[33] Smartphones and their instant access to the Internet amplify this capability. Memories are attachable, detachable, and portable. This is a common view of memory. According to Mayer-Schonberger in a book entitled *Delete*, "externalizing memory has made it possible for us to remember even through generations and across time,"[34] or so it seems.

The linking of the human capability to remember and the electromechanical operations of storing and porting data is seductive, and it's easy to take for granted that information is stored in computer *memory*. Israel Rosenfield's book *The Invention of Memory* provides a helpful antidote to the various myths of memory as storage.[35] We think that "we can accurately remember people, places, and things because images of them have been imprinted and permanently stored in our brains; and that, though we may not be conscious of them, these images are the basis of recognition and hence of thought and action."[36]

Certainly, when I recall a telephone number or try to remember someone's name, it seems like I'm digging up an item of information from a file store. However, one of the keys to understanding memory is *context*: "Note that we generally recall names and telephone numbers in a particular context; each of our recollections is different, just as we use the same word in different sentences."[37] The use of mnemonics, associations that trigger recollections, deployed deliberately or automatically, provides evidence of the importance of context in memory—such as when my PIN comes to mind as I approach an ATM. It's as if the recollection is a dynamic jigsaw that requires components from the environment to complete itself.

We are also better at *recognizing* than *recollecting*.[38] A group can often recall information better than an individual thinking in isolation. Someone may present a fragment of a recollection that awakens in others a recognition that is rapidly confirmed or dismissed. Others fill in the details. The group moves toward a memory by consensual means. Memory has this collective character even when I'm apparently thinking alone. For the early advocate of "collective memory" Maurice Halbwachs (1877–1945), "the individual calls recollections to mind by relying on the frameworks of social memory."[39] Halbwachs speculated on the hypothetical possibility of an individual existing *without* being in society. Without the structuring that derives from social relationships and language, our recollections would have the character of dreams: unrelated and incoherent. After all, it's really only when asleep that you are the supposedly unique individual, away from the support of society. (*Somnio ergo sum.*)

If the process of remembering depends on context, environment, and sociability, then we cannot readily expect online blogging and social media to provide anything other than a *stimulus* to recollection and remembering or an inadvertent trace from which memories get constructed by people in society. Texts, documents, sounds, and pictures are not the memories. We don't code memories into these media, but society constructs its content and media to trigger them. A cherished photograph of a departed friend is not the memory, but it prompts a recollection within me.

If human society were obliterated, then there would be no memories, just a lot of documents (many in digital format) waiting to be interpreted or ignored by the members of a hypothetical alien species with their own memories (if they have them). At the most, electronic devices are memory triggers, or *traces*, not memory stores.

One further antidote to unconsciousness that retains the thrust of the important intellectual movements that feed off it is to understand all inquiry as subject to the workings of interpretation. To "uncover" an unconscious motivation is simply to proffer a particular interpretation, no doubt hard-won and with explanatory power. Insofar as we socialized human beings depend on any kind of cognitive layering, we are at liberty to invert, distort, and confound the structures. As I've already shown, this is one of the ways that ruins affect us, by destabilizing our accepted understandings of objects and their relationships. It's also a property of the haze effect, bringing things into sharp relief and rendering others inconspicuous, as a dynamic, variable, and contingent collection of disorienting processes. If these arguments are effective in dismantling the idea of the unconscious, then what do they say about mood?

Moods are not substrates to human action. The frames in which human action operates are contingent and come into prominence in the context of particular modes of inquiry into human action and emotion. Moods are after all elusive. The terminologies of mood are a linguistic convenience, as are the metaphors we use to activate them. In her book *Unnatural Emotions*, Catherine Lutz is able to assert that "the concepts of emotion can more profitably be viewed as serving complex communicative, moral, and cultural purposes rather than simply as labels for internal states whose nature or essence is presumed to be universal."[40] She appeals to the richness of networks of action and meaning in which words such as happiness, grief, and anger are embedded: "The complex meaning of each emotion word is the result of the important role those words play in articulating the full range of a people's cultural values, social relations, and economic circumstances. Talk about emotions is simultaneously talk about society—about power and politics, about kinship and marriage, about normality and deviance."[41]

Already in this book, I've indicated something of the necessary ambiguity of mood, with more to follow. If moods feature in the way we talk, and in the narratives we construct, then they can also be given account via concepts from theater and scenography, which provide further accounts of mood that rely less on concepts of the unconscious.

Theaters of the Mind

In an earlier section, I referred to my experience as an audience member of a theater production that deployed layers of gauze screens and lighting to reveal and conceal objects on the stage. There's much to be learned about moods from drama and the contrivances of theater and film. Filmmakers speak about the mise-en-scène, the staging of a film scene that sets the mood of the story. According to film theorists Maria Pramaggiore and Tom Wallis, "each element of the *mise en scène*—the setting, the human figure, lighting, and composition—influences the viewer's experience of the story, characters, space, and time. Filmmakers use details in a systematic, integrated manner not only to create a world on screen, but also to indicate character development, present motifs, amplify themes, and establish mood."[42] As I discussed in chapter 4, digital display screens in public places infuse environments with imagery and sounds. Perhaps we are now inclined to see the world through the lens of film and entertainment. The mediatization of the physical environment can turn spaces into television commercials, stage settings, as scenes in a film or as backstage working environments. Media channels also stream to the private realms of smartphones, tablets, and laptops. I conjecture that we urban inhabitants tend to see places as if they are sets in a film or a theater stage.

Setting the Mood

Elements in this mood creation include sound and lighting. According to accepted wisdom, bright images with low contrast and soft shadows (high-key lighting) invoke a "hopeful mood." High-contrast lighting emphasizes shadows (low-key lighting) to create a "somber or forbidding mood."[43] Part of the skill of filmmaking resides in not only the contrasts invoked by any particular scene but also scenes in combination. Pramaggiore and Wallis highlight the transition from the brighter scenes to a lower key, as the action migrates from the happy von Trapp home in *The Sound of Music* (1965) to the threat of being captured by the Nazis.[44]

The term *mise-en-scène* translates as "setting the scene," though it expands to placing in the frame, stage, or setting. Much in art is achieved simply by placement. The surrealists demonstrated the power of incongruous placements—for example, a bicycle wheel on a spindle in an art gallery, a wooden fish in a picture frame, a lost sheep in a music room.[45] Urban design inherits many cinematic devices from cinema, as outlined by urban theorist Richard Koeck.[46] In the temporal medium of film, there's the effect achieved by collage, transitioning between scenes, smoothly or to invoke contrasts. Mood and place is a matter of incongruity, things moving in and out of awareness. The playwright and theorist of theater Bertolt Brecht (1898–1956) introduced the theme of *alien effect* in theater: "A representation that alienates is one which allows us to recognize its subject, but at the same time makes it seem unfamiliar."[47] It also involves "turning an object from something ordinary and immediately accessible into something peculiar, striking and unexpected."[48] As explored in chapter 2, the Situationist International movement thought of mood as a feature of the city, as Guy Debord asserted the importance of "momentary ambiences of life and their transformation into a superior passional quality."[49] The tactics of this movement were to challenge, disrupt, and alienate.

According to sociologists Benford and Hunt, social protest of any persuasion requires staging,[50] and in this resides the impact of effective protest. Think of the iconic banners waved in front of the cameras in lucid English during the Arab Spring uprisings, the careful and symbolic selection of site, and demonstrations staged to lure coverage by the mass media and maximize exposure to the cause. As a bystander at a recent mass demonstration in London, I saw protestors sitting peaceably in front of a theater that at the time was performing *Les Misérables*. That particular protest presented as a deliberate theatrical double irony, a staged performance in front of a staged performance of an iconic protest in Paris in 1832.

Theorists of the theater are invariably interested in incongruity, not least that which requires something from the audience and ambiguates the relationship between audience and performance. Theorist of drama Kimberly Benston identifies what she calls the "theater of differends," which she says juxtaposes "shards of narrative and spectacle to force a constant reciprocal undertow"[51] between audience and performer. For Benston, "dislocation of audience-actor relations implicates the viewer in the mise-en-scène."[52] Playwright and theorist Antonin Artaud says something similar of the theater and the festival.[53] Atmosphere, setting, scene, theater, dislocation, and theatrical effect, with or without haze, smoke, or mirrors: these are the components of mood. The trappings of the theater provide a further alternative to the idea of mood as something simmering within the unconscious.

Data Drama

The everywhere availability of all those apps and files in the data cloud remind us of the incongruity in this haze of ubiquity: always there and enveloping. The current reality of cloud computing, or at least of Wi-Fi access, is that you tend to drift in and out of the cloud; that is, you lose your connection and have to think about whether to switch from Wi-Fi to a cellular phone connection, or perhaps the cloud drifts depending on your location and current network traffic. Haze does something like that. Clambering along the ridge of a mountain range in the Highlands of Scotland, the hill walker is as likely to move in and out of the clouds as he or she is to move in and out of contact with his or her mobile phone network provider. Moods are in these respects like haze and clouds; at the very least, they come and go, and through a series of complex relationships. Complicit in this process is all those stored records, putative recollections, blogs, and archives.

What about data ruin? Perhaps its inability to decay elegantly is what distinguishes data from everything else and removes it from the arena of mood. Bits and bytes don't tend to degrade smoothly. A few bits out of place can corrupt a whole data set. It's a brittle medium without those soft material edges that fray or get colonized gradually by mold or leached by ground water. Malware doesn't add patina. Perhaps we would rather that data fade away with time, like very old photographs, and eventually return to earth. As long as there's a storage medium and a data reader, digital matter is hard to get rid of.[54]

In some respects data already has the character of waste. Data is already "matter out of place."[55] Returning to Second Life (or what's left of it), even though its creators supposed Second Life to be as "real" as the physical world—with added features (it supports flying, mind over matter, action at a distance)—it couldn't help but present as surreal. It's strange without a doubt, as many digital presentations are strange. Think of CGI in this light. Familiarity is the unusual feature, emerging less than occasionally from the entropy and noise of data. Game designers think that haze adds "atmosphere." "Mist," "mystery," and "myth" sound a bit the same but have different etymologies. The evocations of each have not been lost on game developers. The early computer game Myst by Cyan Inc. exploited the necessity for haze to reduce rendering time and increase depth as a game feature, brand, and mise-en-scène of the interactive narrative. The box containing the CD-ROM bore the tagline "the surrealistic adventure game that will become your world."

Digital devices contribute to the haze of place, not just in the ways that they might confound and make things unclear; they render the familiar strange, bringing aspects of the everyday world to light in new ways. Not least, they contribute to the theatricality of place, in Brechtian mode "turning an object from something ordinary and immediately accessible into something peculiar, striking and unexpected."[56]

Summary

In this chapter, I discussed haze as a metaphor for mood, bringing to mind atmosphere and ambience. Moods are ambivalent, like mist. They envelop, drift, and dissipate, and in the process they reveal and conceal. I also discussed memory through the concept of oblivion, the unconscious, and journal records (as in weblogs). After all, the mood of a place pertains to memory. Some people think of moods as resident in the unconscious, as underlying frameworks informing human actions, the substructures of social practices, and that moods even sustain the hegemony of capitalism and class domination. I'm happy with the structuring metaphor—less so with the metaphor of the unconscious. What if we dispense with the unconscious? I presented alternatives. In order to dismantle the unconscious, it's necessary to deal with memory as something other than storage. Dispensing with the unconscious then relocates mood. Theatrical metaphors come to our aid. I showed that the workings of mood in a place ultimately settle on the matter of theatricality and the alienating aspects of theater. It may look as though I've drifted from haze, but not really. It all comes back to the theatricality of atmosphere, the mood of the play.

From haze, I will turn to color in the next chapter. In his cross-cultural analysis of color, historian Robert Finlay says of Japanese art that "color is assimilated to the colorless by dissolving it in similes of moisture—fog, clouds, rain, dew, ocean, streams, and frost."[57] William Gibson's 1984 novel *Neuromancer* begins with the iconic haze metaphor: "The sky above the port was the color of television, tuned to a dead channel."[58]

Coda: Fading to Gray

To illustrate further the disorientating functions of mood, place, and equipment—in July 2012 there was a significant spike in sales of Thomas Tallis's
choral music *Spem in Alium* (Hope in Any Other). The timing corresponded
to the rapid rise in popularity of the erotic novel *Fifty Shades of Grey* by E.
L. James, in which the music sets the mood for a climactic love scene.[59]
The music doesn't play while you are reading, of course, but the author
describes its effects on the characters.[60] The use of music in a fictional erotic
context reminds us of how music can set the mood—that is, provide a setting. The book's narrator says: "Abruptly, the soft silent hiss and pop of
the iPod springs into life. From inside my head, a lone angelic voice sings
unaccompanied a long sweet note, and it's joined almost immediately by
another voice, and then more voices—holy cow, a celestial choir—singing
a capella in my head, an ancient, ancient hymnal. What in heaven's name
is this? I have never heard anything like it."[61]

Several pages later the music is explained: "'What was that Music?' I
mumble almost inarticulately. 'It's called Spem in Alium, a forty-part motet
by Thomas Tallis.' It was . . . overwhelming."[62] For lovers of sacred music,
the juxtaposition is jarring—a deuterocanonical psalm sung as a beautifully
and artfully composed forty-voice motet as the setting for an erotic bond-
age scene in a work of pulp fiction. Moods derive traction from just such
incongruity.

The harmonies of *Spem in Alium* were composed for grand interiors
rather than bedrooms. In this case, the music was composed for one of
Henry VIII's palaces in Surrey, England, now in ruins. By all accounts, the
music was first performed in an octagonal-shaped tower with the choirs
positioned on balconies. The audience members were enveloped by sound
from all directions and unlike the wearer of headphones could turn their
attention to different voices by changing orientation.

Mobile and ambient personalized listening involves listening to music,
radio broadcasts, podcasts, ambient sounds, and even white noise through
headphones and earbuds while walking around, jogging, traveling on public transport, studying, reading, and in just about any situation in which
it's safe to do so, including lovemaking, as described in *Fifty Shades of Grey*.
Personalized listening is used to block out distractions, to signal to others
that you are not available for communication, and adds texture and aural

color to urban existence. For David Beer, "the music becomes a part of the urban experience so the urban experience becomes a part of the experience of listening to the music," a productive experience he terms "tuning out."[63]

Some readers left informative comments on this post:

Comment 1: I have had emotional experiences of architecture. Once, I sat in an alcove of the rotunda in a garden designed by Gertrude Jekyll. There was an essential "rightness" to the proportions that made for a profound spatial experience that has lasted long after the memory of flowers blooming. The space "sang" to me.

Comment 2: In a way, that confirms that we are more comfortable using music to express or talk about emotion than the visual arts. Perhaps gardens are something else again.

Comment 3: We walk around these days playing our own personal soundtracks to represent our moods. The soundtrack for my undergraduate years was symphonic European power metal. As I walk around Edinburgh today, it has to be that same music. I don't think I need to share this music with the world, though.

Comment 4: People share books once they are finished, but no one should ever have to endure the sound track to someone else's life. It would be as if the person next to you on the bus started reading their books out loud, which would be infuriating and, if the book in question is *Fifty Shades of Grey*, incredibly embarrassing!

Comment 5: In a way, you are highlighting a sadistic approach to music, as if some people derive pleasure from afflicting others with their own personal taste preferences. You are also implying that some people are masochistic in listening to substandard music on tinny speakers. Perhaps the solution resides in sadomasochism, in which there's mutuality in the pain and pleasure contract. I say that because *Shades of Grey* is apparently about SM.

Comment 6: For me, it's about texturing the audial field, like erecting a spatial and translucent screen to provide privacy. I select tracks without voice (unless abstract), as that distracts. Rhythm is good, and I avoid minor keys. Sometimes, I overlay white noise from the WhiteNoise app to fill in the gaps. This is all so I can work, of course, and is essential while in a coffee shop or on the train. Walking down the street is something else. In that case, it's sometimes interesting to let the digital sounds interact with the environment.

7 Intoxicated by Color

Computer displays provide unlimited access to colors of all hues, shades, and combinations. Smartphones, e-readers, tablets, laptops, desktop computers, data projectors, and various active surfaces operate with luminous light sources, backlighting, or projection in the home, office, cinema, gallery, or public space, places that are increasingly subject to variable color ambiences. At least one hotel chain claims to provide a "moodpad" in each bedroom from which guests control the color of the ambient lighting.[1] Do colors contribute to mood? If they do, then ubiquitous digital devices indeed provide rich media for the circulation of moods. At the very least, display screens, media facades, light-emitting diode (LED) walls, and projections provide color and movement and "enliven" a space, independently of content and whether or not people are attending to what's on display.[2] Digital displays provide an ambience, a background of flicker, movement, activity, and even excitement. Piccadilly Circus, Times Square, and the Ginza District of Tokyo are iconic, branded environments replicated around the world's cities. They lure crowds with light and color, especially at night. Jaded urban dwellers may be indifferent to the overt content of billboards, neon signs, and luminous display screens, but the covert ambiences of these ubiquitous media deliver some kind of effect, not least through color.

Furthermore, thanks to backlit liquid crystal display (LCD) technology, computer users are now exposed to the dynamic control of color, and in full intensity. Digital photography also contributes to the capture and processing of color. Specialized algorithms manipulate color at source, sharpening color contrasts, and there's the subtle high dynamic range (HDR) photography feature built into many digital cameras and smartphones to even out the colors in high-contrast scenes. There are also popular specialized smartphone apps for distorting and falsely fading digital photographs to give them the patina of age, as if they are faded slides or old, chemically produced prints.[3] Color is now easy to manipulate. Anyone with access to a computer and display screen can present and manage colors, and all colors equally;[4] this was not always the case.

Color in Time

A cursory glance through a catalog of artist's oil paints reveals substantial differences in price between, for example, a tube of "cadmium orange" and the same quantity of "cobalt turquoise," reminding us that different pigments are obtained at different costs, reflecting a wide variety of raw materials and processes. The article "Weaving the Rainbow: Visions of Color in World History" by Robert Finlay provides helpful insights into the history of color.[5] During the later phase of the Roman Empire, purple dye for cloth was extracted from shellfish collected from the Mediterranean at great cost and as a consequence was a color worn only by the extremely wealthy. According to Finlay, thanks to the industrial production of pigments and advances in communications technologies, the situation is different now: "An individual watching color television, strolling through a supermarket, or examining a box of crayons sees a larger number of bright, saturated hues in a few moments than did most persons in a traditional society in a lifetime."[6] Any computer user can manipulate color sliders or a palette to scan across a range of colors and combinations, as long as the output stays on the screen. The digital color designer need pay no regard to the relative cost, complexity of process, or permanence of dyes and pigments. On a computer screen, all colors are equal.

There's a sense in which our contemporary, digitally savvy, color-saturated society has lost the full cultural, symbolic, and emotional resonances of color. Not only are all colors now treated the same, but we lose a sense of the materiality of colors and their pigments, their different reflectance properties, how a glazed blue china cup is different than an unglazed one, and how either changes as you move it about in the light. There's a thickness and viscosity to predigital colors. That's a lament that goes back to the eighteenth century. Isaac Newton (1642–1727) had succeeded in reducing color phenomena to a uniform spectrum derived from the bending of light rays—what we now think of as a range of electromagnetic wavelengths.[7] One hundred years later, the author and artist Johann Wolfgang von Goethe (1749–1832) objected to the mathematical treatment of color and wrote that he wanted to "rescue the attractive subject of the doctrine of colours from the atomic restriction and isolation in which it has been banished, in order to restore it to the general dynamic flow of life and action."[8] Goethe refers to the conditions under which colors emerge and are viewed, including what happens when you press on your eyeball and see red, the yellow halo that sometimes appears around luminous objects, and the relative color properties of worms, feathers, and minerals. By most accounts, Goethe's book *Theory of Colors* is less a scientific document than an attempt to situate color as an everyday phenomenon,[9] which inevitably touches on how we experience colors and what we feel about them, a goal now shared by many artists and designers exploring the unique properties of the medium of ubiquitous digital color.

To restore color to the "flow of life," the scholar now has to probe color through the multiple lenses of art, psychology, language, physiology, and technology. Such study reveals depths and anomalies sufficient to preserve the mysteries of color, or at least its resistance to clear definitions and understanding. Such study also reveals new aspects of the everyday, rendering the familiar experience of color somehow new and enigmatic. In his book-length treatment of the subject of color, the philosopher Ludwig Wittgenstein (1889–1951) presents color as an example of a language game. That is, as a language philosopher he thought that the way people talk about color is really not much different than the behavior of color, and the way we talk about color does reveal anomalies. For example, you can have a red light shining on a surface, but not a gray light. You can speak of a bluish-red color, but not a greenish-red. When it comes to color, he said famously, "we stand there like the ox in front of the newly-painted stall door,"[10] presumably dumbstruck, clumsy, and inept. Playing about with lighting parameters in a computer-rendering application seems to confound these anomalies further. On occasion, I've used a 3-D modeling and rending package that allows you to shine a "black light" onto a surface. It operates like a virtual light source, but sucks out the illumination. It treats light like a shadow, projecting gloom rather than light. The digital manipulation of color introduces new ways of talking about light and color.

Color and Mood

How can a design theorist or scholar approach color and mood? First, there's the question of how we would know if color and mood are related. Evidence that color affects mood would have to come from studies establishing some kind of correspondence between the exposure of individuals to a color (pink, green, gray, etc.) or a particular color palette and the individual's mood states. There is some evidence that the intensity, spectral distribution, and repeated cyclical exposure to certain light conditions throughout the day affect mood, but that's more about light than color. There's a physiological theory that light affects the production of the pigment melanopsin in the retina of the eye, variations in which affect mood.[11] Experimental research does provide some indication that color affects mood, but to date a causal, physiological theory linking color (pink, green, gray, etc.) incontrovertibly to mood proves elusive.

Second, color could affect mood by virtue of the associations and recollections it conjures up in the observer, influenced in turn by variations in cultural context, and this can be different for different individuals. The pale lime green on the walls of hospitals once thought so soothing might produce the opposite effect for someone who has had traumatic experiences in pale lime green rooms. Color would here appear among a range of emotional triggers and relates to people's memories, associations, and "conditioning."[12]

The *culture* of color is important. This leads to a third approach to understanding mood and color, which is to join with Wittgenstein in recognizing that color is part of everyday culture and language. People talk about being blue, having a gray day, being green with envy, being white as a sheet, and having a jaundiced (yellow) view of the world. Whatever the empirical connections, color imbues our emotional language.[13] It seems that color runs deep in the human psyche. For Finlay, human beings respond to color "on the basis of subliminal emotion" rather than "rational consideration."[14] Finlay also notes that the connection between color and emotion is even more pronounced in languages other than English. He writes: "The Chinese word for color, *se*, carried connotations of beauty but also referred to emotion, a baseline from which it came to have overtones of anger, passion, lewdness, and luxury."[15] In everyday English, colorfulness also provides a metaphor for pleasure, health, and vitality. Spring is colorful; winter is gray.

The world of the child is supposedly bright with innocent colors, compared to the dull tones of older age and decline. Correlations and causes here get buried in the wider reaches of cultural practices, attitudes, values, and metaphors, to which any artist, designer, or poet must pay attention if they are to make use of color.

Fourth, color also provides a metaphor for mood. If color is like mood, then perhaps there are lessons for the manipulation of mood from the manipulation of color. For example, if color derives its effects from contrasts, then perhaps mood can be similarly defined as dealing in oppositions and comparisons. If many artists place yellow and its relationships at the epitome of a color hierarchy, then perhaps similarly there's a benchmark mood, such as happiness, melancholy, or anxiety (vertigo). If color is complicit in the identification of pathogens and contamination, then perhaps mood can be understood in terms of noxious byproducts. If there are difficulties in quantifying color, then perhaps there are lessons for the quantification of mood. If mood is influenced by preferences, then perhaps color is as good a medium as any in which to test the relationship between preference and mood.

I recounted the theories of James Russell and others in chapter 1, the idea that moods can be thought of as depending on core affects that have two dimensions: high to low intensity of excitation and pleasant to unpleasant.[16] Similarly, the science of color tells us that we are dealing in just a range or scale of wavelengths and overlaying of wavelengths of vibration in an electromagnetic field. Therefore, color can be studied as a range of intensities, like affect. Color provides a testing ground for such quantification. Insofar as there's some correspondence, color provides further lessons about mood and, thanks to the importance of color on display screens, the relationship with ubiquitous digital media.

Measuring Mood and Color

Goethe wrote that "particular colours excite particular states of feeling."[17] He described yellow as having "a serene, gay, softly exciting character."[18] Blue associates with gloom and melancholy,[19] red inspires "sentiments of awe,"[20] and green is the least demanding and easiest to live with.[21] These are mood terms that color theorists have been keen to ground in the universal experience of color.

Numerous empirical studies attempt to confirm the association between color and mood, a subject of interest to brand and advertising experts who study consumer behavior. According to psychologist Jamie Hyodo, cool colors in the environment "can increase consumer pleasure." He maintains that the evidence confirms this, but his study eliminates the converse hypothesis "that warm colors lead to greater excitement/arousal."[22] In a different domain, a study by medical researcher Helen Carruthers and colleagues investigated "how patients relate their illness or mood to color."[23] The team tested individuals already assessed as healthy, anxious, or depressed. The researchers analyzed the patients' responses to different colors, in terms of the colors they said they were "drawn to" or preferred, and which colors they could identify with their current mood state. The researchers examined responses across a palette of hues and shades. It seems that where people are prepared to admit that they are drawn to a color, the most commonly selected color is yellow, whatever the patient's condition. But when asked about their favorite color, patients more usually selected blue.

The researchers asked if participants could identify a color with their mood. Anxious and depressed people are more likely to feel they can equate their mood to a color, whereas most healthy people find this difficult. When healthy people did associate their mood with a color, it was generally bright yellow. For depressed and anxious subjects, it was invariably gray. The researchers speculate that healthy individuals may relate their mood to saturated (bright) colors, whereas depressed subjects choose dull or washed out (desaturated) colors.[24] It's important to note that the study didn't investigate whether yellow actually made people happy. The most we can say is that people associate yellow with happiness, not that it makes them happy to see yellow.

Some studies have examined the impact of light and color on psychological mood in indoor work environments.[25] In a study that associates color with mood, Valdez and Mehrabian conclude that "pleasure was simply a joint positive function of color brightness and saturation, being influenced more by brightness than by saturation," and "emotional reactions to color hue tended to be weak."[26]

Such studies indicate an indirect relationship between preference and mood states. There's evidence that most people prefer brightness as opposed to darkness. The acquisition of a preference may make people feel more positive, whatever the domain of preference. It's a bit like preferring dogs to cats. If you prefer dogs, then you'll be happier around dogs than when you are in the company of cats. Irrespective of the causes or triggers of our preferences in any particular situation, we are in a more positive mood when we get what we like than if we get what we don't like. Having things we like tends us toward a positive mood state. Having them withdrawn pushes us toward the negative. If for whatever reason we like blue, then we are likely to be in a more positive mood if told to wait in a blue room than if placed in a yellow room. It's difficult to conclude more than this from the empirical evidence on the relationship between mood and color. The most we can say with confidence is this: For most people, when they have what there's evidence they or most people prefer, then they are likely to display evidence of being in a positive mood. Many preferences are biological. Many are shared culturally. Much of the evidence of either is expressed in language—that is, self-reported or elicited indirectly through questionnaires or scenarios.

Color Harmonies

Perhaps colors behave like sounds and thereby operate on the emotions like musical harmonies. According to current color science, the human visual system responds to light as electromagnetic radiation in the approximate wavelength range of 400–800 nanometers (nm; million millionths of a meter). The approximation of the visible light spectrum to a doubling of amplitude from the short to the long wave end of the spectrum does resemble the doubling of sound amplitudes to create the musical octave.[27] Newton thought that light rays vibrate and stimulate the eye to see different colors, but along the length of the ray (like vibrations on the strings of an instrument), rather than as propagating electromagnetic waves.[28] He developed the musical analogy further by wrapping the spectral colors around a circle and explaining the color bands as pitches on the seven-note musical scale. Insofar as musical harmonies affect the emotions, then perhaps color harmonies do the same. However, colors are not experienced simultaneously like chords, and the mixing of colors is not like the mixing of sounds. By most accounts, the music analogy is limited.[29] The strength of any resonances between color and mood resides substantially in the areas of culture and language that will be explored later in this chapter.

Color Mapping

It's worth examining the quantification of color intensity further, for the insights it reveals about the experience of color and its links with the language of mood. Access to such detail is in its own right a product of the digital age. Color is a technical subject about which there is a great deal of information online, from different perspectives (optics, physics, biology, psychology, neuroscience), including among academic articles. The details are now accessible to practical demonstration through digital media, with websites dedicated to the numerical manipulation of color and to experimentation with color.

As discovered by the early vision scientist Thomas Young (1773–1829), the eye contains photoreceptors maximally sensitive to 420, 534, and 564 nm wavelengths, often labeled the short, medium, and long wavelengths, or blue, green, and (approximately) red.[30] The combining of the three visual responses makes up the visible spectrum. Hence, the pixels on a contemporary LCD computer monitor are made up of dots or bands of each of these three colors. That is, pixel screens are engineered to stimulate the human visual system according to the eye's key sensitivities. As Newton demonstrated,[31] white light is actually made up of all wavelengths across the visible light spectrum. White light stimulates all three receptors to about the same degree, and that's what registers to the human visual system as white. Creating colors by mixing light waves in the bands of red, green, and blue (RGB), as on a computer screen, actually "cheats" the eye by presenting the eye's photoreceptors with wavelengths targeted at their particular sensitivities. The white we see on a computer screen is made of RGB. It may look the same as a sheet of white paper in direct sunlight or a cloud or snow, but the spectral distribution will be quite different.

Color and Evolution

The evolution of color vision makes a fascinating story and has explanatory value for those designing with color on display screens. According to theories of evolutionary physiology, it seems that our early ancestors (night-dwelling mammals) had photoreceptors sensitive to just two wavelengths, roughly equal to the blue and the green. This sufficed for night vision. Finlay explains that with the decline of the large predators (dinosaurs), nocturnal mammals emerged into daylight and developed the ability to see in three colors. They had trichromatic vision. This allowed such animals greater discrimination in the long wavelength (green-red) end of the spectrum. This finer discrimination provided a survival advantage. Finlay summarizes several authoritative sources on the subject of evolutionary biology and explains how this adaptation enabled animals to expand their diet from insects to seeds, nuts, fruit, and other high-energy portions of plants: "Against a background of green tropical foliage, fruits stand out as yellow, orange, and red while leaves with the most protein generally have a red or yellowish-red tint. A mammal with dichromatic vision would be effectively blinded to these resources, for anything yellow, orange, or red would appear to its eyes as dark green, signaling that it is not palatable."[32]

Insects have adapted to detect flowers, which have in turn coadapted to attract insects. It seems that human color sensitivity is closest to that of birds and insects: "Like blue jays and bees rather than dogs and cats, human beings see a wide variety of colors."[33] Such developments in vision accompanied perception of depth, frontal vision, hand coordination, and competence in scanning for predators.[34] Therefore, "color first arose to help determine who ate dinner and who ended up on the plate."[35]

There's something special about this adaptation to what we call *yellow* and its ability to grab our attention. What humans register as yellow has a wavelength of around 580 nm, halfway between green (530 nm) and red (630 nm), but there are no photoreceptors for 580 nm—that is, yellow. Red and green wavelengths combined give the impression not of a greenish-red, but a different color sensation, that of yellow. Yellow has all the appearance of a distinct color but is a product of the sensation of green and red in combination. Whereas other parts of the color spectrum offer smooth transitions, yellow stands out as a separator between green and red. We can perceive greenish-yellows, and yellowy-reds, but not greenish-reds. As a perceptual byproduct, yellow intervenes. Yellow quickly grades to orange and brown if you add in blue light or diminish the strength of either the green or the red. Yellow's brightness is reduced by the presence of blue wavelengths. The acquisition of the ability to identify a color we name as *yellow* is indeed a cunning adaptation. Certain nutritious fruits are alluring to birds and insects. In addition to rendering such edible fruits as bright, conspicuous, and alluring to humans, the yellow component enables us to recognize and discriminate among all those rich brown tones, including earth, bark, fur, meat, and those that signal the potential for high nutritional content.

These intricate color adaptations indicate the close coupling between organism and environment. From a biological point of view, the human sensitivity to light and color depends on a finely tuned combination of sensory processes that biology can support efficiently, are calibrated to the particular properties of light on the planet, and enable humans to apprehend features in the environment important for survival, such as identifying foods, dangers, and a mate. Color is ubiquitous, as important to our spatial understanding as a "fifth dimension," according to Finlay.[36] By this reading, our various sensitivities and preferences for colors have a biological basis. There's also evidence that we rely on the contrasts set up by color differences to move about our environment.

Color Contrasts

The theme of color illustrates and amplifies the human attraction to contrasts, which in turn tells us something about mood. The painter Wassily Kandinsky (1866–1944) was an acknowledged practitioner of the use of color as a dynamic and effective medium. He taught at the Bauhaus and published the texts *Concerning the Spiritual in Art* and *Point and Line to Plane*. Kandinsky endorsed the specialness of yellow (which the study by Carruthers and colleagues seems to confirm), in that yellow moves closer to the viewer and is warmer than the other colors, especially blue.[37] For Kandinsky, the opposition between yellow and blue was the "first great contrast," even ahead of that between black and white. That certain colors might draw in the viewer or move closer to the viewer speaks of color's emotional resonances. It also speaks of the relationships between colors.

The transition from RGB color intensities to an accessible mood language is abetted by a mathematical transformation. Anyone using a computer with a display screen can generate a color by manipulating the intensity of red, green, and blue in a patch of pixels, usually by manipulating slider bars in a paint program. Of course, to alter pixel color values or to project colored lights onto a surface is different than mixing paints or pigments. Mixing paints to get different colors is more like overlaying sheets of colored cellophane; it's a subtractive process. As any amateur painter knows, too much mixing tends toward the color of gray sludge. On the other hand, in the RGB system, full white consists of all three colors in full intensity. Grey is simply all three colors combined, but in reduced intensity. For black, all three colors are switched off.

Rather than creating colors by manipulating RGB, it's much easier to manipulate color by starting with a hue (i.e., choose from the continuous color spectrum: red, orange, yellow, green, blue, or violet), then fade it out with varying degrees of gray. For example, a blue that's half gray is a pastel kind of blue. Then, think about how intense is the gray you are combining it with: a very light gray (to produce a powder blue) or a really dark gray (yielding navy blue). With a bit of training, anyone can become good at imagining, manipulating, and controlling colors in this way, by adjusting hue, saturation, and value (HSV).

According to Newton, the hues can be arranged conveniently around a circle. Therefore, any hue is usually specified as an angle between 0 and 360 degrees, with 0 positioned at red. The saturation and value parameters might be indicated as a percentage. In fact, this circular way of specifying colors was developed into a scientific system by the artist and educator Albert Munsell (1858–1918).[38] Munsell's color system did not generate colors via colored light, but deployed meticulously painted and specified swatches of colored pigments, inspected and ordered by human subjects according to the three parameters of hue, saturation, and value (or chroma). This approach grounds the HSV color system in human perception rather than mathematical calculation, though he intended this to be a "sound mathematical basis for the description, comparison and classification of colors."[39]

Digital paint programs usually provide an HSV color-picker option. The HSV method provides access to a more nuanced color-mood language than simply saying that yellow is cheerful, green restful, and so on. It also provides greater access to a language of contrasts and hence mood, as I will show.

Returning to the translation from RGB to HSV, you'll note that the RGB color space can be represented as a cube positioned on a three-dimensional coordinate system with axes labeled red, green, and blue (RGB), selected to correspond to the eye's three sensitivities.[40] Full-intensity light sources each colored red, green, or blue appear white. Turn the lights off, and you get black. Green and blue only (red light off) gives us a greenish-blue color known as cyan. Blue and red without green produce a bluish-red color often called magenta (or purple, as identified by Newton). Red and green gives yellow. The color cube has eight corners, with diametrically opposed corners of white and black, red and cyan, green and magenta, and blue and yellow, with a blending of other colors between these.

This color cube already introduces two anomalous quantities, well-known among color theorists. Magenta is not part of the color spectrum. You won't see magenta in the colors of the rainbow. It does not have a unique wavelength, and yet we recognize it as a color. Newton placed this color intuitively into his color circle by mixing colors from the two ends of the color spectrum, combining the short wavelengths at the dark blue end with red from the long wave end to complete the circle. We do perceive the color magenta, and it occurs in nature. Its presence works mathematically from the mixing of red and blue and the corresponding stimulation of the red and blue photoreceptors in the eye. Therefore, human vision does in fact discriminate every combination from its three key sensitivities (red, blue, and green), as indicated on the color cube. Magenta is simply a blue combined with red, a bluish red, or a reddish blue. Yellow provides a further anomaly. As I've already shown, green and red lights produce yellow. Unlike magenta, though, yellow does exist on the visible color spectrum as a unique wavelength (or band of wavelengths).

A diagonal line through the cube from the white corner to the black corner of the color cube is the gray line, varying from light gray near the white corner to darker gray toward the black corner. Different shades of gray on that line are achieved by varying the intensities of each of the light sources by the same amount.

The cube is of course full of color, grading gradually from gray on the diagonal white-to-black line to the fully saturated hues of red, yellow, green, cyan, blue, and magenta at the other six corners of the cube. However, the color space is much easier to deal with if it's transformed mathematically to the orbital geometry of HSV, as deployed by Newton, Munsell, and others— that is, laying out the six colored vertices onto a plane, as a hexagon, or a circle and imagining the gray line coming out of the page to create a cone, cylinder, or sphere. There are different geometries that can be applied, but they all amount to something similar.[41] A cross-section through the cone, cylinder, or sphere shows the color wheel circumscribed by the hues: red, yellow, green, cyan, blue, and magenta, with orange between red and yellow, and all hues grading to gray at the center of the circle.

With this transformation from a cube to an orbital arrangement, any color can be redefined in terms of the three parameters hue, saturation, and value. The value parameter is sometimes called "lightness" or "brightness" (with a slightly different mapping that's not important here). One of the payoffs of this conversion is that it helps us compare colors in ways that seem intuitive; it provides insights into the qualities of color combinations and brings us closer to the language of color moods.

Contrasts and Moods

It was the painter and color theorist Johannes Itten (1888–1967) who brought the idea of color contrasts to the fore using the HSV system. He taught for a period at the Bauhaus with Kandinsky. Itten was an advocate and practitioner of meditation, and his apparent "mysticism" eventually distanced him from the Bauhaus's bias toward industrial mass production. Itten associated color with mood: "Colors are forces, radiant energies that affect us positively or negatively, whether we are aware of it or not. The artist in stained glass used color to create a supramundane, mystical atmosphere which would transport the meditations of the worshipper to a spiritual plane."[42]

In his book *The Art of Color: The Subjective Experience and Objective Rationale of Color*, Itten outlines and illustrates seven principles of color contrasts.[43] Any artist, designer, or colorist might pay attention to these contrasts, and they can now be explored very easily in paint programs on a computer. They have formed the basis of color exercises for students, and they play a role in diagnosing when color combinations don't seem quite right. The color principles also open the way for thinking about colors in combination rather than just in isolation, and they extend the language of color and mood. For my demonstration here, and without the benefit of his richly colored plates, it's only necessary to attend to the language Itten deploys to articulate these contrasts.

Itten's first contrast was a contrast in hue. Colors on opposite sides of the color wheel have maximum contrast, so red contrasted with cyan, yellow with blue, green with magenta; however, Itten was also referring to any combination of fully saturated colors from widely spaced points around the circumference of the color wheel. A composition made up of such contrasts will be bright and dynamic. Itten remarked that "this contrast involves the interplay of primeval luminous forces," invoking "aboriginal cosmic splendour."[44]

Second is the light–dark contrast. Imagine a desaturated (grayed out) red against a pink that has the same amount of gray, but the gray is lighter. Keeping hue and saturation constant but varying lightness produces something like a black and white (i.e., grayscale) movie, but in which everything has a red tinge. For Itten, "a uniformly gray, lifeless surface can be awakened to mysterious activity by extremely minute modulations of shading."[45]

Munsell makes the obvious distinction between warm and cool colors, the longer and the shorter wavelength colors. Most people think of the yellow-orange side of the color wheel as warm and the cyan side as cool, so Itten's third contrast was of cold against warm colors. He takes the effect literally, citing an experiment involving a horse stable divided into two sections painted in different colors: one blue and the other yellow-orange. Horses in the blue section calmed down after their race, but horses in the yellow-orange section remained restless for some time. As if to soften the claim that colors incontrovertibly affect mood, he adds that there were more flies in the yellow-orange section.[46]

Itten's fourth contrasting principle was of complementary contrast. Goethe highlights the phenomenon of the afterimage. If we focus on a patch of red for a few seconds and then look away from the screen, we tend to see an afterimage in the color on the opposite side of the color wheel, especially if the colors are fully saturated. This observation further grounds the HSV color system in the physiology of the human visual system. The combination of such colors produces interesting effects and contributes to the dynamism of certain color combinations. For Itten, two such opposing colors "incite each other to maximum vividness when adjacent; and they annihilate each other, to gray-black, when mixed—like fire and water."[47]

The fifth principle is simultaneous contrast. The juxtaposition of a fully saturated color to a second color that is close, but not equivalent, to its complement sets up a certain vibration. Under the right conditions, a small patch of color will appear to float above a background made up of its near-simultaneously contrasting color. The stability of the two colors is disturbed, and "they are set in changeable oscillation." The colors "move in an individual field of action of an unreal kind, as if in a new dimension."[48]

His sixth principle is the contrast of saturation. If you want to bring out the brightness of a fully saturated red, then place it near the same color grayed out—that is, its less saturated version. Itten describes the various methods of diluting saturated colors: some pleasant, others less so. For example, diluting yellow with black "deprives yellow of its brilliant character, turning it into something sickly or insidiously poisonous."[49]

Itten's seventh contrast is of extension. Just to show that the appreciation of colors really is contextual, Itten indicates that the extent or size of a color patch in relation to those around it makes a difference in how we see colors. He provides many examples of how a color can look lighter or darker depending on its neighbors. A common rule of thumb in fashion and interior decorating is to restrict fully saturated colors to highlights (i.e., small areas). Imagine the unlikely case of a building facade painted in a fully saturated red. A small door in the facade painted with a less saturated red (pink) would look washed out and even grubby. Of course, the norm would be to reverse the color scheme, a lightly pink facade with a red door as a highlight.

Implicit in Itten's color theory is the idea that the eye of the observer is drawn not only to bright colors, but to areas of contrast. By judicious use of color, a designer can manage the attention of the viewer by varying the extension of a color and also adjusting contrasts according to his seven principles I've just described. A designer may want the eye of the observer to be drawn to areas that are somehow important. Our attention is drawn to areas of contrast, whether created by color contrasts or by shape details and edges.

The way Itten describes such color combinations references mood. A picture made up of fully saturated colors with no variation in lightness or value will look *flat*, possibly too simple and overstimulating, like a child's painting in primary colors. If the colors are less saturated (i.e., grayed out) and with little contrast in saturation or lightness, then we might refer to the picture as *dull*. A picture with large areas of full saturation might appear *vibrant* or *discordant*. A cool palette with highlights might strike the viewer as *mellow*. Here, the language of color draws on the language of affect, emotion, and mood—not just for single colors, but for palettes of colors.

As an illustration of how colors and color combinations affect people, Itten recounts a dinner party in which people were about to embark on their meal. Without warning, the host flooded the room with red light. The meat looked good, but the spinach turned black. Then he changed the light to blue. The meat then looked putrid and the potatoes moldy. A yellow light turned the wine to castor oil, and the guests looked like cadavers. Some had to leave the room. Itten remarks: "Who can doubt that colors exert profound influences upon us, whether we are aware of them of not?"[50]

Color Mood Mapping

The geometrical organization of information in the color cube, HSV cone, cylinder, or sphere brings to mind the importance of gridded representations and axial Cartesian geometries. In chapter 5, when discussing vertigo, I referred to the mythic spatial schema that begins with the gnomon or *axis mundi*, the circle drawn on the ground, and the square with its four cardinal directions, and how this schema is grounded in basic human bodily experience. As all who have navigated round a three-dimensional model of a building on a computer know, there are four major viewing positions on the horizontal plane. You can look at a thing from the front, back, right side, or left side. If you are using GPS in geographical space, then your movement is regulated according to the four cardinal directions of north, south, east, and west. For the mythic imagination, and as expressed in much traditional architecture, these orientations relate to the movement of the sun across the sky and in turn invoke certain resonances. East is the direction of new beginnings, and west symbolizes its conclusion. In the northern hemisphere, the north is the dark aspect, and southern orientations are bright. If you include the movements of the moon, the constellations, and the variations of the seasons, then you discover a series of complex relationships involving ideas about the microcosm and the macrocosm, which in chapter 5 I termed the *vertiginous economy*. Geometry connects together meaning and symbol across different domains, not least those that draw on concepts of color, harmony, personality, and mood.

In an illuminating article published in 1990, psychologists Robert Stelmack and Anastasios Stalikas remind their readers of the many ways that such fourfold geometrical tabulations are expressed in different cultural contexts, both modern and ancient—for example, the four seasons, four ages of man (childhood, youth, prime, and old age), and the four "natural elements" (earth, air, fire, and water).[51] Before the advent of modern science and Enlightenment concepts of reason and empirical evidence, scholars would deploy such fourfold schemas to construct their arguments and explanations and to establish relationships across different phenomena. Church architecture would be organized such that the congregation faces east, oriented optimistically and hopefully to the rising sun. Spring pertains to new beginnings, it relates to childhood, and by a less direct logic it also relates to air—or fresh air, at least. Similar correspondences apply to the other orientations. There's a resonance with the natural elements, but also more than a hint of mood in these orientations. Such mappings between domains would not necessarily be obvious, direct, or automatic. Neither would the correspondences be particularly systematic, agreed, or canonical. There's something about the number four, though.

Poets, philosophers, scientists, and architects ancient and modern latch onto fourfold schemas. There's the four evangelists, the four horses of the apocalypse, four cherubim in Ezekiel, each with four faces, and by extension multiples of these numbers. Following the romantic poets, Martin Heidegger references the "fourfold" of earth, sky, mortals, and divinities. The psychologist Carl Jung's personality model was based on the four psychological functions of sensation, intuition, feeling, and thinking. It's convenient that there are four psychological functions, rather than three, five, or six, as this enables psychometric tables to be drawn up, such as the Myers–Briggs personality mapping system that operates via a four-by-four classification.[52]

Whatever the empirical validity of ancient and modern fourfold schemas, they persist. As I remarked in my explorations of early online culture in the 1990s, *Technoromanticism*, the Internet seems to have unleashed a torrent of web sites dedicated to horoscope readings, explanations of pagan signs and rituals, and pop psychology and nonconformist religious sites, as if giving vent to the pent-up undercurrents of late modernity. A kind of new age medievalism flourishes online, reinventing ancient traditions of number and symbol in modern guise. In any case the fourfold persists in mainstream culture and in language. Color and emotion provide further evidence of this.

Personality Maps

As outlined by Stelmack and Stalikas, four mainstream personality types endure in language, bearing the names *phlegmatic, melancholic, choleric,* and *sanguine.* The phlegmatic person tends to be relaxed and passive. The melancholic is sad, and the choleric is impulsive and restless. The sanguine is cheerful and optimistic. These are the four classical temperaments, explored and explained by the Greco-Roman medical philosopher Claudius Galenus (129–c. 200), known as Galen, and picked up by philosophers such as Immanuel Kant.[53] For Galen, these types pertain to a range of personality traits, such as boldness, timidity, negligence, impertinence, compassion, and envy. Carl Jung credited the origins of his particular characterization of psychological functions to Galen.[54] Here, moods blur into concepts of personality and temperament. Whereas the idea of mood allows for some kind of influence from the environment you are in, temperament implies a predisposition, an emotional condition you are born with.

What's interesting for our study here is that these temperaments have color correlates, and they each pertain to a bodily fluid, or humor. A phlegmatic temperament associates with phlegm (mucus), which ought to be clear. Melancholy is literally "black bile." We moderns know of bile as a product of the gall bladder for the digestion of fats. Black bile was simply any darkening substance detected in the blood or skin. The choleric associates simply with bile, which is ordinarily yellow. The sanguine pertains to blood and, by association, the color red. Stelmack and Stalikas explain how the ancients thought of these substances as excesses left over after the body had taken what it needed from food to form bone and muscle.[55] Blood was thought to be essential, but had a similar function to the other humors in the diagnosis of disease, mainly indicated by changes in color, which in turn relates to an imbalance between the humors. In fact, in keeping with a fourfold axial system, good health was about balance. Stelmack and Stalikas quote Galen: "The best temperate man is he who in the body seems to be in the mean of all extremities, that is skinniness and fatness, heat and coldness . . . and regarding the body this is the best temperate man. Similarly in his soul he is in the middle of boldness and timidity, of negligence and impertinence, of compassion and envy. He is cheerful, affectionate, charitable and prudent."[56]

They further explain the ancient correspondences between the fourfold temperaments and the so-called four elements. Earth relates to black bile (melancholy), air to the blood (sanguine), fire to yellow bile (choleric), and water to phlegm (phlegmatic).[57] There's a cultural correspondence here among color, personality, and mood.

More recent scholars, such as psychologist Hans Eysenck, attempt to provide empirical evidence in support of Galen's categories,[58] though not necessarily the logic of the causal relationships implied or of putative color correspondences.

Sensory Contamination

There are further correspondences between color and the fourfold, which in turn brings us closer to the disruptive effects of ubiquitous digital

media. Philosophers and artists may speak of the harmony among different domains (geometry, architecture, music, color, medicine, temperament,
and mood) and harmony across the senses (sight, sound, touch, taste, and
smell), but there is also a case of confusion across these domains, and even
contamination. I say "contamination" because this itself implies an imbalance. As is well known, there are people who hear colors and see sounds,
which brain scientist Ramachandran describes in terms of cross wiring and
faulty insulation between neurons.[59] This is the phenomenon of *synesthesia*, described as a pathology by neurologists, though it is an idea inspiring
to many artists and in any case speaks of the possibilities available through
metaphor in each of us.

Neurologist Richard Cytowic explains synesthesia as "joined sensation,"
a condition that he relates to anesthesia, which means "no sensation." He
denotes synesthesia as "the rare capacity to hear colors, taste shapes, or
experience other equally startling sensory blendings whose quality seems
difficult for most of us to imagine." He continues: "A synesthete might
describe the color, shape, and flavor of someone's voice, or music whose
sound looks like 'shards of glass,' a scintillation of jagged, colored triangles
moving in the visual field. Or, seeing the color red, a synesthete might
detect the 'scent' of red as well. The experience is frequently projected outside the individual, rather than being an image in the mind's eye."[60]

This alternation or contamination of the senses is a common literary
trope, often described simply as the use of "sensual imagery." Were I to step
indoors after a night stroll and report, "It's dark outside so I can't see the
flowers on the ground," then anyone listening would take it as a statement
of fact, a mundane item of prose. However, from a poet we might hear, "I
cannot see what flowers are at my feet, / Nor what soft incense hangs upon
the boughs."[61] That verse, from John Keats, combines sight, touch, weight,
and smell in one sensory description. Poet as synesthete touches several
senses at once.

Kandinsky was interested in the phenomenon of synesthesia, and he
describes his experience of color with a fairly tortured reference to both the
fourfold geometry of the square and the sensation of heat and of sound. He
refers to the square as the "basic plane" (BP) to which the painter applies
the first horizontal or vertical strokes: "When the one or the other pair
[horizontal or vertical] predominates, either in the width or height of the
BP, this preponderance determines in any particular case the predominance

of the cold or the warm in the objective sound. Thus, from the start, the individual elements are brought into a colder or warmer atmosphere, and later on this condition cannot be completely eliminated due to the greater number of opposing elements—a fact which should never be forgotten." He concludes this difficult paragraph by referring to extremes that "can lead to painful, and, indeed, unbearable sensations."[62] Whatever he means by this and other theories in *Point and Line to Plane*, there's a conflation of the senses: sight, hearing, touch, and the perception of visual imagery, sounds, heat, and pain. All senses are mixed in; each contaminates the other.

Digital media are complicit in the current enthusiasm for synesthetic experience. After all, digital media can give expression to interesting and complex mappings among the senses. Sound signals can be converted to color and movement, video signals mapped to music, and touch transposed to shapes, sounds, and colors. With the eventual introduction of variably heated and textured digital surfaces, Kandinsky's idea of the BP becomes literalized in fully active, touch-sensitive tablet computers and touch screens.

Chemical Reactions

The combining of substances and contamination between elements leads invariably to chemistry, another means of explaining mood. Color relates to alchemy, toxicity, and hazards. Here, I want to rescue color from its inevitable connection with harmony, beauty, joy, and the world of the child bright with innocent colors. There's a malignant and menacing aspect to colors, even bright ones, and this observation helps explain more about mood and the unsettling and alienating aspects of ubiquitous digital media.

Attraction

In his *Theory of Colors*, Goethe makes no reference to the four natural elements as a fourfold, but refers to the variegated colorings of crystals and minerals from the earth, the colorless nature of air, the yellowness of fire, and the various means by which water becomes colored. In keeping with the science of his time, he's more interested in the polarity suggested by electricity, the "striking and powerful" phenomenon of "plus and minus, for north and south . . . in conformity with nature."[63] He explores color polarities, designated as plus and minus: yellow contrasts with blue, action with negation, light with shadow, brightness with darkness, force with weakness, warmth with coldness, proximity with difference, repulsion with attraction, acidic with alkaline.[64] He associates yellow with acids and blue with alkalines.[65]

This line of inquiry brings us to chemistry and emotion. Goethe also wrote an enigmatic novel titled *Elective Affinities*, which involves the relationship between a man and a woman in a kind of love quadrangle. The two characters fall in love and thus feel compelled to leave their current partners. They rationalize their decision in terms of an abstract chemical equation: "With the alkalies and acids, for instance, the affinities are strikingly marked. They are of opposite natures; very likely their being of opposite natures is the secret of their effect on one another—they seek one another eagerly out, lay hold of each other, modify each other's character, and form in connection an entirely new substance."[66]

This use of chemistry is an allegory, though commentators remark that Goethe was referring to the chemical basis of human attraction and human relationships. To this day, people make reference to chemical attraction between people embarking on a love relationship. Chemical reactions carry a certain inevitability and deny rational choice. Chemistry is also a substitute for agency and responsibility. People don't always choose rationally to be passionately attracted to each other, and an appeal to chemistry helps absolve them of responsibility for the consequences.

Color Contamination

Chemistry involves the production of substances with new properties beyond those suggested by the simple addition of the properties of the combined elements, and these new products can be other than those predicted or desired. Color can have this effect. Itten described the transformation of food into something putrid under the wrong light, and the transformation of yellow into poison by the addition of black. Most chemicals in a laboratory are hazardous, and color provides some indication of this.[67] Color is undoubtedly complicit in pleasurable experiences, but it also provides warnings. As was known to the ancients, many synthetic coloring agents turn out to be toxic, as is their means of manufacture and fixing. Think of the medieval and notoriously noxious open pits for dyeing leather in towns such as Fez in Morocco.

There's a language that's developed around color, further suggesting pathology. Finlay refers to the positive and negative experiences of color, sometimes referred to as chromophilia and chromophobia, the love and the fear of color.[68] Much as we enjoy color, in many respects the formal aesthetic tradition (starting with Plato) deprivileges it. The Greeks used color for decorating parts of their buildings, but disparaged the decadent Babylonians for their overuse of color. Renaissance architects adopted the form of classical architecture, but not its colorations. In any case, Plato regarded color as an incidental property of a thing, and he consigned painting to the lower strata of intellectual accomplishment, a bit like his denigration of the emotions. Finlay explains how in ancient times not only were colored materials costly, but the process by which colors were extracted and fixed was sometimes repulsive. Such processes "ordinarily required using ingredients such as stale human or animal urine, dung, saltpeter, rancid olive oil, sour red wine, ox and sheep blood, vinegar, and brine of pickled fish."[69]

On the subject of yellow, there's also an indirect link between yellow and excrement via Freud's ideas about gold and money. He argues that the term "filthy lucre," where "lucre" means gold, derives from an infantile obsession with feces, for which money becomes a substitute later in life, particularly among the rich and miserly.[70]

Color readily associates with the properties of toxic chemicals, poisons, and drugs. As I discussed in chapter 3, in his book *Phaedrus* Plato recounts a story in which the art of writing is equated to the use of a drug. Having the facility to write things down intoxicates the writer and manufactures a sense of intellectual overconfidence and well-being. In his analysis of Plato on this point, Jacques Derrida explains that the word Plato uses for "drug" (*pharmakon*) has many associations.[71] It's the kind of colored makeup applied to corpses before burial. Drugs are also both a means of curing illness and of killing the patient. Cure and killing, panacea and poison, treatment and toxin, all are not so far from vibrant and noxious chromatism—properties also associated with drugs, chemicals, poisons, and colors (and writing, of course, but that's another story).

Galen identified the need to keep the body's humors in balance, ideas that spill into color theory. In explaining complementary colors, Itten observes: "If we gaze for some time at a green square and then close our eyes, we see, as an after image, a red square. . . . The eye posits the complementary color; it seeks to restore equilibrium of itself."[72] The color theory derives from the additive properties of light, and yet the descriptive language of color is of fluids or pigments. The language of chemistry and the mixing of fluids spill over into the language of color. Chemists talk about saturated solutions and dilution. For Itten, "a pure color may be diluted with white," "yellow is cooled by white,"[73] and "when a mixture contains all three primaries, the resulting hue assumes a dim, diluted character."[74]

Itten explains how a small gray square in the middle of a larger area of color of the same brightness will be "tinged, for the eye, with the complementary to the background hue."[75] In other words, a gray square on a yellow background will look bluish. This is a subtle effect, and sets up a vibration or discord, and must be compensated for by tinting the gray slightly to the background color. Itten explains how the customers of a fabric manufacturer complained that a black thread on a particular red background looked green, which was unacceptable to them. Itten says the solution was to dye the thread brown instead of black. Then it would have the appearance of black in that context. In certain combinations, color harmony becomes unbalanced, and colors need correcting.[76] Colors appear in each other's place. They contaminate one another. Color combinations pertain to imbalance, oscillation, vibration, and disequilibrium. Although they have different etymologies, words such as tint, tinge, and taint appear close together in the color lexicon.

Certain color combinations signal alarm, and various organisms use them to deter predators, seeming to deploy what Itten identifies as simultaneous contrast, created when two colors are juxtaposed that are not exactly the complement of each other. Itten describes several such color combinations, one of which involves red-violet and red-orange on a green background. The effect of the simultaneous contrast is a clash, "an irritated simultaneous rubescence."[77] He could be describing an efflorescent rash, or a noxious chemical in the laboratory. Certain colors may not be particularly arresting in isolation, but when combined the simultaneous contrast effects cause oscillations—and even nausea in certain situations, a chemical reaction in effect.

Color vibrancy, so appealing to children and childlike moments in adulthood, derives much of its impact from simultaneous contrasts, jarringly rubescent efflorescences, and conspicuously colored toxifications. Insofar as color pertains to mood, it can do so as a chemical enhancement, no doubt physiologically (as partygoers and addicts imbibe chemicals), but also figuratively. Recall the graphic aura of the 1960s and 1970s, when color was "rediscovered." Think of rainbows, flower power, and early experimentation with recreational drugs. It's now faded, but I recall at the time the record covers were vivid.

Summary

In this chapter, I looked at the phenomenon of color, which is an important component of digital display technologies. People easily relate the language of color to that of mood. Although there really is as yet no firm evidence that color affects mood, there are strong cultural associations. Color provides a powerful metaphor for mood. I looked at the numerical and geometrical understandings of the color spectrum and how human physiology relates to it. The color yellow provides a particularly interesting and dynamic part of the spectrum, helping humans to feed and thrive as a species. Color illustrates and amplifies the human attraction to contrasts, which has a correlate in the idea of mood contrasts. I then related the geometry of the color wheel to various theories about personality, including ancient ideas around the four basic human temperaments, each of which draws on color and fluids. Color enters the chemistry lab, from which we learn about contamination. Synesthesia is a kind of contamination across the senses. Color also warns of toxicity. It's not all harmless joy around the color circle. From an evolutionary point of view, yellow occupies a special position on the mood spectrum the identification of which is an advanced human adaptation. In its brightest form, it signals pleasure and alertness. Its opposites signal melancholy, the subject of the next chapter.

Coda: Fading to White

Now, I can see clouds, little fluffy clouds, distinctly, well-formed and illuminated—or at least I can reproduce skies in digital photography, thanks to the HDR photography feature built into many digital cameras and smartphones.

As anyone knows who has taken a photograph while inside a room during daylight hours, the scenery through the window appears washed out, a white glare. If you set the exposure so that the view outside is clear and visible, then the room appears in darkness. Any camera with HDR capability takes two or more photographs in rapid succession and with different exposure settings. It then combines the images to even out the exposure, in effect reducing extremes of contrast, or at least revealing detail in the extremely light and dark areas. You see the inside of the room and the outside scene without glare or gloom.

The human ocular apparatus is adept at coping dynamically with a wide variation in luminance values in the environment, such as adjustments to the iris and squinting as the eye darts around the scene. When scenes are translated to static images on paper or screen, parts of that range are cut out, producing overexposed areas of white or under-exposed shadow zones—glare and gloom—hence the need for HDR. More sophisticated programs code high dynamic range into the image for later retrieval, for postprocessing, or to reproduce the effect of scanning round a room and reproducing something of the dynamism of the glare effect.

Another consequence of HDR is that external photographs of landscapes on overcast days preserve the brightness of the ground surfaces and the distinctiveness of the sky, showing detail in the formation of clouds. The cost is a "flattening" of the image, the removal of highlights and contrast, not to mention artifacts from the combining of two images, especially when the camera or the subject is in motion.

HDR provides yet another popular medium for testing the application of aesthetic theories. Let's call the object of study the "artless image," unselfconsciously produced, accidental, and everyday. Consider also the target of the image, such as the sky, not as beautiful, picturesque, or pretty, but under the sway of the sublime. HDR is among a species of attempts to capture and codify the sublime characteristics of color, light, shadow, and sky in pictorial form: reproducing the ambitions of romantic painters to represent the unrepresentable, with ever-greater sophistication in the choice of color and composition.

However, the sublime can also be invoked by its opposite: a painting of a white square against a black background by Kazimir Malevich, a child's drawing, the grainy special effects of early movies, and the sometimes carelessly rapid, incidental multiples of amateur digital photography.

Consider another popular medium, that of ambient music. My intuitions about the appeal of the hit remix by Orb in the 1990s, *Little Fluffy Clouds*, lie precisely in the naive, childlike pronouncement on the sublime spoken by singer Rickie Lee Jones during a ripped interview segment: "The sunsets were purple and red and yellow and on fire, and the clouds would catch the colours everywhere." The words are backed by Steve Reich's jaunty Electric Counterpoint III. It seems that words spoken without "artistry" or affectation veer toward the childlike and the pretty, Itten's contrasts of hue, several steps away from the more grown-up "feeling of the sublime." Sometimes, innocent attempts at reproduction project us toward the sublime with ever-greater resolve. Postmodern irony and the pictorial sublime combine.[78]

Contrast the words of *Little Fluffy Clouds* with Edmund Burke on the sublime in architecture: "And in buildings, when the highest degree of the sublime is intended, the materials and ornaments ought neither to be white, nor green, nor yellow, nor blue, nor of pale red, nor violet, nor spotted, but of sad and fuscous colours, as black, or brown, or deep purple, and the like."[79] Catch glimpses of somber skies as spectral hues of gray and dusk, and "a light which by its very excess is converted into a species of darkness."[80]

In the introduction, I alluded to public concerns about mood monitoring and "mood control." Perhaps it is possible to alter how people feel by manipulating news feeds. Critics regard such putative incursions into people's emotional lives with some anxiety; no one likes to feel manipulated. However, for some commentators, all this connectivity places us in the shadows anyway. Sherry Turkle says in her book *Alone Together*: "Suddenly, in the half-light of virtual community, we may feel utterly alone. As we distribute ourselves, we may abandon ourselves."[1] It's as though "we are connected as we've never been connected before, and we seem to have damaged ourselves in the process."[2] There's sadness as she recounts stories of children and adults seeking solace from robot toy companions and flitting among online acquaintances, while friends and families around them physically are given terse recognition. The promises of social media connectivity pale as people fail to make eye contact, lose empathy toward others, and prefer their personal devices to communicating with people around them. She doesn't use the word *melancholy*, but it pervades her book and her reassessment of life online.[3]

Ubiquitous digital media promote a kind of melancholy. Insofar as the Internet channels mass media content and entertainment, it delivers crime dramas, fantasies of zombies, vampires, and werewolves, violent films, and endemically cruel cartoons, not to mention shooter and car crash video games. Sometimes, the content of ubiquitous digital media is just sad, with depressing news and stories and songs of loss and heartbreak. There's optimism and delight online, but tinged, tainted, and laced with heavy doses of melancholy. There's melancholic content, but life online also provides cause for melancholic reflection. As I'll show subsequently, to be depressed about a sad condition speaks to metamoods—moods about moods—the ironic and paradoxical domain of melancholy.

Mood and Melancholy

Melancholy doesn't appear on the standard list generated by psychologists of positive moods, such as being interested, enthusiastic, inspired, excited, strong, proud, alert, determined, or attentive. Nor does melancholy appear among the negative moods, such as being scared, nervous, upset, distressed, guilty, irritable, hostile, ashamed, jittery, or afraid.[4] Psychologists associate melancholy with the extreme conditions of clinical depression and psychosis,[5] but *melancholy* is a term that is most at home in the cultural sphere. Contrary to those who encourage happiness as a social good, there are those literary theorists and poets who advocate for the positive cultural benefits of the mood of melancholy.[6]

Melancholy operates as a seam throughout the discussion of this book so far. It's time now to bring it to the surface. Melancholy is a culturally rich and poetical concept and an interesting and productive kind of mood. Melancholy is often characterized as sadness, a condition without hope, in which pleasures pale into gloom. Shakespeare's play *Hamlet* epitomizes melancholy in its many dimensions. In negative mode, Hamlet asserts: "How weary, stale, flat, and unprofitable seem to me all the uses of this world!"[7] However, melancholy is also a productive, profound kind of sadness. It carries more appealing cultural overtones than happiness, sadness, or depression. For cultural theorist Jonathan Flatley in his book *Affective Mapping*, melancholy is a way of being "interested in the world."[8] I'll also show that melancholy relates to travel and mobility, that it's a state that any of us may encounter, from which we may return with fresh insights. The world looks different to the melancholic and different again when she emerges from her melancholy. I'm interested in this chapter in how the melancholic facets of mood relate to ubiquitous digital media.

The Internet as a Melancholy Medium

Melancholy is really a cluster of symptoms, a *syndrome* in clinical terminology. In cultural terms, melancholy is a collection of concepts. It's also an ambivalent mood. Like the color blue tinted with a little red, melancholy is sadness tinged with pleasure. Being sad is just a part of melancholy, but even sadness captures something of this ambivalent tone. If you search the web for "why do I enjoy being sad?" you get many more hits than "why do I enjoy being bad," or "glad, "happy," "mad," "intelligent," "sexy," "fit," "curious," "funny," or "a winner." There's a contradiction here. How can you have a positive emotion about a negative feeling? One solution to this conundrum is that melancholy can be classed as a *metamood*, a feeling about a mood. To explore melancholy is to add depth to the ontologies of mood explored in chapter 1, as I will examine subsequently.

Melancholy meets ubiquitous digital media in several dimensions. Online media encourage and circulate the autobiographical, the diarist in any of us.[9] The Internet is populated with stories, including the personal narratives of countless bloggers. Blogs sometimes play host to personal tragedies. But there's an inevitable melancholy to autobiography anyway. Autobiography entails memory and loss, and there's always the question of whether anyone is really interested in the author's personal reflections. Forgetting, being forgotten, and the possibility of loss are compatriots of melancholy.

According to a romantic stereotype, poets are melancholics. In part, the Internet is a poetic medium. Insofar as it circulates the products of the poetic imagination, it's a melancholic medium, a feature it shares with cinema, television, books, magazines, and libraries. What makes the Internet so remarkable as a melancholic medium is the ease with which it delivers its content and the extent to which it encourages literary production—and in such quantity, be it professional, amateur, profound, or banal.

In a romantic vein, the poet John Keats (1795–1821) wrote, "in the very temple of Delight / Veil'd Melancholy has her sovran shrine."[10] It seems that melancholy haunts our pleasures. Among its many offerings, the Internet fosters and delivers delights that include poetry in abundance, old and new, with many specialized sites for emerging poets. Commentators remark on the poetic aspects of text messaging and twitter.[11] New poetic forms have emerged, such as micropoetry and twihaiku.[12] The *New York Times* publicized an online application they developed for extracting phrases from the everyday news and turning them into haikus, many of them with the inevitable melancholic twist: "It's really hard to / break bad news without crying / or falling apart."[13]

Submission to the sublime power of melancholy is an abiding theme in romanticism, among the Pre-Raphaelites and the symbolists, and many scholars like to connect creativity with melancholy.[14] Aristotle assumed melancholy was integral to achievement: "Why is it that all men who have become outstanding in philosophy, poetry, or the arts are melancholic?"[15] Prominent people often described as melancholics include Samuel Taylor Coleridge, Vincent van Gogh, Ludwig van Beethoven, Dylan Thomas, Franz Kafka, and John Lennon.[16] Such lists don't of course imply that genius goes with melancholy, though it's evidence that we think it should.

As well as painting, music, and poetry, melancholy accompanies tragedy. As a mass medium for the circulation of stories, the Internet participates in tragic narratives. Melancholics don't necessarily live tragic lives, but they invent and circulate tragic stories and circulate the mood. "How is it that the clouds still hang on you?" asks King Claudius of Hamlet, who is haunted by the ghost of his murdered father. The story of betrayal, murder, loss, and revenge is a template mirrored in many novels, plays, films, and soap operas. Think of Don Quixote in Miguel de Cervantes's novel, Heathcliff in Emily Brontë's *Wuthering Heights*, Ishmael in Herman Melville's *Moby Dick*, and J. R. Ewing in *Dallas*. According to one blogger, recalling the death of the actor Larry Hagman who played J. R.: "The final shot of Bobby, the George Bailey of Southfork Ranch, weeping for J. R. was devastating because it compressed so many different kinds of grief into a single image: a brother crying for a brother, a good man crying for a bad man, an actor crying for a colleague, and a fellow *Dallas* fan mourning the end of an era. Ask not for whom the bell tolls, pardner."[17] That's melancholy.

There's also the music and literature of the *Sturm und Drang* (Storm and Stress) movement in the eighteenth century and the art of the symbol- ists in the late nineteenth century. In the twentieth century, we have the *noir* genre of literature, film, and the graphic novel, featuring the damaged, down-at-heel cynical detective. The iconic melancholic film *Blade Runner* brought tech-noir to the fore. Frank Miller's *Sin City* graphic novels and his film of the same name are melancholic, and the genre migrates to video games. *Limbo* is a grim, award-winning video game in black, white, and gray, involving a small boy's dash through a lethal forest. At one stage, the boy jumps across the corpses of similar little boys bobbing along in a river. Another game, *The Path*, follows similar narrative trajectories, described as a short horror game updating *Little Red Riding Hood*. *American McGee's Alice* is an earlier game in which Alice returns to Wonderland on a slash mission. Such games inherit the intensity of the *noir* genre in film, trading emotional intensity in place of spectacle, evocation instead of lavish costumes and sets, mystery in place of clarity—sometimes blending into horror. Then, there are the melancholic strains of popular music and culture in the genres known as *goth* and *emo*. Note the lyrics to a song by the group Bauhaus: "My heart is a black stone / A streaking mirror of unseen creatures,"[18] and a song by the group My Chemical Romance: "Singin' songs that make you slit your wrists / It isn't that much fun, starin' down a loaded gun."[19] Melancholy permeates all genres. It's also a symptom of so-called teenage angst, reflected in many films and cultural forms.

Melancholy and Loss

Melancholy is associated strongly with loss. Hamlet's depression ostensibly resides in the death of his father. Melancholy is that sad state that accompanies mourning. The Internet purveys stories of all hues. Hamlet provides a good example of how melancholy disseminates itself. Never before has Shakespeare's *Hamlet* been so accessible as it is now online, with several complete stage and film versions on YouTube and of course the full script, with modern English, countless commentaries, and some parodies.

Apart from the many sad stories it contains, the Internet is a medium of reminding and remembrance. Any library or archive conveys an inevitable melancholy: all those dead authors and the stories of times past. Enthusiasts present the Internet as an optimistic medium, but to search the Internet is to alight on so many traces: records, unread and uncommented blog posts, and incomplete stories. Tweets disappear after several months and are forgotten. The Internet is melancholic in the same way that ruins are. Is it worse to be forgotten or ignored? According to Slavoj Žižek, the big anxiety of online privacy, security, and surveillance is that no one is watching after all.[20] The anxiety attached to all those Facebook updates, self-disclosures, blogs, and comments is that perhaps no one is really all that interested.

The melancholy of ubiquitous digital media plumbs new depths. It seems that certain online practices bring other forms of communication to ruin. In his book *Zero Comments*, Geert Lovink writes: "Blogs bring on decay. Each new blog is supposed to add to the fall of the media system that once dominated the twentieth century."[21] Blogging apparently contributes to the erosion of the mass media. It also affects how we consumers think of evidence, truth, and reality: "There is a quest for truth in blogging. But it is a truth with a question mark. Truth has become an amateur project, not an absolute value, sanctioned by higher authorities."[22] For Lovink, blogging is a "nihilistic moment" signaling a decline of "belief in the message," expressing "personal fear, insecurity, and disillusion." Lovink thinks of bloggers as "creative nihilists because they are 'good for nothing,'" but they have turned this futility into a creative force.[23] The Internet purveys loss at the same time that it signals the loss of other media, the unsustainability of old archives, and the loss of traditional concepts of truth and value.

Spectral Presence

Melancholy invokes thoughts of faded recollections and spectral presences. Seeing questions of media through the blue-tinted glass of melancholy encourages us to look at matters differently. The investigations of film theorist Mark Pizzato provide an interesting example of how the theme of melancholy can inflect scholarly analysis. In his book entitled *Ghosts of Theater and Cinema in the Brain*,[24] he explores the theme of ghosts in his detailed analysis of melancholy. Drawing on insights from neuroscience, Pizzato speculates on the phenomenon of phantom limbs. In the same way that an amputee continues to feel an arm or leg that's been removed, as if it's still there, we mask the loss of any aspect of our environment, even fellow human beings and loved ones.[25] The images of the missing person persist after the loss, and such recollections are our ghosts. I think Pizzato is really referring to imagination and memory, but to enlist the explanation of ghosts provides an interesting way of taking the consideration of such phenomena out of the ordinary. It's certainly melancholic.

Pizzato also introduces the metaphor of haunting to account for the idea of collective memory and history. According to Pizzato, we are all haunted by the past, and we in turn will haunt the future.[26] He thereby translates memory, history, legacy, and what the hermeneutical tradition might term "an effective historical consciousness"[27] to the melancholic metaphors of ghosts, haunting, and spirits, as if something otherworldly.

For the philosopher G. W. F. Hegel and his followers, every age has its spirit, which is its *Geist*, or ghost. As I discussed in the introduction, the Spirit of an Age is *the thought of an age*, the *zeitgeist*. Therefore, the telling of history is never far from the melancholic haunting by apparitions. When historians appeal to the spirit of the Information Age, they are inevitably participating in such melancholic reflection, the spirit that haunts the age. As further evidence of this fascination with melancholy, philosopher

Jacques Derrida invokes ghosts to explain the mass media. According to Derrida, the media (or to be precise, the medium in which the media operate) is "neither living nor dead, present nor absent," and its study is a kind of "hauntology." The mass media in general and the age of mass media present and occupy this kind of limbo.[28]

As cognitive extension, the Internet also circulates the presence of ghosts and makes ghosts of us all. Appealing to the character of the mass media and celebrity culture, Pizzato writes: "Thus, the transcendent ghosts of mass-media stars today are built upon the phantom characters of past myths, plus the mimetic specters of particular parental influences in current brains and episodic zombies of preconscious experiences."[29] By this Freudian reading, the mass media simply retell all those stories of trauma and family relationships simmering under the surface of everyone's conscious awareness. As discussed in chapter 4, digital media circulate online entertainment and encourage social networkers to enter into its world. Insofar as the Internet has become a channel for such diversions, it inherits the melancholy of the play, the rise and fall of celebrity, the "ghosts of mass-media stars."

Pursuing the ghost metaphor further, Pizzato suggests that there are two kinds of ghosts. The ghost who wanders about in some kind of limbo is "the impotent, demanding, abject figure with unfinished business."[30] This is the ghost of Hamlet's father, "doom'd for a certain term to walk the night." Then, there are the trickster ghosts, including the "potent, mischievous, godlike trickster."[31] This characterization reminds me of the ghosts in Tim Burton's *Beetlejuice* (1988) or of George and Marion Kerby, the cool, fun-loving ghosts who haunt the otherwise dull life of Cosmo Topper in the vintage CBS sitcom *Topper* (1953–1955).

Pizzato is mainly writing here about ghosts as portrayed in film, though "some film ghosts are dramatic tricksters, like the cyberspace player enjoying the godlike power of rhizomatic hypertext, re-authoring the plots of other characters' lives."[32] Internet users have complained about automated requests from Facebook to befriend users who are no longer alive, as if ghosts from the past.[33] There's also a sense in which active bloggers, tweeters, writers of fanfiction, Internet lurkers, Second Life residents, and social media surfers assume a ghostly, invisible presence in their worlds, appearing when they choose, as Wikipedians or Wikipedia vandals, in Q&A forums and social media sites, and leaving barely a trace that they were ever there. Furthermore, the concept of *haunted media* has currency in media studies. For media theorist Eugene Thacker, haunted media suggest the possibility of communication between two realities: "the natural and the supernatural."[34]

A few years ago, some of us experimented with inserting video images of players into Second Life in real time.[35] We would stream a video image onto a simple, translucent, geometrical form that would move through the Second Life world and interact with other avatars. Inevitably, the video mappings produced spectral forms that floated through the landscapes, adding a ghostly dimension to an already surreal medium. According to Pizzato, both abject and trickster ghosts are trapped in their medium, a medium that extends to ubiquitous digital media.

Melancholy and Irony

Considering how easy it is to insert melancholy into the description of a situation or event, I think it's fair to position melancholy as the quintessential mood, or at least to test its status in that ontology. Without further qualification, mood defaults to the melancholic. To be "in a mood" is to be in a melancholy mood. According to the *Oxford English Dictionary*, someone who is *moody* indulges in "moods of ill humour or depression; melancholy . . . given to unpredictable changes of mood, esp. sudden spells of gloominess or irritable sullenness."[36] By this reading, rather than happiness, melancholy is the mood against which other mood states should be compared. As a further claim to this status, melancholy can be positioned above others in a kind of mood hierarchy. It qualifies as a metamood, a mood about another mood you are having, as in the melancholy that sometimes accompanies success, even success in sport.

Here's an example of success tinged with self-reflective melancholy. In an intellectually astute observation about his Olympic success, the British cyclist Bradley Wiggins said: "There is almost slight melancholy. I realised on the podium that that is it for me. I don't think anything is going to top that. To win the tour and then win Olympic gold in London at 32. I'll look back in 10, 15 years and think that was as good as it got."[37] In the midst of success, there's a kind of sadness. People can be haunted by sadness even in the midst of modest pleasures. Similar themes emerge in film and TV dramas, from *Mad Men* (2007–2015) to *The Dark Knight* (2008). At the start of the film *American Beauty* (1999), the main character, Lester, says in voiceover during a shot of him masturbating in a steam-filled shower: "This will be the high point of my day. It's all downhill from here." That's melancholy.

Moods about Moods

In a seminal paper on emotional awareness, empirical psychologists Peter Salovey and his colleagues defined three metamood conditions, highlighting that it takes a certain skill to deal with moods.[38] The first mood skill is to have an awareness of moods and to be able to talk about them. The second mood skill is to be able to experience moods clearly—that is, to be able to discriminate between being happy, sad, afraid, contented, or jealous. The third is to exhibit the ability to regulate moods—that is, to deliberately snap out of a mood or to know how to induce a pleasurable mood in oneself.

The strong contention is that people who are mood aware in these ways are better able to recover from negative emotional experiences. Salovey and colleagues tested how recovery operates by requiring human participants to watch a frightening movie or a documentary about car accidents and then testing the participants' mood awareness. The researchers extended the idea to actual traumatic life events, such as losing a close relative. They argued that emotional intelligence engenders a kind of resilience. Metamood skills help in coping with stress, abetted by friends, counsellors, and therapists, and we could add online media.[39] Insofar as melancholy indicates mood awareness, we can place it on the positive side of the emotional spectrum, or at least concede that it occupies an ambiguous position.

Plays within Plays

One tactic for managing mood is to make sport of the circumstances one is in, to project a kind of sardonic humor. Hamlet, the melancholic, derives a private mirth from his circumstances at the expense of his antagonists in the play. Here, melancholy delivers sarcasm, a poignant kind of mirth. Most of Hamlet's sarcastic jibes and cruel puns have to be explained to modern ears. (There are now ample websites to help us get the jokes.[40]) Anthropologist Kate Fox provides a more current example. After the tragic 7/7 London bombings in 2005, Americans set up an online forum called "London Hurts," with the tagline, "Today I'm a Londoner and today I hurt." Amid the messages of sympathy from around the world, actual Londoners posted messages such as "If you're all Londoners today that's eight quid each for the congestion charge" and "Southwark cathedral was a bit shaken, and went down the pub with the Imperial War Museum last night."[41] Such responses indicate a pulling back from the circumstances of the grief and even mocking the sympathizers. It's a response that reflects on what people are feeling, what they are supposed to feel, and what people feel about each other's feelings. That's irony—and melancholy.

Thus, melancholy admits a certain kind of humor. As I have already suggested, there's an inevitable backlash to the idea that happiness is always the best mood state to be in. Eric Wilson begins his book *Against Happiness* with a litany of reasons to be depressed: global warming, tsunamis, species depletion, and the threat of nuclear war. He adds to the list the fear of "eradicating major cultural forces, a serious inspiration to invention, the muse behind much art and poetry and music."[42] That is, we are in danger of losing melancholy—so that's something else to be depressed about. Wilson's observation is humorous, a close companion to sarcasm and pathos, and turns a good joke into a book. I would also describe the circumstance of the book as ironic—it's ironic that a book about melancholy should lament the loss of melancholy. The joke is consistent with melancholy as a reflexive condition.[43] Melancholy, irony, and self-reflection are in close alliance.

Hamlet is an ironic play. Like *A Midsummer Night's Dream*, its denouement focuses on the production of a play. *Hamlet* is a play that includes a play, with an onstage audience. Hamlet recruits the play, *The Mousetrap*, to ensnare his murderous uncle the king, who's in the audience. Hamlet thinks that a play, "by the very cunning of the scene," will move guilty parties in the audience to confess their crimes out loud, or at least to flinch uncomfortably when they see their crimes performed by the actors. The play sets the mood, intended to invoke a response in the audience as dramatic as a confession. Through such reflexive indulgence, *Hamlet* (the play) comes across as a melancholic essay in moods, the detection of moods, and mood awareness.

Here's a further literary example. In an often-quoted vignette, "A Melancholy Man," the Victorian novelist and essayist Samuel Butler (1835–1902) says that the melancholic keeps his own company and is "always falling out and quarrelling with himself."[44] In a way, melancholics think "too much" about their condition. Melancholy is a metamood in extremis. Melancholy is also a strong twentieth-century literary theme. Walter Benjamin

(1892–1940), in his study of mourning and tragedy, traces melancholy through several historical transformations. For the premoderns, melancholy related to divination and astronomy, and in turn to the god Saturn, the "protector of the most sublime investigations."[45] Saturn's is also a "spirit of contradictions" that imparts on the soul "sloth and dullness." On the other hand, it's a spirit of "intelligence and contemplation." Melancholy also carries the risk of "depression or manic ecstasy."[46] It's this multifaceted, premodern, and intellectually aware character of melancholy that scholars such as Benjamin would have us restore, or at least recapture afresh.

As a twenty-first-century channel for literary exploration, the Internet serves as a potent medium for the circulation of melancholy in its ironic aspects. As long as people find the Internet new and novel, posts and comments from bloggers and social media networkers elide readily into reflections about the medium. To add a further note of melancholy, we'll know it's lost its impact when the majority of users take digital media for granted and lose the capacity to reflect on and criticize the medium. In the meantime, it's still a medium preoccupied with itself, illustrating the human tendency toward self-reflection and melancholy.

Forgetting

For many scholars, melancholy operates as a response to loss. This is the major feature of melancholy picked up by Jonathan Flatley as a condition of modernity in general. Whether or not the Internet was ever harmless and ingenuous, it contributes to the contemporary lament that things used to be better. It reminds intellectuals of the lost innocence of late modernity. Melancholy has traction in the realms of remembering and forgetting, for which the Internet is an eminently capable medium. For Freud, someone who has lost something of personal value (a loved one, a job, a prize) might reasonably experience *mourning*. On the other hand, someone who is melancholic isn't aware of what he or she has lost: "This would suggest that melancholia is in some way related to an object-loss which is withdrawn from consciousness."[47] According to Flatley, losing the past is a condition of modernity.[48]

Ubiquitous digital media place the art of forgetting in a particular light. In his book *Delete: The Virtue of Forgetting in the Digital Age*, Viktor Mayer-Schonberger argues that with computers it's increasingly difficult to delete information and hence to forget.[49] I think online digital media do help us to forget in several obvious ways. Forgetting is an important aspect of melancholy, so I'll look at it in a little more detail in the next section.

How Computers Help People Forget

Studies into the use of online information sources focus on people's attitudes to knowing things rather than forgetting,[50] but ubiquitous digital media surely also help media-savvy network users to forget. If I store my bank details in my electronic notepad, then I don't need to commit them to memory, so I can forget such details. Thanks to the immediacy of web access and tools such as Wikipedia, I can forget the capital of The Isle of Man; it's easy enough to look up. Digital social media also keep me in touch with a pool of friends, colleagues, and experts who I can consult when I have a query. Because I'm a social being, I can therefore let certain facts drift from my memory. The groups of which I'm a part know things that no individual on his or her own would know. The intellectual skill in harvesting from this memory field is in knowing who to ask and where to look, though there are electronic aids for doing that as well. I don't need to remember so much. I can afford to forget.

Because they are safely itemized on my to-do list, I can forget those essential but challenging tasks ahead of me in which I risk losing time, confidence, or money. My calendar will remind me in good time what I need to know and when. I can forget the mortality rate of men over 30, the rate of global warming, how much nuclear waste is stored along the coast of the British Isles, and when the sun will run out of fuel. It's easy enough to look up these facts (and the disputes that accompany them) when I need to know. As facts fade from memory, I can draw on the collective memory of my network of friends. Many online Q&A forums, such as https://answers .yahoo.com, assist when needed: "How much water should I drink?" "Is this an infection or something worse?" "I just found a cigarette on the pavement. Should I smoke it?" Thanks to such forums, I can afford to forget, as long as I'm prepared to wait for and filter the answers.

Such sites serve as potential regulators of melancholy. As any therapist knows, sometimes the work is done in the framing of the question. In a study into Q&A behavior by Meredith Morris and colleagues, the motivations for asking questions on social media forums include showing trust and being able to connect socially.[51] People who answered queries did so to be helpful and friendly, it was a way of relieving boredom, it enhanced "social capital," it helped keep the network alive, it provided an opportunity to be witty, and it made the answerer feel wanted. Ignorance and forgetfulness provide excuses and opportunities for sociability, a palliative and regulator for melancholy.

Then, there are those painful, embarrassing, and redundant memories that constitute cognitive clutter ready for burial or extinction. Cathartic rituals, such as deleting files, emails, links, to-do items, contacts lists, browser histories, and other memory prompts, can help me forget. I've been careful so far in this chapter not to equate information in a file store with memories. Computer files are of course not memories, but cues, triggers, and traces that prompt memories in social human beings. Their removal prompts my forgetting. Such deletions presumably aid in the erasure of events best forgotten, such as failure, loss, or breakup.

Social Memory

Some scholars claim that forgetting can be coerced in the social realm to affect the mood of a nation. Philosopher Paul Ricoeur and historian Hayden White indicate that genocides and other atrocities are attempts to erase memories of nations and peoples, by removing names, records, and artifacts. Determined communities may rally around those dormant memories and seek to revive and reconstruct them, and thereby rebuild community.[52] There's a sense in which people need to forget in order to remember well. Forgetting is what it is to discriminate, to put things in order, to sift out the unnecessary and redundant. Memory has to be selective. Many narratives we are prepared to describe as melancholic deal with just such remembering and forgetting, such as memorials, museum displays, novels, and films that focus on the Holocaust: *Sophie's Choice* (1982), *Schindler's List* (1993), and *The Pianist* (2002).

For memory theorist Maurice Halbwachs, memories rely on socially constructed frameworks, such as the norms, practices, and language games of family, friends, and belief systems. One way to forget is to remove these frameworks: "Forgetting is explained by the disappearance of these frameworks or of a part of them, either because our attention is no longer able to focus on them or because it is focussed somewhere else."[53] Moving to another city, circle of friends, set of possessions, or culture severs the social ties that sustain memories, turning recollections into disconnected reveries that eventually fade. To this range of environmental displacements, I would add moving from one framework of cognitive and sociotechnical support to another, abandoning one's library, canceling online journal subscriptions, and losing your laptop. A surplus of triggers and traces can also invoke forgetting. Triggers and traces that are too many in number, arbitrarily arranged and disordered, might confuse and thereby engender forgetting. Inheriting someone else's immense digital photo library might produce such a disorienting outcome.

Ultimate Journeys

To forget a story, place, or event is to consign it to oblivion. The usual correlate of oblivion is the melancholic theme of *memento mori*, a recollection that we all die. How do online social media impact on netizens dealings with death? There are online memorials and online support and bereavement groups.[54] Furthermore, people afraid that their illness or parting may go unnoticed can subscribe to online services such as Dead Man's Switch. If the subscriber doesn't report in at some predefined frequency, then an email will be released to a recipient list announcing the possibility that the subscriber may be incapacitated or dead.[55] Many online information sources address death and offer support. Health care professions, insurance companies, probate lawyers, charities, and campaigners deploy the resources of the Internet to deal with death and dying,[56] and information on assisted dying is circulated freely online, even though the practice is illegal in all but a handful of countries.[57]

I only wish to introduce the subject of death here insofar as it casts light on the theme of melancholy as I've described it already. Melancholy also enters the arena of death through humor, as in the case of the response to the London bombings I alluded to earlier. According to theorist of popular culture Keith Durkin, "by rendering death into humor and entertainment, we effectively neutralize it; it becomes innocuous, and thus less threatening, through its conversion and ephemerality in the media."[58] On the one hand, this response appears to trivialize loss and grief. On the other hand, it brings such aspects of life further into the orbit of melancholy. Such loss is serious enough to joke about.

In most traditions, death is a stage in a journey, and most people are reluctant to adopt tropes that indicate it as a termination. We'd rather join with the psalmist's "walk through the valley of the shadow of death."[59] At best, death is an interval of interminable extent. Melancholy draws on the concept of duration—long periods of time, stretching to the infinite—for which journeying becomes a potent emblem and metaphor. Death provides an appropriate segue to the melancholy metaphor of the journey.

Excursion and Return

Walter Benjamin highlights "the melancholic's inclination for long journeys," particularly on the sea.[60] He refers to Albrecht Durer's allegorical illustration entitled *Melancholia*, with the pensive and forlorn angel in the foreground, backed by the sea extending to the horizon, implying long journeys. Eric Wilson concurs. In *Against Happiness* Wilson references Ishmael in Moby Dick: "It is melancholia that inspires this fictional young man to take to ship."[61] But with any journey, there's the hope or expectation of return.

One of the cures for whatever ails the melancholic resides in the idea of the *return*. Melancholy is the process by which we venture into the unknown and from which we return renewed. For Wilson, the melancholic vacillates between sorrow and joy. As if on a journey, brooding leads the melancholic to a more profound state, an eventual understanding of the "rhythms of the whole cosmos, itself a dynamic interplay between opposites."[62] In poetic vein, Wilson diarizes his own awakenings from the social imperative to be always happy, as he gazed into his ultimate aloneness, the brevity of his time on earth, and the melancholy of life in an inhospitable world. Consideration of death brings about an "electrical jolt" that invites him to "seize the day."[63]

I referred to oblivion in chapter 6. When Pope Benedict retired in February 2013, after due ceremony, he made a dramatic helicopter exit from the Vatican. Blogger Dario Morelli of The Huffington Post wrote: "A precise, wise and great director orchestrated the video of Benedict XVI's flight toward *oblivion*."[64] Of course, Benedict returned to the Vatican some days later, but as a quiet emeritus. Considering the authority residing in the figure of the Pope, it's strange to think of this mere "pilgrim" then consigned to an apartment or haunting the corridors he once ruled. In any case, *oblivion* was not the end of the process.

In his essay on oblivion, Marc Augé makes much of the idea of *the return*.[65] As an anthropologist, he writes about customs in tribal Africa in which certain individuals were required to enter into a trance and allow themselves to be possessed by spirits. Such mediums would then return to normalcy and community, and erase what they had just experienced. Hauntings have this transient character. Hamlet's ghost also appears, disappears, and reappears. For Augé, the medium "'re-enters himself' or 'finds his own spirit again.'"[66] That's an excursion and a return into memory and forgetfulness. Travel provides a simpler metaphor. Think of traveling "abroad" as a tourist or pilgrim as a process of excursion and return. Recall a European tourist's journey from home to Singapore and back: Singapore has streets, cars, plazas, shops, and crowds like home, but different, the familiar rendered strange.[67] Life is a journey, characterized by so many returns. The familiar and the unfamiliar oscillate and embed themselves in any aspect of recollection.

Another way to think of a journey is as a series of way stations, instances of our starting position encountered along the way, echoes of home, or moments of familiarity interspersed with the unfamiliar. My colleague Adrian Snodgrass describes travel in this way: "One's prior home is now understood not as a final homestead, a home where one stands steadfast, but a way station, a starting place for entry into the alien; and what was alien is now one's own."[68] If the Pope's exit from Rome was orchestrated by a skilled director, then think also of theater. Playwright Bertolt Brecht said of theater that "it must amaze its public, and this can be achieved by a technique of alienating the familiar."[69] What can be more alien or melancholic than leaving home, or a helicopter ride, Ezekiel-like, to signal departure?

It's easy to confine melancholy to the negative aspects of travel, such as homesickness. In *The Art of Travel*, philosopher Alain de Botton proposes that it's easier to "give way to sadness" in roadside diners, hotel lobbies, and train station cafés, when away from "the false comforts of home."[70] According to sociologist John Urry, for all its positive pleasures and new encounters, travel involves disappointment as tourists encounter "the inevitable gap between what people anticipate will be a place's pleasures and what is actually encountered,"[71] unmotivated hotel staff, depressing, out-of-season seaside resorts, congestion, hawkers, and misrepresentation in the advertising brochures. However, travel has a melancholic aspect even when everything goes as planned.

Melancholy therefore entails a process. It's a journey to a condition of alienation, as if it is an initiation rite, one that is repeated. Pilgrims venture into that condition and emerge renewed, so long as they are able. This is a bit like the pilgrim's emergence from, or evasion of, the Slough of Despair.[72] It's the psalmist's walk through the valley of death.[73] By this reading, there's no need for a cure to melancholy. It's a symptom of thoughtfulness, from which we may never wish to be released. As for happiness, it's not just the melancholic mood state that provides the social good, but the excursion into, and return from, significant emotional experiences. Melancholy is a narrative and literary theme supported by the ubiquity of digital media. Online media have the potential to take digital networkers into and out of cognitive and emotional conditions, not least in the way they provide access to literary sources, music, and film. They also provide a medium for the diarist and a vehicle for remembrance, forgetting, and journeying. Mood, mobility, and melancholy travel together.

Summary

In this chapter, I made the case for a reappreciation of the mood of melancholy and its social and cultural advantages. Autobiography entails memory and loss, and there's always the question of whether anyone is really so interested in our own life stories. Forgetting and being forgotten are compatriots of melancholy. The Internet is a melancholy medium, not least for all the forgotten or ignored personal attempts at minor fame that it harbors. I introduced the idea of ghosts, ghostly presences, memories, and hauntings. I also proposed that melancholy could be at the peak of a mood hierarchy. Melancholy is a metamood, which entails mood awareness. Melancholy deploys reflection, sardonic humor, irony, suspicion, and preoccupation with itself. Melancholy is a self-reflexive mood. It's also a response to loss. Digital social media play a role in helping us forget. I touched on the theme of death, journeying, and the return, in which there's always hope, the subject of the next chapter.

Coda: Orz

Amid the grim images and doleful wails of the North Korean nation mourning the death of its leader Kim Jong-Ill in 2011, we saw grief-stricken citizens enacting the customary orz posture and gestures. It's still a YouTube hit. Orz, with variants, is of course an emoticon popular in Japan, South Korea, China, and elsewhere used to indicate humility, despair, sorrow, submission, shame, regret, and melancholy. When spoken, the text sequence is generally pronounced "oh ar zee," and represents a human body on all fours in profile. If further explanation is needed, then the "o" is a head bowed, the "r" is the arms, and the "z" is the folded legs. This is a customary submissive posture parodied in Orientalist theater. Stage directions in Gilbert and Sullivan's *The Mikado* require Koko and Pitti-Sing to drop to their faces before the Mikado, followed by some slapstick as the dignified and bulky Pooh-Bah tries to do the same.

The contexts in which it is deployed may be different, but orz is a posture that creates unease wherever it occurs. I recall being at a meeting where the somewhat important chairperson crawled on all fours under a table to retrieve some papers. Others were uncomfortable and darted to assist. Perhaps the orz posture suggests a return to the state of an animal "obliged to walk with faces to the ground" as suggested by Vitruvius.[74] It is however a posture that can assume dignity, as when Pope John Paul II would kiss the tarmac on disembarking at an airport.

The orz posture raises some questions. What is the relationship between feeling and action? There is the charge that the North Korean grief was not real, but play acting, a demonstration created under duress. How does this square with the philosopher William James's insight that actions and feelings cannot be so easily separated?[75] A person doesn't get on hands and knees, wail, bend to and fro, and beat the ground *because* they feel sorrowful. We could just as easily assert that people feel sorrowful *because* they so assume this posture and beat the ground; perhaps without the gesture the reception of the event (the mourning) would be "pale, colourless, destitute of emotional warmth," to quote James.[76] The question of sincerity lingers, but it is a question we would probably not be asking were it not for the extreme grief displays captured on camera.

Do groups, crowds, and nations feel something independently of what an individual feels? Is there such a thing as a collective emotion? Here, we can appeal to the idea of a mood or atmosphere that provides the context for personal feelings. This atmosphere is perhaps the *Stimmung*, or social attunement, a prerequisite for whatever emotion we claim. The concept of a corporate mood looks perilously close to Mao Zedong-style collectivism ("the individual is subordinate to the organization"[77]), but the idea that the mood of a people might be manipulated highlights further its importance as a prerequisite for feeling.

An avid user of the orz emoticon had something interesting to say about it:

Comment 1: The orz gesture used to be an important gesture in the etiquette of all ancient Asian cultures. Apart from despair and sorrow, it can also imply great respect. It's almost like a very formal greeting. One explanation for the emergence of this gesture relates to the lack of chairs. People lived on the floor on tatami mats. The orz emoticon is often used in a humorous context by modern Asian youth on the Internet, except in exceptional circumstances calling for extreme expressions of respect.

Comment 2: The tatami reference is interesting. That gives the gesture a particularly spatial significance.

9 Gripped by Suspense

From the depths of melancholy, "hope springs eternal in the human breast,"[1] to quote from a famous poem by Alexander Pope (1688–1744). If we are particularly down, then we can resort to a frivolous song. "Always look on the bright side of life," sang Eric Idle.[2] There's always entertainment to lift the spirits, bring a wry smile, or persuade us that whatever life throws our way, we are in it together. At least, that's a common expectation. Entertainment also illustrates the human propensity to hope for and expect more of the same. If the show is any good, then we want a sequel.

"Sequel baiting" is the practice by optimistic filmmakers to construct their plots in a way that encourages audience demand for a sequel. As well as cliffhanger endings, some filmmakers introduce characters and subplots that invite follow-up once the main story is over. The Harry Potter novels and film series seemed to draw on this tactic to develop an audience and a market for a succession of productions. Although it's not yet in the formal dictionaries, "sequelitis" is a term in usage on the Internet. It's a tendency to produce or expect sequels from a movie or other production, of whatever quality. Such is the virulence of sequelitis that fans make up their own trailers to films they would like a professional filmmaker to produce, and they publish these on YouTube to goad filmmakers into announcing a sequel, as if exhorting James Cameron to produce a sequel to *Avatar* (2009), for example. The amateur trailer is usually assembled from clips out of the original film. There are fake sequel trailers for *Titanic* (1997), *Minority Report* (2002), *Inception* (2010), and *Oblivion* (2013), to name a few. The editing tools for mashing up video content to create user-generated trailers, teasers, mock prequels, and movie trailer parodies are available on anyone's laptop. It seems as though a fake trailer can induce very large numbers of hits to its creator's YouTube channel, though they may have to endure a tirade of negative comments from frustrated visitors who discover the fakery.

In this chapter, I want to situate such expectant phenomena in theories about anticipation and suspense. Continuing the discussion started in chapter 2, mood is a frame of mind in which we are primed with expectations, and there's a structure to these expectations. Ubiquitous digital media invariably influence that mood condition. They circulate and perpetuate moods, and hence the mood of expectation.

Sequencing Tactics

Sequel baiting is a commercial and instrumental indication of a basic human tendency toward hope—that is, to will some event into existence. Not only media but also consumer products succumb to this chain of expectation, such as speculation about an "iPhone 7" long before its development, public announcement, or release. Manufacturers and production teams use naming and numbering to heighten expectation and as an indicator of optimism. There's the role of version numbers in keeping a project open and edging it ever onwards. NASA's Apollo space missions were numbered 1 to 17 and beyond. There's Windows 1.0 to 10.0. Web 2.0 invites expectation of a 2.5, 3.0, and more. The advent of 3-D printing has encouraged a contest for 4-D printing, which could provide any number of innovations—in one case, the printing of rudimentary machines parts that when activated will self-assemble into a functional machine.[3] Claiming to extend a numbered sequence in this way operates in part as a competitive marketing tactic and a way of usurping others' claims on the next generation of computer technologies, printing, presentation, or networking. Seen in the best light, something as ordinary as a number sequence signals healthy competition, a race to claim the next generation of innovation, and is a sign of commercial optimism.

I think of these sequencing tactics as indications of a propensity within the human species to project forward, to anticipate, and to be ever expectant.[4] In a way, they also serve to construct a future and even create the idea of the future. This is also the business of science fiction, one of whose side effects is to heighten anticipation for what might be. Anticipation is also the stock of utopias, through which writers and activists dream of a better future and a better place or disturb us with the opposite of utopia—a pathological, dystopian future.

Along with other commentators, I have already reviewed the utopian aspects of digital media narratives, which I'll recount only briefly here.[5] Utopian narratives and science fiction are as much about the present as the future. They also involve looking back and inventing a past. In a sense, every looking forward is an attempt to get back to something that we think was better than the current condition we are in. The forward look references what's already happened. This is the nature of utopia, looking to a better place and circumstance, which in many ways also transforms our view of the past, commonly to idealize it. The desire to one day arrive at the Celestial City (or the Heavenly Jerusalem) is a desire to return to the Garden of Eden, when life was innocent. The arts and crafts advocate William Morris (1834–1896) proposed a utopian future in which there are no factories and no commercial division of labor. He proposed a return to an idealized preindustrial state.[6]

The dream of betterment by means of, or in spite of, technology permeates narratives about ubiquitous digital media, through television documentaries about science and technology, magazine and press articles, and cultural commentary. This "myth" of progress informs much commercial development and drives research. A recent lecture on a TED video about 4-D printing indicated the future possibilities of printing machine parts that assemble themselves. It replayed a common formula. The technology will bring about medical cures at the scale of nanomachines in the bloodstream, or you can print flexible, self-constructing and adapting machines at the scale of building and engineering components.[7] Irrespective of the capabilities of the emerging technology, this makes good storytelling and is a tactic built into the strategies for marketing products and projects. We consumers expect such optimism. If the story were about an incremental research program with timelines, benefits and costs, problems, challenges, and risks, describing an altogether "wicked" problem domain,[8] then leisure audiences, consumers, and potential backers would probably lose interest.

The theme of this chapter is in opposition to that of chapter 8, which was about melancholy. If melancholy projects a mood of sober reflection, then I am now talking about a mood of hope—a positive disposition and an expectation that circumstances can get better. Hope is the attribute left in the box when Pandora opened it and released all the world's evils.[9] Hope is a positive remnant. In his important book *The Principle of Hope*, philosopher Ernst Bloch anticipated what psychologists say about positive mood states.

He affirmed that hope broadens people's outlook: "The work of this immersion requires people to throw themselves actively into what is becoming, to which they themselves belong."[10] Hope requires effort. The hopeful person trains and tames their daydreams: "It is a question of knowing them deeper and deeper and in this way keeping them trained and unerringly, usefully, on what is right."[11] Bloch's three-volume work captured something of his own position as the sober optimist, a European émigré to the United States in the early 1950s. He affirmed that hope "is in love with success."[12]

Hope makes for good book titles. In 2006, Barack Obama published *The Audacity of Hope*, written to tap into "a running thread of hope that makes our improbable experiment in democracy work," and that can inspire Americans to "pride, duty and sacrifice."[13] Hope pertains to social and cultural virtue, as if to provoke and inspire to action.

Knowing What to Expect

Hope also extends into the everyday: "Will there be anyone at the dinner party we know?" "I hope so." Hope provides a particularly optimistic cultural inflection to the everyday attitude of *anticipation*, or *expectation*. Expectation, as with hope, is far from frivolous or in vain. Expectation is not just an occasional feeling that comes and goes. The tendency of human beings to project, anticipate, and entertain hope is a strong theme in the writing of the philosopher Martin Heidegger,[14] who asserts that without anticipation, or having a "fore-project," there would be no understanding, which is to say that we could never understand anything: a movie, a trailer, a book, or a blog. We are creatures always expecting, with pleasure, dread, or in phlegmatic mood, and it is this concerned projection (into a future) that enables us to make sense of the world we inhabit.

Anticipation is also a to and fro movement in which expectations undergo inevitable revision in light of expectations that are unmet or are realized differently. If it turns out that there is no one at the dinner party I know, then I have to revise my expectations, perhaps thinking that I'll meet someone new to me who is interesting and engaging or with whom I have something in common. By most accounts, this to and fro process of revision is what it means to be open to new interpretations of a film, play, work of art, piece of music, app, building, or just about any situation and to participate in cultural life. Interpretation is what drives much conversation, debate, and human reason.[15]

Expectation can be ill formed and with no particular image of what's in store. Occasionally, while watching a particular television program, I've been known to challenge my fellow audience members to guess what is going to happen next. I frequently draw a blank. We are expecting something, but don't know what; there's no time to process the story; or nobody really cares for the challenge I've set. We'd rather leave it to the filmmaker. Whether we can articulate that expectation or not, we are still expectant, and there is some structure to that expectation.

Moods Frame Expectations

In fact, all expectation has a kind of structure. As I outlined in chapter 2 on moods as frames for action, human expectations fit within some frame or other. The so-called frame problem has occupied researchers in artificial intelligence and cognitive science for some time.[16] We thinking human beings don't need to examine and process every new experience afresh; we pick up on cues in the environment and effectively select from a repertoire of behaviors appropriate to that situation. The oft-cited example is of walking into a restaurant. I know to expect tables, waiters, and food, and I know to take a seat, read the menu, order food, eat it, pay the bill, and eventually leave. The behaviors are different in the situation in which I order popcorn at the cinema or take up a friend's invitation to call round and eat dinner while watching a television program. What is a frame? Sometimes we think of a frame as a scaffolding on which our experience can be assembled. It also operates like a frame around a picture, partitioning that part of the world to which you are to direct your attention. It's also a *frame of mind*. Being expectant—positioned in the right frame—is also a case of being in the mood. A mood is a frame of mind that prepares us for what it's reasonable to hope. The scaffolding is in place, and the organism is primed and receptive. Being required to eat out at a restaurant when you are really in the mood for a night in front of the television requires some kind of frame adjustment.[17]

When the use of mobile phones, smartphones, and digital tablets became widespread, the new social settings they created required people to adjust their mood frames. There once was a time when if you heard someone talking with no one in particular, you would assume that person was talking to himself and would possibly keep a wide berth. With hands-free mobile communication, we now assume the person is conversing with another person on the phone or perhaps dictating a message.

Some people who are accustomed to speaking on the phone in their home or office easily lapse into similar vocal patterns when on public transport. Adjusting the volume of your voice to the setting and technology is a skill many travelers are still learning to develop.

Digital devices frame our expectations in many ways. I was once sitting in a café reading an e-book on my tablet computer, and a family was sitting nearby. The youngest child broke away from the family group, stood near me, and started to stare at the screen. I was distracted by something else, and with no encouragement from me he started to tap at the screen. His parents saw this before I did and then with suitable apology remarked that he was probably looking for his favorite computer game. To the sensibility of the contemporary infant, games are everywhere. There's a mismatch of frames, and part of growing up involves discriminating between frames that relate to the home and those that pertain to public places, or perhaps I have to adjust my frame to expect that everything is potentially available everywhere.

This circumstance also reminded me of the spatial configuration represented by tablet computers, in which the screen is usually positioned horizontally, or at least at an oblique angle, a feature of high-resolution, light, and robust interactive screens found on smartphones and tablet computers. Their use involved a kind of reframing for a generation used to desktop computers. Tablet computers are designed for users to position, hold, view, and touch at all angles. There are major differences between the horizontal and vertical viewing of a flat surface. The vertical screen of a desktop or laptop computer says "hands off," like a vertical wall. It also requires some physical persistence to sustain physical contact with a vertical screen. The horizontal or oblique says "touch me," and "smear me with your fingers." It's like a tabletop or a drawing surface. It invites casual encounter.

One of the earliest advocates of ubiquitous computing, Mark Weiser, imagined the casual, egalitarian office environment, with people reclining on beanbag chairs and reaching for the nearest digital tablet.[18] It's as if the oblique angle is more democratic than the vertical. The geometry of bodily interaction with mobile devices is just one of many frame changes to which users have had to adapt with the introduction of these new media. The rapid rate of change means that those frames do not necessarily have a chance to bed in before requiring the next change in practices. In any case, the technological context is part of the character of a setting, the everyday mise-en-scène that provides the necessary cues to what we expect and how we behave—the mood of a place.

Genre Busting

A similar framing occurs in the case of the consumption of entertainment. If I'm reading a biography of Freud on an e-book, then I don't expect Bob the Builder to appear. When I'm watching a nature documentary, then I won't be expecting Martians. If I'm watching science fiction, then I won't pin my hopes on Lassie. Such frame distinctions are commonly described in terms of *genre*, a term that often appears when selecting movies, television programs, and music on streaming and download services. Mass media entertainment categories are invariably fluid, and many artists, filmmakers, and authors are keen to challenge the expectations of their audiences by playing with genre expectations. Is it a romantic comedy or science fiction, horror, or erotica? I'm thinking of those so-called genre-busting books that excite publishers, such as David Mitchell's *Cloud Atlas* and E. L. James's *Fifty Shades of Grey*.[19] The challenge extends across media: Is it a record album, a game, a film, an interactive entertainment, a social experience, an installation, or an artwork? The interactive smartphone and tablet app *Biophilia* (2011) by the singer Björk also illustrates this kind of genre ambiguity.

Developments in film techniques and CGI effects provide further challenges to audience expectations, and these expectations are in turn undergoing change. Movies provide deliberate and inadvertent cues as to what you can expect next. There was a time when audiences would be forewarned of an impending special effects shot. Think of audience expectations in the film *Jason and the Argonauts* (1963). Cues in the scene would prepare you for what was going to happen. When Hercules and Hylas entered the treasure trove under the gigantic bronze statue of Talos, the audience expected something beyond the ordinary to occur. The giant statue already looked like a physical model in miniature; the static low camera angle and mise-en-scène were optimized so that the live action and the models could appear to blend. The modeling and filming techniques of the effects producer Ray Harryhausen carried a certain signature, and audiences knew the statue would eventually have to start moving. Something similar occurred with the battles involving the animated models of the Harpies, the Hydra, and the skeletons. I think that such films were no less captivating in their day because of these cues and may have been enhanced by them.

The early computer games of *Myst* (1993) and its sequel *Riven* (1997) provide a similar case of telltale production cues forewarning of a particular turn in the narrative. At that stage in the development of the technology, memory and processing limitations on personal computers required certain economies in the design of human–computer interaction. You would know when a wheel was about to turn or the view through the submarine window was about to change by the fact that part of the screen display would become pixelated prior to the playing of a low-resolution animated video. The whole screen would not be animated, just that small part of it where the action was taking place. It was exciting to wait for these animated windows to open up in the game world. The temporary windows were artifacts of the production process rather than part of the game plan. Now, of course, with greater processing power, algorithm design, vast libraries of effects templates, and teams of highly creative designers, virtually anything can happen in any genre of game or film. When it was first released, few audiences realized that the movie *Titanic* (1997) employed a vast range of digital effects. More recently, I recall that at least one reviewer thought Spielberg's *The Adventures of Tintin* (2011) presented live actors in costume, and it's hard to spot that the white trails issuing from the cigarette-smoking monkey in episode 21 of *The Big Bang Theory* (2011) were applied digitally in postproduction.

Filmmakers manipulate audience expectations via a range of different production cues. Audiences are becoming increasingly sophisticated in picking up the nuances of the medium. A film produced in the style of *Jason and the Argonauts* now would fly against current expectations from cinema audiences. It would be identified as a parody or at best some kind of homage to a bygone age of filmmaking.

So framing, frames of mind, and moods are strongly correlated. To be in the mood for dinner, the cinema, a bit of drama, an adventure game, a statue coming to life, some horror, or for love: these imply an emotional disposition, but also sets of expectations comparable to genre, frames, scripts, and landscapes or stage settings in which certain actions can take place and scripts can be enacted.

Repeatable Media

When audiences become habituated to a medium, they get to know the characteristics and nuances of the genre and its violation or disruption.

Online entertainment facilitates such habituation. Digital mass media are now characterized by so much repetition. Modern media consumers can record, rewind, and replay digital media content. You can watch the same film over again or replay highlights. The possibility of a repeat experience is endemic to art and literature, but amplified in the case of digital media. Filmmakers have adapted to the closer scrutiny that this encourages from audiences and have even introduced details in the mise-en-scène, the identification of which invites repeat viewings. I would be surprised if any audience member would grasp all the characters in Disney's CGI animation *Meet the Robinsons* (2007) or the plot the first time, and there's sufficient detail in the city of the future to reward repeat viewings.

So far, I've said little directly about suspense, ostensibly the topic of this chapter. What I've presented to this point provides a preamble, an introduction to the suspense theme. There's an apparent paradox to the idea of suspense, but I'll get to that in a few pages.

Suspense is a genre in film and game play, and critics acknowledge Alfred Hitchcock as the master of suspense. In chapter 5, I referred to Hitchcock's film *Vertigo* (1958), which draws on the power of repetition. At the start of the film, we see a uniformed police officer in pursuit across the rooftops of San Francisco. We don't get to know him or form a strong bond. The officer is accompanied by the main character, Scottie Fergusson, who's also involved in the chase. Scottie slips and clings for his life to the edge of the roof. The uniformed officer tries to rescue him but slips and falls to his death. That implies a pattern of events that the audience might expect to see repeated by Scottie as he hangs from the roof guttering. Later, at the film's denouement, Scottie has to confront his fear and climb to the top of a tower, again repeating the experience of being in a potentially dangerous position above ground. Repetition, and its possibility, heightens suspense. There's similar recourse to the device of repetition in the adventure film *Indiana Jones and the Temple of Doom* (1984). We see someone being sacrificed to a god as that individual is lowered into a fiery pit, so we know that human sacrifice is a possibility. Later on, we see Willie in peril of a similar fate as she's chained to a grille suspended over the same pit.[20] Repetition supports a similar scenario in "slasher" movies and detective stories, particularly those that feature serial killings (who will be the next victim?), but the sequence of fatalities doesn't need to be so extended for the potentially lethal pattern to emerge. Anticipation feeds on repetition and with variation. No two circumstances are exactly the same, and in that resides uncertainly, hope for a particular outcome, and suspense.

In *Vertigo*, the potential victim, Scottie, is not the one in suspense. The audience is in suspense, wanting to know what happens next. Suspense is primarily a narrative device. In fact, literary philosopher Christy Mag Uidhir goes so far as to say that "our work-a-day lives appear largely suspense-free enterprises,"[21] implying that suspense comes in the way you tell a story rather than in actual life events. In his book *The Art of Fiction*, literary theorist David Lodge characterizes suspense as raising questions in the minds of the readers.[22] He identifies two kinds of questions. In the detective story, the typical question is that of who committed the crime. In the adventure story, the question is that of what will happen next. In the thriller, both are combined: "Such narratives are designed to put the main characters repeatedly in situations of extreme jeopardy, thus exciting in the reader emotions of sympathetic fear and anxiety as to the outcome."[23]

According to literary theorists, suspense is a narrative device. It's an emotion we ascribe to a feeling we get while reading or watching a narrative. Should anyone be unlucky enough to find him- or herself suspended from a roof, lost in the mountains, or wrestling with a tiger, it is unlikely that person would describe his or her emotion as one of suspense, wondering how he or she will get out of the situation and when. The overwhelming feeling is likely to be something akin to fear and anxiety about his or her own survival and welfare, not how the story will pan out or end. However, it's also fair to say that we do deploy terms, phrases, and sentiments that indicate *suspense* in everyday life, such as waiting for an exam result, the feelings you get when preparing for a holiday, waiting to receive an online purchase in the post, waiting to hear about the gender of a newborn baby, or anticipating the features of the next generation of smartphones.

A study by psychologists Lars-Olof Persson and Lennart Sjöberg examined the everyday phenomenon of looking forward to a long vacation abroad.[24] They identified a mixture of excitement and fear, happiness and sadness, and a sense of risk, though they didn't resort to *suspense* to describe this phenomenon. Anticipation in everyday life comes with a degree of risk. Looking forward to turning on the television or watching the latest download probably entails little sense of risk, but looking forward to a holiday will involve a mixture of emotions.

The correspondence between everyday suspense and narrative suspense resides in information: the tension between knowing and not knowing.

As Lodge suggests, the suspense element relates to something informational, the answer to questions: Will the goal be reached? What will happen next?[25] The circulation of content in digital media involves the repetition of narrative experiences. Much is available for reviewing through television on demand, music downloads, and online, consumer-led video channels. You don't need to see a film once only; you can revisit it as highlights and commentaries, and even read the script. I don't think this diminishes the suspense potential of media content. As I'll show subsequently, insofar as it deals in information, ubiquitous digital media provides an instinctive setting for suspense.

The Suspense Paradox

I've referred to anticipation and repetition. The idea of suspense entails an apparent paradox. Suspense involves uncertainty about an outcome. We don't know what will happen next. But what if we have already been told the outcome, or have already seen the film, played the game, or read the story? The paradox is that we still feel something akin to suspense. Mag Uidhir calls the kind of suspense in which we already know the outcome "repeater suspense."[26] She thinks that suspense is special as an emotion in accommodating a profoundly different condition once the outcome is known or the question is answered. Suspense is unique as an emotion in this respect.

The repeater question does not arise in the case of other emotions, such as pity or anger. No matter how many times we see or read of Fantine forced into prostitution in *Les Misérables*, the basis of the feeling of pity is not undermined by repeated encounters with the pitiful condition in the story. Nor is our anger undermined by repeat viewings of *The Killing Fields* (1984). Yet, knowing who Madeleine really is in *Vertigo* ought to diminish the suspense element, or the suspense in Hitchcock's *Psycho* (1960) should be reduced if we already know what happens to Lila when she descends into the basement of the spooky old house, but audiences still experience the suspense effect even when they know the outcome in advance. In fact, some murder mysteries and thrillers start with a clear knowledge of who did what to whom. There may be a suspense component in not knowing how the murderer will be found out, but even then, knowing the outcome does not undermine the element of suspense. We still feel it.

Mag Uihir resolves the paradox by maintaining that suspense is something interesting to talk about, is a genre in fiction, and provokes philosophical reflection, but does not exist as an actual emotion: "There can be no genuine, distinct emotion that is the emotion of suspense."[27] Identifying with the character in peril can certainly invoke anxiety or pity as we put ourselves in their position, or excitement, or perhaps we are simply enjoying a good story, but there's no such thing as suspense.

I think that's a provocative proposition, and it has support from the theories advanced by psychologist David Russell, who believes that there are basic core affects along a spectrum of low and high intensity and from unpleasant to pleasant.[28] As I discussed in chapter 1, these constitute axes on a two-dimensional gridded schema. Points on the grid are untagged until we situate such feelings culturally in a context, with words like "happy," "sad," "envious," "bored," or "in suspense."

However, there's another solution to the "repeater paradox." Repetition not only informs our anticipations, but there's a sense in which all narratives are repeat narratives. The ubiquity of repetition comes to our aid in thinking about the issue of what it is to be expectant when you already know the outcome of the story or you've seen it before. Cultural theorists and philosophers have played with the idea that there is never truly a first time. Every interpretive encounter is a reencounter. The philosopher Jacques Derrida develops this view.[29] We are caught up in so many repetitions; some are vicarious, second hand, and prerehearsed. We come to a thriller or horror film we've not seen before carrying the baggage of every other horror film we've ever seen or even every trauma we've experienced in life, of which the film is a reminder.

In chapter 8, I referred to a study of melancholy in which human participants were exposed to traumatic events through film, vicariously. The researchers thought the emotional responses of the audience comparable to life traumas. Even though people know they are only watching a film, their emotional responses are roughly the same, though short-lived and with much milder life consequences. We audience members are good at relating one pattern of events to another.[30]

Therefore, I think the solution to the paradox resides in the observation that all suspense is "repeater suspense." Suspense is simply a case of anticipation, and anticipations build on repetitions of previous situations in which we exercise our necessary capacity for dealing with the world, which is to anticipate. The concept of suspense is simply a literary and cultural realization of what it is to be expectant, codified in a certain literary and narrative fashion and identified with a narrative genre.

It's tempting to think that the audience experience is enhanced by a totally new experience, that it's better not to read the book before seeing the film. We should approach any new situation with a mind cleared of structured anticipations: "I'm open to whatever comes my way." However, as I've already indicated, no one is able to stand back from some object and to understand it without doing so from a frame, a position of belief, assumption, or presumption. Another way of describing this anticipation is negatively as some kind of *prejudice*, a prejudgment. As it happens, though, the idea of an initial raw perception is a chimera, as is reasoning from "first principles" or a position of "objectivity."

The philosopher Hans-Georg Gadamer (1900–2002) brings this issue to the fore, arguing that without prejudice we could never understand anything. He describes the process well in relation to reading a text (book, blog, essay, etc.). We project meanings into the text in front of us: "A person who is trying to understand a text, is always performing an act of projecting. He projects before himself a meaning for the text as a whole as soon as some initial meaning emerges in the text. Again, the latter emerges only because he is reading the text with particular expectations in regard to a certain meaning."[31] Think also of a film. What makes such interpretations meaningful, though, is to be open to revising this preconception: "The working of this fore-project, which is constantly revised in terms of what emerges as he penetrates into the meaning, is understanding what is there."[32]

Gadamer seems to be saying there's a circle of understanding between the text or media experience and the interpreter's prejudice, or perhaps the text and its emergent meaning. There's a moral message here. We need to allow our prejudices to be renewed, transformed, and revised. The bad, or at least culturally limited, kind of prejudice is the intransigent kind. In fact, the ossification of prejudice kills off interpretation, as when we media consumers feel unable to accommodate some new media format, or conversely those newbies who give no credence at all to old media and are indifferent to its qualities.

It seems that in life as with media we are always looking for more or less of the same, and this compels us to think and act and drives people to invent. All this constitutes the fore-projection of understanding: future baiting of a sort. Insofar as suspense is a mood, it runs deep in the human psyche. Research in experimental psychology concurs. According to psychologist Richard Davidson, "Moods provide the affective background, the emotional color, to all that we do."[33] Emotions operate against this background of course, but so does cognition in general: "To the extent that moods are continually present, it can also be said that our cognitive processes are always biased or modulated."[34] Anticipation and suspense constitute bias toward particular outcomes.

In chapter 8, I wrote about melancholy and suggested that emotionally intelligent human beings dip into and out of that mood condition. It's an alien condition in which things don't seem quite right. In similar vein, Dabala says of suspense that it "intensifies the menace, or strangeness, of the event to come, the dramatic effect."[35] We commonly think of melancholy as a condition without hope, perhaps devoid of expectation. This isn't always the case. It's just that the melancholic position is open to outcomes other than those that are entirely positive.

What is the role of ubiquitous digital media in enhancing or modulating our expectations? Insofar as such media trade in knowledge and information, I'll show that they amplify the workings of suspense through their capacity to circulate questions, promote mystery, and instigate delay.

Search Queries

David Lodge characterizes suspense as raising questions in the minds of the readers.[36] Anticipation and suspense are built into the idea of the question. A question demands a next step, the provision of an answer. We expect the answer to follow, and questioning is endemic to online ubiquitous media. The Facebook update field is primed with a question: What's on your mind? What are you doing today? Voice-recognition utilities such as those provided by Apple's Siri interface and Amazon's voice-recognition interface amplify the personable aspect of the question. The classic test for artificial intelligence involves detecting whether the answers to questions sound as though a human being could have delivered them. This is the so-called Turing test.[37] Search engines imply a question: Is there a good restaurant nearby? What does Freud mean by the unconscious? Questioning is a good way to raise anticipation in an audience or in a classroom, to pose a difficult question to get people thinking. I referred to questioning in chapter 3 in the context of curiosity.

The projected, so-called Web 3.0 is supposed to provide semantic awareness and provide contextually meaningful answers to queries. If it were ever to reach realization, it is unlikely that the semantic web would be any less subject to the frames of its inventors and custodians. Will Web 3.0 be a reality? That's an open question. As long as it remains so, then it fuels our suspense about the future of the Internet.

Irrespective of the way answers are framed by particular search engines or the character of Q&A sites, I think the medium promotes the mood of inquiry, of questioning, of curiosity and suspense. Ubiquitous digital media are media of suspense. Behind every question is another question about the future. What will I do with the information, what difference does it make, what will happen next, and when: the components of suspense.

Online Secrets

I've referred to mystery a few times, particularly in relation to curiosity in chapter 3. To raise questions also invokes mystery, and mystery fuels suspense. News reports present headlines such as: "Driver's Mystery Death," "Search for Mystery Naked Reveler," and "Arrest as Cops Probe Mystery Death."[38] Mystery also sells. In the margins of various websites I see so-called clickbait: "5 foods you must not eat" and "Your plastic surgeon will hate you for reading this." If it's alluding to an old remedy that has so far escaped medical science, then all the better: "Lose belly fat with this 1 weird old tip." As for suspense, the sense of mystery is not necessarily diminished when we become aware of or disappointed by its resolution. Reliving, reviewing, and recalling the suspense and the outcome are part of the narrative experience.

Where else is mystery online? I referred to "dark media" in chapter 5. It's also called the "dark web."[39] A display called *Life Online* at the UK's National Media Museum features a chest of drawers, inviting the curious to see what's inside. It's a family venue, so everything is coded for children to consume. In one of the pull-out drawers, we discover the dark web: "Search engines only really search the top layer of the Internet. Underneath the surface lies a space known as the 'dark web.' It does not appear in search engine results. A place to trade illegal pornography, criminal contacts, terrorist plots and viruses in complete anonymity, the dark web requires special software to review it."[40] The family-friendly graphic that accompanies this text shows spider-like web crawlers on the surface of the ground. We see a "No Entry" sign connected to a network of underground pipes. There's a skull and crossbones, a cartoon-style bomb, a head shrouded in a balaclava with the eyes cut out, and three pink Xs, contemporary tokens of illegality, threat, and hiddenness.

Knowing that something is hidden makes some of us all the more curious to find it. A sense of mystery invokes curiosity. As for questioning, it's a useful tool for educators, particularly through storytelling.[41] If deployed successfully, mystery makes the ordinary appear important and can enhance the authority of those who guard the secrets or who hold the key to the rational explanation of mysteries. Mystery can also serve as a mask to occlude the fact that there really is nothing there, or very little. At its worse, the invocation of mystery is a ruse to conceal ignorance and vacuity, and this is not confined to the Internet. This is one of the main charges employed by intellectual movements to discredit one another.[42] For example, the logician Rudolf Carnap (1891–1970) identified the difficult propositions and questions advanced by Martin Heidegger as "pseudo-statements," and therefore "meaningless."[43] Any intellectual ideas that come across as somehow difficult are easily bracketed with the mystical. The writings of Heidegger provide a case in point.[44] Of course, for some of us that makes his writing even more alluring.

As I explore in *Technoromanticism*, the graphic World Wide Web is a medium made for mystery, and in its early days mystery subcultures were among the first to see its potential as a forum for expression.[45] There are many so-called "mystery" traditions and cults with their proponents identified as "mystics." Christian, Jewish, and Arabic mysticism is said to have influenced thinking in the later Middle Ages and the Renaissance, and such influences persist to this day. So-called Eastern mysticism is a hallmark of exoticism and otherness.[46] Mysticism suggests opacity and elitism. The analytic philosopher John Hospers argues that the claims of mysticism have "no justification" and are therefore ultimately "illegitimate."[47] Mysticism links what today we might readily dismiss as "charlatanism," lumped in with pseudoscience, and contemporary New Age speculations. It may even refer simply to a contemplative attitude. Even genuinely radical thinking and radical strands within mainstream philosophy and theology are labeled as "secular mysticism."[48] Contrary to diminishing the appeal of mystery, such criticism seems only to enhance it. Who wants a strictly transparent and logical world anyway? Suspense keeps us interested, and mystery provides plenty of suspense: What will be revealed?

According to scholar of Medieval studies Stanton Lindon, in contrast to scientific explanation, "alchemical discourse is known above all for its obscurity, its deliberate attempts to both reveal and conceal, and—to this end—its extravagant use of abstraction, allegory and analogy, and idiosyncratic displays of bizarrely fanciful images, symbols, and riddles."[49] Alchemical discourse has both an esoteric (unintelligible except to the initiated) and exoteric (a doctrine as presented by the initiates to the external public) aspect. This is also hermetic discourse, secretive and sealed off from dispute.[50]

Hermeticism (other than as a thread in a compelling narrative) of course runs entirely counter to the overt messages of mainstream intellectual developments in philosophy, religion, politics, science, and the arts (at least since the Enlightenment), not to mention the study of hermeneutics (interpretation). There's no room for hidden wisdom in an open and democratic Internet-savvy society that seeks liberty, equality, fraternity, community, and openness to the power of explanation. Fanatical fundamentalism is a subspecies of the hermetic. It purveys the concept of an original and authoritative truth, albeit hidden except to those in the know. This is antithetical to the apparent ethos of the Internet, which champions open-source software, open hardware, and crowd sourcing. However, there's still something appealing about mystery as a vehicle for keeping us in suspense.

In spite of its putative openness, the Internet is already permeated by occult mysteries, though not necessarily delivered in all seriousness. Cultural theorist Stephen O'Leary draws attention to the textual nature of Internet communication and therefore to the amplification of the power of language to invoke all manner of realities, including occult deities, objects, and rituals. He describes many of these emerging online occult and Neopagan traditions as irreverent, ludic, and playful, in that "they revel in pastiche and parody, and they make few (if any) cognitive demands upon the participants," leading inevitably to a kind of commodification of beliefs.[51]

To me, the main characteristic of putative mystical, alchemical, and hermetic sources is that they turn our dependence on logic as an arbiter of reason into a problem. They play with impossibilities and worry over the logical excluded middle: that if A is not B, then A cannot also be B. They develop their impetus from an apparent contradiction or paradox. In a way, there's nothing mystical about that. In light of so much twentieth-century thought, contradiction, paradox, discontinuity, and indeterminacy are basically mainstream, not least for artists and designers who are used to the creative potential of the less than obvious, the peculiar in the ordinary, the difficult, and the paradoxical. In mystery resides an enthusiasm to find out, to know more, to be in suspense, further enhanced when the answers to questions, the resolution to the mysteries, don't come immediately. Matters are on hold. There's a delay.

Delayed Gratification

Withholding information is a technique in fiction to enhance suspense.[52] This element of suspense provides insights into another problem that critics load onto life online, that of addiction. Addicts of online content, game play, shopping, and social media seem unable to wait, even though it's in their own interest to hold fire, to regulate the pleasure, to delay gratification. I'll conclude this chapter by situating so-called Internet addiction within the scenario of delayed gratification.

I've already hinted at the element of delay. The most suspenseful moment in the film *Vertigo* is in the opening scene, in which Scottie hangs by his fingertips, impossibly, from the flimsy guttering. How will he be delivered to safety? Hitchcock doesn't provide an answer. The next scene we see is Scottie in an apartment, on crutches and recovering from the trauma, but we are spared the mechanics of his recovery from his impossible gutter-hanging ordeal. The suspense of the cliffhanging moment is circumvented or delayed indefinitely. The word "suspense" derives from the Latin *suspensum*, to hang or suspend. Like a shirt hanging in the closet, a piñata hanging from a branch, or the sword of Damocles hung over the king's throne by a horse's hair, it's a temporary condition, the significance of which resides in the eventual termination of that condition: the shirt is worn, the booty is retrieved, or the sword falls. It's a position of tension, danger, and uncertainty. Hanging over some peril, as in the film *Vertigo*, provides both a potent metaphor and an illustration of the circumstances of suspense.

According to literary theorist Jacek Dabala, suspense is "a narrative device consisting in delaying the element which is expected by the audience in a state of tension and apprehension."[53] He relates this delay to the intensification of menace. The anticipated event assumes a strange or alien bearing. Having to wait for some event gives scope for the imagination to concoct all manner of variation on the projected scenario. He identifies words related to suspense, such as "delay, expectation, tension, apprehension, intensification, strangeness, menace."[54] As David Lodge asserts, suspense relies on "delaying the answers."[55] To recall yet another encounter with suspense, and suspension, Lodge describes a novel by Thomas Hardy (1840–1928), *A Pair of Blue Eyes*, in which a man, Henry Knight, falls from the edge of a cliff as he tries to rescue his hat. Henry slips and ends up suspended by his fingers on the cliff edge. They are a long way from anywhere, and Elfride, his female companion, has to affect a rescue. Rather than immediately describe such a rescue, Hardy explains how Henry contemplates the geological details of the cliff face he is suspended against, as well as his own mortality. It's several pages before the reader's concern about Henry's welfare, rescue, or death is addressed. Lodge, himself a writer of humorous fiction, teases his readers by compounding the suspense of Hardy's novel. Lodge is not going to tell us how or whether Henry is rescued, but the attempt involves Elfride "taking off all her clothes."[56]

Suspense is a matter of delayed gratification. News reports have drawn attention to the problem of children playing video games and running up huge debts on their parents' credit cards.[57] Neither parent nor child realized that the modest one-off cost of the game is supplemented by subsequent purchases of game components. There's an issue here of game publishers unfairly, though perhaps inadvertently, benefiting from the tendency among small children to go for the immediate gain without thinking long-term. According to a study on Internet addiction by Bryan Saville and his colleagues, "One hallmark of addictive behavior is the tendency toward impulsivity, or the inability to delay gratification even when doing so may produce more positive long-term outcomes."[58]

Psychologists Janet Metcalfe and Walter Mischel draw attention to a simple experimental procedure that tests for addictive tendencies in children and reveals something about the human response to delayed gratification. They investigate the length of time a preschooler is prepared to wait for a food treat.[59] When offered one or two marshmallows, will the child be prepared to wait for a few minutes and be rewarded with two marshmallows, or impatiently go for the immediate option, which the child indicates by ringing a bell, and be rewarded with just a single marshmallow? The experimenter makes the child aware of the consequences of the immediate response versus having to wait. Experimenters vary the protocol with different timings and conditions during the wait. Most children prefer to wait and receive the better outcome (two marshmallows), but will eventually reach some time limit to that period of waiting. What the child does or is encouraged to think about during the wait is also of interest and influences the outcome. Apparently, how the preschooler responds to such tests turns out to be "predictive of cognitive and social outcomes decades later, including Scholastic Aptitude Test (SAT) scores."[60]

Presumably, the experiment works best with preschoolers, before they're of an age at which they develop sophisticated game-playing tactics or try and second-guess the experimenter. Metcalfe and Mischel explain the cognitive process in terms of brain function. There is a "hot system," in which each of us is primed for immediate response. The "cool system" involves reflection and belongs more to the conscious weighing of options, thinking of long-term benefits, and planning. These two systems engage two separate parts of the brain: The amygdala is the more primitive "hot" part of the brain, and the hippocampus is the "cooler" part that deals with problem solving. In Freud's terminology, the waiting game is a battle between the pressure for immediate gratification from the id, our animal nature, versus the more considered deliberations of the ego.[61]

Of particular interest are the various tactics the experimenters deploy to extend the period of the wait. One tactic involves obscuring or ignoring the stimulus, such as covering over or otherwise hiding the reward (the marshmallows) so that the children can't see the reward until they receive it or manage of their own volition to think of something other than the reward. Distraction involves giving the child something to play with to divert her from thinking about the reward. This allows the child to wait longer. Reframing involves changing the meaning of the stimulus, for example by presenting the child with a picture of a marshmallow rather than expose the child to an actual marshmallow sitting on a plate and ready to be eaten. Pictorial representations of the reward apparently engender a more reflective, cooler mode of engagement with the situation: "As one child put it, you can't eat the picture."[62] Seeing a picture is sufficient to remind the child of the promise and yet distant enough to suppress the hot response of making a grab for it.

In some cases, we expectant consumers might want to reduce expectation, to stop looking forward to something, to lessen the suspense for one particular target and increase it for something else. This is a bit like the condition of Henry in the Tomas Hardy novel. Think about the rock face rather than the peril, or at least get the reader to think that way. Distraction provides a method of delaying gratification. In the case of online shopping addiction or succumbing to the many distractions of the Internet, it might be a case of focusing on a picture of a long-term acquisition or life goal (saving for a mortgage) rather than short-term pleasures (buying a jet ski, a new pair of shoes, or the latest game download).

According to Metcalfe and Mischel's theories, instantaneity of online transactions would seem to activate the hot system, especially if the reward is delivered instantly, such as occurs with music downloads, movies, e-books, apps, games, and game elements, and especially if you are already sampling the reward for free, as in the case of free thirty-day software trials, music samples, and book excerpts (e.g., Amazon's "Look Inside"). Where there's a delivery time involved and the book, the DVD, the shoes, or the groceries have to be delivered to your door, then this abstraction provides cause for reflection, activating the cool system. It's not just that you have to wait but that the potential purchaser is making his or her assessment on the basis of a representational abstraction of the goods, such as pictures and descriptions on a screen. You are less inclined to act in the heat of the moment and make a grab for it. After all, online descriptions of the goods are not the goods, and you can't eat pixels.

Summary

I hope I've shown that ubiquitous digital media are the media of suspense. Digital industries encourage certain expectations, in terms of a succession of developments and improvements. This applies to hardware, software, and content. If we examine the media content purveyed by such digital networks and apparatuses, then the narrative device of suspense comes into play. Suspense is a genre of narrative media, be they games, films, novels, documentaries, or interactive apps, and educational practices commonly enlist suspense to maintain audience interest. The components of suspense include hope and anticipation, of course, but also repetition; and ubiquitous digital media are tools of repetition. We media consumers apparently depend less now on programs and schedules, and digital media supports the repeated viewing and listening of content through downloads, pay-per-view, catch-up, and on-demand services. Suspense draws on repetition, which heightens expectations. Plot lines often induce suspense by suggesting a succession or serialization of events. The same thing that happened to one character could happen to another protagonist, and this contributes to the feeling of suspense.

Of course, repetition does not imply exact duplication. Sequences of events entail variation, so there's uncertainty about what will happen next. I touched briefly on the nature of interpretation, which involves approaching any narrative with a set of expectations that then undergo subsequent revision and renewal. This is what it is to be open to new experiences. I examined the issue of questioning as a component of suspense and the workings of mystery. Digital media is a questioning medium, evidenced by search engines and question and answer sites. It's also imbued with mystery, as people trade in rumor, conspiracy theories, and the occult. It's also a medium of delay. Ubiquitous media provide so much promise, but after all we often have to wait for whatever is on offer. In this light, I think that as with any technology, ubiquitous digital media distort or inflect the various fields of human expectation. This influence applies not only to the construction of narratives as content but also to narratives about the way the technology develops.

I've also shown that mood is a frame of mind. We are primed with structured expectations. At our best, we are in the mood for whatever comes our way. Insofar as suspense presents as a mood, there's evidence that ubiquitous digital media modulate that mood condition. They also provide a major contemporary means for the circulation and perpetuation of suspense and hence of mood. As I emphasized in the case of melancholy, the processing of moods has the character of a journey. We enter and leave mood conditions. This raises the issue of the general character and impact of mood: moods are not static. They operate through context and contrasts. Many of the mysteries of mood are resolved if we think of mood transitions and metamoods.

Coda: What's Wrong with the Future?

The book *The New Digital Age* by Google's executive chairman Eric Schmidt and director of Google Ideas Jared Cohen was published in 2013.[63] I read the Kindle edition. As with other books of this genre, there's much we've read before, but it's of interest who is saying it. Google is after all a major player in the "new digital age," and it's good to access the mindset of this particular global brand. According to the book, there are now two civilizations: the physical and the virtual. The latter is still in formation, but it holds promise of being even better than the former. For example, developments in computer graphics and virtual reality "will make the online experience as real as real life, or perhaps even better."[64] There are other improvements in the pipeline. Ever smarter smartphones will provide "insurance against forgetfulness, you will have access to an entire world of ideas."[65] We'll have social robots, thought-controlled motion technology, fairer competition for jobs, new levels of collaboration, and safer roads.

In case you didn't already know it, the book reminds the reader that: "we are facing a brave new world, the most fast-paced and exciting period in human history. We'll experience more change at a quicker rate than any previous generation, and this change, driven in part by the devices on our own hands, will be more personal and participatory than we can even imagine."[66] I think I've read that before. *The New Digital Age* delivers that upbeat technodeterminist utopian futurizing we've come to enjoy, or at least expect, in digital pop publishing.

Data Power

It's easy to get carried away with the power of data. Here's something of interest to designers: apparently, advances in scanning technology will mean that if monuments of world-heritage status are destroyed, as happened when the Taliban dynamited the Bamiyan Buddhas, then they can be restored or replaced. Such monuments "will have been scanned with sophisticated technology that preserves every nook and cranny in virtual memory, allowing them to be rebuilt later by means of 3-D printers, or even projected as a hologram."[67]

Such is the authors' belief in data—not only that it's possible to capture, process, and deploy restorative digital data of building-scaled artifacts in such immaculate detail, but that such data reconstruction constitutes some kind of acceptable substitute for the original. I wonder if the repeated digital restoration of the physical world makes it somehow even more disposable. If artifacts are easier to renew, then you can be more cavalier about their physical preservation. Eventually, the world is replaced by a kind of simulacrum, at least in people's minds. Technology does exhibit this kind of escalating effect in the pages of the book, especially as Schmidt and Cohen turn to statehood, politics, terrorism, and warfare, including cyberwars. I think this is the sober pivot point of the book's narrative.

The book draws attention to technologies such as drones, robotic unmanned aerial vehicles (UAVs). It's a melancholy story and projects a sad future, as countries, rogue states, rebels, and drug cartels send automated military and civilian robots to seek out enemies and do battle with one another. There's also the prospect of "loose drones" falling into the wrong hands or running amok, and decoy UAVs filled with false information and bogus technological components to confound the enemy if captured.[68]

Dreadful Evil

It seems that networked technology "is a source for tremendous good and potentially dreadful evil, and we're only just beginning to witness its impact on the world stage."[69] Evil threads its way through much of the book. It's clear who the enemy is: dictatorships, repressive regimes, failed states, criminal syndicates, cartels, pirates, kidnappers, and rogue individuals. Democracy comes out as the hero of the story. Considering the book's authors, it's no surprise that they don't have in their sights multinationals, avaricious tax-evading global corporations, the fraught finance and banking sector, exploiters of cheap offshore labor, rampant consumerism, materialism, hegemony, or global capital. There's little sense conveyed in the book of any kind of political or collective complicity in the world's problems or those of its future. It's as if no one had ever heard of Theodor Adorno, Herbert Marcuse, Jean Baudrillard, Gilles Deleuze, or even Karl Marx, or read any critical social science or cultural theory. Perhaps that's what's wrong with the future.

This coda prompted the following comments when posted online:

Comment 1: Nice to see not everyone is blown away by rhetoric.

Comment 2: Bang on the money. And talking of money, imagine how valuable "preserved" laser scans will be when the real crumbles, burns, or becomes irrelevant.

Some people think that computers come to our aid in defeating ignorance, in providing correct information, not only to tell us what we don't know, but also to prompt us when we get our facts wrong. According to Google's CEO Eric Schmidt and Jared Cohen, Director of Google Ideas, "By 2025, the majority of the world's population will, in one generation, have gone from having virtually no access to unfiltered information to accessing all the world's information through a device that fits in the palm of the hand."[1] That looks like a double promise: most people and all information, including what's currently offline. Web 2.0 invites everyone to contribute and edit information in crowdsourced forums such as Wikipedia, Q&A forums, and social networks. Thanks to ubiquitous, networked mobile devices, information is available at our fingertips.

On the other hand, this rich information source is prone to corruption. Schmidt and Cohen refer to the threats of cyber-attacks and misinformation campaigns, not just to cover tracks. Cybercriminals attack digital networks, systems, and installations, but also conceal their complicity in the crime. Shrewd criminals who instigate a cyber-attack on data repositories are often able to obscure who they are or give the impression that the source of the attack resides elsewhere.[2] Cybercrime gets complicated and trades in ignorance. Press reports of cybercrimes are becoming as difficult to follow as the afflictions and fortunes of financial markets.[3] Understanding cybercrime seems to require specialized knowledge that aims at a moving target.

Is ignorance a mood, an epistemic state, or a moral condition? Ignorance is not simply an absence of information. It includes the condition of thinking that you know something when you don't. It's a symptom of the false certainties that come with some forms of fundamentalism, and that can pervade a group. It's the opposite of curiosity. It's indifference to information that's new, different, or unexpected. It's useful to think of ignorance as a mood. As every educator knows, ignorance is not overcome simply by providing information, more of it, or information of the right kind. The teacher and the class have to do work in mood shifting, in coaxing themselves into a receptive, curious disposition.

Neither is ignorance always a negative: "Where ignorance is bliss, 'Tis folly to be wise," wrote Thomas Gray (1716–1771) in his "Ode on a Distant Prospect of Eton College."[4] As well as not knowing what might befall (war in this case), ignorance is a cheerful lack of care. You can be kindly to everyone if you don't know what they are up to. That's what it is to be blissfully unaware, blithely ignorant, in a blessed state, and innocent. Search YouTube for meditation routines that encourage you to clear your mind, to assume a state of mind unencumbered by facts and information. Ignorance soothes stress and makes us more receptive to new knowledge. In his book *The Ignorant Schoolmaster*, the philosopher Jacques Rancière shows that a teacher can deliver on a subject he doesn't know anything about by liberating his students so that they are responsible for their own learning.[5] Ignorance is a state of mind, an attitude, an orientation, a mood in its positive and negative aspects.

False memories are also a kind of ignorance, or at least a symptom of ignorance of the negative kind. Recollections recede into a haze, and it's also easy even to forget that you've forgotten. Sometimes "there are things we do not know we don't know."[6] That's also ignorance. If you don't care about your ignorance, then that's a form of apathy or indifference, related moods. A study of ignorance, like curiosity (chapter 3), provides access to apathy, a particularly acquiescent frame of mind.

False Memories

False memories are a good place to start in thinking about ignorance online. Society, the mass media, and the law place great store on eyewitness accounts, such as the reports of victims of domestic and sexual abuse where there are no corroborating third-party witnesses. Apparently, people of violent intent rely on this paucity of witnesses: "It's your word against mine." False memories also become significant politically. George W. Bush reported that he was shocked at the sight of the first plane hitting the World Trade Center. It seems that there was no such footage available at the time he said this, and the chronology of events on that fateful day indicates that there was no time during which he could have seen such a video, even if it existed. It was as if Bush had access to some secret footage that he was concealing from the public. More significantly, some conspiracy theorists thought Bush must have known about the attacks in advance and that cameras were set up to record them. Analysts now insist that Bush was more than likely to have suffered from a "false memory."[7] It's easy enough to get in a muddle about events, especially when our recollections of significant incidents are colored by reports from the mass media, we are speaking off the cuff, in a positive and loquacious mood, and prone to getting carried away by our own rhetoric. However, false memories are not all bad. False memories are indicators of the human capacity for imagining, which I'll demonstrate relates to mood and to ubiquitous digital media.

Vivid Imagination

Considering the importance of eyewitness accounts, it's important to know about the peculiarities of recollection. I referred to memory in chapter 6. To test the operations of remembering, experimenters have succeeded in planting false memories in human interviewees, as a mild kind of "brainwashing." With the right prompting, you can get someone to recall that they concluded their day at Disneyland by shaking hands with someone dressed in a Bugs Bunny costume. Fake posters help, showing the Disney branding and Magic Kingdom promotional material, but with the impossible addition of the rogue Warner Bros. cartoon character.[8] Through similar techniques, experimenters can induce eyewitnesses to falsely recall the details of when the punch bowl got spilt at a wedding, even though it didn't,[9] or that a thief in a shop stole a screwdriver, when in fact the CCTV record shows a wrench being lifted.[10] Unscrupulous counselors can persuade clients that they remember something contrary to the client's initial recollection, and can even induce detailed recollections of so-called past lives or of alien abductions.[11] Any of us can also make false recollections without prompting: that we closed the windows before going out for the day, sent grandma a birthday card, or cc'd the boss in that email. Recollections are populated by misplaced certainties.

Everyone is prone to false memories, because everyone has the capacity to invent and to imagine. Unintended false recollections arise because of human creativity. Experimental psychologists studying memory have debated whether memory involves reproducing or reconstructing events in our minds, but most scholars now think that "all remembering is constructive in nature," as summarized in seminal research by H. Roediger and K. McDermott.[12] In other words, recollection is an act of the imagination.

Conversely, a vivid imagination is inevitably the enemy of factual accuracy. An often-quoted passage from Mark Twain's autobiography indicates something of the ambiguity between recollection and invention: "When I was younger, I could remember anything, whether it had happened or not; but my faculties are decaying now and soon I shall be so that I cannot remember any but the things that never happened."[13] As well as providing an astute observation about memory and imagination, this is actually a slight misquote, and an improvement on the original, that further brings to light the flaws in anthologies of quotations and with online information sources. As an unregulated, crowdsourced medium, the Internet is populated by apparently faulty recollections and misinformation. As I explored in chapter 6, to remember is to invent, together. Crowdsourced online creativity is not dissimilar to the power of the crowd to remember and misremember. It seems that occasional faulty recollection is the price we pay for creativity and sociability.

It appears that the mood you are in also affects recall. As I explored in chapter 1, positive moods enhance our ability to broaden our outlook, to take a bigger view, and to see connections. In technical terms, "positive moods encourage relational processing," according to experimental psychologists Justin Storbeck and Gerald Clorean.[14] The cost of this ability to make connections is that our imaginations kick in and we start to recall things that didn't happen. Storbeck and Clorean demonstrate this with an interesting and simple test.[15] They present human participants with a list of words, such as *bed, dream, blanket,* and *awake.* After a time, they ask the participants to recall the list, perhaps prompted by a set of candidate words to choose from. It's likely that many people will think that the word *sleep* was in the original list. (I've tried this informally with colleagues, and it seems to work in some cases.) "Sleep" wasn't present but is suggested very powerfully by the combination of words in the original list. *Sleep* is here a prototype; it's suggested powerfully by the other words in the list and is a key exemplar around which the other words seem to orbit.[16]

The effect works better if the participants are in a positive mood. If they are in a negative mood state, then they are less likely to make the connection to this invisible key word, *sleep.* According to Storbeck and Clorean, negative mood states suppress the capacity to make connections. Thus, sad or anxious participants are less likely to make this misrecollection. Of course, their experimental studies involved large numbers of subjects and control measures, with different word lists, including random lists. Apparently, the mood of the participants didn't affect their recollection of the *correct* words, just the frequency with which the rogue word, *sleep* (the key), was misrecalled. The experimenters induced the mood states by having the participants listen to music calculated to induce a happy or sad mood state, and they filtered out the results from those participants whose mood was apparently unaffected by the music.[17]

It seems that the false memory effect is even more pronounced when there's a story, a context, and threads of association and meaning, rather than just word lists. Studies by Roediger and McDermott confirm that false memories can arise even when participants are aware of the false memory phenomenon, as is the case when the participants are psychology students. Knowledgeable psychology students are still prone to false memories when they are participants in the studies.[18] Such experiments seem constrained and artificial, but there's good reason to believe that the false memory phenomenon will be even more pronounced outside the lab: "When less of a premium is placed on accurate remembering, and when people know that their accuracy in recollecting cannot be verified, they may even be more easily led to remember events that never happened than they are in the lab."[19] That's likely to be the case in the world of anecdote and opinion that is the domain of Twitter, unmoderated blogging, and citizen journalism. Rumors and half-truths circulate online, where there's little premium set on verification.

Memory researcher Elizabeth Loftus adds that false memories can be compounded when witnesses to an event are asked leading questions—that is, when there's an easy answer resident in the question: Did you see the thief steal the screwdriver? The suggestion plants an image in the mind of the witnesses that skews their response. False memories can also occur when witnesses consult with one another (one may be intent on misleading the others) or if witnesses are subjected to techniques to deliberately encourage misinformation (as in these memory experiments). Exposure to media coverage can also influence the witness's recollection.

All memories are subject to contamination by external sources: "Misinformation can enter consciousness and can cause contamination of memory."[20] However, people in a negative mood state are more likely to find tasks difficult and to have less confidence in their own cognitive abilities and goals. If an office worker thinks a task is difficult, then she will exercise greater care and focus on the more specific aspects of the task.[21] According to this theory, she'll try harder and remember better.

Mental Agility

On the other hand, being in a positive mood encourages mental agility and greater confidence, tending toward overconfidence. It seems that positively disposed and flexible memories offer advantages to the human species. This means that people are open to correction and consensus, which also supports solidarity and the establishment of community. Consider the case of the happy and contented dinner guest, lulled through the pleasant company, background music, or alcohol into flights of anecdotal invention about an enjoyable holiday, only to be informed later of an alternative, less-exaggerated account of the events: the bargain meal wasn't really that cheap, the view was mediocre, and the guide a bit cloying. Then, there's the self-satisfied teacher in front of eager and compliant students who finds herself able to answer any question and deliver facts and insight with supreme confidence, only to discover later that she made a substantial error: that Vanevar Bush invented the World Wide Web, that the first portable stereos were mobile phones, or that Shakespeare wrote a play about Magna Carta.[22] The risk is that such voluble exaggerations from "the ignorant schoolmaster" can generate misleading, if not false, memories and lead people astray, if not into error. On the other hand, being relaxed and positive carries the benefit that we tell each other colorful and memorable stories. Storytelling is an excellent means of communication and of establishing group identity, empathy, and positive mood states. Stories are the stuff of myth and culture, and of history.

Given that false memories are endemic to the human condition, and in a way signs of positive mood states, it's worth reviewing the story of this ignorance over time. The risk is that this turns out to be a false history, but that leads to the question: What is history? Ubiquitous digital media has a history, is the product of history, and is a medium for circulating many histories.

A History of Ignorance

False memories and ignorance are complicit in storytelling and sociability. People can also enlist ignorance as a tactic in the way they present themselves in public. It's sometimes to the polite employee's benefit to be ignorant or to pretend to be ignorant about certain particularities. Having certain facts at his disposal can indicate a kind of knowledge and familiarity, social status, or background. It's bad form to be a know-it-all in any case, but in some contexts the professional doesn't really want others to know that she can name all the main characters in *Game of Thrones*, where you can buy bootlegged Blu-ray disks, the names of porn stars, or the rules of Dungeons and Dragons.

Here's an example of contrived ignorance about history from British politics. Most British people know that *Magna Carta* is a significant document from the thirteenth century according rights to citizens (and that we don't call it "the" *Magna Carta*). On his visit to the United States, Prime Minister David Cameron was asked on a late-night TV program if he knew what the Latin words *Magna Carta* meant in English. He claimed he didn't know and had to bluff.[23] On the subject of the prime minister's apparent lapse, another British politician subsequently claimed that the prime minister was feigning ignorance so as not to appear too comfortable with Latin, which would draw attention to his credentials as a member of the British establishment, someone educated at the elite British school of Eton.[24] It seems that carefully contrived ignorance can help politicians to appear ordinary.

Of course, getting historical facts wrong is a mainstay of British class humor. There's the joke uttered by the British comedian Tony Hancock, who plays a desperately class-conscious dupe trying to assert his scholarly credentials in a jury meeting: "Does Magna Carta mean nothing to you? Did she die in vain?"[25]

As it happens, Magna Carta was formulated to curb the arbitrary will of tyrannical kings and as such served as a prototype for the declarations and constitutions of the Enlightenment that followed many years later. It contains the seeds of what we regard today as liberty and makes reference to the eradication of ignorance. It says that judges and other officials must at least know the law and that no one can be put on trial without credible witnesses (*testibus fidelibus*). The idea of sound evidence lurks within the text. Magna Carta is available online, complete with histories, annotations, and the "credible witness" of over six million mentions on web pages (according to a Google search). As long as you're able to get online, it's easy to feign knowledge—and even to pretend to know some Latin. Thanks to Google Translate, we all now know Latin, Farsi, and Telugu!

As long as you are at a keyboard and online, it's getting harder to pretend ignorance, let alone feign knowledge. By that I mean that unless you are extemporizing and away from a computer, it's hard *not* to know your facts, and it's hard to pretend you don't know. Ignorance is barely an excuse. In the age of the Internet, ignorance becomes something of an empty signifier, were it not that facts don't really constitute knowledge, that ignorance actually signals invention, and ignorance can be a virtue.

We heirs to the Enlightenment think that science increases knowledge and decreases ignorance. That's the usual narrative of technological, scientific, and social progress, of steady increase, with occasional spurts and shifts in frames of reference, sometimes referred to as paradigm shifts.[26] As any philosopher of science will say, science builds on skepticism and its increase as much as the increase in knowledge.

A history of ignorance has yet to be written.[27] It might end with the smartphone, but it would begin by including something about philosophical skepticism. Skeptics question constantly and claim rhetorical superiority by unsettling their adversaries. Skepticism is a felony of which the philosopher Plato (428–427 BC) accused his opponents but in fact practiced himself. To claim that no one can ever know the truth and to unsettle any claims to know the truth are time-honored rhetorical strategies. Ignorance and knowledge of the possibility of ultimate ignorance keep us humble, if not attentive. Skepticism constitutes a persistent intellectual divide. There are those who assert the possibility and benefits of having all the world's information in the palm of your hand,[28] and the skeptics led by Freidrich Nietzsche, Martin Heidegger, and their followers, who resist the idea of a complete world picture.[29] Skepticism offers a palliative to the conceits of the information age.

Things That Think
Such a history of ignorance would also include the idea that things (*res* in Latin) outside of human subjectivity are incapable of thinking. People have knowledge, but the world out there is bereft of thought. Inert, nonsentient objects are ignorant. René Descartes (1596–1615) began his famous philosophical journey with the proposition that the only truth of which he could be certain was his own doubt. What is it that doubts, or thinks doubtfully? His answer was the *thinking thing* (*res cogitans*), *the self*, the entity indulging these skeptical questions.[30] Much reflection on identity and the

importance of online identity[31] stems from Descartes's reflections about the self. Some years after Descartes, Immanuel Kant (1724–1804) wrote about "things in themselves," independently of how we sense them.[32] This is the *noumena*, which turns out to be unknowable—a substrate of unknowable reality, the way things really are, according to some interpreters of Kant. For Descartes, the world is divided into the thinking *thing* and the world outside it, the extended *thing* (*res extensa*). On the other hand, Kant emphasized *things* in themselves. Therefore, there's a history to thinking about *things* that eventually comes into collision with the so-called Internet of *Things*, a series of research and development initiatives that pursue "distributed intelligence for smart objects."[33] The world is to become populated with *things* that think and communicate with one another, constituting a kind of "ambient intelligence." Advocates of the Internet of Things propose that thinking is not constrained to human beings but can move into the extended world (*res extensa*), dislodging even the putative inert ignorance of inanimate objects.

Keeping Silent

Then, there are the Agnostics, a term coined by Thomas Huxley (1825–1895) to describe his position on religion. Huxley defined agnosticism thus: "It is wrong for a man to say that he is certain of the objective truth of any proposition unless he can produce evidence which logically justifies that certainty."[34] You really cannot know if God exists.[35] More recently, the twentieth-century logical positivists observed that people make certain assertions about God, spirit, and deep and invisible underlying truths that are not only unsupportable but meaningless, because there is no way of verifying their truth or falsity. The metaphysical is thus beyond reason and therefore unreasonable, and we can't discuss it sensibly. In keeping with this view, Ludwig Wittgenstein (1889–1951) said at the end of his *Tractatus*, "That about which we cannot speak we must remain silent."[36] Elsewhere, I've reviewed the influence of logical positivism on digital culture.[37] It's a movement that placed logic and calculation at the center of human reason, diminishing the role of emotion and of personal, unverifiable conjecture. In a way, it's treating the mind as a computer. Agnosticism and logical positivism have their places in the history of ignorance. They assert that there are things we really cannot know, or at least, things it makes no sense to speak about.[38]

Lack of Evidence

A history of ignorance ought to include something about evidence. On a practical note, Thomas Huxley made a reference to the condition recognized in Scottish law in which the judge has to pronounce that a verdict of guilt or innocence is not possible. There's insufficient evidence to convict the accused, but there's sufficient doubt about the accused's innocence to pronounce the verdict of "not proven." This is a verdict that carries certain consequences, including the possibility that the case can be reopened at a later date if more evidence comes to light.[39] According to Huxley, "A verdict of 'not proven' is undoubtedly unsatisfactory and essentially provisional, so far forth as the subject of the trial is capable of being dealt with by due process of reason."[40] Such legal frameworks accommodate ignorance on the part of investigators and jurors.

The concept of a provisional verdict suggests a delay or deferral of understanding and truth. Jacques Derrida (1930–2004) developed this form of "ignorance" in his play on the idea of *difference*, which looks a bit like *deferral* in French, so he invents the word *différance*.[41] In fact, a documentary of Derrida's later life includes an apposite anecdote.[42] Derrida's mother overheard a conversation between Derrida and his admirers about his interesting and infamous formulation of the concept of différance. She was taken aback: "You mean you spelt *difference* with an *a*!?" as if this master of linguistic invention was incapable of correct spelling. This is an anecdote about a mother overwhelmed by the need to keep up appearances who remains ignorant of a son's achievements. Derrida's philosophy of the endless referentiality of meaning and the role of paradox and contradiction in human understanding has informed concepts in digital culture from hypertext[43] to critiques of logical positivism.[44]

Fanatical Fundamentalism

A history of ignorance would account for contemporary world events, for which ignorance and fanatical fundamentalism are linked and included as key components.[45] It seems that ignorance can be a force for positive intellectual development, but we still need a term for the bad kind of ignorance that none of Magna Carta's descendants could comfortably endorse, ignorance of the kind many want to ascribe to militant fundamentalists, terrorists, and preachers of hatred, such as the rogue cleric Abu Hamza arrested on terrorism charges in 2004 and haunting the US and UK legal systems and press until his conviction in 2015. Sociologist Antony Giddens says that fundamentalism "has no time for ambiguity, multiple interpretation or multiple identity—it is a refusal of dialogue in a world whose peace and continuity depend on it."[46] We would have to qualify the fundamentalist kind of ignorance. The term "extremely prejudiced" is helpful, but hermeneutical scholars point out that the ability to prejudge is vital before we can develop any kind of understanding or evaluation of anything: a text, a law, a legal case, a work of art. For the bad kind of prejudice, think of the hermeneutical investigation that stops with a prejudgment and is closed to revision, challenge, and renewal, as if all is now decided and beyond dispute. That's the bad kind of ignorance. The philosopher Richard Bernstein affirms, "To risk and test our prejudices is a constant task (not a final achievement)."[47] In this light, ignorance and self-doubt are preferable to blind certainty.

The idea that false memories often emerge as key terms or prototypes also supports the primacy of anticipation, as I outlined in chapter 8 and as developed by hermeneutical scholars. We interpreting human beings are ever expectant. Expectations need to be tested in the situation. In this light, false memories are untested expectations. They are recollections that go unexamined. A history of ignorance would have to include all of these considerations.

From a hermeneutical perspective, the problem is how to deal not with those people who don't know very much, but with those who don't want to know more—those who seem incapable of surrendering to curiosity or who have already circumscribed what they are prepared to be curious about: the intellectually apathetic. Perhaps that's the kind of ignorance that requires our attention—or sympathy. The bad kind of online ignorance is less about misinformation and more about the persistence of intellectual apathy, the palliative for which is to cultivate a vigorous bout of curiosity.

A history of ignorance would need to include the development of theories of interpretation involving Wilhelm Dilthey, Martin Heidegger, and Hans-Georg Gadamer. As it happens, the understanding of history features prominently in hermeneutical scholarship. As I stated in chapter 8, one of the terms Gadamer uses for the arena of expectations is "effective historical consciousness."[48] We interpreters, creators, writers, and readers have a sense of knowing what to expect in any situation by virtue of our access to memories, which are not just personal and private but are influenced by and built on cultural and social fields—and history. Memory and history are intertwined. Therefore, a history of ignorance would need to include a history of history making, historiography, which also includes the philosophy of history. Digital social media have a large investment in history making and the telling and retelling of histories, personal, local, and global, as scholars, educators, and curators of heritage seek to restore the cultural value of recollections, both personal and public.[49]

History as Ignorance

Considering its importance in online culture, it's worth examining further the relationship between history and ignorance. "The past is a construct of the mind. It blinds us. It fools us into believing it," according to Matthias in the sci-fi film *Total Recall* (2012). It's common for films aimed at large markets to include a couple of lines of quotable pop philosophy as an intellectual challenge amid the fights and chases, especially when the film is playing around with ideas about simulation and reality, as in *The Matrix* (1999), and with memory, as in *Total Recall*.

History shares many features with memory. Philosophers of history such as Edward Carr, Hayden White, and Keith Jenkins add support to the arguments I've outlined about the psychology of false memories. The question of the reliability of recollection is similar to the questions they raise about what constitutes a historical fact.[50] Hayden White argues that historians need to "consider historical narratives as what they most manifestly are: verbal fictions, the contents of which are as much *invented* as *found* and the forms of which have more in common with their counterparts in literature than they have with those in the sciences."[51] Edward Carr concurs that the contents of historical narratives are "as much invented/imagined as found."[52]

Historical Skepticism

As for the recollection of events through memory, the facts of history are never "purely objective," according to Carr. Events "become facts of history only in virtue of the significance attached to them."[53] As everyone knows, history is a matter of interpretation. According to Keith Jenkins, in *Re-Thinking History*, "No matter how verifiable, how widely acceptable or checkable, history remains inevitably a personal construct, and manifestation of the historian's perspective as 'narrator.' Unlike memory (itself suspect) history relies on someone else's eyes and voice; we see through an interpreter who stands between past events and our readings of them."[54]

From an even more skeptical point of view, Carr places the concept of fixed historical certainties under question: "The concept of absolute truth is also not appropriate to the world of history—or, I suspect, to the world of science."[55] Evidence for the persistence of uncertainty in the case of historical facts comes from his observation that historians very rarely dispute the facts of history, nor do historians claim that other historians are drawing on or reporting facts that are "absolutely false." A historian would rather dispute an adversary's verdict "as inadequate or one-sided or misleading, or the product of a point of view which has been rendered obsolete or irrelevant by later evidence."[56] Carr concedes that in the case of very simple historical statements we may speak comfortably of absolute truth or falsity—for example, perhaps the fact that King John sealed Magna Carta at Runnymede. Such facts are like the witness statements I alluded to previously: The thief stole the wrench, not the screwdriver, and Bugs Bunny was invented by Warner Bros., not Disney. A historical fact is like a memory that no one is interested in disputing any longer. It's lost its controversial aura, until someone else comes along with new evidence to introduce an element of doubt, like the discovery of the remains of King Richard III in a parking lot in Gloucester, England. Historical facts are like the verdict of not proven in Scots law: innocent until further evidence comes to light, true until proven false.

The History of Now

History is about the present as much as the past. Historian Keith Macfie describes history as a kind of "self-knowledge, constructed (biologically) from a well-stocked brain."[57] The way we tell history says something about ourselves in the present. According to Carr, "Learning from history is never simply a one-way process. To learn about the present in the light of the past means also to learn about the past in the light of the present. The function of history is to promote a profounder understanding of both past and present through the interrelation between them."[58] Macfie confirms that "we cannot actually know a real past, lived or otherwise."[59] All we can know is "an imagined replica of a once-lived present."[60] We human beings experience a "lived present," which we accommodate, make sense of, and retell through imagined or invented histories. The past is something people construct in the present to justify some very present state of affairs.

Evidence from the past has a practical present purpose. For example, guilt or innocence entails deciding something about a current circumstance, requiring the accused to make amends or go free. A plaintiff would rarely say the accused was once innocent of the crime but is now guilty. In a just society, if the law becomes more permissive, then it becomes permissive in retrospect as well. The study of history also exposes something about the present by virtue of the differences it brings to light. The geographer David Lowenthal wrote about the past as a foreign country.[61] To probe the past really is like venturing into a foreign land, as if a tourist, as I discussed in chapter 6. Reading about the past is also analogous to watching a film or playing a computer game. The recollection provides a backdrop to the ordinary aspects of a person's life as lived in the present.

Historian and colleague Adrian Snodgrass speaks of the role of the historian as eliciting from the past individual memories and texts and interpreting them in contemporary terms: "to strengthen remembrance by demonstrating how it contains the possible."[62] The historian broadens the scope of memory by treating the past as "vast unknown territories." The historian returns from this "landscape of oblivion" with new understandings for application in the here and now. The historian "acts to interpret the past for the purposes of the present; the historian translates from one into the other."[63]

In a way, it matters little how philosophers account for the phenomenon of history. According to Macfie, the conviction that a real past exists is unassailable: "So deeply embedded is the human conviction regarding the existence of a real past that can be accessed, primarily by means of memory (the existential foundation of all history), that it is extremely unlikely that human beings will abandon history."[64] The immutability of the past, independently of how we tell it, has practical value and consequences. The world is not yet ready for the kind of extreme skepticism that asserts that the past never really existed, though philosophers do question the utility of absolutism; the past absolutely existed or it absolutely did not.[65] What persists however is the view that history is fallible, subject to retelling, and the narratives that endure are those that provide some kind of cachet for the present, or at least for those storytellers on the side of the powerful. As scholars who are skeptical of canonical and "received" histories say, "history is written by the victors."[66] In many respects, history has a stake in the present, and the kinds of histories we construct reflect the concerns of the time.

Digital Histories

This selective formulation of histories is no less the case with the emerging histories of digital media, which have undergone various transformations at the pen of inventive scholars. I'm thinking of Sadie Plant's reassertion of the role of women and the technologies of weaving into the received history of computing, particularly picking up on the place of Ada Lovelace (1815–1852) and the women of Bletchley Park.[67] In other cases, it's artists collaborating with cyberneticians that provide the thread in contemporary digital narratives.[68] It's interesting, and disconcerting, to read of the historicizing of people and events that are within living memory. The decoders at Bletchley Park have now displaced the atom bomb, the commitment of US military, and the Nazis' decline from within as the catalyst for the end of World War II.[69] The completion and apparent success of the Hadron Collider at CERN in Switzerland seems to have merged with the development of the World Wide Web, which has assumed the status of an invention. At the time of its spread and development in the early 1990s, the web was a window into an aggregation of networks known as the Internet, combining access to all the communications protocols already in existence through a single browser. We early adopters knew that it was developed by researchers at CERN, which was an esoteric science project of which we had little knowledge or interest. That's just one potted account, and there are many others. As for any social history, there's still much to be said about the adoption, use, diffusion, resistance, and mythmaking of society at large and at the scale of the individual. Identifying an origin or originator for an innovation does not complete the historical project. Histories of course do not belong only to professional historians, but are generated, received, curated, and perpetrated as public and private stories. Digital media provides the tools and the impetus for anyone to share artifacts and stories, as attested in recent innovations in heritage and museum studies.[70]

What does this discussion of history have to say about mood? History invariably links with the concept of *zeitgeist*, about which I indicated some skepticism in the introduction. Every time we media-savvy prosumers refer to the digital age, generation Y, the Arab Spring, posthumanism, or other trends, epochs, or places in time and space, we are appealing to the spirit of the age—the mood of the times. In chapter 8, I referred to the zeitgeist that haunts an age, and in chapter 9, to the smaller-scaled framework on which any of us assemble our experiences and expectations as we go about our daily lives: shopping, visiting a restaurant, or typing at a computer. A mood is a frame of mind with a history that primes us with expectation, hope, and trepidation. It's the matrix through which the human organism is prepared and made receptive and in which mobile ubiquitous media play a part.

Ignorance Online

The Internet is an environment in which writers and creators are given scope to broadcast recollections, statements of historical events, interpretations, and assertions without recourse to anything other than their own knowledge, prejudices, and opinions and without the obligation to verify everything that's said, written, or shown.[71] It's a medium in which false recollections can circulate unregulated, as in the world of Twitter, Facebook status updates, comments, blogs, and citizen journalism. Such unregulated memories may circulate through malice and misinformation campaigns, but as suggested by some of the psychological studies I've referred to, in environments without the cross-checking that comes from corroborative witnesses, we can truly believe we are providing an accurate record and telling the truth, even though we are not. In the academic environment with which I'm most familiar, scholars do have a sense of reliable sources online, reputation comes into play, and researchers seek corroboration as a means of getting at the truth online. Trusted sources exist, and we may grant to these sources greater priority in our searching. The Internet is saturated with repetition and redundancy. For facts that matter, we tend to search around to gauge the degree to which they are substantiated.

The more likely source of intellectual falsehood now is to yield to the temptation to take information from the Internet and pretend that it's your own—that is, to plagiarize, either deliberately or due to cut-and-paste carelessness. As long as you're able to get online, it's easy enough to feign knowledge, but then there's a fine line between pretending to be knowledgeable and actually knowing.

I think the mood of ignorance intersects most powerfully with pervasive digital media through the phenomena of imagination and collaboration. I hope I've succeeded in making the case for the strong relationship between ignorance and imagination. Edmund Burke (1729–1797) said, "It is our ignorance of things that causes all our admiration, and chiefly excites our passions."[72] Insights from psychology suggest that ignorance is the norm. Ignorance drives inquiry. That is, we want to know what we don't already know. Ignorance informs the mood of curiosity I explored in chapter 3. In any case, ignorance provides a space for the imagination. We are always projecting (imaginatively) and constructing memories. This works particularly well when those memories are shared, when they rub up against one another and become the products of collaboration, factors abetted by sharing online. Memories and recollections are at core the products of creative coproduction and creative sociability.

Theories about history and recollection typically start with an individualized concept of memory and storytelling, but social media, Web 2.0, prosumerism, and concepts of online cocreation emphasize the collaborative aspects of invention. To reiterate, remembering is inventing, together. The case is perhaps overstated, but the author Don Tapscott presents a seductive image of online knowledge sharing, at least for the next generation:

> I believe that we will see that being immersed in an interactive digital environment has made them smarter than your average TV-watching couch potato. They may read fewer works of literature, but they devote a lot of time to reading and writing online. As we will learn, that activity can be intellectually challenging. Instead of just numbly receiving information, they are gathering it from around the globe with lightning speed. Instead of just trusting a TV announcer to tell us the truth, they are assessing and scrutinizing the jumble of facts that are often contradictory or ambiguous. When they write to their blog or contribute a video, they have an opportunity to synethesize and come up with a new formulation, which leads to a giant opportunity for them. The Net Generation has been given the opportunity to fulfill their inherent human intellectual potential as no other generation.[73]

Crowdsourced online sharing and creativity is not dissimilar to the power of the crowd to remember. False memories need to be corrected, but in any cases are indicators of the more positive human predisposition: the capacity to imagine. Information has this loosely fitting character anyway, as for all language, the interpretation of which depends on context. Language has to fit loosely and to invoke multiple meanings and ambiguities in order to accommodate different contexts.

If it's true that we remember better when in a negative mood state, then perhaps there's some advantage in inducing negative emotions in some contexts—to help people remember better, or at least pay more attention to the accuracy of their recollections. Here, we depart from experimental study and migrate again to the world of speculation. Perhaps a touch of melancholy, vertigo, or frustration enhances attentiveness. Equipment that is not altogether easy to use may fill a similar function, the subject of the next chapter.

Summary

I began this chapter considering false memories. According to key studies, people are more susceptible to misremembering when in a positive mood state. That's when the ability to make connections is most pronounced and the imagination kicks in. If false memories can be induced under laboratory conditions, then they will be even more prevalent when circulated online, given that false memories are endemic and in a way symptomatic of a positive frame of mind. The question of online recollection prompted me to consider history. I presented a potted account of the history of ignorance, alighting eventually on the issue of militant fundamentalism, of which there seem to be many expressions online, a particular kind of ignorance unwilling to reconsider, discuss, and negotiate. I looked at the claims of philosophers of history who wrestle with the idea that historical narratives are as much imagined as found. The issues apply also to emerging histories of digital media. History also relates to the mood of the times and gives accounts of mood transitions over time. I considered history, recollection, and knowing as online, crowdsourced practices.

Coda: Accentuate the Negative

An article on the BBC Science website says that "being physically active can bolster good mental health and help you manage stress, anxiety and even depression."[74] It's good to get out into parks and the countryside, to exercise, eat lots of vegetables, grow plants, and surround yourself with friends. There's lots of evidence in support of these propositions, including some that colleagues and I uncovered through our research project into EEG and outdoor environments.[75] Whether or not everyone practices these principles of healthy living, very few people believe the converse—that being physically active outdoors is bad for you or that the state of our mental health is indifferent to whether or not we are physically active. Many people believe strongly that physical activity is positively related to mental health. Few would search for evidence that supports the opposite case., but from a logical point of view, if rigorously pursued, the failure to find such negative evidence would actually support the positive case even more. (This is one corollary of what Karl Popper asserted about falsification in scientific inquiry.[76])

Confirmation Bias

There are several reasons that people don't tend to look for evidence that might disconfirm their beliefs. It's hard work. It's less work, cognitively, to look for confirming evidence. The positive proposition already contains the information we need to work with.

Is being physically active good for mental health? It's relatively easy to say "yes" and find supporting evidence. The proposition suggests where to look for the evidence. As it happens, physical activity is also something you can see. You can look for people who are physically active (sportspeople, joggers, ramblers, etc.) and even identify people with good mental health (responsible parents, teachers, etc.). The statement contains less information about or encouragement to seek out its converse: lack of physical activity. What is it to be physically inactive: lying in bed all day, watching TV, driving everywhere? What are people in poor mental health like?

Like those survey and referendum questions that incline people toward a particular answer, the proposition linking physical activity to good mental health nudges in the direction of confirmation. There's more "cognitive load" in pursuing the negation, because you have to imagine the converse to what's in the proposition. Negatives are more complicated to process anyway, and negatives are easily compounded: What's not to like about not accentuating the negative? You see what I mean.

In the preceding paragraphs, I've attempted to combine a couple of the many arguments that explain why confirmation bias exists. These are outlined in full in a seminal paper by psychologist Raymond Nickerson.[77] As individuals, we cherish our beliefs, whether positive or negative, and don't give them up easily. It's actually efficient to be conservative to some degree and to resist changes. Imagine the condition we would be in if we changed our beliefs immediately for every new bit of evidence that came to light. Any counsel to guard against confirmation bias is actually advice to consider both sides of any argument, to weigh up evidence for and against. Theories about confirmation bias tell us why this is so difficult.

Against Mood

In investigating mood and ubiquitous digital technologies, I'm starting with the assumption that there is a connection, or a series of connections, between the two (mood and digital technologies). There's lots of direct and indirect evidence from psychological studies, with much of this available online. However, maybe I should look for evidence that there is no connection or that our moods are indifferent to the digital technologies we deploy and how we deploy them. Then, the question becomes: Why would anyone think there ought to be a connection? What establishes such beliefs or disbeliefs in the first place? This is a cultural question.

The connection between color and mood provides a simpler example. There is little if any evidence that a room painted yellow makes us feel happier than being in a gray room, but why do some people even entertain the possibility that it could? Perhaps it's due to several centuries of practice by painters, something about spring and bees, and a host of golden metaphors wandering like clouds through fields of daffodils.

Digital equipment is a bit like yellow. There are deeply embedded reasons for at least entertaining the possibility that technology could provide positive and negative benefits to people's emotional lives and make them more contented, happy, sad, or anxious. Several centuries of industrial development and utopian and dystopian thinking might come into play here. The possibility that mood and computers are connected is sufficient to legitimate the study, even if the evidence was inconclusive.

Contrary Evidence

Here are some candidates for evidence against the proposition that mood and digital technologies are linked in some way, and here evidence and argument get conflated:

- People get emotional about other people and their relationships with them. Computers are not people and don't communicate emotions.
- Giving a severely depressed person a smartphone does not take him or her out of his or her depression.
- Events and life circumstances trigger emotional states: succeeding at a task, being proud of a member of the family, loss, disempowerment, or abuse. These override the effects of any technology.
- Everything in the world around us is somehow complicit in the way we feel: cars, books, teacups, and postage stamps. Asserting the same of ubiquitous computers really tells us very little.

In light of such contrary evidence (or at least assertions), it's difficult to resist marshaling counterevidence. Here are some candidates for counterevidence (and arguments) to each of the preceding negative points:

- Agreed, but computers are channels for people to communicate with one another.
- Neither do severely depressed people necessarily become happy when in the company of happy people.
- The effect of ubiquitous digital media on moods can be subtle. That the effects might be overwhelmed by life circumstances does not constitute evidence against the proposition.
- Ubiquitous digital media are a growing, expensive, and pervasive category of objects, technologies, and systems. The primary proposition that they affect our moods subdivides into other useful questions: in what ways; how do we deploy the link effectively; how do we resist; and so on.

As Nickerson says of the beliefs that matter to people, evidential facts don't really settle the matter: "They tend rather to be beliefs for which both supportive and counterindicative evidence can be found, and the decision as to whether to hold them is appropriately made on the basis of the relative weights or merits of the pro and con arguments."[78]

This post on confirmation bias was triggered by a colleague's insight that our recent study using EEG is unlikely to be refuted by others.[79] Researchers are less likely to invest effort to discount the results from an experiment that confirms what everyone wants to believe anyway. "New Study Shows that There Is No Link between Physical Activity and Mental Health" would be an unlikely headline, and not one that many researchers would necessarily want to develop, except perhaps lobbyists who want to build on parkland. Research is political, after all.

Note that Nickerson's argument follows an analytical line of inquiry.[80] He assumes that reason is ultimately arbitrated by logic, from which human reasoning deviates. The phenomenological perspective of Heidegger, Gadamer, and others is that human reason (or more accurately *understanding*) starts with prejudice, and we can't do without it.

Nickerson also makes the strong point that the initial evidence in a sequence of evidence usually exerts the strongest influence on our beliefs. Thus, arriving in Amsterdam for the first time on a cold, wet day will trigger the belief that Amsterdam is cold and wet, even if it is warm and sunny on subsequent visits. It takes a long time for the initial impression to dissipate. As anyone who has attended a job interview knows, first impressions are important.

When posted online, this coda prompted an interesting discussion about Karl Popper's concept of refutation:

Comment: I think refutation or falsification is slightly different, perhaps more than slightly different, than contrary evidence. For instance, when discussing *The Demarcation between Science and Metaphysics*, Popper suggests "that the refutability or falsifiability of a theoretical system should be taken as the criterion of its demarcation . . . a system is to be considered scientific only if it makes assertions which may clash with observations; and a system is, in fact tested by attempts to produce such clashes, that is to say by attempts to refute it."[81] Later, he is at great pains to emphasize that being untestable and therefore metaphysical does not imply meaninglessness, as suggested by Carnap and Wittgenstein.

Response: Indeed, slightly (or more than slightly) different. Nickerson has a section on Popper. He says: "Although Popper articulated the principle of falsifiability more completely than anyone before him, the idea has many antecedents in philosophy and science. It is foreshadowed, for example, in the Socratic method of refutation (*elenchos*), according to which what is to be taken as truth is whatever survives relentless efforts at refutation . . . the principle of falsifiability was also anticipated by T. H. Huxley (1894/1908), who spoke of 'a beautiful hypothesis killed by an ugly fact.' . . . Hypotheses are strengthened more when highly competent scientists make concerted efforts to disprove them and fail than when efforts at disproof are made by less competent investigators or in are made [sic] half-hearted ways."[82] This is all relevant, including the typo in the original. (Watch out for the perigee moon tonight, by the way.)

Reply: Thanks for the background and reminder about the perigee moon (*perigee* is a new word to me). I think that Popper is also saying something about the way hypotheses should be expressed in a manner that deliberately exposes them to refutation.

If only the nervous, lethargic, and fearful melancholic could flick a switch and be aroused to a state of unalloyed productive positivity—without recourse to intoxicating substances. Philip K. Dick starts his science fiction novel *Do Androids Dream of Electric Sheep?* with the idea of a "mood organ," from which users can select "a creative and fresh attitude" toward their job or even "ecstatic sexual bliss."[1] More ordinary, real-life candidates for such mood modulators include the television set, radio, personal stereo, game console, home entertainment center, and of course the conveniently portable smartphone and tablet computer. Then, there are more exceptional devices, such as virtual reality heads-up displays, augmented reality (AR) glasses (e.g., Google Glass), electromechanically enhanced body suits, electronic body sensors worn on the wrist or elsewhere, and brain-monitoring headsets with feedback, devices that are yet to gain a place in the market, that may be at the experimental stage, or that exist only in science fiction stories.

Prior to digital media, mood-altering machines included fairground rides, jukeboxes, and peep shows: any steam-powered or electromechanical device that excited the senses. In the 1960s, the architect Cedric Price proposed and designed the Fun Palace, a giant, mood-enhancing apparatus. It was a flexible-frame structure the size of an aircraft hanger in which you could "sit out over space with a drink and tune in to what's happening elsewhere in the city. Try starting a riot or beginning a painting—or just lie back and stare at the sky."[2] The unconventional psychiatrist Wilhelm Reich (1897–1957) invented an "orgone accumulator,"[3] a box the size of a phone booth lined with wood, metal, and foam rubber that captured "orgone radiation." The patient would sit in it for a while for the cure of various diseases. The orgone cycle starts with mechanical tension, leading to bioelectric charge, then bioelectric discharge, ultimately ending with mechanical relaxation. After all, "psychic health depends upon orgastic potency, i.e., upon the degree to which one can surrender to and experi- ence the climax of excitation in the natural sexual act."[4] This ambiguous and dubious mechanical economy harnesses the "orgastic potency" that is the life process.[5] Woody Allen parodies the device by placing an "orgas- matron" in his film *Sleeper* (1973). There's also the Excessive Machine in *Barbarella* (1968). Sadly, such parodic fantasies focus on the inducement of pleasurable moods mainly as solitary and short-lived experiences, discon- nected from the everyday.[6]

In this chapter, I'll examine the role of mood-altering devices in the emotional landscape. Just about any physical artifact can claim to trans- form mood. Some of the methods are obvious. It's worth cataloging these before considering some more intriguing underlying mood effects of ubiq- uitous digital devices. Mood effects ultimately depend on the way devices are positioned within constellations of technologies, practices, places, and people, as I'll show.

Mood Machines

"Mood machine" is an appealing alliteration. There's also something intriguing about a machine that claims to put you in the mood, especially a positive mood. I've already discussed music, games, and mass media enter- tainment in chapter 4. Digital devices deliver diversionary and mood-mod- ifying content.[7] It's as if smart consumers can self-prescribe media content to regulate their feelings. People read, watch films, documentaries, sports and comedy shows, play computer games, look at pictures, and listen to radio broadcasts and music as improvised strategies for regulating, modify- ing, softening, intensifying, and sharing a mood. The means of delivering such content and mood regulation include mobile digital devices. Research has shown that mood regulation features in the way people talk and think about entertainment, and in their behaviors and practices—for example, in listening to music to relieve stress or to give vent to a moment of melan- choly.[8] Of course, any claim that media content automatically transforms sadness into joy, as in Dick's "mood organ," is soon tempered by real-world experience. It's convenient to talk about streaming media content as if it flows through pipes like water through a plumbing system. The metaphor of "emotional content" is also convenient shorthand. However, neither are delivered to the human organism as if medication through a catheter, nor are they transmitted and absorbed as if "orgone radiation." Moods are more complex than that, as are technological devices. As with any technology, and as scholars in the field of interaction design and I keep reiterating, digital devices and what they deliver operate in complex, social–cultural constellations, fields, and practices.[9] They don't operate in isolation.

Device Ecologies

Other consumer products are similarly situated.[10] Digital devices are involved in mood adjustment much as any sought-after consumer product. They become objects of desire.[11] Such desire may focus on the device as an object, its beauty and functionality, the artful media content, the software, and the apps, but also the lifestyle, the cultural cachet, and the social codes they entail. Digital devices have symbolic value and position their owners within cultural groups. Their possession contributes to cultural capital that shows you belong. The satisfaction or denial of any desired object influences positive and negative mood conditions. As for the emotional power of media content, objects of desire fit within complex psychosocial and cultural ecologies. Having the latest smartphone doesn't automatically make people happy of course, but it will position them in a social context, in a group.[12] It may help in formulating identity or set them apart. People may also feel that possession of such devices demonstrates participation in the mood of the times or the subculture that fits: the age of network savvy, socially connected urban professionals, design-aware metrosexuals, fitness junkies, hipsters, revolutionaries, aggrieved youths, or members of a gang. There's the mix of emotions that constitutes the accompanying sense of well-being—among them empathy, pride, and a sense of belonging.

More significantly, digital devices provide extra channels of communication and, unsurprisingly, impact directly on sociability. As discussed in chapter 2, communication devices contribute inevitably to the circulation of moods, because social groups share collective mood states. Smartphone and social media users tell each other how they are feeling. They share good and bad news, anxieties, desires, hopes, and disappointments, thereby contributing to collective mood, the mood of the group. Face-to-face physical presence is not necessarily the same as text communication, and online communicants do not necessarily disclose the same information as people do when in the same room, but in the newly nuanced world of digital communication, even being out of contact serves to communicate something.

Mood and Function

Functionality also impinges on mood. Designers and developers generally create digital devices to make some task or other easier, more effective, or more pleasant. Devices function and in so doing make aspects of people's jobs, leisure, or social life easier, and that impacts on people's mood states. It's safe to assume that tools that are designed well, suitable for purpose, and that make tasks easier, quicker, or more pleasurable contribute to positive moods. They make us attentive, focused, and alert. When devices don't work as expected, then users may feel frustrated, angry, or sad, or may simply become bored and cast the device aside. Consumers have certain expectations about their devices, and the achievement or denial of those expectations contributes to moods. When I've spoken with people about the themes of this book, mood and mobility, that's been the most common point of contact with the topic: the mood people get into when files get lost, the Wi-Fi cuts out, and people get overwhelmed with emails. Later in this chapter, I'll challenge that obvious assumption that effective functioning equates to positive moods and poor functionality to negative moods. The contribution of functionality to mood is more nuanced than that.

I like to think of devices that matter as physical, but some of the equipment and software people use support the existence of "virtual objects," and these have mood effects. In some computer games and game environments, the player can acquire objects that are virtual weapons, communicators, mobile phones, e-readers, tablets, and talismans. As I related in chapter 8, during our foray into Second Life, a group of us made folding virtual display screens that received images transmitted from actual mobile phones[13] and mobile avatars that replicated the movement of someone in physical space, presenting ghostly, real-time video projections of their bodies.[14] In Second Life, residents with a modicum of coding skill can make up such devices to their own design, program them, and sell them to other residents. They can also acquire such virtual devices from others. I bought a special virtual surveillance visor that you place on the head of your avatar. It enables the resident (the game player) to see moving images picked up by a camera located somewhere else in Second Life. Interactive virtual devices can also be projected into the physical environment, onto the physical surfaces of walls, onto glass, and through augmented reality (AR), visible via special glasses or light projection.[15] The mood effect pertains as much to the functioning of virtual devices as it does to physical devices in everyday life, and there is increasing overlap between the two.

Product Placement

Sometimes, virtual objects have the appearance of consumer products available on main street and in the shopping mall and are branded as such. Product placement in computer games is a growing business.[16] Some games have in-game hyperlinks to websites on which players can browse complete catalogs and purchase items for real. As well as being able to order home delivery pizzas and tacos from virtual vendors, you can purchase car tires at a pit stop in a car racing game or sports shoes in a basketball video game. Virtualized consumer products are complicit in the formation of mood states, as are any other consumer products, even if only present on the computer screen. They become objects of desire. The portability of ubiquitous digital devices means that such virtual objects can be carried around and accessed at will. The Pokémon game is based on the idea of virtual creatures to be captured, tamed, petted, improved, and set in competition with one another in the environment provided by the portable Gameboy video console.[17] Pokémon is a contraction of "pocket monster," an idea that apparently arose from the inventor Satoshi Tajiri's childhood passion for collecting insects. Owning, collecting, petting, and exchanging connect to basic human emotions and are applicable to living creatures, preserved corpses, and the virtual. The computer game *Spore* encourages similar engagement, with the evolution of whole species that reproduce and evolve in semiautonomous, quasibiological scenarios and campaigns for survival.[18]

Products that Replicate

The idea of autonomously self-replicating machines has been around for a while[19] and features as a common science fiction scenario, as in the *Terminator* (1984) film, which invokes a future dominated by robotic machines. Although it's a long way from dramatic sci-fi lore, the idea of self-replicating machines informs the aspirational mythology of 3-D printers. A RepRap machine is a low-cost printer that can print its own components.[20] The RepRap website claims that if you have one of these machines, then you can use it to print another printer for someone else. For instance, 3-D printers in the home or neighborhood provide the possibility of convenient customization and design variation in the manufacture of physical objects. Consumers can browse the Internet for a pair of shoes, retrieve the file for the shoes, and then print them off at home, or at least the components, and then assemble them. So far, the biggest market for domestic consumers is trinkets and ornaments, children's toys, adult toys, and weapons: toy guns, slingshots, air rifles, and major-league weapons for boys and girls of all ages, or components of these objects—objects of pleasure and for venting aggression. The US Congress has proposed (so far unsuccessfully) putting a ban on 3-D-printable gun magazines that hold bullets.[21] Today 3-D print enthusiasts can produce iPhone cases, mounts for computer screens, cups, trays, lemon juicers, and a miniature Captain Kirk chair. The aspiration for such machines is that they function as factories that make factories,[22] though the components have to be assembled by a human being. Mass production and mass consumption return to the local environment. Consumers can tweak and tune the objects they download and print them to satisfy their personal desires and maximize their particular pleasures. Thus, physical objects move into circulation by digital means and provide another medium for the circulation of moods. Think of navigating across an emotional landscape populated by gadgets, objects of desire, family heirlooms, and secondhand bric-a-brac, both virtual and physical.

As discussed in chapter 9, there are 3-D manufactured objects that have moving parts and become active as machines once manufactured. These are so-called 4-D self-assembling objects. Promoters of the technology appeal to lifestyle and easy living; imagine Ikea flat pack furniture that assembles itself. The promise also extends to emotionally charged health applications, such as self-assembling nanobots that destroy cancer cells, and futuristic space exploration scenarios in which mechanical parts are shot into space and assemble themselves, thereby reducing the risks to human operatives in space. There's something aesthetically appealing about optimally designed objects the design of which exploits the flexibility and resilience of its materials to spring into complex shapes when removed from the box or when tossed into the air, as demonstrated on a TED video by researcher Skylar Tibbits,[23] even if the folded object has no obvious function. Self-replicating machines have emotional entailments. Perhaps they too beget descendants and pass on owners through their generations.

Devices no longer of use may still have aesthetic qualities. Like dead insects, obsolete devices are collectibles, museum pieces, or fetish objects, and would-be users position them within meaning structures. Traditional technology museums invite visitors to admire products laid out on evolutionary tree diagrams and classificatory arrays. The aesthetic dimension encourages emotional attachments, personal, social, and cultural. Even dysfunctional machines arouse the emotions and contribute to mood.

Gain and Pain

As fully functional machines, artifacts can stimulate the senses directly and deliver pleasure or incite aversion simply because of their materials, textures, smells, and the sounds they make. Notice the effects on mood of being in contact with a leather-bound book, a vintage oil lamp, or a satin pillow, compared with a rusty cheese grater, a box of old chalk, a nicotine-stained keyboard, or a fragment of an old circuit board. Some devices are designed to actively stimulate the senses. Digital devices can also be wired to excite the senses directly, delivering pleasure, or arousal. There are apps that deliver relaxing and hypnotic sounds and images, white noise to block out distractions, ambient sounds that transport the listener into a different mood state or that wake the sleeper in the morning when at the optimal stage of the REM cycle, as picked up by movement sensors. There are devices for massage that stimulate the skin with vibrations or mild electric currents and devices that emit odors. Even taste is catered for if we think of e-cigarettes. As well as those oriented to pleasure, there are devices for inflicting pain and discomfort, either for voluntary conditioning or as weapons to intimidate people into submission (e.g., Tasers), evoking extreme negative mood conditions by their direct functioning.

As well as the vicious and the cruel, there are benign examples of devices that stimulate negative sensations and moods. Computer games are not all pleasure and can deliver unpleasant tactile feedback, as do many other everyday objects. The game cycle in any case pits the pleasure of winning against the pain of losing.[24] Musician colleagues have pointed out to me that part of the appeal and value of classical musical instruments resides in the difficulties and challenges they present for the player. Devices can be designed to engender long-term gain at the cost of short-term pain. In fact, as discussed in chapter 10, device users may even be more alert when in a negative mood state, and devices that make you feel uncomfortable may help you to be more alert and effective as a consequence.

Mood Monitoring

Certain digital devices also monitor the moods of their users at a personal level through specialized journal and questionnaire monitoring protocols, such as daily self-reporting on mood. Such devices provide logs for entering mood information according to a scale: mood intensity, sleep quality, the amount of exercise, medication, conflicts encountered, and so on. The information is then monitored by a clinician. A range of such apps exists for people with bipolar disorder, such as Bipolar Bear,[25] Mood Tracker,[26] and Optimism.[27] Motion sensors of various kinds can record how mobile and active are their wearers or carriers. Eye-tracking spectacles can record where the wearer is looking. Skin galvanometry records stress levels, and electroencephalography (EEG) devices such as Emotiv's Epoc and Insight portable neuroheadsets record brain waves,[28] providing an indication of how stressed, bored, or relaxed market testers are as they look at products on supermarket shelves, watch movie previews, or test computer games. EEG devices are now consumer products and can be plugged into computer games as part of an emotional feedback system. If the game player is bored, then the device can pep up the game play a little. My colleagues and I used such devices for recording people's apparent emotional responses as they walk from busy urban streets into parkland.[29]

Digital devices enable self-reporting on mood states. There are long-established means of communicating the emotion and mood of the sender in textual media, such as email, chat, and text messaging. I'm thinking here of emoticons as character combinations, special graphical symbols, and miniature animations that people create or download: cartoon faces that scowl, squint, or laugh hysterically to nuance the text message. Interaction designers experiment with tactile feedback and other sensory means of providing an emotional channel to aid person-to-person communication. TapTap is an experimental wearable fabric shawl, since developed as a wristband, wired with sensors and actuators that when worn conveys touch sensations between individuals across distance.[30] There is also the aggregation of mood data. As I explored in chapter 2, as social media communication tools, mobile devices provide textual data that researchers can mine to construct mood profiles of large groups of people.

Assuming these means of assessing the mood of an individual or a group actually deliver useful information, then clever software can take this information to inflect the computer's interactions with human users. Consumers, researchers, and reviewers are still evaluating the effectiveness of devices with supposed emotional interfaces that exhibit or simulate personality traits and that respond to the mood of the device user.[31] Apple's Siri and Google's Android system provide voice-activated search interfaces and deliver voice answers to queries, providing modes of interaction that give the impression to some users that the device has "personality."[32] The device thereby appears to be sensitive to mood and can exhibit simulated mood states through its responses and through inflexions in its synthetic voice.

Putting all these technologies together provides something like a line of synthetic autonomous entities that reproduce themselves and can detect and exhibit emotions. So far, these mood-modulating features are independent, atomic simulacra of human capability. Their combination would be no mean feat, but encourages thought of synthetic humans, or domestic robots at least, a common enough sci-fi scenario but a proposition that makes many people nervous[33] or perhaps secure in its impossibility. We only have until 2020 to realize Mars colonies, flying cars, and the humanoid replicant robots in Ridley Scott's *Blade Runner* (1984).

Mood Transportation

Devices do not need to be joined-up unitary entities to operate as mood modulators. The responsibility for mood modification needn't reside only in the devices. Digital devices can provide indirect access to emotion by transporting the carrier or wearer to other mood-modifying contexts and environments. Digital maps and navigation tools take visitors, patients, and revelers to where they want to go: the club, the bar, the concert, the clinic, the park, or the countryside, each of which has some impact on mood. Navigation devices can also encourage curiosity and direct desire toward such environments. Documentary content about a great rail journey across the Nullarbor or a hot air balloon ride over the Nile River Valley might just influence the would-be tourist's decision to go there and experience new excitement, peace and quiet, or the intensities and the varieties of mood they seek. Information delivered through the visitor's smartphone might just notch up the pleasure of being at the historic site, the adventure park, or the museum. The device magnifies or attenuates the mood of that

place by providing information, sensory effects, and a "visitor experience."
I referred in the introduction to the mood-modifying effects of speed,
changes in prospect, traveling companions, expectation, and the return.[34]

I hope by now I've made it clear just how complicit ubiquitous digital devices are as instruments to influence, transmit, and transform mood
states, but digital devices are complicit in the provision of even more specialized mood-modulating functions through their potential for erotic arousal.
This will help lead the discussion again toward the sociability of mood,
particularly through Sigmund Freud's ideas about the *pleasure principle*.

Seduction Machines

"I'm in the mood for love," goes the song by librettist Dorothy Fields (1905–
1974) and as sung by Dean Martin and dozens of others. The path to seduction involves getting the other party in the mood. Following the model set
by Casanova, author Robert Greene advises in his book *The Art of Seduction* that "human beings are immensely suggestible; their moods will easily
spread to the people around them. In fact seduction depends on mimesis,
on the conscious creation of a mood or feeling that is then produced by
the other person."[35] This echoes something of the claims made about social
media and emotional contagions with which I began this book. The ability
to seduce is not unlike the relationship between successful orators and their
audiences, as outlined by Aristotle (see chapter 2). According to this formulation, you can't fake seduction. Moods are contagious. So are awkward-
ness and hesitation, the enemies of seduction according to Greene. Perhaps
that's how pornography seduces, when it does. It's anything but subtle. It's
unashamed, brazen, confident, and invites the viewer to share the mood.

Producers of pornography seek to invoke a particularly intense series of
sensations, responses, and interactions in their audiences. Combine this
intensity with smartphones and tablet computers, and you have the ultimate in personal, portable, and private devices to deliver the quintessential
functional mood modulator. It's well-known that whatever the communications medium, the adult entertainment industry will populate it with
content, for which there seems to be unlimited consumer demand. Commentators suggest that online pornography is one of those "killer applications" of the World Wide Web.[36] For some users, it's a kind of bonus, or an
embarrassment. Search engines such as Google provide pages of statistics

that indicate common search terms and their frequency of use, but the figures for pornographic content search are conspicuously absent. In 2011, neuroscientists Ogi Ogas and Sai Gaddam published results from their estimates of pornography usage on the Internet in their book titled *A Billion Wicked Thoughts*. They processed data about the million most visited websites and discovered that only 4 percent were dedicated to sexually explicit content. Web searches for such content rated higher. On their analysis of web searches, it appeared that 13 percent of all searches were for adult content.[37] In reviewing the research, many commentators said they would have expected the figures to be much higher.[38]

Commercial online pornography and its amateur, experimental, not-for-profit sibling known as *netporn* are indeed significant Internet phenomena. Media theorist Susanna Paasonen provides interesting insights into the richly affective dimensions of the genre, and hence its impact on mood and emotion.[39] Commercial pornography and netporn supply online audiences with image galleries, streamed live performances, videos, and short stories. Paasonen observes that in some respects pornography is not so different from other entertainment genres. There's the obvious parallel with extreme dramatic forms, such as horror, melodrama, and comedy. Like these genres, pornography "aims to evoke similar responses in their viewers as the ones they depict."[40] It's about sharing the mood through mimesis and the mirror neuron response.[41] Such dramatic forms go to extremes. They resort to exaggeration to produce significant effects in their audiences, such as sweaty palms, tears, laughter, and sexual arousal, and the emotions that accompany these physiological responses.

Mixed Emotions

Entertainment delivers a range of emotional effects, and audiences don't only simply seek pleasure. Paasonen warns that in the case of pornography, "focus on pleasure easily frames pornography as automatically gratifying and arousing. Yet porn may just as well disgust, titillate, amuse, bore or alienate its viewers."[42] Even the process of searching for pornographic content online prompts certain emotions, such as frustration, due to waiting and delay.[43] There's a great deal of free erotic material online provided as a lure, but much more is for sale. Free content usually includes links to subscription sites, not to mention trails that lead ultimately to sites requiring a credit card number. Users get caught in a frustrating series of pop-up windows, false leads, splash pages, clickbait, and labyrinthine links. Users' devices end up with cached images and history trails that clog up device memory, are stored on backup servers, and reappear again in predictive text prompts due to frequent use. Some browsers provide the option to operate in modes that automatically erase history trails and cookies when the user closes the browser session.[44] It's as if you were never there. Like any navigational encounter, the challenges and frustrations of the journey there and back form part of the emotional experience.

More than other entertainments, pornography takes on a different cast when consumed individually rather than in company, engendering different moods. Cultural theorist and commentator Mark Dery offers an apposite description of one such group experience: "Male viewers who look at them do so with a voyeuristic, high-fiving glee familiar to anyone who has ever watched hardcore videos with a drunken gang of guys at a bachelor party."[45] In fact, Dery is describing the occasion of a veteran showing videos of war atrocities to his mates, making the point that erotic porn also taps the same basic nerve centers as so-called war porn.[46] Paasonen identifies more prosaic responses to pornography, such as "puzzlement, amusement, titillation and dislike."[47] Some responses to pornography also come under the category of *disgust*, as explored by the anthropologist Mary Douglas.[48] Sexual activity and imagery lends itself to descriptions such as "matter out of place." Nothing is disgusting in itself; rather, it's something's relationship to context that's key. A perfectly roasted leg of lamb is appetizing on the dining table but can invoke a disgust response if it's on a vegetarian buffet, it's lying in the gutter, or it's tangled up in hotel bed sheets. There's a time and a place for most things.

Pornography is commonly associated with enjoyment, but also embarrassment, shame, and guilt, feelings that extend beyond its audiences. According to Passonen, the attitudes to pornography involve an array of social responses. There's a protective response, particularly toward children who may come across the material online. According to a recent report by the UK Children's Commissioner, "pornography has been linked to unrealistic attitudes about sex; maladaptive attitudes about relationships; more sexually permissive attitudes; greater acceptance of casual sex; beliefs that women are sex objects; more frequent thoughts about sex; sexual uncertainty . . . and less progressive gender role attitudes."[49] Some people are concerned about exploitation within an industry that is not consistently regulated. There's sympathy for the actors and models and suspicion about coercion. Other responses include moral indignation and concern about addiction among audiences. According to some researches into pornography and youth culture, online pornography fills a void left by a dearth of sex education in schools. The curious can make inquiries online that they would be too embarrassed to reveal to their peers in a classroom setting or to their parents.[50] Curiosity provides a socially acceptable rationale for accessing pornography. Perhaps even the fact that porn exists at all engenders a kind of curiosity. Why does it exist?

Subcultures

Netporn as a subgenre is ostensibly controlled by individuals and independent special interest groups rather than profit-making organizations. At its most interesting for cultural theorists, netporn is a grassroots, producer-consumer-oriented phenomenon. In a sense, it democratizes sexual experience. Critical commentators regard consumer-controlled netporn as more interesting than the commercial variety. In a way, it's more socially consequential. It provides scope for individual expression and community formation. Dery provides an account of what's on offer on netporn sites. There's niche material for aquaphiliacs who like pictures of people fully clothed in swimming pools, neck brace fetishists, representations of putative congress with extraterrestrials, and sites for vomit fetish and hiccup lovers.[51] Outside of the orbit of commercial producers, netporn provides humor, irony, and a sense that there are communities out there who wish to socialize around the theme of erotic arousal, independently of online dating and "hookup" services.

Netporn also becomes emblematic of taboo. It joins with street protest, graffiti, underground movements, and certain mental illnesses, providing a set of ideas and practices to recruit against the establishment, bourgeois values, and capitalism. Amateur pornography represents a form of deviancy that is exciting and transgressive. It contributes to the antibourgeois mood of the libertarian. Netporn also occupies the space of the carnivalesque, in which social priorities are overturned. After all, it's about bodies in extreme postures, objectified into parts, and grotesquely "real" and vertiginous, as I outlined in chapter 5. Dery also thinks netporn provides a medium for those traditionally stigmatized as "abnormal" to express their identity, particularly for those ostracized on the basis of sexual preference. Once it was the case that people labeled as "moral degenerates" were "stigmatized, criminalized, institutionalized. Now, . . . it's the Revenge of the Repressed."[52]

As channels of erotic content, digital devices as seduction machines come into service to support countercultural movements, subcultures, minority groups, and experiments in identity formation. Such applications also fit within the context of larger milieus of invention and innovation that commentators and historians are ready to describe in terms of large-scale social movements. (There's no escaping zeitgeist, after all.) The invention and design of technologies has large-scale mood effects. Marshall McLuhan wrote about the reconfiguration of the whole human sensorium, brought about by the printing press. The electronic age ushers in further reconfiguration. In a way, he was applauding the proliferation and rising influence of the libertarian countercultural tribes of the 1960s. As well as coining the famous phrase "the medium is the message," he affirmed that "the medium is the *massage*,"[53] the title of a book and of a long-playing record, and a phrase that McLuhan admitted could be parsed in several ways, not least in erotic and sensuous terms. Whether or not theorists and historians subscribe to McLuhan's grand narratives of epochal transformations, there's little doubt that technologies and devices contribute to the way human societies define themselves, the visions they have for the future, and their sources of optimism and hope—or pessimism and disorientation.

Life Instinct

The quest for erotic gratification is of course just the flotsam on a current within the human psyche that Sigmund Freud identified as the pleasure principle, or *eros*.[54] Eros is the life instinct, the urge toward sexual pleasure and self-preservation. It's what the misjudged orgone accumulator was supposed to tap into. However, no machine is needed. Freud describes the main purpose of eros as "uniting and binding."[55] It complicates life and preserves it. In his later works, Freud expanded the idea to an account of society at large.[56] He contrasts eros with the death instinct, the most obvious manifestation of which is aggression and hostility. Critical social theorist Herbert Marcuse picks up on this theme in *Eros and Civilization*.[57] For Marcuse, eros is liberating and constructive. Earlier in the chapter, I referred to the link between pornography and depictions of war atrocities. This echoes Freud's characterization of the conflict between the pleasure principle and the death instinct—eros and sadism. Digital devices as mood modulators, not least as seduction machines and purveyors of netporn, remind the astute interpreter of this conflict within every age. The mood of the times speaks of unresolved tensions and varying relationships. In sum, ubiquitous digital technologies highlight further the character of moods by virtue of their positions within constellations of technologies, practices, places, and the psychic economies of human societies.

Things and Objects

Digital devices form into clusters and ecologies. As I type, I'm in the company of a laptop, smartphone, and tablet, each linked by Wi-Fi. Also present are cups, reading glasses, a desk lamp, and even books. In these respects, ubiquitous digital devices as mood modulators are after all simply *things*. This is not to isolate their functioning, but to situate it. The concept of the *thing* has gained some currency in the world of digital consumer products since researchers coined the term "Internet of Things," to invoke a further prevalent machine metaphor.[58] Researchers and developers project the interconnectedness of the hyperlinked World Wide Web onto the world of objects and devices connected by increasingly sophisticated identification tagging technologies. Now, the consumer's refrigerator may communicate with the supermarket to trigger a home delivery when food stocks get low. It's as if the world is about to become populated with smart things that communicate with one another. As I showed in chapter 10, a fascination with *things* and the concept of the *thing* predates sophisticated electronic communications.[59] Literary theorist Steven Connor describes *things* that are particularly significant as *magical*: "Such objects have the powers to arouse, absorb, steady, seduce, disturb, soothe, succour and drug."[60] It's also in the nature of a thing to be interconnected, via not only communications hookups, inventories, and tracking systems, but the rich and varied panoply of devices, habits, spaces, and social relations of which it is a part.

Objects, on the other hand, are things ripped from context. Things are objects that become important to us. This simple insight provides a way of positioning pornography and netporn. Pornography objectifies, which is to say that it treats individuals and sex acts as isolated, unconnected objects, severed from relationships with other activities, things, people, or consequences. Researchers have found for example that men who watch pornography think that dialogue, character development, and getting to know

the people in the scene distract from the arousal potential. Gender stereotypes come into play here. According to Ogas and Gaddam, "men prefer to
watch, women prefer to read and discuss."[61] There's another explanation
of course: that the imagination operates differently in different contexts.
Acts that are objectified and abstracted from personality provide scope for
the imagination. In Ken Russell's melancholic film *Crimes of Passion* (1984),
the sex worker's (China Blue) tormenter and potential client asks, "Who are
you?" She replies, "I'm Cinderella, Cleopatra, Goldie Hawn, Eva Braun. I'm
Little Miss Muffet. I'm Pocahontas. I'm whoever you want me to be—Rev-
erent!"[62] As for silent movies, when the actor does not speak she or he can
have whatever voice the audience can imagine.[63] We imaginative human
beings are capable of making our own connections, of making *things* of
anything.

Real Things

I'll turn to philosophy for a moment in order to advance our understanding
of devices and moods. *Thing* carries connotations of significance, history,
meaning, connection, and memory; this is how I understand philosopher
Martin Heidegger's essay *The Thing*.[64] According to Heidegger, the word
thing means *a gathering*. The serviceable milk jug as heirloom is a thing
around which family and friends gather at the tea table, but as a thing the
jug also gathers together meanings and memories. The *Oxford English Dictionary* concurs. Its first definition for the word "thing" is as a meeting or
assembly, a gathering of sorts. Contrary to *things*, mere *objects* are there for
science, to be dissected and analyzed, commoditized and sold, and perhaps
represented in computer databases. *Things*, on the other, hand carry the
aura, or mood, of authenticity; or at least, we grant them that authenticity.

Heidegger was not content with a comfortable characterization of things
as drawing together meanings, stories, craft processes, and communities.
The *thing* is always open to dispute; the "*thing* means a gathering, and specifically a gathering to deliberate on a matter under discussion, a contested
matter."[65] In Scandinavian countries, the *thing* is the Parliament,[66] a judicial
assembly. Whatever things are, they are situated, contextual, and born of
unresolved contest. No thing is quite as it seems. The mood accompanying
the thing is not always one of blending in and quiet acquiescence. There's
a lesson here for systems design.

Interaction designers draw attention to the trope of "calm computing," introduced by Mark Weiser: "A calm technology will move easily from the periphery of our attention, to the center, and back."[67] However, the reality is bound to be otherwise—and why not? According to Dourish and Bell, "we will always be assembling heterogeneous technologies to achieve individual and collective effects, and they will almost always be messy."[68]

Earlier in this chapter, I suggested that the functional success of a device does not equate automatically to positive mood states for the user. Difficulty can provide a satisfying challenge, and pain sometimes precedes gain. Another way to look at poor device performance is to examine what happens when devices are severed from their usual network of connections. Disconnects occur, and devices do not fit their context. There's a breakdown in the device, but also in the interconnected whole of which it is a part. Rather than tuning in, the device tunes out; it sets up discords. The relationship among machines, mood, and failure helps advance an understanding of mood and mobility. Another of Heidegger's ideas about *things* is the way that equipment is effectively invisible to the person using it until some moment of breakdown.[69]

Typology of Machine Failure

At a conference on the anniversary of the death of Alan Turing (1912–1954), some of us proposed a cultural theory of machine failure,[70] which we've reflected on and developed since. We proposed several creative machine categories that intersect with Turing's theoretical and actual machines, such as his encryption, universal, and cipher machines. We proposed four categories of productive machine failure, each of which has mood correlates.

First is the improving machine. Any machine is on the way to perfection, full and perfect functionality—if not in this generation, then through its successors. Historians of technology invoke Turing's machines in a lineage of devices to situate the computer, to give it a legitimate place in a history of improvement. Think of the transformations of ubiquitous mobile devices that society is quick to describe as indicators of progress. I've discussed the myth of machines that replicate and assemble themselves, the implanting and intensification of Freud's eros function—the pleasure principle—into inanimate objects. Self-replicating and self-assembling machines participate in a celebration of organism, evolution, and improvement. These are the most common machines that reach production, but they are not quite there yet. Any concerns about shortcomings in our consumer devices are assuaged by the promise of something better just around the corner. For such improving machines, full functionality is always just out of reach.[71]

Second is the so-called perfect machine. The improving metaphor suggests progress toward an ideal machine. Turing had such a machine in mind as he broached the concept of the Oracle, the universal machine that could perform "uncomputable" operations. Mathematicians harbor the concept of the ideal machine, the mathematical and logical construct that is theoretically useful but otherwise impractical to build and use. Within this category, there are many machines appearing in so-called thought experiments. One such machine is that advanced by the philosopher Robert Nozick, who proposed the Experience Machine.[72] He conjectured that in the distant future scientists might be able to transport a human brain into a vat of suitable nutrients and wire it up to experience the full richness of human life and interaction, but at a vastly improved level.[73] The scenario is picked up in various philosophical, fictional, and artistic contexts,[74] not least the scenario presented in the film *The Matrix* (1999), in which humans are wired to a perfectly convincing synthetic reality, while serving as a source of bioelectric energy for machines, echoing again the quasi-Freudian theme of erotic energy. Thankfully, such perfect machines don't yet exist; they fail to appear, a particularly persistent and frustrating form of failure.

Third is the subversion machine. As well as carrying out a function, a machine can serve to expose and exploit the dysfunction in other machines.[75] Mark Dery describes the overtly transgressive nature of online pornography in these terms: "For every repressive action from the dominant culture, there is an equal and opposite transgressive reaction from subcultures."[76] Subversion machines operate in much the same way as protest, gorilla action, and radical performance that work to resist, irritate, and transform the dominant culture. The art protest rock group *Pussy Riot* placed themselves and their musical instruments in a sacred space, and deployed sacrilegious and sexually explicit lyrics in their protest songs. The subversion machine operates much as the surrealists regarded the *thing* (or *objet*) as a dramatic intervention into some context: a urinal in an art gallery, an anvil in the company of a sewing machine, or a fish swimming across a desert. Art has the potential to expose something new by virtue of the differences it brings to light, by subverting expectations and challenging the dominant order.

Machines amplify weak signals, transform energy, deliver power, and offer mechanical advantage. Subversion machines also render everyday situations somehow strange by introducing elements that are exaggerated as well as strange. Devices can surprise and shock, even by their very idea. In *Crimes of Passion*, China Blue extracts a series of sex toys from the client's carrier bag, eventually alighting on one of which she asks, "Is this a Cruise Missile or a Pershing?"[77] In chapter 4, I outlined some of the neurological evidence for the effects exaggeration has on mood and emotion. Exaggeration operates subversively in the case of actions, events, settings and devices. Exaggeration provides a socially useful charge, a shift in thinking, the potential for shock. Porn and the devices and channels it recruits trade in exaggeration. According to Dery, "online porn peddlers need to make themselves heard, too, and taking fetishes to gut-lurching extremes is a proven means of grabbing pornsurfers by the eyeballs."[78] As Dery says of so-called inverts and degenerates, they "have to ratchet up their iconoclasm in order to earn the bourgeois seal of disapproval that is the badge of true transgression."[79] In a similar manner, subversion machines exaggerate, disrupt, distort, and provoke.

Fourth is the fully dysfunctional machine. A typology of dysfunction would include machines that do not do what they are supposed to, machines with unexpected behaviors, and machines that fail intermittently and unpredictably, incapacitated machines, imaginary machines that could never work, machines as amusement, machines conceived in ignorance of mechanical operations, machines pushed beyond the limits of their effective functioning, and ambitious prototypes that don't make it to full production (so-called vaporware).[80] In a colorful report relating science fiction to ubiquitous computing research, Dourish and Bell remark on the dysfunctional aspects of certain made-up technologies. For the machines of *Blake's 7* and *Doctor Who*, there was "a form of persistent, niggling, failure to live up to expectations; devices that operate with creaks and groans, or erratically, or not at all. Perhaps they worked once and are simply aging; perhaps they have broken and lie beyond the power of the protagonists to repair."[81] The overt mood-modulating machines outlined previously all have some brush with dysfunction. At the more extreme end of the functional spectrum, Cedric Price's Fun Palace was never built and was an amusing fantasy anyway. The orgone accumulator was a metal box you would sit in so as to harness and amplify sexual energies. Needless to say, it didn't go anywhere. Woody Allen's orgasmatron was of course a joke in a film, incapacitating its occupant. The Excessive Machine in *Barbarella* overheats and implodes. The joke about pleasure-enhancing machines is that you can get too much of a good thing. But then, failure is not necessarily the end of the story.

Disruptive Technologies

In an influential article on disruptive technologies and risk taking, Clayton Christensen and Joseph Bower identified the advantages enjoyed by small firms: "Small, hungry organizations are good at placing economical bets, rolling with the punches, and agilely changing product and market strategies in response to feedback from initial forays into the market."[82] They were writing about firms producing hardware for mass markets: companies that design and manufacture mobile phones and disk drives. Now, we might include app developers and independent game producers.

Christensen and Bower argue that large firms who do all the right things, including listening to their regular customers, may in fact be missing out on the opportunities provided by innovation: "If knowledgeable technologists believe the new technology might progress faster than the market's demand for performance improvement, then that technology, which does not meet customers' needs today, may very well address them tomorrow."[83] As well as affecting businesses, I think that new technologies have the potential to disrupt social and cultural practices. That's why some of us are fascinated by new gadgets. Like a stunning new artwork, they challenge and disturb what we do and think. Some HCI researchers and developers concur. In their investigation of domestic technologies, Genevieve Bell and colleagues assert that "making domestic life and technologies strange provides technology designers with the opportunity to actively reflect on, rather than passively propagate, the existing politics and culture of home life."[84] In part, technologies "defamiliarize," and "will almost always be messy."[85] They have consequences that are unintended.

Countless research and development programs attest to the fact that a computer device may not function as proposed—in providing the intelligent user interface, sympathetic voice interaction, automated self-assembly, or mood modulation. However, failure in all or some of a machine's functioning doesn't invalidate the research program or render it useless. In this light, Turing's machines are interventions into the context of reflections on thought, exposing what human intelligence is or is not. Reflections on mind developed within analytic philosophy, phenomenology, structuralism, and cognitive science offer various forms of accommodation and resistance to the provocation of intelligent machines, which didn't need to be fully functional to provide this role. This is not to champion dysfunctional computer programs and devices, but to recognize that machines have an impact other than via their correct functioning. Mood machines do something similar. Mood modulators have provoked new understandings of life, by not only showing what life is, but also revealing what it is not. At the very least, I think failed mood-modulating machines can assist in exposing failures in our thinking about pleasure, mood, emotion, and cognition. Perhaps, in turn, this failure leads to deeper understanding . . . or unfailing humility about machine capability.

Summary

In this chapter, I began with a reflection on some of the devices that writers, inventors, and filmmakers have imagined for influencing moods. Then, I reviewed the ways that familiar networked digital devices serve this purpose, from the mass media content they deliver to the way they aid people in navigating to new physical places, which in turn influence mood. I concluded that devices do not act alone, but mood effects ultimately depend on the way devices are positioned within constellations of technologies, practices, places, and people. I examined the use of networked digital devices as vehicles for delivering erotic content. Critical commentators regard consumer-generated netporn as more interesting than the commercial variety. The quest for erotic gratification is of course just a breeze on a current within the human maelstrom that Sigmund Freud identified as the pleasure principle (eros). Wanting to participate in pleasurable experiences as well as those that harm is both a private anguish and a feature of social movements writ large. Digital devices are part of this complicity in the mood of the times. Some people want to extend sociability to the relationships among ordinary, nonsentient things, the Internet of Things. Things are connected, but not only through digital networks. The idea of disconnected devices took us to machine failure, different kinds of machines, and various degrees of functioning. I looked at machines that subvert, those that improve, ideal machines, and the outright dysfunctional machine. Machines don't have to function perfectly to have an impact on mood, and failure is also disclosive in any case, confirming yet again the active and socially constructed character of moods and their dependence on interactions among technologies, practices, places, and people.

Coda: The Brain in the City

How does the space you are in affect the way you feel? My colleagues and I published results from a study using head-mounted EEG technology worn by people walking about outdoors in Edinburgh.[86] We think this is a first. Such studies usually take place in a laboratory, with human subjects sitting in front of a computer monitor and looking at pictures of city streets and landscapes. In our study, we took the EEG technology out into the field.

The research was undertaken by Panos Mavros, Jenny Roe, Peter Aspinall, and me. As researchers in architecture, environmental psychology, health studies, and urban design, we are interested in the relationship between the environment and emotions. We conducted a study using mobile EEG as a method to record and analyze the emotional experience of people walking in three types of urban environment, including parkland. Using Emotiv EPOC,[87] a low-cost mobile EEG recorder, participants took part in a twenty-five-minute walk through three different areas of Edinburgh. The areas were a shopping street, a path through green space, and a street in a busy commercial area. The equipment provided continuous recordings from five channels.

The manufacturer of the EEG recorder identifies these channel outputs as "short-term excitement," "frustration," "engagement," "arousal," and "meditation level." In fact, the readings are derived from the faint frequency signals picked up from the human brain, known as alpha, beta, delta, and theta waves. These are the major pulse frequencies at which brain activity takes place and seem to be reliable indicators of the affective state of the person from whom readings are taken.

Our analysis of the data shows evidence of lower frustration, engagement, and arousal as well as higher meditation when moving into the green space zone and higher engagement when moving out of it. Our study provides evidence in support of other perceptual and preference studies based on questionnaires, observations, and the use of other sensor data. We found systematic differences in EEG recordings among the three urban areas, in line with theories about how certain behaviors, environments, and technologies can assist recovery from short-term or long-term periods of stress or illness—that is, restoration theory.

Our study has implications for promoting urban green space to enhance mood, important in encouraging people to walk more or engage in other forms of physical or reflective activity. More green plazas, parkland, trees, access to the countryside, and urban design and architecture that incorporates more of the atmosphere of outdoor open space are all good for our health and well-being. Our study also intersects with the current fascination with global positioning system (GPS) mapping techniques, providing new avenues for experimentation. The recordings from the portable EEG were tagged with location data and later turned into maps showing the relative levels of readings at different points along the journeys.

Even without producing useful data, wearing a head-mounted device for monitoring putative affective states renders the familiar experience of walking strange, and for the design researcher provokes new thoughts about mood and mobility.

This coda prompted the following discussion when posted online.

Comment 1: Perhaps the technology or methodology could become a form of sick building diagnosis, with data extracted and medication prescribed by interior architects, designers, and so on.

Comment 2: Good idea, though wearing and adjusting head-mounted EEG is not currently practical (or desirable) on a day-to-day basis. May be plausible for a research study, except that there are many stress factors in the workplace other than the interior design.

Comment 3: Is heart rate relevant?

Comment 4: I think so, but heart rate changes with physical activity and other factors. Or, were you thinking that changes in outdoor exertion might affect the EEG result?

Comment 5: Given that current debate in many cities considers connectivity within urban centers to be important, as well as the importance of green networks, I imagine that this could have applications in both design and postoccupancy studies.

Comment 6: We are also analyzing data from screen-based studies of urban visual preferences using EEG, but it's too early to report on that yet. It will be interesting to see if others replicate the results from our outdoor study.

Epilogue: From Head to World

I've attempted to navigate the emotional spaces of digital social networks, so it's appropriate to conclude with a spatial question[1] or, more specifically, a question about location: Where do emotions happen? It's a common query. Roberta Flack asked in an old 1970s hit, "Where is the love?" The Google Ngram website shows that the phrases "find love" and "find happiness" occur much more frequently than "find sorrow" and "find anger" in Google's database of book contents.[2] Of course, designers, philosophers, psychologists, and other scholars ask the question about where things happen within a different frame of reference. Here are some candidate answers to the research question of where emotions take place. The answers lead inevitably to propositions about mood.

First, some think that emotions are planted firmly in the head, particularly at the core of the limbic system, in the almond-shaped structure known as the *amygdala*. According to introductory texts such as *The Brain: A Beginner's Guide*, this structure "has a crucial and important role in the mediation and control of major emotions like friendship, love, rage and aggression; emotions that are essential for self-preservation."[3] Most popular books explaining "the new science of the brain" resort at some stage to diagrams of where things happen. The main purpose is to show the evolution of brain function, from those functions that are the most primitive and are shared among species (e.g., the fear response) to higher functions, such as advanced problem solving. The proximity between functioning parts also provides clues about their mutual dependencies. For example, someone who has a damaged amygdala may recognize another person, but won't be able to decide whether or not he or she likes that person.

However, brain maps only take us so far. An online article by philosopher Andy Clark called "Out of Our Brains" provides a lighthearted account of brain function mapping: "'brain blob' pictures that show just where activity (indirectly measured by blood oxygenation level) is concentrated as we attempt to solve different kinds of puzzles: blobs here for thinking of nouns, there for thinking of verbs, over there for solving ethical puzzles of a certain class, and so on, ad blobum."[4] I hope that in this book I've been able to demonstrate the limited scope of brain function mapping by emphasizing the cultural aspects of emotional life and action.

Second, most scholars concur that the whole body is complicit in emotional responses. As I've shown, the philosopher William James famously conflated bodily actions and basic human emotions, such as fear. The stimulus encounter (a bear), running for your life, and the attendant feelings are what constitutes the emotion of fear. But then, most emotions map onto actions, postures, and expressions exhibited by bodies: happiness with agitation, sadness with stooping, and anger with tension.

An emotion indicates an attitude, after all, which is something the body does. As well as suggesting a mental view or opinion, "attitude" suggests a bodily posture, pose, disposition, or orientation. To have an attitude toward something is simply to orient one's body in relation to it, often to face it. A person or thing can have "an attitude," or simply "attitude" in its own right. A person "with attitude" is opinionated in a way that is unselfconscious. I think designers can learn a great deal from studying what bodies do rather than just focusing on claims about the emotions people are experiencing.

Third, for some researchers, emotions are *out there*. Andy Clark and David Chalmers propose that the mind is not only in the brain, the head, and the human body, but that human beings are already wired in to the world as an extended, thinking entity.[5] The human organism is very economical in its deployment of cognitive activity, and in order to resolve problems it latches onto aspects of the world to which it is already in tune. Extending the extended mind proposition, if thought is out there, then so are emotions.

Fourth is the relational position. Experimental psychologist Joseph de Rivera and colleagues have demonstrated that "an emotion may be viewed as a relationship between the person and other rather than as something within the person. . . . An emotion is not an internal response to an external situation but a transaction between person and situation."[6] After all, you can be angry with the bank teller at the same time you love your kids. Some emotions are obviously relational, such as anger, horror, and love, each of which is directed at an object. However, de Rivera indicates that "me" emotions also exist, such as depression, guilt, and a sense of security. In the case of such self-oriented emotions, an *other* is at least implied. What we characterize as "internal processes" derive from something relational and grounded in social interaction.[7]

The fifth proposition about the site of emotions brings questions of environment into play. Emotions are in the environment, including architecture and equipment. Here, I'll requote the philosopher Otto Bollnow about mood: "Mood is itself not something subjectively 'in' an individual and not something objective that could be found 'outside' in his surroundings, but it concerns the individual in his still undivided unity with his surroundings. . . . One speaks of a mood of the human temperament as well as of the mood of a landscape or a closed interior space, and both are, strictly speaking, only two aspects of the same phenomenon."[8] I hope this book has marshaled sufficient evidence to demonstrate how digital devices, as part of our environment, are complicit in the formation of moods and emotions.

Six, emotions are in language. There are different ways of talking about emotion. Certain words are encouraged and accepted in some contexts but not others. Anthropologist Catherine Lutz undertook fieldwork into community life on a Micronesian island. She found her own European-American practices of venting grief at a funeral under challenge. She was exhorted by locals to "cry big," rather than just sniffle. If she didn't cry big, she would "be sick."[9] Emotions are circulated, validated, and even created through a host of linguistic practices, metaphors, and tropes.

Seventh, as long as we think of language as performance, then emotions are in our actions. We human beings make, create, and trigger moods in the contexts of our actions. That includes social interactions, the uses of language, and artifacts: all the paraphernalia of human sociability. We are reflexive creatures. We don't only have emotions, but also talk about them, and have feelings about our feelings. I discussed metamoods in chapter 8.

The eighth and final proposition asserts the phenomenological, ontological position that we need to understand emotions in relation to our whole being. This is a position more accurately directed to moods. Emotions draw on our immersion in a primordial condition of *Stimmung*—that is, mood. This proposition provided the stimulus for this book. Getting down to moods touches on basic aspects of the human condition and our place in the world.

Writers, inventors, and filmmakers have imagined various devices for adjusting people's moods. I have reviewed the ways that familiar networked digital devices serve this purpose, including in the delivery of mood-altering entertainment and media content. Devices do not act alone, but mood effects ultimately depend on the way devices are positioned within constellations of technologies, practices, places, and people. Moods generated within groups and crowds even incite people to action, protest, and revolution. Moods are mobile. They circulate, ebb, and flow, abetted by communities connected through networked digital media. Space is filled with devices and technologies that really do have a role in the way moods happen.

Notes

Introduction

1. Do digital devices influence your mood? In the course of my research, I put this question to a class of students whose specialty is digital media and culture. Nearly all supported the view that technologies influence the way you feel, and networked, social media–enabled mobile and laptop devices offer more than other technologies. At the very least, they provide channels for mood-altering entertainment. The responses from the admittedly biased sample referred to content, functionality, dysfunction, intensity of engagement, rapid emotional transitions, realism, controlling your emotions, dependency, addiction, persuasion, being in contact with others through these media, isolation, having desires met, experiencing a lack, assault, and the personality of the user. I provide evidence to support these responses in the rest of this book.

2. See Kramera, Guillory, and Hancock, "Experimental Evidence of Massive-Scale Emotional Contagion through Social Networks," 8788. The emotional content of the news feeds was based on word usage, to be discussed in chapter 4. The idea was to test whether or not Facebook users pick up on and "transmit" the mood of their news feed to others. Also see Krämer, Wiewiorra, and Weinhardt, "Net Neutrality: A Progress Report," 794.

3. Meyer, "Everything We Know About Facebook's Secret Mood Manipulation Experiment," http://www.theatlantic.com/technology/archive/2014/06/everything -we-know-about-facebooks-secret-manipulation-experiment/373648/ (accessed April 12, 2015).

4. Thrift, "Intensities of Feeling: Towards a Spatial Politics of Affect." Thrift argues that ubiquitous media screens now provide something similar. We are being encouraged toward positive attitudes to the built environment and civic life. Writing prior to the widespread adoption of social media, Thrift indicated how politicians and citizens are encouraged to think of cities as vibrant and exciting, engendering a kind of creativity that in turn enhances economic prosperity. On the subject of the intelligent and prosperous digital city and "affective urbanism," see de Lange, "The Smart

City You Love to Hate: Exploring the Role of Affect in Hybrid Urbanism." Also see O. Jones, "An Ecology of Emotion, Memory, Self, and Landscape."

5. Packard, *The Hidden Persuaders*.

6. Season 1, episode 1 of *Mad Men*. Quoted in *The Telegraph* (20 of the most memorable *Mad Men* quotes) and elsewhere; see http://www.telegraph.co.uk/ culture/tvandradio/8170937/20-of-the-most-memorable-Mad-Men-quotes.html (accessed April 12, 2015).

7. Ling, "From Ubicomp to Ubiex(pectations)," 177; Ling, *New Tech, New Ties: How Mobile Communication Is Reshaping Social Cohesion*.

8. Chomsky and Herman, *Manufacturing Consent: The Political Economy of the Mass Media*.

9. Pariser, *The Filter Bubble: What the Internet Is Hiding from You*, 122.

10. Fox, *Watching the English: The Hidden Rules of English Behavior*, "Grooming-talk," under "Bonding-talk."

11. Ling, "From ubicomp to ubiex(pectations)."

12. A. Wilson, "Phantom Vibration Syndrome: Word of the Year."

13. Lovink, "Hermes on the Hudson: Notes on Media Theory after Snowden," http// www.e-flux.com/journal/hermes-on-the-hudson-notes-on-media-theory-after -snowden/ (accessed April 12, 2015). "Snowden events" refers to the leaking of classified documents by Edward Snowden while working as a National Security Agency (NSA) contractor. More significantly, the documents revealed massive global covert surveillance of the communications of ordinary citizens.

14. Ibid. For similar dark reflections on the current age, see Bratton, "The Black Stack."

15. Historicism is largely attributed to German idealism, exemplified in the historical theorizing of Johann Gottfried von Herder (1744–1803), Wilhelm von Humboldt (1767–1835), Georg Wilhelm Friedrich Hegel (1770–1831), Leopold von Ranke (1795–1886), and Friedrich Schleiermacher (1768–1834). In my discipline of architecture, historicism treats interpretation and history as the processes of uncovering the grand idea. Great architecture gives expression to the spirit, mood, and aspirations of a people, and history presents it as such. We discuss the issue in relation to hermeneutics in the introduction to Snodgrass and Coyne, *Interpretation in Architecture: Design as a Way of Thinking*.

16. Although Onion Inc. is based in Madison, WI.

17. http://www.theonion.com/video/internet-scam-alert-most-kickstarter-projects -just,28655/ (accessed April 12, 2015).

18. http://www.theonion.com/video/braindead-teen-only-capable-of-rolling-eyes -and-te,27225/ (accessed April 12, 2015).

19. www.youtube.com/watch?v=CK62I-4cuSY (accessed April 12, 2015).

20. This is the message that appears at theonion.com when a reader reaches the limit of his or her access to free content (accessed March 2015).

21. For accounts of the relationships between emotion, space, place, and the body, see the collection of articles by Davidson, Bondi, and Smith, *Emotional Geographies*. Phil Hubbard provides an interesting account of the urban phenomenon of "going" out as an experience that's both emotional and embodied. See P. Hubbard, "The Geographies of 'Going Out': Emotion and Embodiment in the Evening Economy." Also see van Liempt, van Aalst, and Schwanen, "Introduction: Geographies of the Urban Night."

22. James, "What Is an Emotion?"

23. De Botton, *The Art of Travel*, 41.

24. Apparently, this is an example of the "ethics of disappearance," according to Paul Virilio in *The Aesthetics of Disappearance*.

25. For interesting research into the representation of and notation for such travel experiences, see Kamvasinou, "Notation Timelines and the Aesthetics of Disappearance."

26. Mansikka, "Can Boredom Educate Us? Tracing a Mood in Heidegger's Fundamental Ontology from an Educational Point of View." Mansikka refers to the example provided by Martin Heidegger of waiting impatiently for the arrival of a train. Jeff Malpas also provides an interesting account of boredom: "Boredom is one of the ways in which we can find ourselves in the world, and, in boredom, the world and our situatedness in the world come to evidence in a striking way through the way in which nothing in the world seems to matter to us. Of course, in boredom it is not that nothing matters, but rather that the only thing that seems to matter is that the world appears as not mattering to us. In this sense, boredom provides one way into philosophical questioning—one way into a grasp of our prior situatedness." Malpas, *Heidegger's Topology: Being, Place, World*, section 2.1, "Philosophy and 'Life.'"

27. Here, I don't want to equate restricted movement to the mobility practices of the differently abled.

28. Attributed to the British Foreign Secretary Edward Grey on the evening Britain entered into the World War I.

29. As I refer to mapping a few times in this book, it's worth elaborating a little on the role of maps. Maps are active media, made with some purpose in mind. In mathematics, the verb *to map* is to associate the elements of one set with those in another. For example, all of the alphabetical characters (a, b, c, etc.) map onto

numbers (97, 98, 99, etc.) through the ASCII chart of correspondences. I find it helpful to think of maps in this way, as one set of interrelated symbols corresponding to (mapped on to) some other set of interrelated symbols. Maps map to other maps: models map to models; one term in a metaphor maps to another; this maps as that; one frame of reference maps against another frame. Mapping practices (and cartography) are contingent on the circumstances in which a map is made and deployed. Maps also derive from instruments of measurement, sensors, observational practices, symbolic conventions, rules, and algorithms. Accuracy and usefulness are matters of fit between the systems being mapped and the repeatability of the mapping processes. The same applies to the discursive mapping functions in this book.

30. Lutz, "Emotion, Thought, and Estrangement: Emotion as a Cultural Category."

31. Psychological researchers are familiar with the charge that they are telling us what we know already. A short article by Tom Stafford provides a helpful response: "The purpose of psychological science is making findings about the human mind and behaviour available—obvious!—to everyone. By explicitly, rigorously, stating propositions about psychology and laying them open to testing we are democratising knowledge. We are making knowledge public, explicit and usable by everyone. That means stating the obvious, so that anyone can come and disagree with it (and so that we can be sure we aren't deluding ourselves about what is true or what we know)." Stafford, "Isn't It All Just Obvious," 95.

32. See "The Digital Humanities Manifesto 2.0," 6. Also see Fish, "The Digital Humanities and the Transcending of Mortality."

33. See, for example, Mavros et al., "Engaging the Brain: Implications of Mobile EEG for Spatial Representation"; Aspinall et al., "The Urban Brain: Analysing Outdoor Physical Activity with Mobile EEG"; Roe et al., "Engaging the Brain: The Impact of Natural versus Urban Scenes Using Novel EEG Methods in an Experimental Setting"; Coyne, "Nature versus Smartphones."

34. Darwin, *The Expression of the Emotions in Man and Animals.*

35. Freud, *On Dreams.*

36. W. Benjamin, "The Work of Art in the Age of Mechanical Reproduction." For connections between aura and atmosphere, see Böhme, "Atmosphere as the Subject Matter of Architecture"; Böhme, "Atmosphere as the Fundamental Concept of a New Aesthetics."

37. Norberg-Schulz, *Genius Loci: Towards a Phenomenology of Architecture.*

38. See Snodgrass and Coyne, *Interpretation in Architecture: Design as a Way of Thinking*; Malpas and Gander, *The Routledge Companion to Hermeneutics.*

39. Karandinou, *No-Matter: Theories and Practices of the Ephemeral in Architecture.*

40. Koeck, *Cine-Scapes: Cinematic Spaces in Architecture and Cities.*

41. Coyne, *The Tuning of Place: Sociable Spaces and Pervasive Digital Media*.

42. See, for example, Picard, *Affective Computing*.

43. Dourish and Bell, *Divining a Digital Future: Mess and Mythology in Ubiquitous Computing*, chapter 4, under "Affect."

44. Ibid.

45. Ling, "From Ubicomp to Ubiex(pectations)."

46. Available at http://richardcoyne.com (accessed April 12, 2015).

47. Access to online resources has increased dramatically in my field of architecture. See Coyne, "Even More than Architecture."

48. Russell, "Core Affect and the Psychological Construction of Emotion."

49. Kaplan, "The Restorative Benefits of Nature: Toward an Integrative Framework."

50. Gadamer, *Truth and Method*. For a fuller account of the implications of Gadamer's thinking for design, see Snodgrass and Coyne, *Interpretation in Architecture: Design as a Way of Thinking*.

51. Heidegger, *Being and Time*. I've examined the implications for digital networks of Heidegger's philosophy in various places, including Coyne, "Cyberspace and Heidegger's Pragmatics." Heidegger's thinking underlies the investigations of this book, though I resist the temptation to bring him in at every turn.

52. Massumi, *Parables for the Virtual: Movement, Affect, Sensation*.

53. Flatley, *Affective Mapping: Melancholia and the Politics of Modernism*.

54. Freud, "The Ego and the Id."

55. Picard, *Affective Computing*; Picard, "What Does It Mean for a Computer to 'Have' Emotions?" Also see Scheirera et al., "Frustrating the User on Purpose: A Step toward Building an Affective Computer." This strand of research seems driven by the desire to make computers more emotionally intelligent, as if to echo the desire to make them more cognitively intelligent. Also of note are "affective engineering" approaches, based on translating "the customer's feelings into design specifications." Nagamachi, *Kansei: Affective Engineering*, 3.

56. Norman, *Emotional Design: Why We Love (or Hate) Everyday Things*.

57. Dourish and Bell, *Divining a Digital Future: Mess and Mythology in Ubiquitous Computing*.

58. Gadamer, *Truth and Method*; Snodgrass and Coyne, *Interpretation in Architecture: Design as a Way of Thinking*.

1   What Is a Mood?

1. I'll discuss in later chapters the more recent trends in architectural practice and scholarship to deal overtly with emotion, mood, and the atmosphere of a place; see chapter 6.

2. See, for example, Beesley et al., *Responsive Architectures: Subtle Technologies.*

3. Mithen, *The Singing Neanderthals: The Origins of Music, Language, Mind and Body*, 2.

4. See, for example, neurological research by Juslin and Västfjäll, "Emotional Responses to Music: The Need to Consider Underlying Mechanisms"; Schaefer, K. Overy, and P. Nelson, "Affect and Non-Uniform Characteristics of Predictive Processing in Musical Behaviour."

5. Ranking high in the happy songs list at http://www.popculturemadness.com (accessed July 2012).

6. Philosopher Ronald da Sousa puts this position succinctly: "If you want to change your emotional state, you might try changing either the ambient scene or your physiological state, whichever is more easily manipulated." De Sousa, *The Rationality of Emotion*, 51.

7. Laird, "Self-Attribution of Emotion: The Effects of Expressive Behavior on the Quality of Emotional Experience." For a review of the theories and controversies, see McIntosh, "Facial Feedback Hypotheses: Evidence, Implications, and Directions."

8. Strack, Martin, and Stepper, "Inhibiting and Facilitating Conditions of Facial Expressions: A Nonobtrusive Test of the Facial Feedback Hypothesis."

9. Finzi, *The Face of Emotion: How Botox Affects Our Moods and Relationships*, 3. For an academic discussion of the topic, see Alam et al., "Botulinum Toxin and the Facial Feedback Hypothesis: Can Looking Better Make You Feel Happier?"

10. Riskind and Gotay, "Physical Posture: Could It Have Regulatory or Feedback Effects on Motivation and Emotion?"

11. Dövelin, von Scheve, and Konijn, *The Routledge Handbook of Emotions and Mass Media.*

12. Cohen, "Music as a Source of Emotion in Film," 249. Also see Cubitt, *The Cinema Effect.*

13. BARB is the Broadcasters Audience Research Board: http://www.barb.co.uk/ (accessed April 12, 2015).

14. According to the Audit Bureau of Circulations (ABC): http://www.abc.org.uk/ (accessed April 12, 2015).

15. Maslov and Redner, "Promise and Pitfalls of Extending Google's PageRank Algorithm to Citation Networks."

16. Hochschild, *The Managed Heart: Commercialization of Human Feeling*, 8. Also see Highmore and Bourne Taylor, "Introducing Mood Work."

17. Hochschild, *The Managed Heart: Commercialization of Human Feeling*, 8.

18. Ibid., 11.

19. Ibid.

20. Coyne, *Technoromanticism: Digital Narrative, Holism, and the Romance of the Real*.

21. Clark, *Natural-Born Cyborgs: Minds, Technologies, and the Future of Human Intelligence*.

22. Gere, "Brains-in-Vats, Giant Brains and World Brains: The Brain as Metaphor in Digital Culture."

23. Ramachandran, *The Tell-Tale Brain: Unlocking the Mysteries of Human Nature*.

24. For an exploration of fMRI and design, see Alexiou et al., "Exploring the Neurological Basis of Design Cognition Using Brain Imaging: Some Preliminary Results."

25. Norman, *Emotional Design: Why We Love (or Hate) Everyday Things*, 8.

26. Dourish and Bell, *Divining a Digital Future: Mess and Mythology in Ubiquitous Computing*, chapter 4, under "Affect." They also draw on the influential insights of Catherine Lutz. See Lutz, "Emotion, Thought, and Estrangement: Emotion as a Cultural Category."

27. Picard, *Affective Computing*, x.

28. Dourish and Bell, *Divining a Digital Future: Mess and Mythology in Ubiquitous Computing*, chapter 4, under "Affect."

29. Spinoza, *Ethics*, 83. For further discussion relating Spinoza's concepts to city life, see Thrift, "Intensities of Feeling: Towards a Spatial Politics of Affect." For a discussion of Spinoza's concept of *affectus*, geometry, and space, see Rawes, "Spinoza's Geometric Ecologies."

30. Norman, *Emotional Design: Why We Love (or Hate) Everyday Things*, 11.

31. Wundt, *Outlines of Psychology*.

32. Wundt introduced a third dimension that contemporary theorists think of in terms of *attention*. It matters whether you are attending to the feeling or if it's somehow in the background of our awareness, like a mood.

33. Russell and Pratt, "A Description of the Affective Quality Attributed to Environments."

34. Russell, "Core Affect and the Psychological Construction of Emotion," 149.

35. Ibid., 148.

36. Freud, "Civilization and Its Discontents," 264.

37. Saussure, *Course in General Linguistics*.

38. Dourish and Bell, *Divining a Digital Future: Mess and Mythology in Ubiquitous Computing*, chapter 4, under "Affect."

39. Massumi, *Parables for the Virtual: Movement, Affect, Sensation*, 27.

40. Russell, "Core Affect and the Psychological Construction of Emotion," 149.

41. Flatley, *Affective Mapping: Melancholia and the Politics of Modernism*, 19.

42. Mithen, *The Singing Neanderthals: The Origins of Music, Language, Mind and Body*, 90.

43. Isaacson, *Steve Jobs: The Exclusive Biography*, 350.

44. Mithen, *The Singing Neanderthals: The Origins of Music, Language, Mind and Body*, 90.

45. deNora, *Music and Everyday Life*, 57.

46. One example is the sequence of notes A, B, C, E, F, and A in the key of C major as they appear in the Japanese song *Sakura*. Many listeners would regard the Japanese mode as setting a melancholic mood.

47. Aristotle, *The Politics*, 10340a18.

48. Cooke, *The Language of Music*.

49. In the Japanese example (Sakura), that would be the A note, the "tonic" note appearing at the start and end of the melody to which the melody gravitates. The A note may even feature as a bass drone. If a composition used the same range of notes but started and ended on the C note or had the C as a base drone, then the mood would be very different.

50. Dourish and Bell, *Divining a Digital Future: Mess and Mythology in Ubiquitous Computing*, chapter 4, under "Affect."

51. I discuss voice at length in Coyne, *The Tuning of Place: Sociable Spaces and Pervasive Digital Media*.

52. *Blade Runner* (1982), directed by Ridley Scot, screenplay by Hampton Fancher and David Peoples. In fact, as a subjunctive the sentence is incomplete, with an implied completion something like "then you would know what I've been through," or something similar, though that's best left to the imagination. In his book on effective writing, Ernest Gowers says of the subjunctive, "it denotes a greater call on the imagination." Gowers, Greenbaum, and Whitcut, *The Complete Plain Words*, 138.

53. Consider this sentence: "Researchers think that mood is emotion without an object." This requires less effort to process than, "Mood is thought to be emotion without an object." The latter version raises the question of who is doing the thinking (the major actant of the verb "to think"), which arguably halts the flow of the sentence. It instils a mood of uncertainty, hesitancy, and perhaps modesty in the claim, or perhaps exercises less control over mood, because we don't know who is doing what to whom. However, mood as I've described it in this chapter is emotion without identifiable agency. Mood is emotion in the passive voice.

54. http://www.oed.com/ (accessed April 12, 2015).

55. Ibid.

56. Wigley, "The Architecture of Atmosphere," 18. For a survey of the ephemeral in architecture, see Karandinou, *No-Matter: Theories and Practices of the Ephemeral in Architecture*. For an examination of Karl Marx's use of "atmosphere" and the term's ambiguity and multiple uses, see Anderson, "Affective Atmospheres."

57. Wigley, "The Architecture of Atmosphere," 18.

58. The traceur is the free runner who jumps over street furniture and scales buildings as sport.

59. Kozel, "Conference Presentation Notes."

60. The codas to chapters are adapted from blog posts and comments available at http://richardcoyne.com (accessed April 12, 2015).

61. Juslin and Västfjäll, "Emotional Responses to Music: The Need to Consider Underlying Mechanisms."

62. Ibid., 564.

63. Ibid.

64. Ibid., 566.

65. Ibid., 560.

66. Ibid., 567.

2 Moved by the Mob

1. Carey, *Communication as Culture: Essays on Media and Society.*

2. Kramera, Guillory, and Hancock, "Experimental Evidence of Massive-Scale Emotional Contagion through Social Networks." For an example of the petri dish metaphor applied to social media, see Becker, "Welcome to the Petri Dish: A Great Big Thumbs Up."

3. Carey, *Communication as Culture: Essays on Media and Society*, 43.

4. Ibid., 21.

5. Aristotle, *The Art of Rhetoric*, 141(1378a).

6. Heidegger, *Being and Time*, 178. Michael Hyde and Craig Smith explain Heidegger on emotion in *Being and Time*: "Heidegger recognizes that emotions function primordially as vehicles for the active sensibility of human beings; that is, they provide the perspectives for seeing the world as interesting, as something that matters and that warrants interpretation. Emotions are not primarily psychical phenomena originating purely from one's inner condition; rather, they take form in the interaction between a person and the world, as the world is perceived by the person through an act of consciousness. In this way, an emotion orients a person toward the world in a 'concernful' manner." They go on to write about mood as "generalised emotions permeating a person's existence" (Hyde and Smith, "Aristotle and Heidegger on Emotion and Rhetoric: Questions of Time and Space," 74). They then explain Heidegger's insistence that we are always projecting forward, anticipating and in a condition of "not yet." This discussion links concepts of time with emotion. Hyde and Smith make the connection with rhetoric and Aristotle on knowing your audience before you speak to them. I think the language connection is also strengthened in Heidegger's later writing, in which he affirms language as "the house of Being." See Heidegger, "Building, Dwelling, Thinking," 143.

7. Dourish and Bell, *Divining a Digital Future: Mess and Mythology in Ubiquitous Computing*, chapter 4, under "Affect."

8. Sook Kwon and Sung, "Follow Me! Global Marketers' Twitter Use."

9. "Twitter Co-Founder Says There's More to Life than Tweets."

10. For an account linking sympathy to empathy in the arts, see Spuybroek, *The Sympathy of Things: Ruskin and the Ecology of Design*, 146.

11. Smith, *The Theory of Moral Sentiments*, 10.

12. Ibid., 14.

13. Smith, *An Inquiry into the Nature and Causes of the Wealth of Nations*, 22.

14. *The Iron Lady* (2011), directed by Phyllida Lloyd, screenplay by Abi Morgan.

15. Green, "Reviews."

16. http://www.bbc.co.uk/news/uk-politics-17815769 (accessed April 11, 2015).

17. Ibid. Insofar as the accusation is about lack of empathy, it's also a criticism of their economic prowess. Empathy can also involve emulation. Smith writes about the propensity of the poor to emulate the rich, which leads to merely following

fashion. See A. Smith, *An Inquiry into the Nature and Causes of the Wealth of Nations*, 64. See also a social theory based on this by Veblen, *The Theory of the Leisure Class*.

18. Carlyle and Tanizaki, *Past and Present*.

19. I expand on this theme in relation to electronic commerce in Coyne, *Cornucopia Limited: Design and Dissent on the Internet*.

20. Khalil, "The Mirror Neuron Paradox: How Far Is Understanding from Mimicking?"

21. Al-Chalabi, Turner, and Delamont, *The Brain: A Beginner's Guide*.

22. He also develops and critiques Smith's ideas about emotional pitch—a nice resonance with tuning. For an account of the MNS in music, see Molnar-Szakacs and Overy, "Music and Mirror Neurons: From Motion to 'E'motion," and in architecture, Mallgrave, *The Architect's Brain: Neuroscience, Creativity, and Architecture*.

23. Rizzolatti and Craighero, "The Mirror-Neuron System."

24. But see Roger Caillois on "involuntary" mimicry in insects. Caillois, "Mimicry and Legendary Psychasthenia."

25. Rizzolatti and Craighero, "The Mirror-Neuron System," 180.

26. The moral lesson from the MNS hypothesis is that those who call the shots ought to exhibit the behavior they want of others. Considering our propensity to mimicry, there's not much use in demanding austerity in others if we don't practice it ourselves.

27. Clark, "Where Brain, Body and World Collide," 15–16.

28. McLuhan, *The Gutenberg Galaxy: The Making of Typographic Man*, 47.

29. The saying is mostly attributed to the self-help author William W. Purkey. See Purkey and Siegel, *Becoming an Innovative Leader: A New Approach to Professional and Personal Success*.

30. Bollnow, *Human Space*.

31. Ibid., 236.

32. Ibid., 237.

33. Ibid.

34. Ibid., 217.

35. Smith, *The Theory of Moral Sentiments*, 27.

36. Coyne, *The Tuning of Place: Sociable Spaces and Pervasive Digital Media*.

37. For further discussion of the concept of *Stimmung* in relation to architectural design, see Teal, "Dismantling the Built Drawing: Working with Mood in Architectural Design." In its relationship to location-based social media, see Evans, "Being-towards the Social: Mood and Orientation to Location-Based Social Media, Computational Things and Applications."

38. Bollnow, *Human Space*, 217.

39. Smith, *The Theory of Moral Sentiments*, 9.

40. Ibid., 110.

41. Ibid., 89–90.

42. Wordsworth, *The Collected Poems of William Wordsworth*, 219.

43. Philosopher Jonathan Flatley relates the condition to William James's understanding of the primacy of bodily engagement in understanding emotion. See Flatley, *Affective Mapping: Melancholia and the Politics of Modernism*.

44. Ratcliffe, "Heidegger's Attunement and the Neuropsychology of Emotion" 289.

45. Heidegger, *Being and Time*, 176. See also Heidegger, *Being and Time*, 172, and Dreyfus, *Being-in-the-World: A Commentary on Heidegger's Being and Time Division I*, 171. See also Heidegger, "What Is Metaphysics?," 100.

46. Aristotle, *The Art of Rhetoric*.

47. Heidegger, *Being and Time*, 178.

48. Ratcliffe, "Heidegger's Attunement and the Neuropsychology of Emotion," 290.

49. Schutz, "Making Music Together," 177.

50. Ibid., 176.

51. Smith, *The Theory of Moral Sentiments*, 316.

52. Gieseking and Mangold, *The People, Place and Space Reader*, 107.

53. Debord, *Report on the Construction of Situations and on the International Situationist Tendency's Conditions of Organization and Action*, 10. Also see McDonough, *Guy Debord and the Situationalist International: Texts and Documents*.

54. Debord, *Report on the Construction of Situations and on the International Situationist Tendency's Conditions of Organization and Action*, 12.

55. Ling, "From Ubicomp to Ubiex(pectations)."

56. Ghannam, *Social Media in the Arab World: Leading up to the Uprisings of 2011*, 23.

57. Ibid.

58. Ghannam, *Social Media in the Arab World: Leading up to the Uprisings of 2011*, 21.

59. http://battletracker.com/index.php?page=CoD5GameInfo (accessed April 11, 2015).

60. Giumetti and Markey, "Violent Video Games and Anger as Predictors of Aggression," 1241.

61. Cohen, *Folk Devils and Moral Panics*.

62. Watson, Clark, and Tellegen, "Development and Validation of Brief Measures of Positive and Negative Affect: The PANAS Scales."

63. For a full PANAS list of emotions, see ibid., 1070.

64. Deignan, "Corpus Linguistics and Metaphor," 280.

65. Ibid., 281.

66. Xenakis, *Formalized Music: Thought and Mathematics in Music*, 9. I also quote this passage in *The Tuning of Place*, in a discussion on noise and entropy. See Coyne, *The Tuning of Place: Sociable Spaces and Pervasive Digital Media*, 234.

67. Topping, "Looting 'Fuelled by Social Exclusion.'"

68. Lewis et al., "Rioters Say Anger with Police Fuelled Summer Unrest."

69. Lutz and White, "The Anthropology of Emotions."

70. Ibid.

71. Berger and Luckmann, *The Social Construction of Reality: A Treatise in the Sociology of Knowledge*.

72. Lutz and White, "The Anthropology of Emotions," 420.

73. Ibid., 417.

74. Dourish and Bell, *Divining a Digital Future: Mess and Mythology in Ubiquitous Computing*, chapter 4, under "Affect."

75. Bateson, *Naven*, 2.

76. Ibid., 33.

77. Morris and Schnurr, *Mood: The Frame of Mind*, 8–9.

78. Schank and Abelson, *Scripts, Plans, Goals and Understanding: An Inquiry into Human Knowledge Structures*; Black, *Models and Metaphors: Studies in Language and Philosophy*.

79. They probably wouldn't label them as moods, but scientists and philosophers of science talk of *models*, which are formalized and diagrammatized sets of relationships and analogies. The idea of the *paradigm* was advanced by the philosopher of science Thomas Kuhn; it includes, formulas, procedures, and methods, but also

laboratory practices, rules about gaining academic tenure, and even how to format and present publications. See Kuhn, *The Structure of Scientific Revolutions.*

80. Deignan, "Corpus Linguistics and Metaphor," 287.

81. Joffé, "The Arab Spring in North Africa: Origins and Prospects," 311.

82. Morozov, *The Net Delusion: How Not to Liberate the World.*

83. Rittel and Webber, "Dilemmas in a General Theory of Planning." The article was an antidote to Herbert Simon's influential book *The Sciences of the Artificial.* The first edition of Simon's book appeared about four years earlier and followed the path of the founder of systems theory Ludwig Bertalanffy and others in proposing a "science of design, a body of intellectually tough, analytic, partly formalizable, partly empirical, teachable doctrine about the design process," with empirical science, mathematics, logic, and algorithmic methods as the models. See Simon, *The Sciences of the Artificial,* 58.

84. Morozov, *The Net Delusion: How Not to Liberate the World,* 311.

85. "Let us try to characterize the way in which the wide-awake grown up man looks at the intersubjective world of daily life within which and upon which he acts as a man amidst his fellow-men. This world existed before our birth, experienced and interpreted by others, our predecessors, as an organized world. Now it is given to our experience and interpretation. All interpretation of this world is based on a stock of previous experiences of it, our own or those handed down to us by parents or teachers; these experiences; in the form of 'knowledge at hand' function as a scheme of reference." Schutz, *Collected Papers I. The Problem of Social Reality,* 7.

86. Ratcliffe, "Heidegger's Attunement and the Neuropsychology of Emotion," 299.

87. Ibid.

88. See video "Project Loon: New Zealand Pilot Test," available at https://www.youtube.com/watch?v=LNCFc00oejE (accessed April 12, 2015).

89. http://www.oed.com/ (accessed April 12, 2015).

90. Cunningham, "Weather, Mood and Helping Behavior: Quasi Experiments with the Sunshine Samaritan," 1950.

91. Flaherty, *Howling (and Bleeding) at the Moon: Menstruation, Monstrosity and the Double in Ginger Snaps Werewolf Trilogy,* 11.

92. I've not seen the *Ginger Snaps Werewolf Trilogy,* but in the Pixar-Disney animated feature *Brave* (2012), Merida's mother is transformed into a huge bear. It's a contemporary made-up story about *ursusthropy* rather than lycanthropy, but it helps sustains the myth of beastly transformations, coming of age, and puberty, with a bit of sugar added.

3 Captivated by Curiosity

1. Hooper-Greenhill, *Museums and the Shaping of Knowledge*; Yates, *The Art of Memory*.

2. Fredrickson, "The Broaden-and-Build Theory of Positive Emotions."

3. Vast, Young, and Thomas, "Emotion and Automaticity: Impact of Positive and Negative Emotions on Novice and Experienced Performance of a Sensorimotor Skill."

4. Fredrickson, "The Broaden-and-Build Theory of Positive Emotions," 1372.

5. In chapter 10, I present the view that negative emotions are beneficial, in that they encourage more accurate memory recall.

6. Diener and Diener, "Most People Are Happy," 184.

7. Silvia, *Exploring the Psychology of Interest*, 15.

8. Silvia, "Interest: The Curious Emotion," 57.

9. Vitruvius, *Vitruvius: The Ten Books on Architecture*, 38.

10. Flatley, *Affective Mapping: Melancholia and the Politics of Modernism*, 19.

11. Rousseau, *Émile*.

12. Ibid.

13. Thoreau, *Walden: Or, Life in the Woods*, 68–69.

14. Kellert and Wilson, *The Biophilia Hypothesis*, 45.

15. Deakin, *Wildwood: A Journey through Trees*, 24.

16. See Coyne, "Nature versus Smartphones."

17. Cockain, "Students' Ambivalence toward Their Experiences in Secondary Education: Views from a Group of Young Chinese Studying on an International Foundation Program in Beijing."

18. Silvia, "Interest: The Curious Emotion," 59.

19. Stein and Visel, "Mao, King Kong, and the Future of the Book."

20. Silvia, *Exploring the Psychology of Interest*, 22.

21. Carey, *Communication as Culture: Essays on Media and Society*, 16.

22. Freud, "Leonardo da Vinci and a Memory of His Childhood," 170. Also see Loewenstein, "The Psychology of Curiosity: A Review and Reinterpretation."

23. Turkle, *Alone Together: Why We Expect More from Technology and Less from Each Other*; Turkle, *Evocative Objects: Things We Think With*; Turkle, *Life on the Screen:*

Identity in the Age of the Internet; Turkle, *Psychoanalytic Politics: Jacques Lacan and Freud's French Revolution*; Stone, *The War of Desire and Technology at the Close of the Mechanical Age*. For a further argument about the ephemeral and addictive nature of online friendships, see Scruton, "Hiding behind the Screen."

24. http://www.oed.com/ (accessed April 12, 2015).

25. Unlike earlier, standalone computer applications, social media applications require you to create profiles of yourself and multiply those profiles. Second Life requires users (residents) to invest effort in creating their own personas as 3-D humanoid avatars, complete with clothing and accessories. Something similar (though less like dressing up) is required of Google+, LinkedIn, WordPress, and many other websites and applications with a social aspect. Reputation among one's peers is clearly a factor when any group comes together. It is fair to say that until social media and Web 2.0, it was unusual for computer applications to incorporate tools for managing online identities.

26. To educate is to bring up or to rear; to edify is to build up, or *Bildung*, in the phenomenology literature.

27. Gadamer, *Truth and Method*.

28. "This entity which each of us is himself and which includes inquiring as one of the possibilities of its Being, we shall denote by the term 'Dasein.'" Heidegger, *Being and Time*, 27.

29. Thoreau, *Walden: Or, Life in the Woods*, 6.

30. Diener and Diener, "Most People Are Happy."

31. Available at https://nightwalk.withgoogle.com/en/home.

32. Koeck, *Cine-Scapes: Cinematic Spaces in Architecture and Cities*, 1.

33. Saussure, *Course in General Linguistics*.

34. Foucault, *Discipline and Punish: The Birth of the Prison*, 184.

35. Derrida, "Différance," 3.

36. Macfarlane, *Mountains of the Mind: A History of a Fascination*, 203. For an example of how architecture participates in this intrigue, see Hollis, *The Secret Lives of Buildings: From the Parthenon to the Vegas Strip in Thirteen Stories*.

37. Goffman, *The Presentation of Self in Everyday Life*; Goffman, *Ritual Interaction: Essays on Face-to-Face Behavior*.

38. Coyne, *Cornucopia Limited: Design and Dissent on the Internet*.

39. Playwright Bertolt Brecht said of theater: "It must amaze its public, and this can be achieved by a technique of alienating the familiar." Brecht, "A Short Organum for the Theatre," 9.

40. Rousseau, *Émile*, 158.

41. http://richardcoyne.com/2011/12/03/almost-to-infinity/ (accessed April 11, 2015).

42. Romans 6:1.

43. Heidegger, "The Origin of the Work of Art," 17.

44. Ibid., 17.

45. Ibid., 36.

46. Ibid., 39.

47. Heidegger, "What Are Poets for?, 91.

48. Heidegger, "Building, Dwelling, Thinking, 143.

49. Ibid.

50. Heidegger, "The Thing," 165.

51. Landow, "Hypertext as Collage-Writing"; Landow and Delany, "Hypertext, Hypermedia and Literary Studies: The State of the Art," 3.

52. Coyne, *Derrida for Architects*.

53. Derrida, "Plato's Pharmacy."

54. Toesenberger, "Homosexuality at the Online Hogwarts: Harry Potter Slash Fanfiction."

55. http://www.farfilm.com/films/white-light-black-rain-learn.html (accessed April 11, 2015).

4   Piqued by Pleasure

1. Michael Bozarth provides a helpful summary. See Bozarth, "Pleasure Systems in the Brain."

2. Coyne, *Technoromanticism: Digital Narrative, Holism, and the Romance of the Real*.

3. "Digital Sales Break £1bn Barrier."

4. Adorno and Horkheimer, *Dialectic of Enlightenment*, 123.

5. Ibid., 154.

6. Artaud, *The Theater and Its Double*, 60.

7. Ibid., 84.

8. Dyer, *Only Entertainment.*

9. Ibid., 176.

10. Ibid.

11. Postman, *Amusing Ourselves to Death: Public Discourse in the Age of Show Business*, 4.

12. Veblen, *The Theory of the Leisure Class.*

13. Thin, *Social Happiness: Theory into Policy and Practice*, 97.

14. For a Twitter-based sentiment analysis, see Quercia et al., "Tracking 'Gross Community Happiness' from Tweets."

15. Mislove et al., *Pulse of the Nation: U.S. Mood Throughout the Day Inferred from Twitter.*

16. Cuff, "Immanent Domain: Pervasive Computing and the Public Realm," 48.

17. Bradley and Lang, *Affective Norms for English Words (ANEW): Instruction Manual and Affective Ratings (Technical Report C-1).*

18. Aggarwal and Zhai, *Mining Text Data.*

19. Hence the therapist's advice: "While dressing or shaving or getting breakfast, say aloud a few such remarks as the following: 'I believe this is going to be a wonderful day. I believe I can successfully handle all problems that will arise today. I feel good physically, mentally, emotionally. It is wonderful to be alive.'" Peale, *The Power of Positive Thinking*, 83.

20. Thin, *Social Happiness: Theory into Policy and Practice.*

21. Kramer, "An Unobtrusive Behavioral Model of 'Gross National Happiness.'"

22. Freud, "Beyond the Pleasure Principle."

23. Vorderer, Klimmt, and Ritterfeld, "Enjoyment: At the Heart of Media Entertainment"; Zillmann, "Mood Management through Communication Choices."

24. Dövelin, von Scheve, and Konijn, *The Routledge Handbook of Emotions and Mass Media.*

25. Ibid. For a discussion of how it is that gamers apparently derive pleasure from failure in video games, see Juul, *The Art of Failure: An Essay on the Pain of Playing Video Games.*

26. Salovey et al., "Emotional Attention, Clarity, and Repair: Exploring Emotional Intelligence Using the Trait Meta-Mood Scale," 136.

27. Cupchik, "Reactive and Reflective Responses to Mass Media," 340.

28. Although boredom can be a productive state, according to Heidegger. See Mansikka, "Can Boredom Educate Us? Tracing a Mood in Heidegger's Fundamental Ontology from an Educational Point of View."

29. Cupchik, "Reactive and Reflective Responses to Mass Media," 339.

30. Freud, *Jokes and Their Relation to the Unconscious*.

31. "Thousands Killed in Asian Tsunami."

32. The program shows carefully edited shots of groups of people talking while watching other programs. See http://www.channel4.com/programmes/gogglebox (accessed April 12, 2015).

33. Dövelin, von Scheve, and Konijn, *The Routledge Handbook of Emotions and Mass Media*, 304.

34. Ibid., 186.

35. Carey, "Introduction," xxi.

36. Eliade, *The Two and the One*, 114.

37. Bakhtin, *Rabelais and His World*, 21.

38. Rabelais, Gargantua and Pantagruel, 37.

39. Ibid., 99.

40. Bakhtin, *Rabelais and His World*, 194.

41. Buck and Renfro Powers, "Emotion, Media and the Global Village," 189.

42. Ramachandran, *The Tell-Tale Brain: Unlocking the Mysteries of Human Nature*.

43. Huizinga, *Homo Ludens: A Study of the Play Element in Culture*.

44. Takahashi et al., "When Your Gain Is My Pain and Your Pain Is My Gain: Neural Correlates of Envy and Schadenfreude," 938.

45. Ibid., 408.

46. Cross and Littler, "Celebrity and Schadenfreude: The Cultural Economy of Fame in Free Fall," 396.

47. Ibid., 408.

48. The risks of extremes will be elaborated in chapter 5.

49. According to digital commentator Andrew Keen, celebrity is now "democratized and we are reinventing ourselves as self-styled celebrities, even going so far as to deploy online services like YouCeleb that enable us to dress like twentieth-century mass media stars." Keen, *Digital Vertigo: How Today's Online Social Revolution*

Is Dividing, Diminishing, and Disorienting Us, chapter 1, under "Our Age of Great Exhibitionism."

50. Dyer, *Only Entertainment*, 68. Also see the discussion of netporn in chapter 11 of this book.

51. Hinnant, "'We Are All Hooligans': Protests for Pussy Riot."

52. "How Sister Feng Became Famous."

5 Addicted to Vertigo

1. NordiCHI is a conference for human–computer interaction research and is held in a Nordic country each year.

2. For a clear explanation of the human body's relationships within space from a phenomenological perspective, see Bollnow, *Human Space*, 44–54.

3. Smith, "Introduction: The Quest in Guest," 1.

4. Heidegger explores anxiety. See Heidegger, *Being and Time*, chapter 6.

5. Benedikt, *Cyberspace: First Steps*, 121.

6. Keen, *Digital Vertigo: How Today's Online Social Revolution Is Dividing, Diminishing, and Disorienting Us*, chapter 3, under "Privacy Concerns."

7. Jones, *Design Methods: Seeds of Human Futures*, 5.

8. Brandt, Dietricj, and Strupp, *Vertigo and Dizziness: Common Complaints*, 1.

9. http://www.oed.com/ (accessed April 12, 2015).

10. Caillois, *Man, Play, and Games*, 23.

11. Wilkes, "Queue Here to Conquer Everest: Chilling Photo Shows Bottleneck on Mount Everest as Dozens of Climbers Try to Reach Summit on Weekend When Four Died."

12. Chmielewska, "Vectors of Looking: Reflections on the Luftwaffe's Aerial Survey of Warsaw, 1944"; Dorrian, "The Aerial Image: Vertigo, Transparency and Miniaturization"; Dorrian, "On Google Earth"; Dorrian and Pousin, *Seeing from Above: The Aerial View in Visual Culture*.

13. Further evidence for the popularity of views from on high come from those reckless amateur videos taken from the tops of tall buildings. It's important in these images that the photographer is in the frame, as evidence of their presence. The vertiginous effect is enhanced by the use of a handheld monopod camera extension known as a "selfie stick." So climbers hold their cameras about a meter away from their extended arm. The climber sees herself in the flat screen viewfinder, and of

course the resultant still image or video positions the climber in the surrounding scene. If it's a video, then the inevitable sweep of the arm comes into play, vertiginously. Such photography presents a highly contemporary and dynamic expression of the sublime, an amplified variant of the iconic romantic painting *Wanderer in the Mists* (1818) by the German idealist Caspar David Friedrich—the sublime view from the mountaintop featuring the singular contemplative artist.

14. Derrida, "Différance," 22. The philosopher Soren Kierkegaard wrote: "Anxiety may be compared with dizziness. He whose eye happens to look down into the yawning abyss becomes dizzy. But what is the reason for this? It is just as much in his own eye as in the abyss, for suppose he had not looked down. Hence anxiety is the dizziness of freedom." Kierkegaard, *The Concept of Anxiety: A Simple Psychologically Orienting Deliberation on the Dogmatic Issue of Hereditary Sin*, 61. Also see Bollnow, *Human Space*, 48.

15. Thacker, "Dark Media," under "The Realism of the Unseen."

16. Ibid.

17. Heidegger, *Being and Time*.

18. The repeated opening arpeggiated chord is D-Bb-Gb down to D up to Gb up to Bb, according to a blog post by Wrobel, "The Nature of Bernard Herrmann's Music."

19. See, for example, the philosopher Gaston Bachelard's essay, "The Phenomenology of Roundness," which concludes his book *The Poetics of Space*.

20. According to a *New York Times* article on problems with the euro. See Taylor, "A European Debt Crisis with an Italian Twist."

21. I need hardly say that economists and sociologists from Karl Marx onward write about the *circulation* of capital.

22. Plato, "Timaeus," 1238.

23. Plato, *Symposium*.

24. Vitruvius, *Vitruvius: The Ten Books on Architecture*, 38.

25. Ibid., 73.

26. Ibid., 26–27.

27. Da Vinci was in the company of other artists and protoscientists keen to draw the figure, sometimes as illustrations for the publication of Vitruvius's book—for example, by Francesco di Giorgio (1439–1502), Cesare Cesariano (1400s–1500s), and Fra Giocondo (1433–1515).

28. Wittkower, *Architectural Principles in the Age of Humanism*, 25.

29. Gem, "Leonardo's Vitruvian Man, Renaissance Humanism, and Nicholas of Cusa," 104. Da Vinci doesn't explain how he constructed his geometrical figure. It's likely that he was following a standard gross approximation to the problem of squaring the circle. There are other symbolic aspects to da Vinci's figure and those of his contemporaries. The male body is often depicted with an erection. In da Vinci's diagram, the circle centers on the umbilicus and the square is centered on the groin, hence reinforcing the nascent cosmology of Renaissance humanism: man as the generator, the geometer, the producer of the universe. If our bodies really are located in the circle, then it's a container of paradoxical character, infinite extent, and boasts of the body's generative capabilities, as well as the alien character of Renaissance thinking to the twenty-first-century mind.

30. Burke and Boulton, *A Philosophical Enquiry into the Origin of our Ideas of the Sublime and Beautiful*, 91.

31. Burke and Boulton, *A Philosophical Enquiry into the Origin of our Ideas of the Sublime and Beautiful*.

32. Bentham, *The Works of Jeremy Bentham, Volume 4.*

33. Any architect could spot the many "utilitarian" reasons for the lack of success of the panoptic plan form as detailed by Bentham, not least the waste of space around the tower; the difficulty of accommodating other necessary spaces that are not part of the panoptic arrangement, such as staff quarters, kitchens, recreation areas, eating and service zones, access points, circulation, and fire escape stairs; and the problems of fitting ducts and furniture against curved walls. There's also that vertigo-inducing three- to four-story inspection tower in the middle of the arrangement and the high-level walkways serving the cells.

34. See the "Thriller" YouTube video, available at https://www.youtube.com/watch?v=hMnk7lh9M3o (accessed April 12, 2015).

35. Levin, Frohne, and Weibel, *CTRL [SPACE]: Rhetorics of Surveillance from Bentham to Big Brother.*

36. Foucault, *Discipline and Punish: The Birth of the Prison*, 204.

37. Ibid., 202.

38. Ibid., 261.

39. Derrida and Bass, "The Linguistic Circle of Geneva," 682.

40. Quoted by Koyré, in *From the Closed World to the Infinite Universe*, 17.

41. Anzaldúa, "Speaking in Tongues: A Letter to Third World Women Writers," 205, quoted by Bastian, in "The Contradictory Simultaneity of Being with Others: Exploring Concepts of Time and Community in the Work of Gloria Anzaldúa," 155.

42. The Lacanian philosopher Slovoj Žižek provides an account of this story in psychological terms—the unattainability of the desired object and looking into the eyes of another as encountering the ultimate abyss—but doesn't engage with the geometry of vertigo. See Žižek and Miller, "Hitchcock."

43. For a fascinating experiment indicating the close relationship between sexual arousal and vertigo, see Dutton and Aron, "Some Evidence for Heightened Sexual Attraction under Conditions of High Anxiety." Questionnaires completed on a "fear-arousing suspension bridge" elicited significantly greater sexual content than those that took place on a regular bridge.

44. Lovejoy, *The Great Chain of Being: A Study of the History of an Idea*, 24.

45. Gell, "The Gods at Play: Vertigo and Possession in Muria Religion," 230.

46. According to T2India, an events news website: "Teej is the festival of swings celebrated in August. Dedicated to the Goddess Parvati, it marks the advent of the monsoon. Swings are hung from trees and decorated with flowers. Young girls and women dressed in green clothes sing songs in celebration of the advent of the monsoon. Goddess Parvati is worshipped by seekers of conjugal bliss and happiness. An elaborate procession is taken out on the streets of Jaipur for two consecutive days on the festive occasion." Available at http://www.t2india.com/west-india-festivals.aspx (accessed April 12, 2015).

47. Gell, "The Gods at Play: Vertigo and Possession in Muria Religion," 211. James Frazer also mentions the importance and ubiquity of swings in religious experience. See Frazer, *The Golden Bough*. Also see Lavondés, "A Polynesian Game of Swings."

48. Gell, "The Gods at Play: Vertigo and Possession in Muria Religion," 223.

49. Gell, "The Gods at Play: Vertigo and Possession in Muria Religion," 226. Gell references Weiner, *The Human Use of Human Beings*.

50. Caillois, *Man, Play, and Games*, 53.

51. Ofcom, *Communications Market Report: UK*.

52. Ibid., 4.

53. Ito, Okabe, and Matsuda, *Personal, Portable, Pedestrian: Mobile Phones in Japanese Life*.

54. Bull, "The Intimate Sounds of Urban Experience: An Auditory Epistemology of Everyday Mobility," 171.

55. Coyne, *The Tuning of Place: Sociable Spaces and Pervasive Digital Media*.

56. Breivik, "Being-in-the-Void: A Heideggerian Analysis of Skydiving."

57. Strehovec, "Vertigo—on Purpose: Entertainment in Simulators," 206.

6   Enveloped in Haze

1. Zumthor, *Atmospheres: Architectural Environments—Surrounding Objects*, 13.

2. A related term is "spirit of place," or *genius loci*. See Norberg-Schulz, *Genius Loci: Toward a Phenomenology of Architecture*.

3. "Blur Building—Diller Scofidio and Renfro."

4. M. Kennedy, "Gormley's installation is a mist-see."

5. Pizzato, *Ghosts of Theater and Cinema in the Brain*, 121.

6. See Walters, *Tennyson: Poet, Philosopher, Idealist*, 13. Walters also discusses the related line, "Distance lends enchantment to the view."

7. Simmel, "Two Essays: The Handle and the Ruin," 383.

8. Ibid. Also see Hetzler, "Ruin Time and Ruins."

9. Simmel, "Two Essays: The Handle and the Ruin," 384.

10. Leggio, "The Paradoxes of Piranesi."

11. Jones, "No Way Out."

12. Hill, "The Weather in Architecture: Soane, Turner and the 'Big Smoke.'"

13. Edensor, "Waste Matter: The Debris of Industrial Ruins and the Disordering of the Material World," 320.

14. Ibid., 321.

15. McCullough, *Ambient Commons: Attention in the Age of Embodied Information*.

16. Turbayne, *The Myth of Metaphor*.

17. Dreyfus, *Being-in-the-World: A Commentary on Heidegger's Being and Time, Division I*.

18. Ibid.

19. Zumthor, *Atmospheres: Architectural Environments—Surrounding Objects*, 13.

20. Till, *Architecture Depends*.

21. Cultural geographer Owain Jones provides an apposite spatial account of memory: "Each spatialized, felt, moment or sequence of the now-being-laid-down is (more or less), mapped into our bodies and minds to become a vast store of past geographies which shape who we are and the ongoing process of life. The becoming-of-the-now is not distinct from this vast volume of experience, it emerges from it, and is coloured by it, in ways we know and ways we don't know. If we are all vast repositories of past emotional-spatial experiences then the spatiality of humanness

becomes even deeper in extent and significance." Jones, "An Ecology of Emotion, Memory, Self and Landscape," 206. He then proceeds to challenge this proposition.

22. Augé, *Oblivion*, 15.

23. Ibid.

24. Nowlis and Nowlis, "The Description and Analysis of Mood," 352; Morris and Schnurr, *Mood: The Frame of Mind*; Lormand, "Nonphenomenal Consciousness."

25. Freud, "A Note upon the 'Mystic Writing Pad,'" 211.

26. Freud, *Jokes and Their Relation to the Unconscious*.

27. Bachelard, *The Poetics of Space*, 8.

28. Hawkes, *Structuralism and Semiotics*.

29. Tafuri, *Architecture and Utopia: Design and Capitalist Development*, 179.

30. Ibid., 169.

31. In fact, according to philosopher Paul Ricoeur, it's their common interest in a stratum of "unconsciousness" that allows these three intellectual movements to cross-reference each other with ease. See Ricoeur, *Freud and Philosophy: An Essay in Interpretation*.

32. Ibid.

33. Speed, "An Internet of Things That Do Not Exist."

34. Mayer-Schonberger, *Delete: The Virtue of Forgetting in the Digital Age*, 14.

35. Rosenfield, *The Invention of Memory: A New View of the Brain*.

36. Ibid., 3.

37. Ibid., 163.

38. Ibid., 162.

39. Halbwachs, *On Collective Memory*, 182.

40. Lutz, *Unnatural Emotions: Everyday Sentiments on a Micronesian Atoll and their Challenge to Western Theory*, 5.

41. Ibid., 6.

42. Pramaggiore and Wallis, *Film: A Critical Introduction*, 60.

43. Ibid., 81.

44. Ibid., 82. Pramaggiore and Wallis include still images from well-known films. In *The Sound of Music* (1965), von Trapp plays the guitar with children at his feet, while Maria leans against a wall. The countess is seated and composed, but at a distance.

45. The last example is from Luis Buñuel's film *Exterminating Angel* (1962).

46. Koeck, *Cine-Scapes: Cinematic Spaces in Architecture and Cities*.

47. Brecht, "A Short Organum for the Theatre," 192.

48. Ibid, 143. This is quoted by Diamond, in "Brechtian Theory/Feminist Theory: Towards a Gestic Feminist Criticism," 84.

49. Debord, *Report on the Construction of Situations and on the International Situationist Tendency's Conditions of Organization and Action*, 10.

50. Benford and Hunt, "Dramaturgy and Social Movements: The Social Construction and Communication of Power."

51. Benston, "Introduction: Being There: Performance as Mise-en-Scène, Abscene, Obscene, and Other Scene," 440.

52. Ibid., 441.

53. Artaud, *The Theater and Its Double*.

54. Concern about "bit rot" focuses on storage media and file formats, and the prospect that there'll be no way of reading all those old files. See Samuel Gibbs, "What Is 'Bit Rot' and Is Vint Cerf Right to Be Worried?," *Guardian Newspaper*, February 13, 2015, http://www.theguardian.com/technology/2015/feb/13/what-is-bit-rot-and-is-vint-cerf-right-to-be-worried.

55. Douglas, *Purity and Danger: An Analysis of Concepts of Pollution and Taboo*, 36.

56. Brecht, "A Short Organum for the Theatre" 143. This is quoted by Diamond, in "Brechtian Theory/Feminist Theory: Towards a Gestic Feminist Criticism," 84.

57. Finlay, "Weaving the Rainbow: Visions of Color in World History," 406.

58. Gibson, *Neuromancer*, 9.

59. James, *Fifty Shades of Grey*.

60. The movie version of the book *Fifty Shades of Grey* doesn't include "Spem in Alium" in its track list.

61. James, *Fifty Shades of Grey*, chapter 25.

61. Ibid.

62. Beer, "Tune Out: Music, Soundscapes and the Urban Mise-en-Scène," 860.

7 Intoxicated by Color

1. Available at http://www.citizenm.com (accessed April 12, 2015).

2. Mcquire, "Rethinking Media Events: Large Screens, Public Space Broadcasting and Beyond."

3. See https://instagram.com.

4. See, for example, the app *Interaction of Color by Josef Albers* by Yale University, based on Albers, *Interaction of Color*.

5. Finlay, "Weaving the Rainbow: Visions of Color in World History."

6. Ibid., 398.

7. Newton, *Opticks: Or a Treatise of the Reflections, Inflections, and Colors of Light*.

8. Goethe, *Theory of Colors*, 297–298.

9. Judd, "Introduction." For applications of color theory to architecture, see McLachlan, *Architectural Color in the Professional Palette*.

10. Wittgenstein, *Remarks on Color*, 16e; McGinn, "Wittgenstein's 'Remarks on Colour.'"

11. Rosenthal et al., "Seasonal Affective Disorder: A Description of the Syndrome and Preliminary Findings with Light Therapy."

12. Regina Lee Blaszczyk describes the history of "mood conditioning" through color. See Blaszczyk, *The Color Revolution*, 215. On neural theories of conditioning, see Ramachandran, *The Tell-Tale Brain: Unlocking the Mysteries of Human Nature*. For an amusing take on color attributions, see Fforde, *Shades of Grey*. There's an angry mob scene in which "a large crowd of Greys had turned up from the fields, glasshouse and factory. Some even carried tools. The mood had grown darker" (331).

13. In her summary of Wittgenstein's position, Marie McGinn writes: "The grammar of the language in which we describe the colours of objects in a natural scene diverges quite radically from the grammar of colour concepts that are introduced in connection with flat, monochrome samples of colour arranged in the colour circle." McGinn, "Wittgenstein's 'Remarks on Colour,'" 443.

14. Finlay, "Weaving the Rainbow: Visions of Color in World History," 394.

15. Ibid., 410.

16. Russell, "Emotion, Core Affect, and Psychological Construction."

17. Goethe, *Theory of Colors*, 305.

18. Ibid., 307.

19. Ibid., 311.

20. Ibid., 315.

21. Ibid., 316.

22. Hyodo, "Can Colors Make Me Happy? The Effect of Color on Mood: A Meta-Analysis," 864.

23. Carruthers et al., "The Manchester Color Wheel: Development of a Novel Way of Identifying Color Choice and Its Validation in Healthy, Anxious and Depressed Individuals," 1.

24. Ibid., 10.

25. Küller et al., "The Impact of Light and Colour on Psychological Mood: A Cross-Cultural Study of Indoor Work Environments."

26. Valdez and Mehrabian, "Effects of Color on Emotions," 406.

27. Westland et al., "Colour harmony."

28. Newton, *Opticks: Or a Treatise of the Reflections, Inflections, and Colors of Light.*

29. Westland et al., "Colour harmony."

30. Finlay, "Weaving the Rainbow: Visions of Color in World History," 387. The peak of the sensitivity of the L receptors do not correspond exactly to red, but the L receptors are the ones able to pick up the red part of the spectrum, about 620–740 nm.

31. Newton, *Opticks: Or a Treatise of the Reflections, Inflections, and Colors of Light.*

32. Finlay, "Weaving the Rainbow: Visions of Color in World History," 392.

33. Ibid., 391.

34. Ibid., 392.

35. Ibid., 389.

36. Ibid., 393.

37. Kandinsky, *Concerning the Spiritual in Art*; Kandinsky, *Point and Line to Plane.*

38. Munsell, "A Pigment Color System and Notation."

39. Ibid., 244.

40. I first heard this explained in a conference presentation by Robert Norman. See R. B. Norman, "Color Contrast and CAAD: The Seven Color Contrasts of Johannes Itten."

41. Munsell and Johannes Itten mapped this space as a sphere.

42. Itten, *The Elements of Color: A Treatise on the Color System of Johannes Itten Based on His Book The Art of Color*, 12.

43. Itten, *The Art of Color: The Subjective Experience and Objective Rationale of Color.*

44. Itten, *The Elements of Color: A Treatise on the Color System of Johannes Itten Based on His Book The Art of Color*, 34.

45. Ibid., 37.

46. Ibid., 45.

47. Ibid., 49.

48. Ibid., 54.

49. Ibid., 55.

50. Ibid., 83.

51. Stelmack and Stalikas, "Galen and the Humour Theory of Temperament."

52. Available at http://www.myersbriggs.org (accessed April 12, 2015).

53. Kant, *Observations on the Feeling of the Beautiful and the Sublime.*

54. Jung, *Psychological Types*, 510.

55. Stelmack and Stalikas, "Galen and the Humour Theory of Temperament," 257.

56. Ibid., 259.

57. Ibid., 258. Also see Bowring, *A Field Guide to Melancholy.*

58. Eysenck, "Principles and Methods of Personality Description, Classification and Diagnosis."

59. Ramachandran, *The Tell-Tale Brain: Unlocking the Mysteries of Human Nature*, chapter 3.

60. Cytowic, "Synesthesia: Phenomenology and Nauropsychology—A Review of Current Knowledge."

61. The example is from John Keats's poem "Ode to a Nightingale," 218–220.

62. Kandinsky, *Point and Line to Plane*, 115.

63. Goethe, *Theory of Colors*, 295–296.

64. Ibid., 276.

65. Contrary to the blue and red produced from litmus tests.

66. Goethe, *Elective Affinities*, 39.

67. Note Artaud's reference to alchemy and theater (Artaud, *The Theater and Its Double*). Vials of colored iridescent liquids are among the film clichés of the chemistry laboratory.

68. Finlay, "Weaving the Rainbow: Visions of Color in World History," 394.

69. Ibid., 397.

70. Freud, "Character and Anal Eroticism."

71. Derrida, "Plato's Pharmacy." Many prominent philosophers have written on color and prodded the certainty of its sciences, not least among them Gilles Deleuze. I found a recent paper by Carolyn Kane very helpful in providing an up-to-date summary of the approaches taken by each, within the context of a long color tradition that includes Plato, Kant, Hegel, and Goethe. See Kane, "The Synthetic Color Sense of Pipilotti Rist, or, Deleuze Color Theory for Electronic Media Art."

72. Itten, *The Art of Color: The Subjective Experience and Objective Rationale of Color*, 21.

73. Ibid., 55.

74. Ibid., 58.

75. Ibid., 52.

76. Ibid., 54.

77. Ibid., 89.

78. Lyotard, *The Postmodern Condition: A Report on Knowledge*. On further amusing association between rainbows and childlike innocence, see series 2, episode 21, of Dreamworks' animated series *The Penguins of Madagascar*, where Private achieves "quantum hypercute at 130% adorability" and assumes a doe-eyed penguin pose while hugging a toy unicorn—all beneath a rainbow.

79. Burke and Boulton, *A Philosophical Enquiry into the Origin of our Ideas of the Sublime and Beautiful*, 75.

80. Ibid., 74.

8   Haunted by Media

1. Turkle, *Alone Together: Why We Expect More from Technology and Less from Each Other*, introduction, under "The Robotic Moment."

2. Ibid., conclusion, under "Forbidden Experiments."

3. For a comparison with her earlier book on the subject, see Turkle, *Life on the Screen: Identity in the Age of the Internet*.

4. Watson, Clark, and Tellegen, "Development and Validation of Brief Measures of Positive and Negative Affect: The PANAS Scales."

5. Hagnell et al., "Are We Entering an Age of Melancholy? Depressive Illnesses in a Prospective Epidemiological Study over 25 Years: The Lundby Study, Sweden."

6. For example, see Bowring, *A Field Guide to Melancholy*; Wilson, *Against Happiness: In Praise of Melancholy*.

7. *Hamlet*, William Shakespeare, act 1, scene 1. I adopt *Hamlet* as the leitmotif of this chapter on haunting from Pizzato, *Ghosts of Theater and Cinema in the Brain*.

8. Flatley, *Affective Mapping: Melancholia and the Politics of Modernism*, 2.

9. For an account of melancholy as despair and helplessness in the face of an oppressive social order and given vent through blogging, see Keren, "Blogging and the Politics of Melancholy."

10. Keats, "Ode on Melancholy," 233–234.

11. Kennedy, "How Do I Love Thee? Count 140 Characters."

12. Available at https://twitter.com/twihaiku (accessed November 2014).

13. Ellis, "Not an April Fool's Joke: The New York Times Has Built a Haiku Bot."

14. Wilson, *Against Happiness: In Praise of Melancholy*.

15. As translated and excerpted from Aristotle's *Problems* in Radden, *The Nature of Melancholy*, 57.

16. For a fuller list, see Wilson, *Against Happiness: In Praise of Melancholy*, 101–102.

17. Seitz, "A Requiem for Dallas's J. R. Ewing."

18. Lyrics to "Black Stone Heart" by Daniel Gaston Ash, Kevin Michael Dompe, Peter John Murphy, and David John Haskins.

19. Song lyrics from "Cemetery Drive" by My Chemical Romance.

20. Žižek, "Big Brother, or, the Triumph of the Gaze over the Eye."

21. Lovink, *Zero Comments: Blogging and Critical Internet Culture*, 17.

22. Lovink, "Blogging, the Nihilist Impulse."

23. Lovink, *Zero Comments: Blogging and Critical Internet Culture*, 22.

24. Pizzato, *Ghosts of Theater and Cinema in the Brain*, 111. Gilbert Ryle (1900–1976) described Descartes's formulation of the mind in the human brain as "the ghost in the machine," as if the mind were of a different substance than the material world. See Ryle, *Concept of Mind*.

25. Pizzato, *Ghosts of Theater and Cinema in the Brain*, 56.

26. Ibid., 65.

27. Gadamer, *Truth and Method*, 301.

28. Derrida, *Specters of Marx: The State of the Debt, the Work of Mourning*, 63.

29. Pizzato, *Ghosts of Theater and Cinema in the Brain*, 231.

30. Ibid., 10.

31. Ibid.

32. Ibid., 9.

33. Wortham, "As Facebook Users Die, Ghosts Reach Out."

34. Thacker, "Dark Media," under "On What Cannot Be Said."

35. The inventors of the method were Henrik Ekeus and Mark Wright. See Wright et al., "Augumented Duality: Overlapping a Metaverse with the Real World.

36. http://www.oed.com/ (accessed April 12, 2015).

37. Reported in several newspaper articles in August 2012. See "Olympic Champion Bradley Wiggins on His Cycling Gold Medal," *The Telegraph*, August 2, http://www .telegraph.co.uk/sport/olympics/olympicsvideo/9445835/London-2012-Olympic -champion-Bradley-Wiggins-on-his-cycling-gold-medal.html (accessed April 12, 2015).

38. Salovey et al., "Emotional Attention, Clarity, and Repair: Exploring Emotional Intelligence Using the Trait Meta-Mood Scale," 136. Also see experiments from the 1970s based on typical metamood descriptors, as when people say: "My thinking hasn't changed," "It has altered my outlook," "It is coloring everything I look at," "I shouldn't feel this way," "I know this feeling is wrong," "It's a normal way to feel," "I don't know why I feel it," or "I almost never feel like this." See Mayer and Stevens, "An Emergent Understanding of the Reflective (Meta-) Experience of Mood." In a different vein, Jacques Derrida includes this kind of reflexivity in his account of the contradictory working of emotion. According to commentator Rei Terada, "we don't feel to the extent that our experience seems immediate, but to the extent that it doesn't—not to the extent that other experiences remind us of our own, but to the extent that our own seem like someone else's." Terada, "Imaginary Seductions: Derrida and Emotion Theory," 197.

39. As explored in chapter 4, entertainment and the mass media also provide means of regulating mood. Sometimes, we read a book, look at pictures, watch television shows, or listen to music to modify our moods.

40. Hamlet says to his mother: "Assume a virtue if you have it not." His mother had married his father's murderer. Subtly and sarcastically, Hamlet tells his mother to pretend to be virtuous even if she's not. In another act, as advice to his distraught female companion Ophelia, Hamlet says: "If thou wilt needs marry, marry a fool." It's better to marry a fool, because he won't know when you cheat on him.

41. Fox, *Watching the English: The Hidden Rules of English Behaviour*, "Humour Rules," under "The Importance of Not Being Earnest Rule." The congestion charge is a toll to be paid on entering the center of London by car. Southwark Cathedral and the Imperial War Museum are two important London buildings.

42. Wilson, *Against Happiness: In Praise of Melancholy*, 4.

43. Shakespeare's *Hamlet* is similarly laced with metathemes involving suspicion, intense observation, second-guessing, spying, and surveillance. Polonius spies on Hamlet through a tapestry, through which, in a bitter irony, he is pierced by Hamlet's sword.

44. Butler, "A Melancholy Man." Also see Radden, *The Nature of Melancholy*, 158.

45. Benjamin, *The Origin of German Tragic Drama*, 151.

46. Ibid., 149.

47. Freud, "Mourning and Melancholia," 258.

48. Flatley, *Affective Mapping: Melancholia and the Politics of Modernism*.

49. Mayer-Schonberger, *Delete: The Virtue of Forgetting in the Digital Age*. However, there are in fact no memories in computers. Social beings are the bearers of memory. The cues, triggers, prompts, and traces of computer databases may be difficult to delete, but forgetting is a distinctly human capability more complicated, profound, and nuanced than erasing a file.

50. Morris, Teevan, and Panovich, "What Do People Ask Their Social Networks, and Why? A Survey Study of Status Message Q&A Behavior."

51. Ibid.

52. Ricoeur, *Memory, History, Forgetting*; White, "Review Article: Guilty of History? The Longue Durée of Paul Ricoeur."

53. Halbwachs, *On Collective Memory*, 172.

54. For an interesting discussion of "techno-spiritual practices," some of which relate to funerary rites, see Bell, "No More SMS from Jesus: Ubicomp, Religion and Techno-Spiritual Practices." Also see Walter et al., "Does the Internet Change How We Die and Mourn? Overview and Analysis."

55. Karrim, "Digital Death Planning for Dummies."

56. In spite of such measures, apparently ours is a "death-denying" society according to some reports, inept at planning for the perpetuation or termination of our personal data legacies. See http://www.dyingmatters.org (accessed April 12, 2015).

57. See http://www.dignitas.ch (accessed April 12, 2015).

58. Durkin, "Death, Dying, and the Dead in Popular Culture," 47.

59. Psalm 23:4.

60. Benjamin, *The Origin of German Tragic Drama*, 149.

61. Wilson, *Against Happiness: In Praise of Melancholy*, 32.

62. Ibid., 90.

63. Ibid., 44.

64. Morelli, "The Pope's Last Flight: A Media Masterpiece."

65. Augé, *Oblivion*.

66. Ibid., 56.

67. Urry, *The Tourist Gaze: Leisure and Travel in Contemporary Societies*.

68. Snodgrass and Coyne, *Interpretation in Architecture: Design as a Way of Thinking*, 244.

69. Brecht, "A Short Organum for the Theatre," 9.

70. De Botton, *The Art of Travel*, chapter 2.

71. Urry, "The Place of Emotions within Place," 79.

72. Bunyan, *Pilgrim's Progress and Grace Abounding to the Chief of Sinners*.

73. Psalm 23:4.

74. Vitruvius, *Vitruvius: The Ten Books on Architecture*.

75. James, "What Is an Emotion?"

76. Ibid., 190.

77. Tsetung, *Quotations from Mao Tsetung*.

9   Gripped by Suspense

1. Pope, "An Essay on Man," 274.

2. "Always Look on the Bright Side of Life" was written by Eric Idle and performed in *Monty Python's Life of Brian* (1979).

3. See http://selfassemblylab.net (accessed April 12, 2015).

4. Coyne, *Technoromanticism: Digital Narrative, Holism, and the Romance of the Real*.

5. Ibid.; Wertheim, *The Pearly Gates of Cyberspace: A History of Space from Dante to the Internet*.

6. Morris, *News from Nowhere*; Coyne, *Technoromanticism: Digital Narrative, Holism, and the Romance of the Real*.

7. Tibbits, "The Emergence of '4D Printing.'"

8. The key text on wicked problems is by Rittel and Webber, "Dilemmas in a General Theory of Planning." See also Buchanan, "Wicked Problems in Design Thinking"; Coyne, "Wicked Problems Revisited."

9. The text of *Hesiod: Works and Days* (written around 700 BC) tells the story of Pandora's box and is freely available on the web. Pandora was a kind of female archetype. Hephaestus, Athena, and Aphrodite gave her form, arts, and graces, but the god Hermes put in her "a shameless mind and a deceitful nature." Her curiosity got the better of her. She opened the tempting box (or jar) gifted to her and unleashed plagues and evils, leaving hope behind.

10. Bloch, *The Principle of Hope*, 3.

11. Ibid.

12. Ibid.

13. Obama, *The Audacity of Hope: Thoughts on Reclaiming the American Dream*, 8.

14. Heidegger, *Being and Time*, 395–396.

15. Gadamer, *Truth and Method*, 551.

16. Schank and Abelson, *Scripts, Plans, Goals and Understanding: An Inquiry into Human Knowledge Structures*; Goffman, *Frame Analysis: An Essay on the Organisation of Experience*.

17. Referring back to chapter 6, notice that there's no need to posit the unconscious to support the idea of a "frame of mind."

18. Weiser, "The Computer for the 21st Century."

19. Tagholm, "Genre-Busting Trends in the UK."

20. We suspect that she too could be consumed by the flames. We have already witnessed the fatal event, but with a different person, and that informs our anticipation of her fate.

21. Uidhir, "The Paradox of Suspense Realism," 161.

22. Lodge, *The Art of Fiction*, 14.

23. Ibid.

24. Persson and Sjöberg, "Mood and Positive Expectations," 171.

25. Lodge, *The Art of Fiction*, 14.

26. Uidhir, "The Paradox of Suspense Realism," 162.

27. Ibid., 169.

28. Russell, "Core Affect and the Psychological Construction of Emotion"; Russell, "Emotion, Core Affect, and Psychological Construction."

29. Derrida, *Of Grammatology*.

30. When you know the result, then you know what to expect, and with some certainty. Your expectations are clearly formed. It seems as though not only do audiences relive the sense of expectancy, but they are capable of experiencing again their first viewing, the sense of excitement that arose from not being certain of the outcome. As reflective beings, we relive the anticipation.

31. Gadamer, *Truth and Method*, 263.

32. Ibid.

33. Davidson, "On Emotion, Mood, and Related Affective Constructs," 52.

34. Ibid.

35. Dabala, *Mystery and Suspense in Creative Writing*, 98.

36. Lodge, *The Art of Fiction*, 14.

37. Hodges, *Alan Turing: The Enigma of Intelligence*.

38. These headlines are taken from an exhibition called *London Pictures* by the artists Gilbert and George.

39. Chen, *Dark Web: Exploring and Data Mining the Dark Side of the Web*.

40. Life Online installation at the National Media Museum in Bradford, England, described at http://www.nationalmediamuseum.org.uk/PlanAVisit/Exhibitions/Life OnlineExhibition/PermanentGallery.aspx (accessed April 12, 2015).

41. See advice to educators in Green, "Storytelling in Teaching." Also see Gall, "The Use of Questions in Teaching."

42. Sokal and Bricmont, *Intellectual Impostures: Postmodern Philosophers' Abuse of Science*; Bricmont and Sokal, *Impostures Intellectuelles*.

43. Carnap, "The Elimination of Metaphysics through Logical Analysis of Language," 75.

44. John Caputo's book *The Mystical Element in Heidegger's Thought*, published in 1986, explores the way Heidegger draws on the sayings of Meister Ekhardt (ca. 1260–ca. 1327), Angelus Silesius (1624–1677), and of course the Pre-Socratics, all of whom have been variously described as belonging to the mystical tradition.

45. Coyne, *Technoromanticism: Digital Narrative, Holism, and the Romance of the Real*.

46. One of the problems with the term "mysticism" is that it aggregates a range of practices, theories, ideas, and beliefs that might in fact be very different. Traditions such as astrology, alchemy, magic, and other practices might variously be equated with early or protoscience. It's well-known that Robert Boyle (1627–1691) and Isaac Newton (1642–1727), key figures in the development of science, practiced and wrote about alchemy.

47. Hospers, *An Introduction to Philosophical Analysis*, 482–483.

48. Sokal and Bricmont, *Intellectual Impostures: Postmodern Philosophers' Abuse of Science*, 34.

49. Lindon, *The Alchemy Reader: From Hermes Trismegistus to Isaac Newton*, 19.

50. Hermetic and occult texts are now more available to a general readership than ever. *The Emerald Table* is a short explanation, apparently by Hermes Mercurius Trismegistus, about the philosopher's stone. It begins: "True it is, without falsehood, certain and most true. That which is above is like to that which is below, and that which is below is like to that which is above, to accomplish the miracle of one thing." See Lindon, *The Alchemy Reader: From Hermes Trismegistus to Isaac Newton*, 28.

51. O'Leary, "Cyberspace as Sacred Space: Communicating Religion on Computer Networks," 55.

52. Dabala, *Mystery and Suspense in Creative Writing*, 106.

53. Ibid., 98.

54. Ibid.

55. Lodge, *The Art of Fiction*, 14.

56. Ibid., 16.

57. Insley, "FarmVille User Runs Up £900 Debt."

58. Saville et al., "Internet Addiction and Delay Discounting in College Students," 274.

59. Metcalfe and Mischel, "A Hot/Cool-System Analysis of Delay of Gratification: Dynamics of Willpower."

60. Ibid., 3.

61. Freud, "The Ego and the Id."

62. Metcalfe and Mischel, "A Hot/Cool-System Analysis of Delay of Gratification: Dynamics of Willpower," 12.

63. Schmidt and Cohen, *The New Digital Age: Reshaping the Future of People, Nations and Business*.

64. Ibid., introduction.

65. Ibid.

66. Ibid., conclusion.

67. Ibid.

68. Ibid., chapter 6, under "Automated Warfare."

69. Ibid., introduction.

10 Fogged by Ignorance

1. Schmidt and Cohen, *The New Digital Age: Reshaping the Future of People, Nations and Business*, introduction.

2. Schmidt and Cohen, *The New Digital Age: Reshaping the Future of People, Nations and Business*.

3. "Cybercriminals 'Drained ATMs' in $45m World Bank Heist."

4. Gray, *Thomas Gray: Selected Poems*, 43.

5. Rancière, *The Ignorant Schoolmaster: Five Lessons in Intellectual Emancipation*.

6. To précis a famous statement by Donald Rumsfeld.

7. Simons, "Remarkable False Memories."

8. Loftus, "Planting Misinformation in the Human Mind: A 30-Year Investigation of the Malleability of Memory."

9. Pomeroy, "Guest Blog: How to Instill False Memories."

10. Loftus and Hoffman, "Misinformation and Memory: The Creation of New Memories," 365.

11. Clancy et al., "Memory Distortion in People Reporting Abduction by Aliens."

12. Roediger and McDermott, "Creating False Memories: Re-membering Words Not Presented in Lists," 812.

13. The quotation actually runs: "When I was younger, I could remember anything, whether it had happened or not; but my faculties are decaying now and soon I shall be so I cannot remember anything but the latter." Twain, *Autobiography of Mark Twain: Volume 1, Reader's Edition*, 30.

14. Storbeck and Clore, "With Sadness Comes Accuracy; with Happiness, False Memory: Mood and the False Memory Effect," 786.

15. Built on a study by Loftus and Hoffman, "Misinformation and Memory: The Creation of New Memories."

16. McClelland, "Constructive Memory and Memory Distortions: A Parallel-Distributed Processing Approach."

17. Using music to induce moods poses challenges anyway. See the coda to chapter 1. On the use of emotionally suggestive films and stories as a way to induce mood in

experimental conditions, see Phillips, Smith, and Gilhooly, "The Effects of Adult Aging and Induced Positive and Negative Mood on Planning."

18. Roediger and McDermott, "Creating False Memories: Re-Membering Words Not Presented in Lists."

19. Ibid., 812.

20. Loftus and Hoffman, "Misinformation and Memory: The Creation of New Memories," 365.

21. Storbeck and Clore, "On the Interdependence of Cognition and Emotion."

22. Those three propositions are of course false.

23. Watt, "David Cameron Fluffs Citizenship Test on David Letterman's Late Show."

24. Ibid.; "Boris Johnson: David Cameron 'Knew Full Well' What Magna Carta Meant."

25. Script from "Twelve Angry Men," an episode of the BBC's *Hancock's Half Hour* (1959), by Ray Galton and Alan Simpson.

26. Kuhn, *The Structure of Scientific Revolutions*.

27. Ignorance is given treatment as a central theme in texts such as Vitek and Jackson, *The Virtues of Ignorance: Complexity, Sustainability, and the Limits of Knowledge*.

28. Schmidt and Cohen, *The New Digital Age: Reshaping the Future of People, Nations and Business*, introduction.

29. Heidegger, "The Age of the World Picture."

30. "I think therefore I am," wrote Descartes. Descartes, *Discourse on Method and the Meditations*, 19.

31. Turkle, *Life on the Screen: Identity in the Age of the Internet*.

32. Kant, *Immanuel Kant's Critique of Pure Reason*, 271.

33. Atzori, Iera, and Morabito, "The Internet of Things: A Survey," 1.

34. Huxley, *Collected Essays Volume V*, 107.

35. Lightman, "Huxley and Scientific Agnosticism: The Strange History of a Failed Rhetorical Strategy"; Huxley, *Collected Essays Volume V*.

36. Wittgenstein, *Tractatus Logico Philosophicus*.

37. Coyne, *Technoromanticism: Digital Narrative, Holism, and the Romance of the Real*, 92–95.

38. We discuss the logical fallacy of this position in Snodgrass and Coyne, *Interpretation in Architecture: Design as a Way of Thinking*.

39. Coyne, "Space without Ground."

40. Huxley, *Collected Essays Volume V*, 9.

41. Derrida, "Différance."

42. Dick and Ziering Kofman (directors), *Derrida*.

43. Landow and Delany, "Hypertext, Hypermedia and Literary Studies: The State of the Art."

44. Coyne, *Derrida for Architects*.

45. Giddens, *Runaway World: How Globalisation Is Shaping Our Lives*.

46. Ibid., 49.

47. Bernstein, *Beyond Objectivism and Relativism*, 129.

48. Gadamer, *Truth and Method*, 301.

49. Giaccardi, *Heritage Matters: Understanding and Experiencing Heritage through Social Media: Understanding Heritage in a Participatory Culture*.

50. Carr, *What Is History?*.

51. White, *Tropics of Discourse: Essays in Cultural Criticism*, 82.

52. Jenkins, *On 'What Is History': From Carr and Elton to Rorty and White*, 144.

53. Carr, *What Is History?*, 159.

54. Jenkins, *Re-Thinking History*, 14.

55. Carr, *What Is History?*, 159.

56. Ibid.

57. Macfie, "Review of Keith Jenkins Retrospective."

58. Carr, *What Is History?*, 86.

59. Macfie, "Review of Keith Jenkins Retrospective."

60. Ibid.

61. Lowenthal, *The Past Is a Foreign Country*.

62. Snodgrass and Coyne, *Interpretation in Architecture: Design as a Way of Thinking*, 143.

63. Ibid.

64. Macfie, "Review of Keith Jenkins Retrospective."

65. Bernstein, *Beyond Objectivism and Relativism*.

66. This is an aphorism of unknown origin.

67. Plant, *Zeros and Ones: Digital Women and the New Technoculture*.

68. Brown et al., *White Heat Cold Logic: British Computer Art, 1960–1980*.

69. The afterword at the conclusion of the film *The Imitation Game* (2014) attests to the proposition that Allan Turing and the decoders shortened the war by two years, a sentiment also expressed on several interpretation boards at the Bletchley Park visitor center.

70. See Giaccardi, "Cross-Media Interaction for the Virtual Museum: Reconnecting to Natural Heritage in Boulder, Colorado"; Silberman, "Chasing the Unicorn? The Quest for 'Essence' in Digital Heritage"; Speed, "An Internet of Things That Do Not Exist"; Giaccardi, *Heritage Matters: Understanding and Experiencing Heritage through Social Media: Understanding Heritage in a Participatory Culture*; Speed, "Mobile Ouija Boards."

71. Perhaps the Internet encourages online researchers to be superficial in their reading: "What the net seems to be doing is chipping away my capacity for concentration and contemplation." Carr, *The Shallows: What the Internet Is Doing to Our Brains*, 6. The opposing view to Carr's celebrates the fact that habituated web users don't rely on the linear narratives provided by texts as presented by their authors but construct their own narratives. See Tapscott, *Grown Up Digital: How the Net Generation Is Changing Your World*.

72. Burke and Boulton, *A Philosophical Enquiry into the Origin of Our Ideas of the Sublime and Beautiful*, 57.

73. Tapscott, *Grown Up Digital: How the Net Generation Is Changing Your World*, 98.

74. "Healthy Living: How to Live Longer."

75. Aspinall et al., "The Urban Brain: Analysing Outdoor Physical Activity with Mobile EEG."

76. Popper, *Conjectures and Refutations: The Growth of Scientific Knowledge*.

77. Nickerson, "Confirmation Bias: A Ubiquitous Phenomenon in Many Guises."

78. Ibid., 209.

79. Aspinall et al., "The Urban Brain: Analysing Outdoor Physical Activity with Mobile EEG."

80. The usual example of confirmation bias is that of horoscopes and fortune tellers able to capitalize on people's tendency to confirm what they want to believe on the

slimmest of evidence. Horoscopes are a legitimate area of academic study, especially if we ask why it is that many people start off with the assumption that the stars can influence life events. There are deeply developed cultural reasons for the supposed connection.

81. Popper, *Conjectures and Refutations: The Growth of Scientific Knowledge*, 256.

82. Nickerson, "Confirmation Bias: A Ubiquitous Phenomenon in Many Guises," 206.

11   Aroused by Machines

1. Dick, *Do Androids Dream of Electric Sheep?*, 10. For an account of the domestic context of the machine, see Fortin, *Architecture and Science Fiction Film: Philip K. Dick and the Spectacle of Home*, 94.

2. Price, *Cedric Price: The Square Book*, 30.

3. Williams, *Sex and Buildings: Modern Architecture and the Sexual Revolution*; Reich, *The Function of the Orgasm: Sex-Economic Problems of Biological Energy*.

4. Reich, *The Function of the Orgasm: Sex-Economic Problems of Biological Energy*, 6.

5. Ibid., 4.

6. Architecture is no less captivated by the fantasy of erotic, empathic environments. Neil Spiller describes an architectural project by Philip Beesley as follows: "Implant Matrix is an interactive geo-textile that could be used for reinforcing landscapes and buildings of the future. The matrix—fabricated by laser-cutting direct from digital models—is capable of mechanical empathy. A network of mechanisms reacts to human occupants as erotic prey. The structure responds to the human presence with subtle grasping and sucking motions, ingesting organic materials and incorporating them into a new hybrid entity. Implant Matrix is composed of interlinking filtering 'pores' within a polymer structural system. Primitive *interactive* controls employ distributed microprocessors with capacitance sensors and shape-memory alloy-wire actuators." Implant Matrix was installed at the InterAccess Media Arts Centre in Toronto in 2006. See Spiller, *Digital Architecture Now: A Global Survey of Emerging Talent*, 40. For an extended account of organic, fleshy, sensual, and grotesque architectures, see Cruz, *The Inhabitable Flesh of Architecture*.

7. For a further account of imaginative apps that channel entertainment, see Miller and Matviyenko, *The Imaginary App*.

8. DeNora, *Music and Everyday Life*.

9. Paul Dourish develops this theme of the importance of context. See Dourish, *Where the Action Is: The Foundations of Embodied Interaction*, 19–20. Also see Hughes,

"The Evolution of Large Technological Systems"; Williams and Edge, "The Social Shaping of Technology."

10. Ahmed, "Happy Objects."

11. Desire is one of the major themes of psychoanalytic philosopher Jacques Lacan. See Lacan, *The Four Fundamental Concepts of Psychoanalysis*; Bowie, *Lacan*; Žižek, *Enjoy Your Symptom! Jacques Lacan in Hollywood and Out.*

12. I examined the social pressures to adopt new technologies in the introduction and chapter 1, drawing on Ling, "From Ubicomp to Ubiex(pectations)."

13. Coyne et al., "Virtual Flagships and Sociable Media."

14. Wright et al., "Augmented Duality: Overlapping a Metaverse with the Real World."

15. Aurigi and de Cindio, *Augmented Urban Spaces: Articulating the Physical and Electronic City.*

16. Cowley, "As a Backdrop, Part of the Game, or a Goal in a Game: The Ubiquitous Product Placement."

17. Shinn, *Case Study: First Generation Pokémon Games for the Nintendo Game Boy.*

18. Available at http://www.spore.com (accessed November 2014).

19. Kemeny, "Man Viewed as a Machine."

20. See http://reprap.org (accessed November 2014).

21. Greenberg, "Congressman Says He'll Propose Ban on 3D-Printable Gun Magazines."

22. Available at http://www.reprap.org/wiki/Main_Page (accessed April 12, 2015).

23. Wainwright, "4D-Printing: From Self-Assembling Chairs to Cancer-Fighting Robots"; Tibbits, "The Emergence of '4D Printing.'"

24. Kay, *Obliquity: Why Our Goals Are Best Achieved Indirectly*, 14.

25. Available at http://mybpbear.com (accessed November 2014).

26. Available at https://www.moodtracker.com (accessed November 2014).

27. Available at http://www.findingoptimism.com (accessed November 2014).

28. Available at http://www.emotiv.com (accessed November 2014). Skin galvanometry and other monitoring techniques have been used to assess audience's emotional responses to particular "viral" online videos. See Bardzell, Bardzell, and Pace, *Emotion, Engagement and Internet Video.*

29. Aspinall et al., "The Urban Brain: Analysing Outdoor Physical Activity with Mobile EEG"; Mavros et al., "Engaging the Brain: Implications of Mobile EEG for Spatial Representation."

30. Heiss, "Empathy over Distance: Wearables as Tools for Augmenting Remote Emotional Connection." Also see http://www.taptap.me/ (accessed 12 April 2015).

31. Picard, *Affective Computing*; Trappl, Petta, and Payr, *Emotions in Humans and Artifacts*.

32. Queena, "Google Speaks Up on Desktops and Laptops."

33. As in the case of Sherry Turkle's misgivings about surrogate companions, with which I began chapter 8. See Turkle, *Alone Together: Why We Expect More from Technology and Less from Each Other*.

34. I don't think I need to elaborate further on the role of digital photography and video recording via hand-held devices to share a mood.

35. Greene, *The Art of Seduction*, 65.

36. Paasonen, "Pornography, Affect and Feminist Reading"; Paasonen, "Online Pornography: Ubiquitous and Effaced."

37. Ogas and Gaddam, *A Billion Wicked Thoughts: What the World's Largest Experiment Reveals about Human Desire*.

38. Ruvolo, "How Much of the Internet Is Actually for Porn."

39. Paasonen, "Pornography, Affect and Feminist Reading"; Paasonen, "Online Pornography: Ubiquitous and Effaced"; Paasonen, *Carnal Resonance: Affect and Online Pornography*.

40. Paasonen, "Pornography, Affect and Feminist Reading," 46.

41. See chapter 2; see also Rizzolatti and Craighero, "The Mirror-Neuron System."

42. Paasonen, "Pornography, Affect and Feminist Reading," 50.

43. Paasonen, "Online Pornography: Ubiquitous and Effaced," 434.

44. For example, the Chrome browser's "incognito mode."

45. Dery, "Paradise Lust: Pornotopia Meets the Culture Wars," 136.

46. The "porn" suffix has come to apply to any obsessive, fetishistic, or objectifying treatment of a subject that privileges the visual and ignores the contextual economic, political, and social context of the phenomenon. This much has been said of so-called ruin-porn, which promotes romantic and evocative images of decaying buildings, or of war-porn depicting carnage. See DeSilvey and Edensor, "Reckoning with Ruins."

47. Paasonen, "Pornography, Affect and Feminist Reading," 52.

48. Douglas, *Purity and Danger: An Analysis of Concepts of Pollution and Taboo.*

49. Horvath et al., *"Basically . . . Porn Is Everywhere": A Rapid Evidence Assessment on the Effects that Access and Exposure to Pornography has on Children and Young People*, 7.

50. Daneback and Löfberg, "Youth, Sexuality and the Internet: Young People's Use of the Internet to Learn about Sexuality."

51. Dery, "Naked Lunch: Talking Realcore with Sergio Messina."

52. Dery, "Paradise Lust: Pornotopia Meets the Culture Wars," 130.

53. McLuhan, *The Medium Is the Massage.*

54. Freud, "The Ego and the Id."

55. Ibid., 386.

56. Freud, "Civilization and Its Discontents."

57. Marcuse, *Eros and Civilisation: A Philosophical Inquiry into Freud.*

58. Atzori, Iera, and Morabito, "The Internet of Things: A Survey," 1.

59. The *thing* is of course the *res* of which Descartes wrote, as I suggested in chapter 10.

60. Connor, *Paraphernalia: The Curious Lives of Magical Things*, introduction, under "Magical Things."

61. Ogas and Gaddam, *A Billion Wicked Thoughts: What the World's Largest Experiment Reveals about Human Desire*, chapter 1, under "The Genie of a Million Squicks."

62. Russell (director) and Sandler (scriptwriter), *Crimes of Passion.*

63. Chion, *The Voice in Cinema.*

64. Heidegger, "The Thing."

65. Ibid., 174.

66. Later in the essay, Heidegger says, "Whatever becomes a thing occurs out of the world's mirror play." Ibid., 182.

67. Weiser and Brown, "The Coming Age of Calm Technology," 79.

68. Dourish and Bell, *Divining a Digital Future: Mess and Mythology in Ubiquitous Computing*, chapter 2, under "Ubicomp Is Really about Messiness."

69. Heidegger, *Being and Time.*

70. Wiszniewski, Coyne, and Pierce, "Turing's Machines"; Hodges, *Alan Turing: The Enigma of Intelligence.* The mathematician and parent of modern computational

theory Alan Turing famously constructed formal theories about computational machines and their categories.

71. On the subject of the "proximate future" implied by current technologies, see Dourish and Bell, *Divining a Digital Future: Mess and Mythology in Ubiquitous Computing*, chapter 2, under "Envisioning the Future."

72. Nozick, *Anarchy, State, and Utopia*.

73. He argued that human beings would never prefer such a state and thereby demonstrated that humans do not only seek to maximize their pleasure.

74. Gere, "Brains-in-Vats, Giant Brains and World Brains: The Brain as Metaphor in Digital Culture."

75. Turing's early encounter with encryption machines was as strategic instruments of war. Military operations were only effective if internal communications could go undetected. The encryption machine exploited the weakness in enemy communications.

76. Dery, "Paradise Lust: Pornotopia Meets the Culture Wars," 130.

77. Russell (director) and Sandler (scriptwriter), *Crimes of Passion*.

78. Dery, "Paradise Lust: Pornotopia Meets the Culture Wars," 130.

79. Ibid.

80. Atkinson, *Delete: A Design History of Computer Vaporware*.

81. Dourish and Bell, "'Resistance Is Futile': Reading Science Fiction Alongside Ubiquitous Computing," 774.

82. Christensen and Bower, "Disruptive Technologies: Catching the Wave," 51.

83. Ibid., 50.

84. Bell, Blythe, and Sengers, "Making by Making Strange: Defamiliarization and the Design of Domestic Technologies," 169.

85. Dourish and Bell, *Divining a Digital Future: Mess and Mythology in Ubiquitous Computing*, chapter 2, under "Ubicomp Is Really about Messiness."

86. Aspinall et al., "The Urban Brain: Analysing Outdoor Physical Activity with Mobile EEG."

87. Cernea, Kerren, and Ebert, "Detecting Insight and Emotion in Visualization Applications with a Commercial EEG Headset."

Epilogue

1. "Space" is a conveniently ambiguous term, referring to a space of intellectual inquiry, a physical space, information space, and other spaces that are tangible, virtual, and imaginary.

2. See https://books.google.com/ngrams (accessed April 2015).

3. Al-Chalabi, Turner, and Delamont, *The Brain: A Beginner's Guide*, 68–69.

4. Clark, "Out of Our Brains."

5. Clark, *Being There: Putting Brain, Body and World Together Again*; Clark and Chalmers, "The Extended Mind."

6. De Rivera and Grinkis, "Emotion as Social Relationships," 366.

7. The relational thesis about emotions gains support from studies in ethnopsychology and related disciplines. According to Catherine Lutz, "ethnopsychology is concerned with the way people conceptualize, monitor and discuss their own and others' mental processes, behaviour and social processes . . . All ethnotheories explain some aspect of variability in the world; ethnopsychologies explain inter- and intrapersonal variation in the world and they both construct and derive from people's observations of changes in consciousness, action, and relationships." Lutz, *Unnatural Emotions: Everyday Sentiments on a Micronesian Atoll and Their Challenge to Western Theory*, 83.

8. Bollnow, *Human Space*, 217.

9. Lutz, *Unnatural Emotions: Everyday Sentiments on a Micronesian Atoll and Their Challenge to Western Theory*, 100.

Bibliography

Adorno, Theodor W., and Max Horkheimer. *Dialectic of Enlightenment*. Translated by John Cumming. London: Verso, 1979. First published in German in 1944.

Aggarwal, Charu C., and ChengXiang Zhai, eds. *Mining Text Data*. New York: Springer, 2012.

Ahmed, Sara. "Happy Objects." In *The Affect Theory Reader*, edited by Melissa Gregg and Gregory J. Seigworth, 29–51. Durham, NC: Duke University Press, 2010.

Alam, Murad, Karen C. Barrett, Robert M. Hodapp, and Kenneth A. Arndt. "Botulinum Toxin and the Facial Feedback Hypothesis: Can Looking Better Make You Feel Happier?" *Journal of the American Academy of Dermatology* 58, no. 6 (2008): 1061–1072.

Albers, Josef. *Interaction of Color*. New Haven, CT: Yale University Press, 2006. First published in 1963.

Al-Chalabi, Ammar, Martin R. Turner, and R. Shane Delamont. *The Brain: A Beginner's Guide*. Oxford: Oneworld, 2008.

Alexiou, Katerina, Theodore Zamenopoulos, Jeffrey Johnson, and Sam Gilbert. "Exploring the Neurological Basis of Design Cognition Using Brain Imaging: Some Preliminary Results." *Design Studies* 30, no. 6 (2009): 624–647.

Anderson, Ben. "Affective Atmospheres." *Emotion, Space and Society* 2, no. 2 (2009): 77–81.

Anzaldúa, Gloria. "Speaking in Tongues: A Letter to Third World Women Writers." In *This Bridge Called My Back: Writings by Radical Women of Color*, edited by Cherríe Moraga and Gloria Anzaldúa, 163–172. New York: Kitchen Table/Women of Colour Press, 1983.

Aristotle. *The Art of Rhetoric*. Translated by H. C. Lawson-Tancred. London: Penguin, 1991. Written in the third century BC.

Aristotle. *The Politics*. Translated by T. A. Sinclair. London: Penguin, 1981. Kindle edition.

Artaud, Antonin. *The Theater and Its Double*. Translated by Mary Caroline Richards. New York: Grove, 1958.

Aspinall, Peter, Panagiotis Mavros, Richard Coyne, and Jenny Roe. "The Urban Brain: Analysing Outdoor Physical Activity with Mobile EEG." *British Journal of Sports Medicine*, 2013. doi:.10.1136/bjsports-2012-091877

Atkinson, Paul. *Delete: A Design History of Computer Vapourware*. London: Bloomsbury, 2013.

Atzori, Luigi, Antonio Iera, and Giacomo Morabito. "The Internet of Things: A Survey." *Computer Networks* 54 (2010): 2787–2805.

Augé, Marc. *Oblivion*. Translated by Marjolijn de Jager and James E. Young. Minneapolis: University of Minnesota Press, 2004.

Aurigi, Alessandro, and Fiorella de Cindio, eds. *Augmented Urban Spaces: Articulating the Physical and Electronic City*. Aldershot, UK: Ashgate, 2008.

Bachelard, Gaston. *The Poetics of Space*. New York: Orion Press, 1964.

Bakhtin, Mikhail. *Rabelais and His World*. Translated by Hélène Iswolsky. Bloomington: Indiana University Press, 1984.

Bardzell, Jeffrey, Shaowen Bardzell, and Tyler Pace. *Emotion, Engagement and Internet Video*. Charlestown, MA: OTO Insights, 2008.

Bastian, Michelle. "The Contradictory Simultaneity of Being with Others: Exploring Concepts of Time and Community in the Work of Gloria Anzaldúa." *Feminist Review* 97 (2011): 151–167.

Bateson, Gregory. *Naven*. Stanford, CA: Stanford University Press, 1958.

Becker, Rich. "Welcome to the Petri Dish: A Great Big Thumbs Up." *Words, Concepts, Strategies Blog*, 2014. http://www.richardrbecker.com/2014/07/welcome-to-petri -dish-great-big-thumbs.html.

Beer, David. "Tune Out: Music, Soundscapes and the Urban Mise-en-Scène." *Information Communication and Society* 10, no. 6 (2007): 846–866.

Beesley, Philip, Sachiko Hirosue, Jim Ruxton, Marion Trankle, and Camille Turner. *Responsive Architectures: Subtle Technologies*. Toronto: Riverside Architectural Press, 2006.

Bell, Genevieve. "No More SMS from Jesus: Ubicomp, Religion and Techno-Spiritual Practices." *UbiComp 2006: Ubiquitous Computing* 4206 (2006): 141–158.

Bell, Genevieve, Mark Blythe, and Phoebe Sengers. "Making by Making Strange: Defamiliarization and the Design of Domestic Technologies." *ACM Transactions on Computer-Human Interaction* 12, no. 2 (2007): 149–173.

Benedikt, Michael. *Cyberspace: First Steps*. Cambridge, MA: MIT Press, 1994.

Benford, Robert D., and Scott A. Hunt. "Dramaturgy and Social Movements: The Social Construction and Communication of Power." *Sociological Inquiry* 62, no. 1 (1992): 36–55.

Benjamin, Walter. *The Origin of German Tragic Drama*. Translated by George Steiner and John Osborne. London: Verso, 2003.

Benjamin, Walter. "The Work of Art in the Age of Mechanical Reproduction." In *Illuminations*, edited by Hannan Arendt, 1–58. London: Fontana,1992.

Benston, Kimberly W. "Introduction: Being There: Performance as Mise-en-Scène, Abscene, Obscene, and Other Scene." *PMLA* 107, no. 3 (1992): 434–449.

Bentham, Jeremy. *The Works of Jeremy Bentham, Volume 4*. London: John Bowring, 1787.

Berger, Peter, and Thomas Luckmann. *The Social Construction of Reality: A Treatise in the Sociology of Knowledge*. New York: Anchor, 1966.

Bernstein, Richard J. *Beyond Objectivism and Relativism*. Oxford: Basil Blackwell, 1983.

Black, Max. *Models and Metaphors: Studies in Language and Philosophy*. Ithaca, NY: Cornell University Press, 1962.

Blaszczyk, Regina Lee. *The Color Revolution*. Cambridge, MA: MIT Press, 2012.

Bloch, Ernst. *The Principle of Hope*. Oxford: Blackwell, 1986.

"Blur Building—Diller Scofidio and Renfro." *Arcspace.com*, 2001. http://www.arcspace.com/features/diller-scofidio--renfro/blur-building/.

Böhme, Gernot. "Atmosphere as the Fundamental Concept of a New Aesthetics." *Thesis Eleven* 36 (2005): 113–126.

Böhme, Gernot. "Atmosphere as the Subject Matter of Architecture." In *Herzog and De Meuron: Natural History*, edited by Philip Ursprung, 398–406. Montreal: Lars Müller, 2005.

Bollnow, Otto Friedrich. *Human Space*. Translated by Christine Shuttleworth. London: Hyphen Press, 2011.

"Boris Johnson: David Cameron 'Knew Full Well' What Magna Carta Meant." *The Guardian*, 2012.

Bowie, Malcolm. *Lacan*. London: Fontana, 1991.

Bowring, Jacky. *A Field Guide to Melancholy*. Harpenden, UK: Oldcastle, 2008.

Bozarth, Michael A. "Pleasure Systems in the Brain." In *Pleasure: The Politics and the Reality*, edited by David M. Warburton, 5–14. New York: John Wiley and Sons, 1994.

Bradley, Margaret M., and Peter J. Lang. *Affective Norms for English Words (ANEW): Instruction Manual and Affective Ratings (Technical Report C-1)*. Gainesville: The Center for Research in Psychophysiology, The University of Florida, 1999. http://www.uvm .edu/~pdodds/files/papers/others/1999/bradley1999a.pdf.

Brandt, Thomas, Marianne Dietricj, and Michael Strupp. *Vertigo and Dizziness: Common Complaints*. London: Springer-Verlag, 2005.

Bratton, Benjamin. "The Black Stack." *E-flux*, 2014. http://www.e-flux.com/journal/ the-black-stack/.

Brecht, Bertolt. "A Short Organum for the Theatre." In *Brecht on Theatre: The Development of an Aesthetic*, edited by John Willett, 179–205. London: Methuen, 1964.

Breivik, Gunnar. "Being-in-the-Void: A Heideggerian Analysis of Skydiving." *Journal of the Philosophy of Sport* 37 (2010): 29–46.

Bricmont, Jean, and Alan Sokal. *Impostures Intellectuelles*. Paris: Odile Jacob, 1997.

Brown, Paul, Charlie Gere, Nicholas Lambert, and Catherine Mason. *White Heat Cold Logic: British Computer Art, 1960–1980*. Cambridge, MA: MIT Press, 2008.

Buchanan, Richard. "Wicked Problems in Design Thinking." In *The Idea of Design*, edited by Victor Margolin and Richard Buchanan, 3–20. Cambridge, MA: MIT Press,1995.

Buck, Ross, and Stacie Renfro Powers. "Emotion, Media and the Global Village." In *The Routledge Handbook of Emotions and Mass Media*, edited by Katrin Dövelin, Christian von Scheve, and Elly A. Konijn, 181–194. London: Routledge, 2010.

Bull, Michael. "The Intimate Sounds of Urban Experience: An Auditory Epistemology of Everyday Mobility." In *A Sense of Place: The Global and the Local in Mobile Communication*, edited by Kristóf Nyíri, 169–178. Vienna: Passagen Verlag, 2005.

Bunyan, John. *Pilgrim's Progress and Grace Abounding to the Chief of Sinners*. London: Penguin, 1987. First published in 1666.

Burke, Edmund, and James Boulton, eds. *A Philosophical Enquiry into the Origin of our Ideas of the Sublime and Beautiful*. Notre Dame: University of Notre Dame Press, 1958. First published in 1757.

Butler, Samuel. "A Melancholy Man." In *Characters and Passages from Note-Books*, edited by A. R. Waller, 59–60. Cambridge, UK: Cambridge University Press, 1908.

Caillois, Roger. *Man, Play, and Games*. New York: Free Press, 1961.

Caillois, Roger. "Mimicry and Legendary Psychasthenia." *October* 31 (Winter 1984): 17–32. First published in *Minotaure* in 1935.

Caputo, John D. *The Mystical Element in Heidegger's Thought*. New York: Fordham University Press, 1986.

Carey, James W.*Communication as Culture: Essays on Media and Society*. London: Routledge and Kegan Paul, 1989.

Carey, John. "Introduction." In *The Joke and Its Relation to the Unconscious*, edited by Sigmund Freud, vii–xxviii. London: Penguin, 2002.

Carlyle, Thomas, and Takaaki Tanizaki, eds. *Past and Present*. Tokyo: Yamagushi Shoten, 1984.

Carnap, Rudolf. "The Elimination of Metaphysics through Logical Analysis of Language." In *Logical Positivism*, edited by Alfred J. Ayer, 60–81. New York: Free Press, 1932.

Carr, Edward Hallett. *What Is History?* Harmondsworth: Penguin, 1964.

Carr, Nicholas. *The Shallows: What the Internet Is Doing to Our Brains*. New York: W. W. Norton, 2011.

Carruthers, Helen R, Julie Morris, Nicholas Tarrier, and Peter J. Whorwell. "The Manchester Color Wheel: Development of a Novel Way of Identifying Color Choice and Its Validation in Healthy, Anxious and Depressed Individuals." *BMC Medical Research Methodology* 10, no. 12 (2010): 1–13.

Cernea, Daniel, Andreas Kerren, and Achim Ebert. "Detecting Insight and Emotion in Visualization Applications with a Commercial EEG Headset." *Proceedings of SIGRAD Linköping Electronic Conference*, Stockholm, Sweden, 2011.

Chen, Hsinchun. *Dark Web: Exploring and Data Mining the Dark Side of the Web*. New York: Springer, 2012.

Chion, Michel. *The Voice in Cinema*. Translated by Claudia Gorbman. New York: Columbia University Press, 1999. First published in French in 1982.

Chmielewska, Ella. "Vectors of Looking: Reflections on the Luftwaffe's Aerial Survey of Warsaw, 1944." In *Seeing from Above: The Aerial View in Visual Culture*, edited by Mark Dorrian and Frédéric Pousin. London: IB Tauris, 2013.

Chomsky, Noam, and Edward Herman. *Manufacturing Consent: The Political Economy of the Mass Media*. London: Random House, 2010. First published in 1988.

Christensen, Clayton M., and Joseph L. Bower. "Disruptive Technologies: Catching the Wave." *Harvard Business Review* (January–February 1995): 43–53.

Clancy, Susan A., Richard J. McNally, Daniel L. Schacter, Mark F. Lezenweger, and Roger K. Pitman. "Memory Distortion in People Reporting Abduction by Aliens." *Journal of Abnormal Psychology* 111, no. 3 (2002): 455–461.

Clark, Andy. *Being There: Putting Brain, Body and World Together Again*. Cambridge, MA: MIT Press, 1997.

Clark, Andy. *Natural-Born Cyborgs: Minds, Technologies, and the Future of Human Intelligence*. Oxford: Oxford University Press, 2003.

Clark, Andy. "Out of Our Brains." *The Opinionator*, 2010. http://opinionator.blogs.nytimes.com/2010/12/12/out-of-our-brains/.

Clark, Andy. "Where Brain, Body and World Collide." *Journal of Cognitive Systems Research* 1 (1999): 5–17.

Clark, Andy, and David Chalmers. "The Extended Mind." *Analysis* 58, no. 1 (1998): 7–19.

Cockain, Alex. "Students' Ambivalence toward Their Experiences in Secondary Education: Views from a Group of Young Chinese Studying on an International Foundation Program in Beijing." *China Journal* 65 (January 2011): 101–118.

Cohen, Annabel J. "Music as a Source of Emotion in Film." In *Music and Emotion: Theory and Research*, edited by Patrik N. Juslin and John A. Sloboda, 249–272. New York: Oxford University Press, 2001.

Cohen, Stanley. *Folk Devils and Moral Panics*. St. Albans: Paladin, 1973.

Connor, Steven. *Paraphernalia: The Curious Lives of Magical Things*. London: Profile, 2011. Kindle edition.

Cooke, Deryck. *The Language of Music*. Oxford: Clarendon Press, 1989. First published in 1959.

Cowley, Elizabeth. "As a Backdrop, Part of the Game, or a Goal in a Game: The Ubiquitous Product Placement." In *The Psychology of Entertainment Media: Blurring the Lines between Entertainment and Persuasion*, edited by L. J. Shrum, 37–63. New York: Routledge, 2012.

Coyne, Richard. *Cornucopia Limited: Design and Dissent on the Internet*. Cambridge, MA: MIT Press, 2005.

Coyne, Richard D. "Cyberspace and Heidegger's Pragmatics." Special issue (Heidegger and Information Technology), *Information Technology and People* 11, no. 4 (1998): 338–350.

Coyne, Richard. *Derrida for Architects*. Abingdon: Routledge, 2011.

Coyne, Richard. "Even More than Architecture." In *Design Research in Architecture: An Overview*, edited by Murray Fraser, 185–203. Farnham, UK: Ashgate, 2013.

Coyne, Richard. "Nature versus Smartphones." *Interactions Magazine* 21, no. 5 (2014): 24–31.

Coyne, Richard. "Space without Ground." In *Architecture in Scotland*, edited by Morag Bain, 94–99. Glasgow: The Lighthouse Trust, 2006.

Coyne, Richard. *Technoromanticism: Digital Narrative, Holism, and the Romance of the Real*. Cambridge, MA: MIT Press, 1999.

Coyne, Richard. *The Tuning of Place: Sociable Spaces and Pervasive Digital Media*. Cambridge, MA: MIT Press, 2010.

Coyne, Richard. "Wicked Problems Revisited." *Design Studies* 26, no. 1 (2005): 5–17.

Coyne, Richard, Mark Wright, James Stewart, and Henrik Ekeus. "Virtual Flagships and Sociable Media." In *Flagship Marketing: Concepts and Places*, edited by Anthony Kent and Reva Brown, 46–62. London: Routledge, 2009.

Cross, Steve, and Jo Littler. "Celebrity and Schadenfreude: The Cultural Economy of Fame in Free Fall." *Cultural Studies* 24, no. 3 (2010): 395–417.

Cruz, Marcos. *The Inhabitable Flesh of Architecture*. Farnham:Ashgate, 2013.

Cubitt, Sean. *The Cinema Effect*. Cambridge, MA: MIT Press, 2005.

Cuff, Dana. "Immanent Domain: Pervasive Computing and the Public Realm." *Journal of Architectural Education* 57, no. 1 (2003): 43–49.

Cunningham, Michael R. "Weather, Mood and Helping Behavior: Quasi Experiments with the Sunshine Samaritan." *Journal of Personality and Social Psychology* 37, no. 11 (1979): 1947–1956.

Cupchik, Gerald C. "Reactive and Reflective Responses to Mass Media." In *The Routledge Handbook of Emotions and Mass Media*, edited by Katrin Dövelin, Christian von Scheve, and Elly A. Konijn, 332–346. London: Routledge, 2010.

"Cybercriminals 'Drained ATMs' in $45m World Bank Heist." *BBC News US and Canada*, 2013. http://www.bbc.co.uk/news/world-us-canada-22470299.

Cytowic, Richard E. "Synesthesia: Phenomenology and Neuropsychology—A Review of Current Knowledge. *PSYCHE* 2, no. 10, 1995. http://www.theassc.org/files/assc/2346.pdf.

Dabala, Jacek. *Mystery and Suspense in Creative Writing*. Vienna: Lit Verlag GmbH and Co, 2012.

Daneback, Kristian, and Cecilia. Löfberg. "Youth, Sexuality and the Internet: Young People's Use of the Internet to Learn about Sexuality." In *Youth Culture and Net Culture: Online Social Practices*, edited by Elza Dunkels, Gun-Marie Frånberg, and Camilla Hällgren, 190–206. Hershey, PA: IGI Global, 2011.

Darwin, Charles. *The Expression of the Emotions in Man and Animals*. New York: Appleton, 1899.

Davidson, Joyce, Liz Bondi, and Mick Smith. *Emotional Geographies*. Aldershot, UK: Ashgate, 2005.

Davidson, Richard J. "On Emotion, Mood, and Related Affective Constructs." In *The Nature of Emotion: Fundamental Questions*, edited by Paul Ekman, 51–55. New York: Oxford University Press, 1994.

Deakin, Roger. *Wildwood: A Journey through Trees*. London: Penguin, 2008.

Debord, Guy. *Report on the Construction of Situations and on the International Situationist Tendency's Conditions of Organization and Action*. Translated by Ken Knabb. Pamphlet. Publisher unknown, 1957.

de Botton, Alain. *The Art of Travel*. London: Penguin, 2002. Kindle edition.

Deignan, Alice. "Corpus Linguistics and Metaphor." In *The Cambridge Handbook of Metaphor and Thought*, edited by Raymond W. Gibbs, 280–294. Cambridge: Cambridge University Press, 2008.

de Lange, Michiel. "The Smart City You Love to Hate: Exploring the Role of Affect in Hybrid Urbanism." In *Proceedings of The Hybrid City II: Subtle rEvolutions*, edited by Dimitris Charitos, Iouliani Theona, Daphne Dragona, and Charalampos Rizopoulos. Athens: University Research Institute of Applied Communication, 2013. http://www.bijt.org/wordpress/wp-content/uploads/2006/01/Michiel_de_Lange-The-smart-city-you-love-to-hate-exploring-the-role-of-affect_Hybrid_City-Athens_styled_edit-v2.pdf (accessed May 28, 2015).

deNora, Tia. *Music and Everyday Life*. Cambridge: Cambridge University Press, 2000.

de Rivera, Joseph, and Carmen Grinkis. "Emotion as Social Relationships." *Motivation and Emotion* 10, no. 4 (1986): 351–369.

Derrida, Jacques. "Différance." In *Margins of Philosophy*, 3–27. Chicago: University of Chicago Press, 1982.

Derrida, Jacques. *Of Grammatology*. Translated by Gayatri Chakravorty Spivak. Baltimore, MD: Johns Hopkins University Press, 1976.

Derrida, Jacques. "Plato's Pharmacy." In *Dissemination*, 61–171. London: Athlone, 1981.

Derrida, Jacques. *Specters of Marx: The State of the Debt, the Work of Mourning*. New York: Routledge, 1994.

Derrida, Jacques, and Alan Bass. "The Linguistic Circle of Geneva." *Critical Inquiry* 8, no. 4 (1982): 675–691.

Dery, Mark. "Naked Lunch: Talking Realcore with Sergio Messina." In *C'Lick Me: A Netporn Studies Reader*, edited by Katrien Jacobs, Marije Janssen, and Matteo Pasquinelli, 17–30. Amsterdam: Institute of Network Cultures, 2007.

Dery, Mark. "Paradise Lust: Pornotopia Meets the Culture Wars." In *C'Lick Me: A Netporn Studies Reader*, edited by Katrien Jacobs, Marije Janssen, and Matteo Pasquinelli, 125–148. Amsterdam: Institute of Network Cultures, 2007.

Descartes, René. *Discourse on Method and the Meditations*. Translated by F. E. Sutcliffe. Harmondsworth, UK: Penguin, 1968.

DeSilvey, Caitlin, and Tim Edensor. "Reckoning with Ruins." *Progress in Human Geography* 37, no. 4 (2012):465–485.

de Sousa, Ronald. *The Rationality of Emotion*. Cambridge, MA: MIT Press, 1990.

Diamond, Elin. "Brechtian Theory/Feminist Theory: Towards a Gestic Feminist Criticism." *TDR* 32, no. 1 (1988): 82–94.

Dick, Kirby, and Amy Ziering Kofman (directors). *Derrida* (film). Zeitgeist Films, 2002.

Dick, Philip K. *Do Androids Dream of Electric Sheep?* London: Voyager, 1996.

Diener, Ed, and Carol Diener. "Most People Are Happy." *Psychological Science* 7, no. 3 (1996): 181–185.

"The Digital Humanities Manifesto 2.0." *Humanities Blast*, 2011. http://www.humanitiesblast.com/manifesto/Manifesto_V2.pdf.

"Digital Sales Break £1bn Barrier." *BBC UK News*, 2013. http://www.bbc.co.uk/news/uk-20885506.

Dorrian, Mark. "The Aerial Image: Vertigo, Transparency and Miniaturization." *Parallax* 15, no. 4 (2009): 83–93.

Dorrian, Mark. "On Google Earth." In *Seeing from Above: The Aerial View in Visual Culture*, edited by Mark Dorrian and Frédéric Pousin, 290–307. London: IB Tauris, 2013.

Dorrian, Mark, and Frédéric Pousin. *Seeing from Above: The Aerial View in Visual Culture*. London: IB Tauris, 2013.

Douglas, Mary. *Purity and Danger: An Analysis of Concepts of Pollution and Taboo*. London: Routledge and Kegan Paul, 1966.

Dourish, Paul. *Where the Action Is: The Foundations of Embodied Interaction*. Cambridge, MA: MIT Press, 2001.

Dourish, Paul, and Genevieve Bell. *Divining a Digital Future: Mess and Mythology in Ubiquitous Computing*. Cambridge, MA: MIT Press, 2011. Kindle edition.

Dourish, Paul, and Genevieve Bell. "'Resistance Is Futile': Reading Science Fiction Alongside Ubiquitous Computing." *Perspectives on Ubiquitous Computing* 18: 769–778.

Dövelin, Katrin, Christian von Scheve, and Elly A. Konijn, eds. *The Routledge Handbook of Emotions and Mass Media.* London: Routledge, 2010.

Dreyfus, Hubert L. *Being-in-the-World: A Commentary on Heidegger's Being and Time, Division I.* Cambridge, MA: MIT Press, 1991.

Durkin, Keith. "Death, Dying, and the Dead in Popular Culture." In *Handbook of Death and Dying,* edited by Clifton D. Bryant, 43–49. Newbury Park, CA: Sage, 2003.

Dutton, Donald G., and Arthur P. Aron. "Some Evidence for Heightened Sexual Attraction under Conditions of High Anxiety." *Journal of Personality and Social Psychology* 30, no. 4 (1974): 510–517.

Dyer, Richard. *Only Entertainment.* London: Routledge, 2002.

Edensor, Tim. "Waste Matter: The Debris of Industrial Ruins and the Disordering of the Material World." *Journal of Material Culture* 10, no. 3 (2005): 311–332.

Eliade, Mercea. *The Two and the One.* Translated by John Michael Cohen. London: Harvill Press, 1965.

Ellis, Justin. "Not an April Fool's Joke: The New York Times Has Built a Haiku Bot." *Nieman Journalism Lab,* 2013. http://www.niemanlab.org/2013/04/not-an-april -fools-joke-the-new-york-times-has-built-a-haiku-bot/.

Evans, Leighton. "Being-towards the Social: Mood and Orientation to Location-Based Social Media, Computational Things and Applications." *New Media & Society,* 2014, 1–16. http://nms.sagepub.com/content/early/2014/01/20/1461444813518183 .full.pdf+html.

Eysenck, H. J. "Principles and Methods of Personality Description, Classification and Diagnosis." *British Journal of Psychology* 55 (1964): 284–293.

Fforde, Jasper. *Shades of Grey.* London: Hodder and Stoughton, 2010.

Finlay, Robert. "Weaving the Rainbow: Visions of Color in World History." *Journal of World History* 18, no. 4 (2007): 383–431.

Finzi, Eric. *The Face of Emotion: How Botox Affects Our Moods and Relationships.* New York: Palgrave Macmillan, 2013.

Fish, Stanley. "The Digital Humanities and the Transcending of Mortality." *Opinionator,* January 2012. http://opinionator.blogs.nytimes.com/2012/2001/2009/the -digital-humanities-and-the-transcending-of-mortality/?_php=true&_type=blogs&_r =2010.

Flaherty, Erin M. "Howling (and Bleeding) at the Moon: Menstruation, Monstrosity and the Double in Ginger Snaps Werewolf Trilogy." Master's thesis, Pace University, 2008. http://digitalcommons.pace.edu/honorscollege_theses/67.

Flatley, Jonathan. *Affective Mapping: Melancholia and the Politics of Modernism*. Cambridge, MA: Harvard University Press, 2008.

Fortin, David T. *Architecture and Science Fiction Film: Philip K. Dick and the Spectacle of Home*. London: Ashgate, 2011.

Foucault, Michel. *Discipline and Punish: The Birth of the Prison*. London: Penguin, 1977.

Fox, Kate. *Watching the English: The Hidden Rules of English Behavior*. 2nd ed. Boston; London: Nicholas Brealey Publishing, 2014. Kindle edition.

Frazer, James. *The Golden Bough*. London: Penguin, 1996. First published in 1922.

Fredrickson, Barbara L. "The Broaden-and-Build Theory of Positive Emotions." *Philosophical Transactions of the Royal Society of London. Series B, Biological Sciences* 359, no. 1449 (2004): 1367–1377.

Freud, Sigmund. "Beyond the Pleasure Principle." In *The Penguin Freud Library, Volume 11: On Metapsychology*, edited by Angela Richards, 269–338. Harmondsworth, UK: Penguin, 1990.

Freud, Sigmund. "Character and Anal Eroticism." In *The Penguin Freud Library, Volume 7: On Sexuality*, edited by Angela Richards, 205–215. Harmondsworth, UK: Penguin, 1991.

Freud, Sigmund. "Civilization and Its Discontents." In *The Penguin Freud Library, Volume 12: Civilization, Society and Religion*, edited by Albert Dickson, 243–340. London: Penguin, 1985.

Freud, Sigmund. "The Ego and the Id." In *The Penguin Freud Library, Volume 11: On Metapsychology*, edited by Angela Richards, 339–407. Harmondsworth, UK: Penguin, 1990.

Freud, Sigmund. *Jokes and Their Relation to the Unconscious*. New York: W. W. Norton, 1960.

Freud, Sigmund. "Leonardo da Vinci and a Memory of His Childhood." In *The Penguin Freud Library, Volume 14: Art and Literature, Jensen's Gradiva, Leonardo da Vinci and Other Works*, edited by Albert Dickson, 151–231. London: Penguin, 1953.

Freud, Sigmund. "Mourning and Melancholia." In *Penguin Freud Library, Volume 11: On Metapsychology*, edited by Angela Richards, 251–268. Harmondsworth, UK: Penguin, 1990.

Freud, Sigmund. "A Note upon the 'Mystic Writing Pad.'" In *Complete Psychological Works of Sigmund Freud, Volume 19*, edited by James Strachey, 227–232. London: Vintage, 1925.

Freud, Sigmund. *On Dreams*. Translated by James. Strachey. London: Hogarth Press and the Institute of Psycho-Analysis, 1952.

Gadamer, Hans-Georg. *Truth and Method*. Rev. ed. Translated by Joel Weinsheimer and Donald G. Marshall. New York: Continuum, 2004. Originally published in German in 1960.

Gall, Meredith D. "The Use of Questions in Teaching." *American Education Research Association* 5, no. 40 (1970): 707–721.

Gell, Alfred. "The Gods at Play: Vertigo and Possession in Muria Religion." *Man* 15, no. 2 (1980): 219–248.

Gem, Martin. "Leonardo's Vitruvian Man, Renaissance Humanism, and Nicholas of Cusa." *[umĕní] Art* 55, no. 2 (2007): 102–107.

Gere, Charlie. "Brains-in-Vats, Giant Brains and World Brains: The Brain as Metaphor in Digital Culture." *Studies in History and Philosophy of Biological and Biomedical Sciences* 35 (2004): 351–366.

Ghannam, Jeffrey. *Social Media in the Arab World: Leading Up to the Uprisings of 2011*. Washington, DC: Center for International Media Assistance, 2011.

Giaccardi, Elisa. "Cross-Media Interaction for the Virtual Museum: Reconnecting to Natural Heritage in Boulder, Colorado." In *New Heritage: New Media and Cultural Heritage*, edited by Yehuda E. Kalay, Thomas Kvan, and Janice Affleck, 112–131. London: Routledge, 2008.

Giaccardi, Elisa, ed. *Heritage Matters: Understanding and Experiencing Heritage through Social Media: Understanding Heritage in a Participatory Culture*. London: Routledge, 2012.

Gibbs, Samuel. "What Is 'Bit Rot' and Is Vint Cerf Right to Be Worried?" *Guardian Newspaper*, February 13, 2015. http://www.theguardian.com/technology/2015/feb/13/what-is-bit-rot-and-is-vint-cerf-right-to-be-worried.

Gibson, William. *Neuromancer*. London: Harper Voyager, 1995.

Giddens, Anthony. *Runaway World: How Globalisation Is Shaping Our Lives*. London: Profile Books, 1999.

Gieseking, Jen Jack, and William Mangold. *The People, Place and Space Reader*. New York: Routledge, 2014.

Giumetti, Gary W., and Patrick M. Markey. "Violent Video Games and Anger as Predictors of Aggression." *Journal of Research in Personality* 41, no. 6 (2007): 1234–1243.

Goethe, Johann Wolfgang von. *Elective Affinities*. Translated by David Constantine. New York: Henry Holt, 1883. First published in German in 1809.

Goethe, Johann Wolfgang von. *Theory of Colours*. Translated by Charles Lock East-lake. Cambridge, MA: MIT Press, 1970. First published in German in 1810.

Goffman, Erving. *Frame Analysis: An Essay on the Organisation of Experience*. New York: Harper and Row, 1974.

Goffman, Erving. *The Presentation of Self in Everyday Life*. London: Penguin, 1969.

Goffman, Erving. *Ritual Interaction: Essays on Face-to-face Behavior*. New York: Pantheon, 1967.

Gowers, Ernest, Sidney Greenbaum, and Janet Whitcut. *The Complete Plain Words*. Boston: D. R. Godine, 1988.

Gray, Thomas. *Thomas Gray: Selected Poems*, edited by John Heath-Stubbs. Manchester, England: Carcanet Press, 1981.

Green, Ewen. "Reviews." *Twentieth Century British History* 16, no. 3 (2005): 342–347.

Green, Melanie C. "Storytelling in Teaching." *Observer: The Association for Psychological Science*17, no. 4 (2004): 37–54.

Greenberg, Andy. "Congressman Says He'll Propose Ban on 3D-Printable Gun Magazines." *Forbes*, 2013. http://www.forbes.com/sites/andygreenberg/2013/01/16/congressman-says-hell-propose-ban-on-3d-printable-gun-magazines/.

Greene, Robert. *The Art of Seduction*. London: Profile, 2003.

"Healthy Living: How to Live Longer." *BBC Science*, 2013. http://www.bbc.co.uk/science/0/22019289 (accessed April 2015).

Hagnell, Olle, Jan Lanke, Birgitta Rorsman, and Leif Öjesjö. "Are We Entering an Age of Melancholy? Depressive Illnesses in a Prospective Epidemiological Study over 25 Years: The Lundby Study, Sweden." *Psychological Medicine* 12 (1982): 279–289.

Halbwachs, Maurice. *On Collective Memory*. Chicago: University of Chicago Press, 1992.

Hawkes, Terrence. *Structuralism and Semiotics*. London: Routledge, 2003.

Heidegger, Martin. "The Age of the World Picture." *The Question Concerning Technology and Other Essays*, 115–154. New York: Harper and Row, 1977.

Heidegger, Martin. *Being and Time*. Translated by John Macquarrie and Edward Robinson. London: SCM Press, 1962.

Heidegger, Martin. "Building, Dwelling, Thinking." In *Poetry, Language, Thought*, 143–161. New York: Harper and Row, 1971.

Heidegger, Martin. "The Origin of the Work of Art." In *Poetry, Language, Thought*, 15–87. New York: Harper and Rowe, 1971.

Heidegger, Martin. *Poetry, Language, Thought*. Translated by Albert Hofstadter. New York: Harper and Row, 1981.

Heidegger, Martin. "The Thing." In *Poetry, Language, Thought*, 165–186. New York: Harper and Row, 1971.

Heidegger, Martin. "What Are Poets For?" In *Poetry, Language, Thought*, 91–142. New York: Harper and Rowe, 1971.

Heidegger, Martin. "What Is Metaphysics?" In *Martin Heidegger: Basic Writings*, edited by David. Farrell Krell, 93–110. London: Routledge, 1978.

Heiss, Leah. "Empathy over Distance: Wearables as Tools for Augmenting Remote Emotional Connection." *Proceedings of SIGRADI*, Santiago, Chile, 2006.

Hetzler, Florence M. "Ruin Time and Ruins." *Leonardo* 21, no. 1 (1988): 51–55.

Highmore, Ben, and Jenny Bourne Taylor. "Introducing Mood Work." *New Formations* 82 (2014): 5–12.

Hill, Jonathan. "The Weather in Architecture: Soane, Turner and the 'Big Smoke.'" *Journal of Architecture* 14, no. 3 (2009): 361–376.

Hinnant, Lori. "'We Are All Hooligans': Protests for Pussy Riot." *Bloomberg Business Week*, 2012. http://www.businessweek.com/ap/2012-08-17/nudity-masks-and-color-protests-for-pussy-riot.

Hochschild, Arlie Russell. *The Managed Heart: Commercialization of Human Feeling*. Berkeley, CA: University of California Press, 2012.

Hodges, Andrew. *Alan Turing: The Enigma of Intelligence*. London: Unwin Paperbacks, 1985.

Hollis, Edward. *The Secret Lives of Buildings: From the Parthenon to the Vegas Strip in Thirteen Stories*. London: Portobello, 2011.

Hooper-Greenhill, Eilean. *Museums and the Shaping of Knowledge*. London: Routledge, 1992.

Horvath, Miranda A. H., Llian Alys, Kristina Massey, Afroditi Pina, Mia Scally, and Joanna R. Adler. *"Basically . . . porn is everywhere": A Rapid Evidence Assessment on the Effects that Access and Exposure to Pornography Has on Children and Young People*. Office of the Children's Commissioner, London, 2013. http://www.cypnow.co.uk/digital_assets/BasicallyporniseverywhereReport%5B1%5D_copy.pdf.

Hospers, John. *An Introduction to Philosophical Analysis*. London: Routledge, 2013.

"How Sister Feng Became Famous." *Chinahush*, 2010. http://www.chinahush.com/2010/04/24/how-sister-feng-became-famous/.

Hubbard, Phil. "The Geographies of 'Going Out': Emotion and Embodiment in the Evening Economy." In *Emotional Geographies,* edited by Joyce Davidson, Liz Bondi, and MickSmith, 117–134. Aldershot, UK: Ashgate, 2005.

Hughes, Thomas P. "The Evolution of Large Technological Systems." In *The Social Construction of Technological Systems: New Directions in the Sociology and History of Technology,* edited byWiebe E. Bijker, Thomas P. Hughes, Trevor Pinch, and Deborah G. Douglas, 45–76. Cambridge, MA: MIT Press, 1990.

Huizinga, Johan. *Homo Ludens: A Study of the Play Element in Culture.* Boston: Beacon Press, 1955.

Huxley, Thomas H.*Collected Essays.* Vol. 5. New York: D. Appleton and Company, 1902.

Hyde, Michael J., and Craig R. Smith. "Aristotle and Heidegger on Emotion and Rhetoric: Questions of Time and Space." In *The Critical Turn: Rhetoric and Philosophy in Postmodern Discourse,* edited by Ian Angus, and Lenore Langsdorf, 68–99. Carbondale: Southern Illinois University Press, 1993.

Hyodo, Jamie. "Can Colors Make Me Happy? The Effect of Color on Mood: A Meta-Analysis." *Advances in Consumer Research* 39 (2011): 858–867.

Insley, Jill. "FarmVille User Runs Up £900 Debt." *The Guardian,* 2010. http://www.theguardian.com/money/2010/apr/07/farmville-user-debt-facebook.

Isaacson, Walter. *Steve Jobs: The Exclusive Biography.* London: Hachette Digital, 2011.

Ito, Mizuko, Daisuke Okabe, and Misa Matsuda, eds. *Personal, Portable, Pedestrian: Mobile Phones in Japanese Life.* Cambridge, MA: MIT Press, 2006.

Itten, Johannes. *The Art of Color: The Subjective Experience and Objective Rationale of Color.* Translated by Ernst von Haagen. New York: Wiley, 1973.

Itten, Johannes. *The Elements of Color: A Treatise on the Color System of Johannes Itten Based on His Book The Art of Color.* New York: Van Nostrand Reinhold, 1970.

James, E. L. *Fifty Shades of Grey.* London: Arrow, 2012. Kindle edition.

James, F. William. "What Is an Emotion?" *Mind* 9 (1884): 188–205.

Jenkins, Keith. *On "What Is History"': From Carr and Elton to Rorty and White.* London: Routledge, 1995.

Jenkins, Keith. *Re-Thinking History.* London: Routledge, 1991.

Joffé, George. "The Arab Spring in North Africa: Origins and Prospects." *Journal of North African Studies* 16, no. 4 (2011): 507–532.

Jones, John Chris. *Design Methods: Seeds of Human Futures.* London: Wiley, 1970.

Jones, Jonathan. "No Way Out." *The Guardian*, November 6, 2001. http://www
.theguardian.com/culture/2002/nov/06/artsfeatures.highereducation.

Jones, Owain. "An Ecology of Emotion, Memory, Self and Landscape. In *Emotional Geographies*, edited by Joyce Davidson, Liz Bondi, and Mick Smith, 205–218. Aldershot, UK: Ashgate, 2005.

Judd, Deane B. "*Introduction.*" In *Johann Wolfgang von Goethe's Theory of Colours*, *v–xvi*. Cambridge, MA: MIT Press, 1970.

Jung, Carl G.*Psychological Types*. Translated by Helton Godwin Baynes. London: Kegan Paul, 1944.

Juslin, Patrik N., and Daniel Västfjäll. "Emotional Responses to Music: The Need to Consider Underlying Mechanisms." *Behavioral and Brain Sciences* 31 (2008): 559–621.

Juul, Jesper. *The Art of Failure: An Essay on the Pain of Playing Video Games*. Cambridge, MA: MIT Press, 2013.

Kamvasinou, Krystallia. "Notation Timelines and the Aesthetics of Disappearance." *Journal of Architecture* 15, no. 4 (2010): 397–423.

Kandinsky, Wassily. *Concerning the Spiritual in Art*. Translated by M. T. H. Sadler. New York: Dover, 1977.

Kandinsky, Wassily. *Point and Line to Plane*. Translated by Howard Dearstyne and HillaRebay. New York: Dover, 1979. First published in German in 1926.

Kane, Carolyn L. "The Synthetic Color Sense of Pipilotti Rist, or, Deleuze Color Theory for Electronic Media Art." *Visual Communication* 10, no. 4 (2011): 475–497.

Kant, Immanuel. *Immanuel Kant's Critique of Pure Reason*. Translated by Norman Kemp Smith. London: Macmillan, 1950.

Kant, Immanuel. *Observations on the Feeling of the Beautiful and the Sublime*. Translated by John T. Goldthwait. Berkeley, CA: University of California Press, 1960.

Kaplan, Stephen. "The Restorative Benefits of Nature: Toward an Integrative Framework." *Journal of Environmental Psychology* 15 (1995): 169–182.

Karandinou, Anastasia. *No-Matter: Theories and Practices of the Ephemeral in Architecture*. London: Ashgate, 2013.

Karrim, Qudsiya. "Digital Death Planning for Dummies." *Mail and Guardian*, May 10, 2012. http://mg.co.za/article/2012-05-10-digital-death-planning-for-dummies.

Kay, John. *Obliquity: Why Our Goals Are Best Achieved Indirectly*. London: Profile, 2011.

Keats, John. "Ode on Melancholy." In *The Complete Poems of John Keats*, 233–234. Ware, Hertfordshire, UK: Wordsworth Editions Limited, 1994.

Keen, Andrew. *Digital Vertigo: How Today's Online Social Revolution Is Dividing, Diminishing, and Disorienting Us*. London: Constable and Robinson, 2012. Kindle edition.

Kellert, Stephen R., and Edward O. Wilson. *The Biophilia Hypothesis*. Washington, DC: Island Press, 1993.

Kemeny, John G. "Man Viewed as a Machine." *Scientific American* 192, no. 4 (1995): 58–67.

Kennedy, Maev. "Gormley's Installation Is a Mist-See." *The Guardian*, May 15, 2007. http://www.theguardian.com/artanddesign/artblog/2007/may/15/gormleysinstallationisamis.

Kennedy, Randy. "How Do I Love Thee? Count 140 Characters." *The New York Times*, March 20, 2011. http://www.nytimes.com/2011/03/20/weekinreview/20twitterature.html?_r=0.

Keren, Michael. "Blogging and the Politics of Melancholy." *Canadian Journal of Communication* 29, no. 1 (2004). http://www.cjc-online.ca/index.php/journal/article/view/1401/1491.

Khalil, Elias L. "The Mirror Neuron Paradox: How Far Is Understanding from Mimicking?" *Journal of Economic Behavior & Organization* 77 (2011): 86–96.

Kierkegaard, Soren. *The Concept of Anxiety: A Simple Psychologically Orienting Deliberation on the Dogmatic Issue of Hereditary Sin*. Translated by Reidar Thomte. Princeton, NJ: Princeton University Press, 1980.

Koeck, Richard. *Cine-Scapes: Cinematic Spaces in Architecture and Cities*. Abingdon, UK: Routledge, 2013.

Koyré, Alexandre. *From the Closed World to the infinite Universe*. New York: Harper and Row, 1958.

Kozel, Susan. "Conference Presentation Notes." *Proceedings of Invisibility and Unawareness: Ethico-Political Implications of Embeddedness*, Copenhagen, 2011.

Kramer, Adam D. I. "An Unobtrusive Behavioral Model of 'Gross National Happiness.'" In *Proceedings of the 28th International Conference on Human Factors in Computing Systems*, 287–290. New York: ACM, 2010.

Krämer, Jan, Lukas Wiewiorra, and Christof Weinhardt. "Net Neutrality: A Progress Report." *Telecommunications Policy* 37, no. 9 (2013): 794–813.

Kramera, Adam D. I., Jamie E. Guillory, and Jeffrey T. Hancock. "Experimental Evidence of Massive-Scale Emotional Contagion through Social Networks." *Proceedings of the National Academy of Sciences of the United States of America* 111, no. 24 (2014): 8788–8790.

Kuhn, Thomas. *The Structure of Scientific Revolutions.* Chicago: University of Chicago Press, 1970.

Küller, Rikard, Seifeddin Ballal, Thorbjörn Laike, Byron Mikellides, and Graciela Tonello. "The Impact of Light and Colour on Psychological Mood: A Cross-Cultural Study of Indoor Work Environments." *Ergonomics* 49, no. 14 (2013): 1496–1507.

Lacan, Jacques. *The Four Fundamental Concepts of Psychoanalysis.* Translated by Alan Sheridan. London: Penguin, 1979.

Laird, James D. "Self-Attribution of Emotion: The Effects of Expressive Behavior on the Quality of Emotional Experience." *Journal of Personality and Social Psychology* 29, no. 4 (1974): 475–486.

Landow, George P. "Hypertext as Collage-Writing." In *Hypermedia and Literary Studies*, edited by Paul Delany and George P. Landow, 150–170. Cambridge, MA: MIT Press, 1994.

Landow, George P., and Paul Delany. "Hypertext, Hypermedia and Literary Studies: The State of the Art." In *Hypermedia and Literary Studies*, edited by Paul Delany and George P. Landow, 3–50. Cambridge, MA: MIT Press, 1994.

Lavondés, Henri. "A Polynesian Game of Swings." *Journal of the Polynesian Society* 105, no. 2 (1996): 201–216.

Leggio, Gail. "The Paradoxes of Piranesi." *American Arts Quarterly* 27, no. 2 (2010). http://www.nccsc.net/legacy/the-paradoxes-of-piranesi.

Levin, Thomas Y., Ursula Frohne, and Peter Weibel, eds. *CTRL [SPACE]: Rhetorics of Surveillance from Bentham to Big Brother.* Cambridge, MA: MIT Press, 2002.

Lewis, Paul, Tim Newburn, Matthew Taylor, and James Ball. "Rioters Say Anger with Police Fuelled Summer Unrest." *The Guardian*, December 5, 2011. http://www.theguardian.com/uk/2011/dec/05/anger-police-fuelled-riots-study.

Lightman, Bernard. "Huxley and Scientific Agnosticism: The Strange History of a Failed Rhetorical Strategy." *British Journal for the History of Science* 35, no. 3 (2002): 271–289.

Lindon, Stanton J., ed. *The Alchemy Reader: From Hermes Trismegistus to Isaac Newton.* Cambridge: Cambridge University Press, 2003.

Ling, Rich. "From Ubicomp to Ubiex(pectations)." *Telematics and Informatics* 31 (2014): 173–183.

Ling, Rich. *New Tech, New Ties: How Mobile Communication Is Reshaping Social Cohesion.* Cambridge, MA: MIT Press, 2008.

Lodge, David. *The Art of Fiction*. London: Vintage, 1992.

Loewenstein, George. "The Psychology of Curiosity: A Review and Reinterpretation." *Psychological Bulletin* 116, no. 1 (1994): 75–98.

Loftus, Elizabeth F. "Planting Misinformation in the Human Mind: A 30-Year Investigation of the Malleability of Memory." *Learning & Memory* 12 (2013): 361–366.

Loftus, Elizabeth F., and Hunter G. Hoffman. "Misinformation and Memory: The Creation of New Memories." *Journal of Experimental Psychology* 118, no. 1 (1989): 100–104.

Lormand, Eric. "Nonphenomenal Consciousness." *Noûs* 30, no. 2 (1996): 242–261.

Lovejoy, Arthur O. *The Great Chain of Being: A Study of the History of an Idea*. Cambridge, MA: Harvard University Press, 1936.

Lovink, Geert. "Blogging, the Nihilist Impulse." *Eurozine*, January 2, 2007. http://www.eurozine.com/articles/2007-01-02-lovink-en.html.

Lovink, Geert. "Hermes on the Hudson: Notes on Media Theory after Snowden." *E-flux*, 2014. http://www.e-flux.com/journal/hermes-on-the-hudson-notes-on-media-theory-after-snowden/.

Lovink, Geert. *Zero Comments: Blogging and Critical Internet Culture*. London: Routledge, 2003.

Lowenthal, David. *The Past Is a Foreign Country*. Cambridge: Cambridge University Press, 1985.

Lutz, Catherine. "Emotion, Thought, and Estrangement: Emotion as a Cultural Category." *Cultural Anthropology* 1, no. 3 (1988): 287–309.

Lutz, Catherine. *Unnatural Emotions: Everyday Sentiments on a Micronesian Atoll and Their Challenge to Western Theory*. Chicago: University of Chicago Press, 1998.

Lutz, Catherine, and Geoffrey M. White. "The Anthropology of Emotions." *Annual Review of Anthropology* 15 (1986): 405–436.

Lyotard, Jean-François. *The Postmodern Condition: A Report on Knowledge*. Manchester, UK: Manchester University Press, 1986.

Macfarlane, Robert. *Mountains of the Mind: A History of a Fascination*. London: Granta, 2003.

Macfie, Keith. "Review of Keith Jenkins Retrospective." *Reviews in History*, 2009. http://www.history.ac.uk/reviews/review/1266.

Mallgrave, Harry Francis. *The Architect's Brain: Neuroscience, Creativity, and Architecture*. Chichester, UK: John Wiley, 2010.

Malpas, Jeff. *Heidegger's Topology: Being, Place, World.* Cambridge, MA: MIT Press, 2006. Kindle edition.

Malpas, Jeff, and Hans-Helmuth Gander, eds. *The Routledge Companion to Hermeneutics.* Abingdon, UK: Routledge, 2015.

Mansikka, Jan-Erik. "Can Boredom Educate Us? Tracing a Mood in Heidegger's Fundamental Ontology from an Educational Point of View." *Studies in Philosophy and Education* 28 (2008): 255–268.

Marcuse, Herbert. *Eros and Civilisation: A Philosophical Inquiry into Freud.* London: Routledge and Kegan Paul, 1987.

Maslov, Sergei, and Sidney Redner. "Promise and Pitfalls of Extending Google's PageRank Algorithm to Citation Networks." *Journal of Neuroscience* 28, no. 44 (2008): 11103–11105.

Massumi, Brian. *Parables for the Virtual: Movement, Affect, Sensation.* Durham, NC: Duke University Press, 2002.

Mavros, Panagiotis, Richard Coyne, Jennifer Roe, and Peter Aspinall. "Engaging the Brain: Implications of Mobile EEG for Spatial Representation." In *Digital Physicality Proceedings of the 30th eCAADe Conference,* edited by Henri Achten, Jiri Pavlicek, Jaroslav Hulin, and Dana Matejdan, 657–665. Czech Technical University in Prague, MOLAB, 2012.

Mayer, John D., and Alexander A. Stevens. "An Emergent Understanding of the Reflective (Meta-) Experience of Mood." *Research in Personality* 28 (1994): 351–373.

Mayer-Schonberger, Viktor. *Delete: The Virtue of Forgetting in the Digital Age.* Princeton, NJ: Princeton University Press, 2009.

McClelland, James L. "Constructive Memory and Memory Distortions: A Parallel-Distributed Processing Approach." In *Memory Distortion: How Minds, Brains, and Societies Reconstruct the Past,* edited by Daniel L. Schacter, 69–90. Cambridge, MA: Harvard University Press, 1995.

McCullough, Malcolm. *Ambient Commons: Attention in the Age of Embodied Information.* Cambridge, MA: MIT Press, 2013.

McDonough, Tom, ed. *Guy Debord and the Situationalist International: Texts and Documents.* Cambridge, MA: MIT Press, 2002.

McGinn, Marie. "Wittgenstein's 'Remarks on Colour.'" *Philosophy* 66, no. 258 (1991): 435–453.

McIntosh, Daniel N. "Facial Feedback Hypotheses: Evidence, Implications, and Directions." *Motivation and Emotion* 20, no. 2 (1996): 121–147.

McLachlan, Fiona. *Architectural Colour in the Professional Palette*. Abingdon, UK: Routledge, 2012.

McLuhan, Marshall. *The Gutenberg Galaxy: The Making of Typographic Man*. Toronto: University of Toronto Press, 1962.

McLuhan, Marshall. *The Medium Is the Massage*. Columbia Records CS 9501, CL2701, 1968.

Mcquire, Scott. "Rethinking Media Events: Large Screens, Public Space Broadcasting and Beyond." *New Media & Society* 12, no. 4 (2010): 567–582.

Metcalfe, Janet, and Walter Mischel. "A Hot/Cool-System Analysis of Delay of Gratification: Dynamics of Willpower." *Psychological Review* 106, no. 1 (1999): 3–19.

Meyer, Robinson. "Everything We Know About Facebook's Secret Mood Manipulation Experiment." *The Atlantic*, June 28, 2014. http://www.theatlantic.com/technology/archive/2014/06/everything-we-know-about-facebooks-secret-mood-manipulation-experiment/373648/.

Miller, Paul D., and Svitiana Matviyenko, eds. *The Imaginary App*. Cambridge, MA: MIT Press, 2014.

Mislove, Alan, Sune Lehmann, Yong-Yeol Ahn, Jukka-Pekka Onnela, and J. Niels Rosenquist. *Pulse of the Nation: U.S. Mood throughout the Day Inferred from Twitter*. Northeastern University, College of Computer and Information Science, 2010. http://www.ccs.neu.edu/home/amislove/twittermood/.

Mithen, Steven. *The Singing Neanderthals: The Origins of Music, Language, Mind and Body*. London: Orion, 2005.

Molnar-Szakacs, Istvan, and Katie Overy. "Music and Mirror Neurons: From Motion to 'E'motion." *SCAN* 1 (2006): 235–241.

Morelli, Dario. "The Pope's Last Flight: A Media Masterpiece." *The World Post*, February 28, 2013. http://www.huffingtonpost.com/dario-morelli/popes-last-flight-a-media-masterpiece_b_2783626.html?utm_hp_ref=world&ir=World.

Morozov, Evgeny. *The Net Delusion: How Not to Liberate the World*. London: Allen Lane, 2011.

Morris, Meredith Ringel, Jaime Teevan, and Katrina Panovich. "What Do People Ask Their Social Networks, and Why? A Survey Study of Status Message Q&A Behavior." In *Proceedings of CHI 2010: Using Your Social Network*, 1739–1748. New York: ACM, 2010.

Morris, William. *News from Nowhere*. London: Routledge and Kegan Paul, 1970.

Morris, William N., and Paula P. Schnurr. *Mood: The Frame of Mind*. New York: Springer-Verlag, 1989.

Munsell, Albert Henry. "A Pigment Color System and Notation." *American Journal of Psychology* 23, no. 2 (1912): 236–244.

Nagamachi, Mitsuo. *Kansei: Affective Engineering*. Boca Raton, FL: CRC Press, 2011.

Newton, Isaac. *Opticks: Or a Treatise of the Reflections, Inflections, and Colours of Light*. New York: Prometheus, 2003.

Nickerson, Raymond S. "Confirmation Bias: A Ubiquitous Phenomenon in Many Guises." *Review of General Psychology* 2, no. 2 (1998): 175–220.

Norberg-Schulz, Christian. *Genius Loci: Towards a Phenomenology of Architecture*. New York: Rizzoli, 1980.

Norman, Donald A. *Emotional Design: Why We Love (or Hate) Everyday Things*. New York: Basic Books, 2004.

Norman, Richard B. "Color Contrast and CAAD: The Seven Color Contrasts of Johannes Itten." In *The Electronic Design Studio: Architectural Knowledge and Media in the Computer Era*, edited by Malcolm McCullough, William J. Mitchell, and Patrick Purcell, 469–478. Cambridge, MA: MIT Press, 1990.

Nowlis, Vincent, and Helen H. Nowlis. "The Description and Analysis of Mood." *Annals of the New York Academy of Sciences* 65 (1956): 345–355.

Nozick, Robert. *Anarchy, State, and Utopia*. New York: Basic Books, 1974.

O'Leary, Stephen. "Cyberspace as Sacred Space: Communicating Religion on Computer Networks." In *Religion Online: Finding Faith on the Internet*, edited by Lorne L. Dawson and Douglas E. Cowan, 37–58. New York: Routledge, 2004.

Obama, Barack. *The Audacity of Hope: Thoughts on Reclaiming the American Dream*. Edinburgh: Canongate Books, 2007.

Ofcom. *Communications Market Report: UK*. London: Ofcom, 2011. http://stakeholders.ofcom.org.uk/binaries/research/cmr/cmr11/UK_CMR_2011_FINAL.pdf.

Ogas, Ogi, and Sai Gaddam. *A Billion Wicked Thoughts: What the World's Largest Experiment Reveals about Human Desire*. New York: Penguin, 2011. Kindle edition.

"Olympic Champion Bradley Wiggins on His Cycling Gold Medal." *The Telegraph*, August 2, 2012. http://www.telegraph.co.uk/sport/olympics/olympicsvideo/9445835/London-2012-Olympic-champion-Bradley-Wiggins-on-his-cycling-gold-medal.html.

Paasonen, Susanna. *Carnal Resonance: Affect and Online Pornography*. Cambridge, MA: MIT Press, 2011.

Paasonen, Susanna. "Online Pornography: Ubiquitous and Effaced." In *The Handbook of Internet Studies*, edited by Robert Burnett, Mia Consalvo, and Charles Ess, 424–439. Chichester, UK: Wiley-Blackwell, 2011.

Paasonen, Susanna. "Pornography, Affect and Feminist Reading." *Feminist Theory* 8, no. 1 (2007): 43–57.

Packard, Vance. *The Hidden Persuaders*. Brooklyn: Ig Publishing, 2007. First published in 1957.

Pariser, Eli. *The Filter Bubble: What the Internet Is Hiding from You*. London: Penguin, 2011.

Peale, Norman Vincent. *The Power of Positive Thinking*. Kingswood, UK:Cedar, 1953.

Persson, Lars-Olof, and Lennart Sjöberg. "Mood and Positive Expectations." *Social Behavior and Personality* 13, no. 2 (1985): 171–181.

Phillips, Louise H., Liz Smith, and Ken J. Gilhooly. "The Effects of Adult Aging and Induced Positive and Negative Mood on Planning." *American Psychological Association* 3, no. 2 (2002): 263–272.

Picard, Rosalind W. *Affective Computing*. Cambridge, MA: MIT Press, 1998.

Picard, Rosalind W. "What Does It Mean for a Computer to 'Have' Emotions?" In *Emotions in Humans and Artifacts*, edited by Robert Trappl, Paolo Petta, and Sabine Payr, 213–235. Cambridge MA: MIT Press, 2002.

Pizzato, Mark. *Ghosts of Theatre and Cinema in the Brain*. New York: Palgrave, 2006.

Plant, Sadie. *Zeros and Ones: Digital Women and the New Technoculture*. London: Fourth Estate, 1998.

Plato. *Symposium*. Translated by Robin Waterfield. Oxford: Oxford University Press, 1994.

Plato. "Timaeus." In *Complete Works*, edited by John M. Cooper, 1224–1291. Indianapolis, IL: Hackett, 1997.

Pomeroy, Steven Ross. "Guest Blog: How to Instill False Memories." *Scientific American*, February 19, 2013. http://blogs.scientificamerican.com/guest-blog/2013/02/19/how-to-instill-false-memories/.

Pope, Alexander. "An Essay on Man." In *The Major Works: Including* The Rape of the Lock *and* The Dunciad, 270–308. Oxford: Oxford University Press, 2006.

Popper, Karl Raimund. *Conjectures and Refutations: The Growth of Scientific Knowledge*. London: Routledge, 2002.

Postman, Neil. *Amusing Ourselves to Death: Public Discourse in the Age of Show Business*. New York: Penguin, 1985.

Pramaggiore, Maria, and Tom Wallis. *Film: A Critical Introduction*. London: Laurence King, 2005.

Price, Cedric. *Cedric Price: The Square Book*. London: Wiley-Academy, 2003. Originally published in 1984 as *Cedric Price: Works II, Architectural Association*.

Purkey, William W., and Betty Siegel. *Becoming an Innovative Leader: A New Approach to Professional and Personal Success*. Lake Worth, FL: Humanics Publishing, 2002.

Queena, Kim. "Google Speaks Up on Desktops and Laptops." *Marketplace*, 2013. http://www.marketplace.org/topics/tech/google-speaks-desktops-and-laptops.

Quercia, Daniele, Jonathan Ellis, Licia Capra, and Jon Crowcroft. "Tracking 'Gross Community Happiness' from Tweets." In *Proceedings of the ACM 2012 Conference on Computer Supported Collaborative Work*, 965–968. New York: ACM, 2012.

Rabelais, François. *Gargantua and Pantagruel*. Translated by John Michael Cohen. London: Penguin, 1955. First published in French in 1530–1534.

Radden, Jennifer. *The Nature of Melancholy*. New York: Oxford University Press, 2000.

Ramachandran, V. S. *The Tell-Tale Brain: Unlocking the Mysteries of Human Nature*. London: William Heinemann, 2011. Kindle edition.

Rancière, Jacques. *The Ignorant Schoolmaster: Five Lessons in Intellectual Emancipation*. Translated by Kristin Ross. Stanford, CA: Stanford University Press, 1991. First published in French in 1987.

Ratcliffe, Matthew. "Heidegger's Attunement and the Neuropsychology of Emotion." *Phenomenology and the Cognitive Sciences* 1 (2002): 287–312.

Rawes, Peg. "Spinoza's Geometric Ecologies." *Interstices: Journal of Architecture and Related Arts* 13 (2012): 60–69.

Reich, Wilhelm. *The Function of the Orgasm: Sex-Economic Problems of Biological Energy*. Translated by Vincent R. Carfagno. New York: Farrar, Straus and Giroux, 1973.

Ricoeur, Paul. *Freud and Philosophy: An Essay in Interpretation*. Translated by Denis Savage. New Haven, CT: Yale University Press, 1970.

Ricoeur, Paul. *Memory, History, Forgetting*. Translated by Kathleen Blamey and David Pellauer. Chicago: University of Chicago Press, 2004. Kindle edition.

Riskind, John H., and Carolyn C. Gotay. "Physical Posture: Could It Have Regulatory or Feedback Effects on Motivation and Emotion?" *Motivation and Emotion* 6, no. 3 (1982): 273–298.

Rittel, Horst, and Melvin Webber. "Dilemmas in a General Theory of Planning." *Policy Sciences* 4 (1973): 155–169.

Rizzolatti, Giacomo, and Laila Craighero. "The Mirror-Neuron System." *Annual Review of Neuroscience* 27 (2004): 169–192.

Roe, Jenny J., Peter A. Aspinall, Panagiotis Mavros, and Richard Coyne. "Engaging the Brain: The Impact of Natural versus Urban Scenes Using Novel EEG Methods in an Experimental Setting." *Environmental Sciences* 1, no. 2 (2013): 93–104.

Roediger, H., and K. McDermott. "Creating False Memories: Remembering Words not Presented in Lists." *Journal of Experimental Psychology: Learning, Memory, and Cognition* 21 (1995): 803–814.

Rosenfield, Israel. *The Invention of Memory: A New View of the Brain*. New York: Basic Books, 1988.

Rosenthal, Norman E., David A. Sack, J. Christian Gillin, Alfred J. Lewy, Frederick K. Goodwin, Yolande Davenport, Peter S. Mueller, David A. Newsome, and Thomas A. Wehr. "Seasonal Affective Disorder: A Description of the Syndrome and Preliminary Findings with Light Therapy." *Archives of General Psychiatry* 41, no. 1 (1984): 72–80.

Rousseau, Jean-Jacques. *Émile*. Translated by Barbard Foxley. London: Everyman, 1993. First published in French in 1762.

Russell, James A. "Core Affect and the Psychological Construction of Emotion." *Psychological Review* 110, no. 1 (2003): 145–172.

Russell, James A. "Emotion, Core Affect, and Psychological Construction." *Cognition and Emotion* 23, no. 7 (2009): 1259–1283.

Russell, James A., and Geraldine Pratt. "A Description of the Affective Quality Attributed to Environments." *Journal of Personality and Social Psychology* 38, no. 2 (1980): 311–322.

Russell, Ken (director), and Barry Sandler (scriptwriter). *Crimes of Passion* (film). New World Pictures, 1984.

Ruvolo, Julie. "How Much of the Internet Is Actually for Porn." *Forbes*, September 2011. http://www.forbes.com/sites/julieruvolo/2011/09/07/how-much -of-the-internet-is-actually-for-porn/.

Ryle, Gilbert. *Concept of Mind*. Harmondsworth, UK: Penguin, 1963.

Salovey, Peter, John D Maye, Susan Lee Goldman, Carolyn Turvey, and Tibor P Palfai. "Emotional Attention, Clarity, and Repair: Exploring Emotional Intelligence Using the Trait Meta-Mood Scale." In *Emotion, Disclosure and Health*, edited by James Pennebaker, 125–154. Washington, DC: American Psychology Association, 1995.

Saussure, Ferdinand de. *Course in General Linguistics*. Translated by Roy Harris. London: Duckworth, 1983. Originally published as *Cours de Linguistique Générale*, Payot, Paris, in 1916.

Saville, Bryan K., Amanda Gisbert, Jason Kopp, and Carolyn Telesco. "Internet Addiction and Delay Discounting in College Students." *Psychological Record* 60 (2010): 273–286.

Schaefer, Rebecca S., Katie Overy, and Peter Nelson. "Affect and Non-Uniform Characteristics of Predictive Processing in Musical Behaviour." *Behavioral and Brain Sciences* 36, no. 3 (2013): 226–227.

Schank, Roger C., and Robert P. Abelson. *Scripts, Plans, Goals and Understanding: An Inquiry into Human Knowledge Structures*. Hillsdale, NJ: Erlbaum, 1977.

Scheirera, Jocelyn, Raul Fernandeza, Jonathan Klein, and Rosalind W. Picard. "Frustrating the User on Purpose: A Step toward Building an Affective Computer." *Interacting with Computers* 14 (2002): 93–118.

Schmidt, Eric, and Jared Cohen. *The New Digital Age: Reshaping the Future of People, Nations and Business*. London: John Murray, 2013. Kindle edition.

Schutz, Alfred. "Making Music Together." In *Alfred Schutz, Collected Papers II: Studies in Social Theory*, edited by Arvid Brodersen, 159–178. The Hague: Martinus Nijhoff, 1964.

Schutz, Alfred. *Collected Papers I: The Problem of Social Reality*. Hingham, MA: Kluwer, 1982.

Scruton, Roger. "Hiding Behind the Screen." *New Atlantis*, Summer 2010, 48–60.

Seitz, Matt Zoller. "A Requiem for Dallas's J. R. Ewing." *Vulture*, March 2013. http://www.vulture.com/2013/03/seitz-a-requiem-for-dallass-jr-ewing.html.

Shinn, Gini. *Case Study: First Generation Pokémon Games for the Nintendo Game Boy*. Stanford University, March 16, 2004. http://www.stanford.edu/group/htgg/cgi-bin/drupal/sites/default/files2/gshin_2004_1.pdf.

Silberman, Neil. "Chasing the Unicorn? The Quest for 'Essence' in Digital Heritage." In *New Heritage: New Media and Cultural Heritage*, edited by Yehuda E. Kalay, Thomnas Kvan, and Janice Affleck, 81–111. London: Routledge, 2008.

Silvia, Paul J. *Exploring the Psychology of Interest*. Oxford: Oxford University Press, 2006.

Silvia, Paul J. "Interest: The Curious Emotion." *Current Directions in Psychological Science* 17, no. 1 (2012): 57–60.

Simmel, Georg. "Two Essays: The Handle and the Ruin." *Hudson Review* 11, no. 3 (1958): 371–385.

Simon, Herbert. *The Sciences of the Artificial*. Cambridge, MA: MIT Press, 1969.

Simons, Daniel. "Remarkable False Memories." *The Invisible Gorilla*, November 16, 2010. http://theinvisiblegorilla.com/blog/2010/11/16/remarkable-false-memories/.

Smith, Adam. *An Inquiry into the Nature and Causes of the Wealth of Nations*. Oxford: Oxford University Press, 1998. First published in 1776.

Smith, Adam. *The Theory of Moral Sentiments*. Indianapolis: Liberty Fund, 1984. First published in 1759.

Smith, Valena. "Introduction: The Quest in Guest." *Annals of Tourism Research* 19 (1992): 1–17.

Snodgrass, Adrian, and Richard Coyne. *Interpretation in Architecture: Design as a Way of Thinking*. London: Routledge, 2006.

Sokal, Alan D., and Jean Bricmont. *Intellectual Impostures: Postmodern Philosophers' Abuse of Science*. London: Profile Books, 2003.

Sook Kwon, Eun, and Yongjun Sung. "Follow Me! Global Marketers' Twitter Use." *Journal of Interactive Advertising* 12, no. 1 (2011): 4–16.

Speed, Chris. "An Internet of Things That Do Not Exist." *Interaction* 18, no. 3 (2011): 18–21.

Speed, Chris. "Mobile Ouija Boards." In *Heritage and Social Media: Understanding Heritage in a Participatory Culture*, edited by Elisa Giaccardi, 179–196. London: Routledge, 2012.

Spiller, Neil. *Digital Architecture Now: A Global Survey of Emerging Talent*. London: Thames and Hudson, 2008.

Spinoza, Baruch. *Ethics*. Translated by Andrew Boyle and G. H. R. Parkinson. London: Everyman, 1997. First published in Latin in 1677.

Spuybroek, Lars. *The Sympathy of Things: Ruskin and the Ecology of Design*. Rotterdam, NL: NAi Publishers, 2011.

Stafford, Tom. "Isn't It All Just Obvious?" *Psychologist* 20, no. 2 (2007): 94–95.

Stein, Bob, and Dan Visel. "Mao, King Kong, and the Future of the Book." *Triplecanopy*, 2010. http://canopycanopycanopy.com/issues/9/contents/mao__king _kong__and_the_future_of_the_book.

Stelmack, Robert M., and Anastasios Stalikas. "Galen and the Humour Theory of Temperament." *Personality and Individual Differences* 12, no. 3 (1991): 255–263.

Stone, Allucquere Rosanne. *The War of Desire and Technology at the Close of the Mechanical Age*. Cambridge, MA: MIT Press, 1996.

Storbeck, Justin, and Gerald L. Clore. "With Sadness Comes Accuracy; with Happiness, False Memory: Mood and the False Memory Effect." *Psychological Science* 16, no. 10 (2005): 785–791.

Storbeck, Justin, and Gerald L. Clore. "On the Interdependence of Cognition and Emotion." *Cognition and Emotion* 21, no. 6 (2007): 1212–1237.

Strack, Fritz, Leonard L. Martin, and Sabine Stepper. "Inhibiting and Facilitating Conditions of Facial Expressions: A Nonobtrusive Test of the Facial Feedback Hypothesis." *Journal of Personality and Social Psychology* 54 (1988): 768–776.

Strehovec, Janez. "Vertigo—on Purpose: Entertainment in Simulators." *Journal of Popular Culture* 31, no. 1 (1997): 199–209.

Tafuri, Manfredo. *Architecture and Utopia: Design and Capitalist Development*. Translated by Barbara Luigia La Penta. Cambridge, MA: MIT Press, 1996. First published in Italian in 1973.

Tagholm, Roger. "Genre-Busting Trends in the UK." *Publishing Perspectives*, 2012. http://publishingperspectives.com/2012/10/genre-busting-trends-in-the-uk/.

Takahashi, Hidehiko, Motoichiro Kato, Masato Matsuura, Dean Mobbs, Tetsuya Suhara, and Yoshiro Okubo. "When Your Gain Is My Pain and Your Pain Is My Gain: Neural Correlates of Envy and Schadenfreude." *Science* 323 (2009): 937–939.

Tapscott, Don. *Grown Up Digital: How the Net Generation Is Changing Your World*. New York: McGraw Hill, 2009.

Taylor, Paul. "A European Debt Crisis with an Italian Twist." *The New York Times*, January 24, 2012. http://www.nytimes.com/2012/01/24/business/global/24iht -inside24.html?_r=3&scp=1&sq=going round in circles&st=cse&.

Teal, Randall. "Dismantling the Built Drawing: Working with Mood in Architectural Design." *Journal of Art and Design Education* 29, no. 1 (2010): 8–16.

Terada, Rei. "Imaginary Seductions: Derrida and Emotion Theory." *Comparative Literature* 51, no. 3 (1999): 193–216.

Thacker, Eugene. "Dark Media." In *Excommunication: Three Inquiries in Media and Mediation*, edited by Alexander R. Galloway, Eugene Thacker, and McKenzie Wark. Chicago: University of Chicago Press, 2013. Kindle edition.

Thin, Neil. *Social Happiness: Theory into Policy and Practice*. Bristol, UK: Policy Press, 2012.

Thoreau, Henry David. *Walden: Or, Life in the Woods*. Princeton, NJ: Princeton Paperbacks, 1989.

"Thousands Killed in Asian Tsunami." *The Guardian*, 2004. http://www.theguardian .com/environment/2004/dec/26/naturaldisasters.climatechang.

Thrift, Nigel. "Intensities of Feeling: Towards a Spatial Politics of Affect." *Geografiska Annaler: Series B, Human Geography* 86, no. 1 (2004): 57–78.

Tibbits, Skylar. "The Emergence of '4D Printing.'" *TED video*, 2013. https://www.ted .com/talks/skylar_tibbits_the_emergence_of_4d_printing.

Till, Jeremy. *Architecture Depends*. Cambridge, MA: MIT Press, 2009.

Toesenberger, Catherine. "Homosexuality at the Online Hogwarts: Harry Potter Slash Fanfiction." *Children's Literature* 36 (2008): 185–207.

Topping, Alexandra. "Looting 'Fuelled by Social Exclusion.'" *The Guardian*, August 8, 2011. http://www.theguardian.com/uk/2011/aug/08/looting-fuelled-by -social-exclusion.

Trappl, Robert, Paolo Petta, and Sabine Payr, eds. *Emotions in Humans and Artifacts*. Cambridge, MA: MIT Press, 2003.

Tsetung, Mao. *Quotations from Mao Tsetung*. Peking, China: Foreign Languages Press, 1976.

Turbayne, Colin M. *The Myth of Metaphor*. Columbia: University of South Carolina Press, 1970.

Turkle, Sherry. *Alone Together: Why We Expect More from Technology and Less from Each Other*. New York: Basic Books, 2011. Kindle edition.

Turkle, Sherry, ed. *Evocative Objects: Things We Think With*. Cambridge, MA: MIT Press, 2007.

Turkle, Sherry. *Life on the Screen: Identity in the Age of the Internet*. London: Weiden-feld and Nicolson, 1995.

Turkle, Sherry. *Psychoanalytic Politics: Jacques Lacan and Freud's French Revolution*. New York: Guilford, 1992.

Twain, Mark. *Autobiography of Mark Twain: Volume 1, Reader's Edition*. Berkeley: University of California Press, 2012.

"Twitter Co-Founder Says There's More to Life than Tweets." *The Star.com*, 2012. http://www.thestar.com/news/world/2012/02/22/twitter_cofounder_says_theres _more_to_life_than_tweets.html.

Uidhir, Christy Mag. "The Paradox of Suspense Realism." *Journal of Aesthetics and Art Criticism* 69, no. 2 (2011): 161–171.

Urry, John. *The Tourist Gaze: Leisure and Travel in Contemporary Societies*. London: Sage, 1990.

Urry, John. "The Place of Emotions within Place." In *Emotional Geographies*, edited by Joyce Davidson, Liz Bondi, and Mick Smith, 77–83. Aldershot, UK: Ashgate, 2005.

Valdez, Patricia, and Albert Mehrabian. "Effects of Color on Emotions." *Journal of Experimental Psychology* 123, no. 4 (1994): 394–409.

van Liempt, Ilse, Irina van Aalst, and Tim Schwanen. 2015. "Introduction: Geographies of the Urban Night." *Urban Studies* 52, no. 3 (2015): 407–421.

Vast, Robyn, Robyn Young, and Patrick R. Thomas. "Emotion and Automaticity: Impact of Positive and Negative Emotions on Novice and Experienced Performance of a Sensorimotor Skill." *International Journal of Sport and Exercise Psychology* 9, no. 3 (2011): 227–237.

Veblen, Thorstein. *The Theory of the Leisure Class.* Amherst, NY: Prometheus, 1998. First published in 1899.

Virilio, Paul. *The Aesthetics of Disappearance.* Translated by Philip Beitchman. Cambridge, MA: MIT Press, 2009.

Vitek, Bill, and Wes Jackson, eds. *The Virtues of Ignorance: Complexity, Sustainability, and the Limits of Knowledge.* Lexington, KY: University Press of Kentucky, 2008.

Vitruvius, Pollio. *Vitruvius: The Ten Books on Architecture.* Translated by Morris Hicky Morgan. New York: Dover Publications, 1960. Written circa 50 AD.

Vorderer, Peter, Christoph Klimmt, and Ute Ritterfeld. "Enjoyment: At the Heart of Media Entertainment." *Communication Theory* 14, no. 4 (2004): 388–408.

Wainwright, Oliver. "4D-Printing: From Self-Assembling Chairs to Cancer-Fighting Robots." *The Guardian*, April 10, 2013. http://www.theguardian.com/artanddesign/ architecture-design-blog/2013/apr/10/4d-printing-cancer-nano-robots.

Walter, Tony, Rachid Hourizi, Wendy Moncur, and Stacey Pitsillides. "Does the Internet Change How We Die and Mourn? Overview and Analysis." *Omega* 64, no. 4 (2012): 275–302.

Walters, John C. *Tennyson: Poet, Philosopher, Idealist.* New York: Haskell House Publishers, 1893.

Watson, David, Lee Anna Clark, and Auke Tellegen. "Development and Validation of Brief Measures of Positive and Negative Affect: The PANAS Scales." *Journal of Personality and Social Psychology* 54, no. 6 (1988): 1063–1070.

Watt, Nicholas. "David Cameron Fluffs Citizenship Test on David Letterman's Late Show." *The Guardian*, September 27, 2012. http://www.theguardian.com/ politics/2012/sep/27/david-cameron-letterman-late-show.

Weiner, Norbert. *The Human Use of Human Beings.* Cambridge, MA: Da Capo Press, 1950.

Weiser, Mark. "The Computer for the 21st Century." *Scientific American* 265, no. 3 (1991): 66–75.

Weiser, Mark, and John Seely Brown. "The Coming Age of Calm Technology." In *Beyond Calculation: The Next Fifty Years of Computing*, edited by Peter J. Denning, and Robert M. Metcalfe, 75–85. New York: Springer, 1997.

Wertheim, Margaret. *The Pearly Gates of Cyberspace: A History of Space from Dante to the Internet.* London: Virago, 1999.

Westland, Stephen, Kevin Laycock, Vien Cheung, Phil Henry, and Forough Mahyar. "Colour Harmony." *Colour: Design and Creativity* 1, no. 1 (2007): 1–15.

White, Hayden. *Tropics of Discourse: Essays in Cultural Criticism*. Baltimore: Johns Hopkins University Press, 1978.

White, Hayden. "Review Article: Guilty of History? The Longue Durée of Paul Ricoeur." *History and Theory* 46 (2007): 233–251.

Wigley, Mark. "The Architecture of Atmosphere." *Daidalos* 68 (1998): 18–27.

Wilkes, David. "Queue Here to Conquer Everest: Chilling Photo Shows Bottleneck on Mount Everest as Dozens of Climbers Try to Reach Summit on Weekend When Four Died." *Mail Online*, 2012. http://www.dailymail.co.uk/news/article-2151418/ The-traffic-jam-30-000-feet-Chilling-photo-shows-dozens-climbers-trying-reach -summit-Mount-Everest-died-stuck-bottleneck.html.

Williams, Richard J. *Sex and Buildings: Modern Architecture and the Sexual Revolution*. London: Reaktion, 2013.

Williams, Robin, and David Edge. "The Social Shaping of Technology." In *Information and Communication Technologies*, edited by William H. Dutton, 53–67. Oxford: Oxford University Press, 1996.

Wilson, Aidan. "Phantom Vibration Syndrome: Word of the Year." *Crikey*, February 7, 2013. http://blogs.crikey.com.au/fullysic/2013/02/07/phantom-vibration-syndrome -word-of-the-year/.

Wilson, Eric G. *Against Happiness: In Praise of Melancholy*. New York: Macmillan, 2008.

Wiszniewski, Dorian, Richard Coyne, and Christopher Pierce. "Turing's Machines." In *Proceedings of Architectural Computing from Turing to 2000 eCAADe Conference*, edited by A. Brown, M. Knight, and P. Berridge, 25–32. Liverpool: eCAADe, 1999.

Wittgenstein, Ludwig. *Tractatus Logico Philosophicus*. Translated by C. K. Ogden. London: Routledge and Kegan Paul, 1922.

Wittgenstein, Ludwig. *Remarks on Colour*. Translated by Linda L. McAlister and Margaret Schättle. Oxford: Basil Blackwell, 1977.

Wittkower, Rudolf. *Architectural Principles in the Age of Humanism*. Chichester, UK: Academy Editions, 1998.

Wordsworth, William. *The Collected Poems of William Wordsworth*. Ware, Hertfordshire, UK: Wordsworth Editions Limited, 1994.

Wortham, Jenna. "As Facebook Users Die, Ghosts Reach Out." *The New York Times*, July 18, 2010. http://www.nytimes.com/2010/07/18/technology/18death.html ?adxnnl=1&adxnnlx=1408986589-W4YydFIZUOyStD1pExri/w.

Wright, Mark, Henrik Ekeus, Richard Coyne, James Stewart, Penny Travou, and Robin Williams. "Augmented Duality: Overlapping a Metaverse with the Real

World." In *Proceedings of the International Conference on Advances in Computer Entertainment Technology, ACE 2008*, edited by Masa Inakage and Adrian David Cheok, 263–266. Yokahama, Japan: ACM, 2008.

Wrobel, Bill. "The Nature of Bernard Herrmann's Music." *Society for the Appreciation of the Music of Bernard Herrmann—1911–1975*, 2008. http://www.bernardherrmann.org/articles/misc-nature/.

Wundt, Wilhelm. *Outlines of Psychology*. Translated by C. H. Judd. Leipzig: Engelmann, 1897.

Xenakis, Iannis. *Formalized Music: Thought and Mathematics in Music*. Stuyvesant, NY: Pendragon Press, 1992.

Yates, Frances A. *The Art of Memory*. London: Routledge and Kegan Paul, 1966.

Zillmann, Dolf. "Mood Management through Communication Choices." *American Behavioral Scientist* 31, no. 3 (1988): 327–340.

Žižek, Slavoj. "Big Brother, or, the Triumph of the Gaze over the Eye." In *CTRL [SPACE]: Rhetorics of Surveillance from Bentham to Big Brother*, edited by Thomas Y. Levin, Ursula Frohne, and Peter Weibel, 224–227. Cambridge, MA: MIT Press, 2002.

Žižek, Slavoj. *Enjoy Your Symptom! Jacques Lacan in Hollywood and Out*. London: Routledge, 2001.

Žižek, Slavoj, and Richard Miller. "Hitchcock." *October* 38 (1986): 99–111.

Zumthor, Peter. *Atmospheres: Architectural Environments—Surrounding Objects*. Basel: Birkhäuser, 2006.

Index

Printed in the United States
by Baker & Taylor Publisher Services